HOLISTIC WEl
A PARADIGM. ᴖᴎᴇᴛ

Third Edition

Nourish your BODY
Free your MIND
Awaken your SPIRIT

A Practical & Balanced Approach to Nutrition,
Natural Health & Holistic Living
*now written with consideration to
the principles of German New Medicine*

by
Danielle M. Bryant
with contributions by
Lloyd Bryant and Beth Bryant

Published by Impetus Books

DISCLAIMER:

This book is not intended as a substitute for advice or recommendations from medical health care professionals. It is intended to offer information as a complement to that of a health care professional.

This book or the information herein is not intended to treat, diagnose or cure any illness, condition or disease.

If you have any health concerns it is recommended that you visit your GP or regular health care professional.

Neither the publisher nor the author are responsible for any goods and/or services referred to in this book, and disclaim all liability in connection with damages, loss or expense to person or property arising from the use of information or products.

Published by IMPETUS BOOKS
www.impetusbooks.co.uk
email: info@impetusbooks.co.uk

ISBN 978-0-9575952-4-8

Front cover image by Marcel S.
Cover Design by Danielle M. Bryant
Political artwork by David Dees
Illustrations by Danielle M. Bryant

Dedicated to:

My Children,

My Children's Children

My Children's, Children's, Children,

and so on...

so that they may always have access to this information,

and so they know that

I tried to make a positive difference to their world

in my own small way.

xxXxx

CONTENTS

Acknowledgements

I could not have written this book without the love and support of my family. My amazing husband, Lloyd, who has done a wonderful job in taking over much of my chores and tasks at work and at home, proof-reading, editing, advising, checking facts – and making sure I look after myself! To my beautiful 3 children Beth, Connor and Olivia and my gorgeous baby grandson, Kylo, who have all inspired me so much each in their own individual and very special ways. Thank you all for your patience, help, for being so wonderful, making me feel both proud and humble at the same time, and showing me the true meaning of life!

To my parents, grandparents, my brother, Matthew and sister-in-law, Mair, thank you all for accepting me as the black sheep of the family and not trying to change me. Thank you for all your help, love and support through my hard times and for sharing with me my good times, and for everything you have done and still do!

Thank you to my Mum-in-law, late Dad-in-law, Vanessa, Chris, Wayne and Paul for believing in me, supporting me and accepting me as I am.

I appreciate and thank my past and present Yoga students and clients who have each helped me to grow as a teacher and therapist, and have confidence in myself, many of whom are now dear friends.

My heartfelt thanks to all those who have touched my life for the better and helped me to overcome life's hurdles including (but not limited to!) Linda & Eddie, Kim & Graham, Saffronne, Lorraine, Anthony, Sonya,

Nicola J, Damien, Mi'chal, Joanne, Jayne, Steve M, Davy, Karen, Ann, Cary, Nicola M, Marion, Sarah H, Glenda, Kyle D, Shell, Omar, Jamie S, Danielle, Narissa, Emily, Yvonne, Peter, Menna, Jean and Val.

I am so thankful for my kinesiologist and friend, Dr Bill Seage, who has worked with me throughout my journey back to health, inspired me to become a kinesiologist, and continues to assist me.

Sincere gratitude to the late Dr Ryke Geerd Hamer for his outstanding research for which he received so much persecution, and to Dr Caroline Markolin who has dedicated her life to sharing Dr Hamer's work in its pure, unadulterated state as Dr Hamer would have wanted.

Heartfelt appreciation to Richard D Hall, who has played his part in my awakening, for supporting my business and assisting us in introducing GNM to the UK, and has since become a good friend.

I'm grateful to my first Yoga teacher Sue Wakefield who sparked my love of Yoga and introduced me to the fascinating holistic world that I had long been curious about but too scared to enter!

Thank you to Scott Tips for allowing me to use his interview, and to David Dees for adapting his amazing political images for me to use.

I also wish to extend my gratitude to everyone who has played their part in making me aware of controversial issues, and for your continued selfless efforts in spreading awareness of the truth. I would particularly like to mention Ian R Crane, Brian Gerrish, Scott Tips, Sean Maguire, Sandra Barr and Andrew Johnson.

Last, but by no means least, my appreciation and thanks goes to those who proof-read and offered advice and guidance on relevant chapters: Graham deVall who proof-read the first edition, Helen Delingpole and Linda Reed who partially proof-read the second edition, Marion Bader who read my first draft, and provided me with a wonderful book review; Joy Warren of West Midlands Against Fluoridation and Jay Newman of Invision International who checked facts and figures in the relevant chapters; and Val Ruston who proof read my third edition.

Foreword
(and About the Author)

Danielle and I are a husband-and-wife team who are both passionate about cutting-edge truth and health issues. We own and run a natural health mail order shop called Shop Holistic which we started in 2004 as a small home-based business. It has since grown organically but we still remain a small family business.

Danielle is qualified in Nutritional Therapy, Kinesiology, Homeopathy, Holistic Diagnosis, Yoga teaching, Reflexology and is a Reiki Master/Teacher. At the time of writing she is also a student of Advanced Aromatherapy and Massage. She started practising Yoga in 1997, and later qualified as a Yoga teacher in 2006, teaching various local Yoga classes, and several weekend Yoga & Healing retreats at a Buddhist retreat centre. She became a Reiki Master/teacher in 2005 and after receiving various Angel attunements, ran Angel and Reiki workshops before deciding to offer 1-2-1 tuition and healing. In 2011, Danielle was ordained as a Health Minister of the Genesis II Church of Health & Healing, a non-secular organisation whose beliefs are to uphold our rights to choose how we manage our health and have access to any substance we deem necessary for this purpose, and as a result, she is now entitled to use the title Reverend, if she wishes!

She has given various public talks on Healthy Eating, Health Freedom (along with myself), Yoga and Angels both at health shows and at our own organised events. In 2008 she was asked to talk about and demonstrate nasal cleansing and Yogic breathing in a DVD self-help programme called Botau (www.botau.com). Botau is a stress-relief programme based around optimising your breath and was devised by Dr David Lewis, a research and media psychologist who regularly appears on T.V.

Since before opening the shop, both Danielle and I have extensively researched into the alternative health arena and related issues. Our research became more aggressive when we discovered Codex Alimentarius and the threat this was posing on the natural health industry (as explained in Chapter 91). It is through this research that we became involved with the National Health Federation, and served as co-Executive Directors of the NHF in Wales. We have met some excellent researchers, received 'cutting edge' health information, and have run information campaigns on various health issues such as fluoridation, vaccines, artificial sweeteners, the corporate corruption of "Big Pharma", etc. This led us to further our research into other areas such as politics and spirituality.

Danielle has studied several diploma courses in order to better understand the products and methods we have researched from a qualified perspective. Her passion is for helping and guiding others to not only realise their own potential, but also to be aware that there is an alternative to the mainstream pharmaceutical and medical systems that have so sadly become corrupt and controlled. This approach has helped to empower many of our customers and her clients to become more responsible for their own health without fear, and many have found a lot of benefit with their chronic conditions and quality of life. The reason she chose not to study to become a doctor in the conventional way is because she did not want to be indoctrinated! Instead she has attempted to accumulate as much information and knowledge that she deemed necessary from unbiased and trusted sources and studies (and continues to do so!). In this way her advice and guidance remain pure and intuitive.

Danielle's desire to help others shines through in everything she does, and she often gives advice and assistance freely with no expectation of any return. In the past this has even been to the detriment of her own health, for example at health shows where she has been vulnerable to negative energies while healing others! She has freely offered advice and guidance many times in the past, and continues to do so when her schedule allows as her belief is that the knowledge of Holistic and Natural Health should be available to all.

I must add in relation to product sales: yes, we sell products that are mentioned in this book, but the content of this book is not based around the promotion of these products at all. Our shop policy is not to plan what we are going to sell. We sell high quality products after becoming aware of them either from personal recommendations or through our research into relief of ailments and conditions. Once we are made aware of beneficial products, we research the market for the most ethical, cost efficient, most health beneficial and best quality products. So the advice is pure and honest with the only intention being to help you achieve optimum well-being.

At times, this book may challenge some of your preconceptions. Not least, it suggests that some organizations put profit and control above anything else, at the expense of the rest of us. It would be easy to conclude that for this to happen, everyone in these organizations must be evil and knowledgeable about the corruption! This is unlikely to be the case. Research has shown that when decisions are made as part of a group, the individuals feel their responsibility for that decision is absolved or at least considerably diluted, so when a scenario of business/profit versus ethics arises, this makes it easier for people to be more relaxed with their morals. It is also understood that only a few people at the top may realise the extent of the corruption. The workforce are merely obeying commands, or trained to believe that the work is for the greater good. So as it stands, it falls upon us as individuals to make the right decisions based upon our morals and beliefs, and this book will hopefully provide information to help light the way for you.

Lloyd Bryant

About the Author – My Mother, Danielle M. Bryant

I would be lying if I said having a Mum that is so passionate about our health wasn't annoying at times! Although she has never told her children that they can't do or eat anything, she has told us that we shouldn't! Growing up, watching friends eat at fast food chains and being allowed sweets and sugary snacks whenever they felt like it was torture. We were too young to understand the seriousness of our health-care. If our friends were allowed to do it, then why couldn't we? Mum was just strict and boring! But the more I grew, the easier it became to thank her for everything she had done for my siblings and I. She paved the way to a healthier, knowledge-rich life. Having parents like mine has made me ask "Why?" to absolutely everything. And we SHOULD be asking why. We should always ask why and we should always want to find the answer. Now I have started a family of my own, I am so grateful to have parents that can guide me and help me make the best decisions for my children's health and future, both from what they've already taught me and what they continue to teach me every day.

My mum is the most giving, selfless person I have ever had the fortune of knowing. She will work endlessly to help whoever she can, always before her self. She is the living example of the quote "Always leave people better than you found them." And this is what she does, every day. Whether it be a physical or emotional problem, she always has just the right thing! Because of my Mum, I have acquired a taste of forever learning and growing. I have studied and qualified in Nutritional Therapy, Aromatherapy and Massage, and I play a major role in the family business. She has taught me that helping people in any way we can, either through sharing our knowledge or taking our time to give the person what they need, is truly the most rewarding thing we can do as humans. I am proud to call this woman my mother. I couldn't ask for a better Mum, best friend and Grandmother to son and future children.

Beth Bryant

Introduction

The advice enclosed in this book is based upon my studies, mine and Lloyd's research but most importantly, our own experience. We are all different and therefore we will find different things work for us, but please reflect upon the advice in this book and use it as a foundation. If something doesn't feel right to you, research and find your own way as nobody will know your body like you do.

It is not intended to be a comprehensively detailed account of every subject I have written about, and I in no way offer myself as an expert in any of these fields. I have simply compiled what I consider to be well-rounded and common sense advice based upon how I see things myself, and what I believe to be on the right path to truth.

It is a minefield of information out there including so much disinformation linked to product sales, professionals who have their own agenda (or who are indeed sponsored to give biased advice) and many written by unqualified people who intend well but may not have a true understanding. I am not saying I understand everything, as after my years of research (which began in 2004), including taking 9 diplomas (at time of writing), I have realised that much of it is actually based upon different beliefs rather than wisdom and fact. I have tried my best to stick with the information and beliefs that have been confirmed by either science or experience and factual research programmes, and I have combined this with my own experiences of healing myself of fibromyalgia, treating myself, my family and friends, and the experience and feedback I have received from clients and shop customers.

Originally this book was intended as a way of making the health advice available after having to remove the information from my shop website due to the EU Health Claims Directive. However, as it was being written it grew organically into something much more profound! Some chapters were originally stand-alone articles so there may be a little duplication of information. In addition, please be aware that some of these articles were written by myself over the last 12 years. I have attempted to trawl the internet for instances whereby I may have used quotes from other websites including previous product suppliers and information websites. However, the majority of my previous wording has now been re-written and updated.

During my search I came across some instances of my original wording used on various blogs and websites without my knowing or acknowledgement, and some since even copyrighting the wording (although their copyright post-dates my original article, some by 6 years!). So I have attempted to re-word my work so that it may remain original, however some phrasing may remain.

I have not approached these people as I am happy to let bygones be bygones and am happy that the information and research concerned has been shared for the benefit of others (even though some is on commercial sites). I truly hope this has been of benefit to readers that these websites have reached and I otherwise would not have been able to get the information to! After all, in a way it is not really that important who put the information out there in the first place – unless there is ego involved! What's most important is that it does get out there! However, it is a different story when published in a book, so I hope that my copyright and original wording here are respected!

I hope you find the information in this book helpful. Think of it as a journey – you may wish to revisit some chapters in the future that were first dismissed as a little bizarre. This is quite understandable and natural as our minds generally need time to absorb and accept new concepts, especially when the viewpoints are contraindicative to how we believe things are, or have been. It took me a while to begin letting go of my conditioned belief that all is what it appears to be and fully open my mind, accepting that which is beyond my perception and understanding. Yet I am still discovering completely mind-blowing research as my journey continues!

"Life is a journey – enjoy the ride and remember to take in the scenery as you go!"

Danielle, January 2013

Second & Third Editions

Subsequent editions are not intended as an addition to the original first edition, but replacements to it. The new editions have been quite thoroughly updated and revised each time, not only with more up-to-date information, but also where my continuing research and experiences have lead me to understand certain subjects in more detail, or even in a different way. My mind continues to be open to learning, and flexible to change – as it should be!

Before each edition, I would find myself at a crossroads. Do I write a new book or update the current edition? Each time I wanted to change a lot, add even more and explain some things in a lot more detail and I feared that this would have made the already-hefty book much too big! So, in the second edition, I added as much information as I could fit in without making it a massive tome. I had felt it was fairly complete – and I could move on to writing another volume with additional information if needed. That was until I studied German New Medicine which turned everything upside down and back to front! It was not my first choice to replace a book and make the old versions invalid, but my integrity would not let me continue to sell a book that I knew was written from my 'old' perspective had therefore had incorrect information in it. Hence the Third Edition was born late 2019 which has undergone extensive changes throughout!

I also think it is important to mention that I have written this book with the intention that it is read through in its entirety at least once before it is used as a reference book. You will get a lot more from it this way! It was apparent from feedback from many readers of the first edition that this book was not read in its entirety, but only used as a reference book. This can cause misunderstandings of my advice and message, as those readers didn't have the full picture they would have had from reading it in full. I have attempted to mention other relevant chapters where information crosses over throughout, however I wrote most of the book in a way that flows and builds upon understanding, subjects given later on often relying on concepts already covered. While some of the chapters in this book act as a stand-alone reference, I did not want to repeat myself too much through the book, so many chapters do not alone give the full picture.

Since writing the first edition, I have become qualified in kinesiology and have opened a new therapy centre (Lotus Therapy Centre) in Caerphilly, and also studied German New Medicine, including attending a GNM training conference in Austria.

Also, I have faced a rather big and scary health challenge of my own. I discovered I had early stages of Breast Cancer in the summer of 2016 (which I have now recovered from naturally, of course!). I have written an additional chapter briefly outlining my journey back to health how I had thought it had played out at the time, and then a reassessment of the journey through my new understanding since studying GNM.

It really has been a roller-coaster ride – in particular the unlearning of everything I thought I knew. I have seen my journey as a gift for which I am extremely grateful, and utilising this experience to help others will make the difficult times I had really worthwhile!

I really hope you enjoy reading my book and gain something from my work!

Danielle, December 2019

The German New Medicine Perspective

This new edition is re-written based upon the suppressed science of German New Medicine (GNM). It is important that there is an understanding of GNM before reading this book as some information is likely to be in contrary to mainstream (and even most alternative) health information you may have read, as these are generally based upon a belief that diseases are a malfunction of our body.

GNM is an entirely new perspective of our health, and I therefore often refer to it as 'the new perspective'. It redefines so-called disease and cancer as meaningful Biological Special Programmes of Nature that are designed to assist our body in times of trauma. The irrefutable science is based upon Five Biological Laws which have no hypothesis. It is challenging to learn as much of what we have been brought up to believe is pulled into question, and much of it is actually disproved. Learning GNM (which anyone can do at an amazing website called LearningGNM.com) created a massive paradigm shift for me (which ironically, this book has also had to experience, despite its original name of "A Paradigm Shift!")

This is an introduction to the wisdom of GNM, I've expanded on its various aspects throughout the book in relevant chapters and sections. Keep your mind open to learning when you read this, as you may realise, as I have, that this is awakening what we truly and instinctively know.

History

This information is based upon 40 years of scientifically and clinically correlated research by Dr. med. Ryke Geerd Hamer. Dr Hamer was a German doctor who developed testicular cancer shortly after his son Dirk died after being accidentally shot. He wondered if the cancer was linked to the shock of losing his son, and after discovering all his cancer patients had also experienced unexpected, traumatic shocks before their disease occurred, he set about his research and German New Medicine was born.

Dr Hamer stated that if there was just one exception to a theory, then it was incorrect. No guesswork or assumptions, every discovery had to be found to be 'without exception' before it was stated as fact. GNM leaves no question unanswered and studying it reveals how many assumptions, unanswered questions and unproven science exists in the modern conventional medical world. It has been stated that Dr Hamer had a success rate of 98% of full recovery with his patients, which reduced to 92% if the patient had previous conventional treatment. The small percentage who did not pull through may have simply been due to the fact that they could not shake the fear of the so-called disease they were confronting.

In 1981, Dr Hamer completed a thesis which he submitted to the University of Tuebingen for evaluation, but it was rejected and he was told if he didn't renounce his findings that he would lose his job. Not willing to abandon this life-saving research, he continued to work privately. However a few years later he lost his doctor licence on the grounds that he would not renounce his findings and conform to the conventional paradigm. He continued working privately, relying on other doctors for brain scans and patient records to continue his research despite continued attacks and intimidation, extradition to France, and even 2 unjustified stints in prison. He continued his work until he sadly died at age 82 in 2017 from a stroke. It is due to his persecution and the suppression of his findings, that this life-saving research is little-known today.

After analysing over 40,000 cases, Dr Hamer discovered the purpose of every so-called 'disease' and developed the 'Five Biological Laws'. The science of German New Medicine is bound by the science of embryology (the development of the embryo) and follows evolutionary logic. His research proves without doubt that diseases are not malfunctions of our body but meaningful biological programmes set into motion by a specific conflict shock or trauma (which he calls a DHS or Dirk Hamer Syndrome after his late son Dirk). The conflict shock causes a lesion in the brain at the control relay of a specific body part that is instrumental in assisting our survival in coping with the specific trauma experienced. He also discovered that all of these biological processes run in 2 phases, a conflict-active phase and a healing phase which runs after the conflict is resolved, and this is when most symptoms will occur. This means that when we experience symptoms, we are actually healing and not malfunctioning!

To explain GNM, we can look at the Five Biological Laws:

The First Biological Law (the Iron Rule of Cancer)

The 3 criteria of the 1st Biological Law are:

1. Every 'disease' is a Biological Special Programme which is set off by an "unexpected, highly acute, and isolating conflict shock that occurs simultaneously in the psyche, the brain, and on the corresponding organ."

A conflict shock is something that occurs unexpectedly and catches us unprepared and off-guard. This is very subjective and occurs entirely on a subconscious level. The type of conflict that is experienced depends on the person's perception of the situation which is based upon their beliefs, upbringing, emotional state, etc.

For example, a divorce may be experienced as an abandonment conflict (affecting the kidneys), self- devaluation conflict (affecting the muscles, lymphs nodes or bones), separation conflict (affecting the skin), starvation conflict (affecting the liver), indigestible morsel (affecting the digestive system/GI tract), etc. – or a combination of these.

The conflict theme is directly related to the function of the related organ, e.g. a morsel conflict would affect the alimentary canal (either unable to catch, eliminate or digest a morsel). As humans are emotional, complex beings, the conflict can be of a figurative nature. For example, a death fright conflict can be experienced when a cancer diagnosis is received. We can even suffer a conflict on behalf of someone else!

2. The type of the conflict determines which organ will be affected and from which area of the brain the biological programme will be controlled. Specific conflicts will trigger a specific biological programme to run, the purpose of which is to make the organ stronger or more efficient so we can cope with and survive the unexpected trauma. For example, a death-fright conflict will trigger extra cells to grow in the lung to enable more surface area for more oxygen to be brought into the body to help prevent death.

3. Every Biological Programme runs simultaneously on the level of the psyche, the brain, and the correlating organ.

> *"The differentiation between the psyche, the brain, and the body is purely academic. In reality, they are one." - Dr Ryke Geerd Hamer*

The Second Biological Law states that "Every Biological Special Program runs in two phases provided there is a resolution of the conflict."

Phase 1 is known as the **Conflict-active phase**. It is a time of stress, difficulty sleeping, cold hands, and generally no physical symptoms. While the conflict is active, the biological programme is facilitating the survival and coping of the conflict on a primitive, subconscious level by either creating more cells (to increase surface area for more absorption, for example) or cell loss (ulceration) to widen a vessel (to allow more flow of bodily fluid through, for example), or function loss.

xiv

Once the conflict is resolved, the **Healing Phase** begins. This is the body's way of getting back to normal, and is where the symptoms of 'disease' as we know them begin. The intensity of the healing phase depends on the intensity of the conflict and the length of time we were in the conflict-active phase.

The healing process is assisted by bacteria such as TB, fungi such as Candida and other microbes which, until activated by the brain, remain dormant (if not wiped out by overuse of antibiotics and vaccines). These microbes either help to break down additional cells or replenish cells depending on the biological programme that is running.

There is inflammation in this phase, and thus often pain, as the body actually requires a fluid environment for the healing to take place. There are also sweats, particularly night sweats if TB bacteria is involved, and tiredness, often fatigue. This is because our body needs minimal movement and to rest in order to heal.

Where there are night sweats indicating TB bacteria is involved, it is important to consume more protein as TB use up a lot of protein. What we see in patients that appear to be wasting away with a serious disease, is actually protein loss caused by the bacteria, and this can be fatal.

The main point to take from this phase is that our symptoms are nothing to fear. They are purposeful and are an indication that we are actually in healing. Conventionally we try to turn away from symptoms through inconvenience and fear. But working with the symptoms, supporting the process and allowing the healing to happen with a positive mindset is what is required to ensure the healing phase is completed.

Once the first part of healing phase is complete, the body needs to push out the waste. So the body temporarily goes back into the 'stress' phase in what is known as an **'Epileptoid Crisis'**. At this phase we see symptoms such as nose bleeds, coughing fits, abdominal cramps, etc. depending on the biological programme that is running its course.

Then the second part of the healing phase sees discharges, sometimes bleeding, mucous, pus, diarrhoea, etc. as the body rids itself of the toxins and waste products produced during healing, and finally the scarring and healing of the tissue.

Chronic conditions are caused by a 'hanging healing' which is when the body cannot complete the healing phase. This can be due to conflict relapses, poor diet, certain medications, and stimulants which can push the body back into the conflict-active phase by taking the body out of the vagatonic (relaxed, unstressed) state. This may cause symptoms to disappear (due to there being no symptoms in the conflict-active phase). This can create a belief that the medication/stimulant is helping – but in reality it is not allowing the biological programme to complete.

Allergies are caused when 'tracks' are created that are basically triggers of the original conflict. When these triggers are experienced, the biological programme is reactivated.

The Third Biological Law

In line with embryology, the control relays of our organs are found in the part of the brain that developed at the same time as the organ. All organs controlled from the same part of the brain will run the same biological programme. For example: in all organs that are controlled from the old brain (the brainstem and cerebellum) there will be cell proliferation in the conflict-active phase and cell removal by TB bacteria and fungi in the healing phase; in all organs that are controlled from the 'new brain' (the cerebral medulla and the cerebral cortex), there will be cell loss in the conflict-active phase, which will be replenished during the healing phase). Some organs and tissues may also suffer function loss rather than cell proliferation or loss in conflict active.

The Fourth Biological Law

Microbes don't cause diseases but play instead a vital role during the healing phase. Bacteria such as TB, streptococcus, staphylococcus, and fungi such as Candida will become active in order to remove the additional cells that are no longer required or to assist the replenishing of tissue. Each type of microbe has its own specific task. So-called "infections" such as a Candida infection (commonly known as candidiasis) occur therefore in the healing phase. Its intensity is proportional to the length and intensity of the conflict-active phase. Microbes require an acidic environment in which to thrive and work. Therefore the acidic imbalance is not the cause of disease, but an essential part of healing.

The Fifth Biological Law

"Every so-called disease is part of a Significant Biological Special Program of Nature created to assists an organism (humans and animals alike) during unexpected distress."

> "All so-called diseases have a special biological meaning. While we used to regard Mother Nature as fallible and had the audacity to believe that She constantly made mistakes and caused breakdowns (malignant, senseless, degenerative cancerous growths, etc.) we can now see, as the scales fall from our eyes, that it was our ignorance and pride that were and are the only foolishness in our cosmos. Blinded, we brought upon ourselves this senseless, soulless and brutal medicine. Full of wonder, we can now understand for the first time that Nature is orderly and that every occurrence in Nature is meaningful, even in the framework of the whole. Nothing in Nature is meaningless, malignant or diseased." - Dr Hamer

So as we understand this new perspective, we can begin to accept that many things we once thought were causing cancer, cannot cause or increase the risk of cancer, as cancer is not a malfunction. This has been the biggest paradigm shift this book has undergone! However, they can all hinder or even prevent healing. Maybe this is what the undeniable statistics show? Maybe biological programmes would go undetected if they complete healing in a healthy, balanced body? In any case, it now becomes clear that what we considered risk factors are in fact stresses on our system, either poisoning us, or robbing us of energy and preventing our Biological Special Programmes from running correctly.

Therefore, where there are undeniable statistics and quotes linked to cancer and disease throughout this book, they need to be considered in this new light. But remember, with a firm understanding of GNM, we now know that: **no substance can CURE a disease and no substance can CAUSE a disease.**

Glossary of GNM Terms

DHS – Conflict shock, the shocking isolating moment of a trauma

Biological Special Programme / Biological Programme – 'disease'

Conflict Active – the first phase of a biological programme, when we are active with the conflict

Healing phase / "in healing" – the Healing phase of a biological programme

Epi Crisis / Epileptoid Crisis – the stress peak during the Healing phase of a biological programme

Hanging Healing – stuck in a biological programme

Track – a trigger which is a subconscious association of a particular substance, place, person, etc and a Conflict Shock

Constellation – 2 active conflicts involving both brain hemispheres

Vagotonia – a non-stress state, when the parasympathetic nervous system is dominant in the Healing Phase

Sympathicotonia – a stress state, fight or flight, when the sympathetic nervous system is dominant in the Conflict-active Phase

SECTION I.....Nourish Your Body

CHAPTERS:

From the perspective of GNM:

Nutritional therapy takes a new meaning with this new perspective. Biological Special programmes and our susceptibility to experience intense conflict shocks (meaning intensive healing symptoms) can depend upon our general health. When our body is under constant stress, which can be from a poor diet and consuming unnatural, highly processed foods, we can hinder our healing, and could even cause hanging healing and chronic conditions.

Harmful foods and unnatural additives POISON our body on a physical level. Poisons can cause symptoms without a conflict shock!

1

CHAPTER 1...
We Really Are What We Eat

This phrase has been quite overdone, but it really is so very true as our bodies are constantly renewing and repairing themselves (apart from our brain and eyes). The lifespan and renewal rate of our cells goes from 2-3 days for our intestines, up to 20 years for our heart muscles. Where do you think our bodies obtain the elements with which to renew our cells? From our food! So we really ARE what we eat!

Metabolic Typing

It is my firm belief that we are all different and we therefore require a different balance of nutrients to thrive.

At the turn of the millennium, a book by William Wolcott and Trish Fahey was published called 'The Metabolic Typing Diet'. This book was the result of 100 years research (which was taken over in 1977 and completed by William Wolcott) into how differently and individually our bodies can process foods, and therefore what we require is different to each other. His book attempts to break through the mainstream myths of 'one size fits all' diets but has received resistance to make it into the mainstream. Many feel this is due to the corporations failing to be able to market their 'one diet fits all' products.

Metabolic typing takes into account many aspects of the body including the blood type, electrolyte balance, anabolic balance, constitutional type, acid/alkaline type, oxidative type, endocrine type, autonomic type and prostaglandin balance. As each of these aspects display certain traits, reactions, characteristics, features and tendencies, an extensive questionnaire was designed to ascertain the correct balance of nutrients required by the individual and which foods would be beneficial or not to the individual's well-being. The basic results are found as 'Protein', 'Mixed' or 'Carb' type individuals, the diet further being tweaked on an individual level. To ascertain your correct balance of nutrients I offer Metabolic Typing that is based upon William Wolcott's research. A comprehensive quiz is available free on my own website (www.holisticdani.co.uk) under 'Free Resources'.

Finding a Nutritional Therapist

I have found that some nutritional therapists try to push their own beliefs through their advice. For example you will have those who believe in raw and juicing, those who are veggie or vegan, those who are anti glutenous grains, those who are anti dairy, those who are pro paleo diet, etc. You will find that many have their own agenda. My viewpoint is that I am anti whatever-is-not-right-for-the-individual and pro whatever-is-right-for-the-individual, and I strongly believe that is how it should be as we are all different!

If you wish to seek advice from a nutritional therapist (or a naturopath) then I advise you ask their stance on dairy, vegan, etc. as you will then get an idea whether they advocate the one rule for all mentality. Have a chat, and ask as much as you like, as above all you must be comfortable with them!

CHAPTER 2...
Understanding Good Eating Basics

This chapter provides a summary of the basic rules that I deem are the most important points to follow – some of these points are discussed in greater detail throughout this book.

1. Avoid any artificial sweeteners (aspartame, neotame, Truvia, saccharin, Splenda, sucralose, Acesulfame K, etc.).

2. Avoid MSG (monosodium glutamate) or flavour enhancers, foods high in glutamate, or preservatives such as sodium and potassium nitrite.

3. Eat organic as much as possible as the pesticides, weed killers and pharmaceutical drugs (in meat) used in today's foods will remain on and in your vegetables and meat and place your body under a lot of stress.

4. Avoid processed foods and ready made meals – the nutrients in these are almost non-existent. Opt for making meals from scratch using whole foods (unprocessed foods that look like they do in the garden!)

5. Do not use a microwave! Microwaves basically 'nuke' your food and you will end up with your food having little nutritional value and enriched with radiation!!

4

6. It is highly recommended that you take a metabolic typing test (as previously mentioned available on my website) as you may be causing unnecessary stress and imbalance to your body by not eating the correct balance of foods. **This is particularly important if you are vegetarian or vegan.** I am not saying that you need to eat meat, but you MAY need to. Please keep an open mind about this for your body's sake, and read Chapter 5, The Veggie/Vegan Debate. For now, a good indication for vegetarians is looking at the fundamental ruling of the blood type diet: type O particularly need animal protein (in particular high purines which cannot be obtained from plants such as those found in red meat and organ meat), type A & B are generally more suited to vegetarianism, but a combination like AO will usually need some animal protein.

7. Drink enough clean water you know if you are drinking enough if your wee is clear! I do not go by the usual "2 Litres per day" as this can greatly depend on you, your size, your exercise levels and the amount of fresh fruit and veg you eat, and also the time of year and outside temperature. Please see Chapter 4.

8. Reduce consumption of caffeine beverages to 1-2 cups per day, or eliminate them completely, although organic ground coffee in the morning can have some benefits.

9. Reduce alcohol intake to an occasional tipple, or eliminate it. In addition you may wish to consider the information on alcohol in Chapter 87. However, a moderate amount of sulphate-free organic red wine can be healthful for its resveratrol content.

10. Only use good quality healthful saturated fats like butter, ghee or coconut oil to cook with. Never use hydrogenated oil or so-called 'healthy' spreads. Only use olive oil and nut oils cold, or slightly warmed.

11. Always opt for wholegrain and avoid refined and bleached flours. Avoid non-organic wheat and wheat products. Modern wheat is a hybrid plant and most people cannot truly tolerate it.

12. Reduce sugars, and especially refined sugar. A healthy option is Xylitol which is a natural plant based sugar substitute.

13. Take care with plastic containers – when disposable plastic containers become hot they can leach chemicals from the plastic into the drink or food (unless they are formulated for hot beverages). If you warm food wrapped or covered with cling film, you are basically melting the plastic onto your food. Look at the number in the recycling triangle on your plastic containers. Plastic numbers 3, 6 and 7 will usually contain hazardous chemicals which are released upon warming (such as in hot sun), cooking, age, washing and re-using the bottles.

14. Take care with tinned foods – many tinned products such as sweetcorn, tomatoes and others react to the tin so the inside of the tin has a white coating. This is Bisphenol-A (BPA) which is linked to drastic hormone changes as it imitates the hormone oestrogen. These products are generally available in jars at good health stores. Alarmingly, BPA is used in the production of some baby bottles!

15. Change all your salt to Himalayan Salt and use freely. This acts as a completely balanced mineral supplement and reacts with your body in a completely different way to ordinary salt. Also change your vinegar to organic Apple Cider Vinegar, one of the benefits is it will help to regulate your stomach acid.

16. Eat the Rainbow – I believe the best way to ensure our bodies have a plethora of goodness from our fruit and vegetables is to 'Eat the Rainbow' every day (i.e. at least one food of every colour – red, orange, yellow, green, blue, purple, white). This is something I always strive to do, particularly when I understand that I am in a healing phase.

Our wise Grandparents!

I think we have come almost full circle regarding nutrition. In many ways I believe our grandparents ate the most healthy diet – everything was organic then, they used unprocessed fats, and traditional food combinations like thick butter on bread, tomatoes with egg, etc. All of which make perfect sense the more I learn.

We have been so confused by fads, extremists, fake science through propaganda by food corporations trying to pass their rubbish unhealthy products off as healthy, taking notice of supplement sales information and studies into certain aspects of nutrients without understanding the full antagonistic and synergistic effects, etc. I think the more we listen to our bodies and eat what is right for us as individuals and ignore all this 'science', the better we will all be for it! Of course I am not putting down the way nutrition can be used therapeutically by holistic programmes such as the Gerson Therapy, but this would be only for therapeutic use and not long term general use!! Diets should also be followed with a knowledge of the GNM perspective and our body's healing process, and adapted to suit what is needed at each stage in the biological programme.

Anything done to extremes can be harmful and I have been very dubious about some of the fads emerging, with people all trying to promote a 'one rule fits all' mentality. An example of this is the raw and juicing fad, which I believe to be cherry-picked from the Gerson Therapy. But this therapy is a holistic programme and cherry-picking destabilises and causes imbalance. Many vegetables and foods are actually harmful if eaten raw such as cabbage, spinach, broccoli, kale, etc. due to oxalic acid and others for many other reasons. And yet I find it alarming that these fads are promoted by some nutritional therapists!

I have found myself almost going back in time in my mind to remember what people used to eat and how they used to cook before all the corporate propaganda began, and in the same way how people used to treat and heal themselves before Big Pharma! This enables me to see past what we have come to believe. Propaganda exists in both the corporate mainstream and the alternative health industries. There is disinformation and misinformation in both and it can be so confusing for anyone looking to manage their own health.

CHAPTER 3...The Way we Eat

The way you eat is also important as your digestion is the key to the release of energy and efficient use of the nutrients in your foods.

For optimum digestion it is better to take small bites and chew your food thoroughly before swallowing. Chewing the food breaks it down into simple sugars for easy digestion – you will notice your food becoming sweeter the more you chew and this will satisfy your sweet taste buds. It is believed that if you have cravings for dessert, it is because you haven't chewed your food properly! Do not allow yourself to rush and gulp your food. Do not drink with your meal as this will dilute your stomach acid and can cause poor digestion. Slow your eating down as it takes a while for your brain to receive the signal that you do not need to eat any more. I generally try to eat until I am no longer hungry rather than stopping when I am full (there is a difference!). This is good practice as the energy from the food will otherwise be taken up with the processing and digesting of unwanted food and this can have a huge impact on your energy levels and the use of the nutrients by your body. Think how tired you feel after a big meal! This is why!

You need to get out of the habit of finishing everything on your plate, even if it is delicious! This comes from our instinct of filling up while we have food in front of us as we do not know when our next meal will be, but we need to re-train ourselves to understand that we have plentiful food, and can leave our dinner and go back to it later if needed – even if that is in half hour!

Timing

After 6pm it is good practice not to eat much at all. After this time our bodies begin storing the sugars and energy for the following day in a 'reserve tank'. Generally, we go to bed much later than we are designed to which is ideally between 9pm and 10pm (7pm-8pm for children). This forces our bodies to release tomorrow's stored energy to keep us going (usually known as the Second Wind). This leaves us depleted of energy for the following day and causes unhealthy carb cravings for quick release energy. It also causes a depletion in brain function and our concentration and clarity of thought is greatly affected.

Fasting

Not eating after 6pm will also help our digestive systems to rest. For thousands of years fasting has been practised in traditions such as Yoga for this very reason. You will be giving your digestion a 12-hour (at least) break every day! Additionally, eating too regularly can keep us in a state of being dependant on the glycogen in our liver for energy rather than using it once it has been stored in our fat. This keeps our weight up and can force us into insulin resistance (pre-diabetes). The body can basically 'turn off' the ability to use fat for energy as it doesn't get the chance to, due to always having a supply in the liver! At one point it was discovered by my kinesiologist that my body was not producing Lipase, the enzyme that breaks down fat, so the fat was just being stored rather than processed. Could this be a result of my grazing and evening eating, I wonder? The antidote for this is to regularly fast (having clear liquids only such as herbal tea or water) for a minimum of 12 hours to reset the body's fat metabolism, making no-eating-in-the-evening even healthier for you!

Breakfast is touted to be the most important meal of the day, however it has been discovered that studies showing this were funded by cereal companies! Many nutritional experts advocate intermittent fasting for a slightly longer period, one method being to skip breakfast so the body is fasting each day for around 18 hours. This is ideal, though I think a happy medium is needed. Maybe have a later breakfast, consisting of a vegetable juice sweetened with a pear or apple, organic porridge or organic eggs with some tomatoes fried in coconut oil, or maybe fruit and nuts with yoghurt. For me, fasting in this way (which appears to happen naturally for me) seems to work fairly well.

Fasting for longer periods often claims therapeutic benefits and I can understand this as it gives the digestion a total rest and allows healing in the absence of foods that may be causing symptoms. However, from the new perspective, if you are in a healing phase it is imperative that you eat regularly to give yourself the nourishment and energy to heal.

There is much controversy over whether it is best to eat main meals without snacks or if it is best to graze, eating little and often. My answer to this is to do what is best for you while bearing in mind the above information, and if you are diabetic or have a compromised metabolic rate, unless you are following a therapeutic 'ketogenic diet' it is good to eat something every few hours or so, even if it is just a small bite.

Also bear in mind that thirst is often mistaken for hunger. Try to drink plenty of fresh, clean water (see next chapter). Also bear in mind that hunger pangs could be sugar/carb cravings! I personally think that it should be quite possible to go without food for 18-24 hours without much ill affect for anyone with a healthy metabolism and who is not in a healing programme, although it maybe a small challenge. If it isn't possible, maybe you are relying on sugar and glycogen in your liver too much.

CHAPTER 4...Water

It is very important to drink water but also just as important to drink the correct water! As a rough guide for the amount of fluid your body requires just divide your body weight in pounds by 2. This gives an idea of the fluid ounces of clear fluids such as water or herbal tea that you need for optimum hydration. However, it depends a lot on the type of foods you eat as raw fresh vegetables and fruit can help to hydrate you meaning you don't need so much fluids, but you will require more fluids for hydration if you consume salty foods or drink caffeinated beverages. Also it depends on exercise and the weather, and whether you are in a biological programme. In this case, you would want to reduce your fluid intake (without getting dehydrated) in the first phase of healing, particularly if inflammation is a problem, as any extra fluid will just increase the inflammation. In the second phase of healing after the Epi Crisis, you can increase fluids to assist in the ridding of the waste products. So only use this as a guide. The best indication that you are having enough fluid is that a) you feel well and b) your wee is either very pale or clear.

Water Purity

I recommend filtering tap water to remove large impurities. Despite water purification processes at the water treatment plants, there are many hidden dangers in tap water. Chlorine, which is added to the water to destroy pathogens, remains in the water reaching our taps, and worst of all fluoride is added in many areas. Fluoride is a poison that has a huge negative impact on our bodies. There have been no unbiased tests to prove that fluoride is even good for our teeth, and despite this lack of sound independent research, it is promoted as safe and healthy by the dental profession and health authorities. There is much available information on the negative health conditions caused by consuming fluoride on the Internet and in Chapters 30 & 31. In England and the Irish Republic, the fluoride used in water fluoridation programmes is derived from the poisonous Hydrogen Fluoride gas which dissolves into a solution of generally Sodium Fluosilicate or Hydrofluorosilicic Acid. Many parts of England are now fluoridated including the West Midlands and the North East. Even if you do not live in a fluoridated area, the existence of residual chemicals is a good enough reason not to drink water straight from your tap!

There are a few ways of removing the chemicals and pharmaceuticals from your drinking water and that is by distillation, reverse osmosis filtration or activated alum filtration. I have had a distiller and a reverse osmosis filter and so have personal experience of two of these systems. Small counter-top distillers can be found from about £60, reverse osmosis filter systems will probably cost from £100 and don't need professional plumbing if you are handy – Lloyd fitted ours himself ....eventually (private joke there). The activated alum are usually plumbed in professionally for whole or part house filtration. In my opinion, it is a very worthwhile investment to have a purification system in place – and an essential one if you are in a fluoridated area. Please note that your standard jug-style water filter will not remove fluoride or chlorine, but it is better than nothing!

Re-mineralisation of Water

Distillation and Reverse Osmosis filtration will leave you with water devoid of anything including essential minerals (if you were to use a TDS meter to measure particles in the water it should read close to 0 parts per million). If you drink 'empty' water in the long term this will draw minerals out of your body (scientifically proven through hair mineral analysis and bone density testing). Some people use it in the short term to help with detox but I honestly would not recommend this. Anyone who promotes the drinking of pure distilled water is either selling water distillers, or does not understand the true science behind water chemistry. A good friend has a Ph.D. in this field and has assured me that water needs to be re-mineralised. The best way of doing this is by adding a pinch of Himalayan Salt. See Chapter 6 for more info.

Re-energising

Water acts like a crystal because it holds energy. When we distil it, it also becomes devoid of living energy, however reverse osmosis filtered water will retain some of its living energy. Water is energised naturally by the Earth's energy along with flowing and movement, and is especially energised near a natural waterfall or from a running stream. This is why we feel so good near a waterfall, it is due to the negative ions that are being released by the moving water and the living energy that it is collecting from the earth. We can energise our drinking water by swirling the water in a clockwise vortex for a few seconds.

But also it is worth noting it is believed that when we give the water love and gratitude the water particles change and become symmetrical and beautiful. When given hate or anger they are malformed and lacking in symmetry. Look at the work of Dr Masaru Emoto for more information on this! It is actually very interesting as our bodies are up to 70-80% water! So bear this in mind for your water and your self!!

CHAPTER 5...The
Veggie / Vegan Debate

There is much debate over vegetarianism and veganism and I thought from a qualified perspective that I would bring some information together in one place to help ascertain whether eating meat or being vegetarian is right for you. The purpose of this article is to bring a balanced view. If you are a vegetarian or vegan, no matter how strict, I would implore that you read this with an open mind especially if you are experiencing any health concerns.

First I must point out that I am neither an advocate of vegetarianism, veganism or eating meat. I am an advocate of eating what our bodies need, whether that be a fruit salad or a huge beef steak! There *are* issues with eating meat, and these need to be addressed, however our priority must be for ourselves as how can we begin to bring about peace and well-being to our world if we do not have peace and well-being within?

I first wrote this chapter as an article for my website as I was receiving an increasing number of clients who were vegetarians experiencing health problems and according to their metabolic type and blood type they should have been eating meat, so it may appear in places to be biased towards meat eating. I have since tried to adapt it to include more balanced information.

I will be explaining how I transitioned from being a very strict vegetarian (well I was vegan apart from eating eggs) into a meat eater for my own health and the way that meat can be eaten with compassion based upon Buddhist teachings from respected monks if that is what you need for your own optimum health. I will also be looking into the fallacies and myths surrounding vegetarianism and veganism for a more balanced view.

Some Background Science

Vegetarianism and veganism is becoming increasingly popular in the Western world, but this is actually concerning me and the reason is that in the Western world we are primarily O type blood – it is believed that some 70% of the western population has O type blood. O type blood is the oldest type on the earth and is directly descended from carnivores. Therefore O type bloods require animal protein – it is in their genetic make-up. I agree that we can evolve to become less dependent on meat but this would realistically happen over generations, not in a single lifetime. I must add that this is only an indication and it is possible that an A or B type blood has the metabolic type to require animal protein, or an O type blood may thrive on a primarily (but usually not completely) vegetarian diet, in rare cases especially if meat has not been consumed since very early in life.

The original advocates of vegetarianism are the spiritual Eastern religions, such as Buddhism and the Yoga philosophy which is the core of many Indian religions. A & B type bloods are believed to have originated in the East and therefore the Eastern people are predominantly A & B bloods. These blood types do not rely so much on animal protein, and they can generally be suited to a vegetarian or vegan diet. So you can see just from this that by bringing a tradition that is tailored around the natives of a foreign land to another country, it is not always the best thing. It is a fact that the food our bodies will benefit the most from are the foods that can be grown and sourced locally to the land we are native to. Our needs even change depending on the season to cope with seasonal produce. So foreign and imported foods in general are not as great for us as they may be for the natives of the country from which they originate, and this is also true in the case of being vegetarian or not.

Despite the science, I know some strict vegetarians who have not eaten meat since they were very young, some are O type blood and yet their health does not appear to have suffered. I believe that in these cases, as they have developed and grown without meat, or with very little meat, their body and digestion has adapted to going without it and therefore the blood typing rules may not apply. This is why I do not advocate the blood typing diet alone, but only use it as a guide. The diet I advocate is the metabolic typing diet which takes so much more into account. I also believe that if a child (whose mind and food preferences are unconditioned and pure) naturally has an aversion to meat then it is this instinct we should follow, providing correct research is carried out to ensure their nutritional needs are being met.

If an adult has grown and developed eating meat and then becomes vegetarian once they are fully grown, I do not believe that their body can adapt to vegetarianism over time without health issues if they are a blood type or metabolic type that requires meat. Through my studies I have come to the conclusion that it would take generations to alter a bloodline's requirements.

My Personal Transition

As an O type blood, I discovered that I required meat when I studied nutritional therapy. It was a huge thing for me to begin eating meat after being such a strict vegetarian and it took me months to come to terms with the fact that my body needs animal protein. Not only was I

Buddhist but I had studied about all the ethical and spiritual reasons for being veggie through my Yoga diploma and the Yoga philosophy and teachings, so I was therefore utterly convinced that eating meat was cruel, unnecessary and damaging to my body and the environment. I basically had to de-programme my conditioning once I fully realised the damage I was doing to myself! When I first started studying nutritional therapy one of the first things I learned about was blood typing and metabolic typing as we are all individuals with different needs, and therefore there is no such thing as" one diet fits all". But due to my denial and despair in the fact that I was carnivore and needed animal protein, I halted my studies so I could search for the information I wanted to tell me that I was OK to continue being vegetarian. I just couldn't see how I could bring myself to eat meat again, to even smell meat cooking was like smelling a scorched animal, searing flesh, not food at all, and it made me heave at the very thought of having to consume it.

As I was also fearful of the effects on my spiritual progress which I firmly believed relied upon a vegetarian diet, I decided to also take counsel from some highly respected Buddhist monks, directors and a Lama on this subject (none of whom told me what I wanted to hear either!). Over those few months, I will summarise what I learned in light of what they told me along with a degree of self-realisation.

Realisation

I must practice compassion but this must be with wisdom. One without the other will cause imbalance and problems. To practice compassion by being vegetarian is not wise when my body requires animal protein. If it is what my body requires, then it is my medicine and not my food. We cannot promise to give compassion to all sentient beings when this does not include ourselves, as we are also sentient beings. We must begin in our compassion work by being compassionate to ourselves as if we do not we are not practising with wisdom. Wisdom is to know how we may eat what we need to with compassion and with respect to those whose lives have been sacrificed in order to nourish us. If we are carnivore, that is what we must be and we are trying to be something we are not by being veggie. We are denying ourselves to be who we truly are.

Not eating meat will not make us more spiritual or help us on our spiritual path if these issues are present. We will not progress spiritually if we are denying who we truly are. We will not progress if we are stopping ourselves from being truly nourished and well, as decreased well-being will lower our vibrations and this is contra-indicative of spiritual advancement. We must eat without guilt but acceptance, without fear but with wisdom, and most importantly – without greed but with need. Even H.H. the Dalai Lama eats meat for his well-being!

A fine example of compassion without wisdom is (believe it or not) through Gandhi! He was a very strict vegan. His daughter-in-law became very ill and he was told she would die if she did not receive protein. She was advised that consuming eggs would save her life, but he refused to give them to her. It was then pointed out to him that if she consumed unfertilized eggs there would be no life sacrifice and so he agreed to give her unfertilized eggs and she was saved.

Being vegetarian or vegan is often practised for ethical and compassionate reasons, many of which I agree with, and yet some still continue to purchase cosmetics, toiletries and other foods that are cruelly tested on animals. Additionally, some have vaccines which contain animal, insect and even human cells from aborted foetuses, so are definitely not vegetarian, let alone vegan. To me, this is a good example of compassion without wisdom and I think condoning animal testing by buying and using these products, and having vaccines with these ingredients is far worse than consuming ethically sourced meat if we need to for our health and well-being!

Eating Meat Ethically and with Compassion

An ethical way of eating meat is by choosing organic and free range, and knowing where it has come from. So a local farm would be a good choice, or an organic network such as Abel & Cole or Riverford. We should also be choosing meat that comes from larger animals so that there is a lesser life sacrifice. For example, a cow is vegetarian, so only 1 life is sacrificed to feed about 150 people. Whereas a prawn will eat millions of living micro-organisms and you need at least 50 of them for a meal, so all those lives have been sacrificed for just 1. Also while you are preparing or eating the meat, it is good practice to bless the animal from which it came and give appreciation and love for the fact it is going to nourish your body. This is the underlying message that the Buddhist monks gave me.

Organic, Free Range, Cost & Quality

I know it may seem expensive, but you do not need much if you are having quality meat. I personally found that I can only eat about a 4-5oz organic rump steak whereas I was eating 8-10oz of non-organic steak! The same with organic sausages, they are so dense that I only need 1 where I would need 2-3 or sometimes 4 of the "cheapy" ones. I prefer to buy from the organic networks when I can, but when my budget is tight I cut each steak in 2 and that will provide 4 meals.

The way I see it is this. Animals should be free range, they should be fed and treated naturally, and not forced to grow beyond how they would naturally grow. So the cost of free range organic meat and dairy is what the actual cost *should* be. Anything cheaper is compromising on something such as animal welfare, or quality. Besides animals that are fed nutritiously and killed humanely will have much better nutritious meat and produce.

When an animal feeds, any toxins such as pesticides or herbicides that have been used to treat the feed will be stored in the tissues of the animal along with growth hormones and drugs (routine antibiotics, etc.). These toxic chemicals that are stored in the animals meat become our food and we will then have concentrated levels of these toxins to cope with. Organic animals are fed with vegetation that has not had these harmful chemicals sprayed onto it, are not genetically modified and they are treated naturally, generally homeopathically, and only when they are ill.

Important Points

Organic does not necessarily mean the animal welfare is good, and this needs to be investigated before you choose your meat supplier if you have this concern. However if a farmer is organic it generally means he has his animals' welfare at heart. Likewise, non-organic does not necessarily mean that the animal will have been subject to these chemicals and not treated well. There are many local farms that take all these factors into account but are not registered as organic for some reason (quite often cost).

The humane killing is important as the negative emotions such as pain and fear that the animal experiences upon an inhumane slaughter is stored in its cells, and those energies are transferred to us when we eat it. It is believed that this is where our fear of death comes from. In addition, I have read that many non-organic cows are given a 'tenderiser' injection 24 hours before slaughter which causes them horrendous pain and suffering.

The Vegan 'Agenda'

The vegan agenda is pushed upon us so much through fallacies which are tools used to alter our beliefs and logical thinking – more information is in Chapter 80. Now I am not saying that these issues are not real, but if those who need to eat meat practice eating meat and dairy with compassion these issues will no longer be issues.

I believe this is being done to push the processed vegan meat alternatives in a drive similar to the crazes of 'Low fat spread' and 'Low sugar / artificial sweetener', paying no attention to health, but demonising natural foods to replace them with highly profitable, processed, often genetically modified junk! I've even experienced someone saying to me that a chocolate bar was healthy as it was vegan, and this is a big misconception brought on by this propaganda!

Not only are we subject to this vegan/healthy misappropriation fallacy, we are also 'guilted' into giving up meat and dairy through animal welfare which is all based upon an appeal to our emotions. Animal welfare is a very real issue indeed and I highly commend those who campaign tirelessly to expose animal cruelty and attempt to improve the welfare of farm animals. However, you can see by what I have written above how this can be overcome without resorting to vegetarianism if it is not right for you. I find it a shame that the animal rights groups go to the extreme and promote that the only way to solve the problem is to go veggie or vegan. On the other hand, if your blood type or metabolic type suggests you can be a vegetarian, then I strongly recommend that you give up meat and fish. The less the demand for animal products, the less need for the mass-production of these products there will be.

So-called 'health' propaganda causes us to believe that red meat causes health problems, well actually this is a fallacy based upon half-truth. Maybe if you consume large amounts of red meat and you are an A or B type blood then you are not eating right for your type, and then yes it probably will cause you to have health problems. But this is only going to be relevant to approximately 30% of the population in the UK! And a

22

mass-produced steak from a cow that has been scared and caged all its life, fed a genetically modified diet and given growth hormones and antibiotics as routine is a far cry from a pasture-raised, organic, grass-fed cow that has led a happy life.

So many common beliefs are based upon propaganda by corporations and those who do not want us to be fully well. Even environmentalists are jumping on the bandwagon with vegetarianism and veganism. They claim that methane from cattle is causing an increase in greenhouse gases. Well I am not going into the climate change/greenhouse gas scam here (we will save that for another time, shall we?).

Use of land is another argument. But I believe this is based upon a *perceived* opinion that there is a shortage of land. People are being crammed into cities and suburbs with decreasing greenbelt land and we perceive there is not enough land to farm the food required by the world's population. That is until we actually see the amount of undeveloped land that there actually is in the world! I am not saying we should develop loads of unspoilt land, not at all. Here is where one of my favourite Gandhi quotes comes in:

> *"Earth provides enough to satisfy every man's need, but not every man's greed"*

In an ideal world, those of us eating meat that don't need to would become veggie, those who need meat would only eat organic (requiring less meat) and only the amount that they actually need. Then there would be no issues! It is the mass-production, mass-consumption and greed that creates the problems!

In addition I believe that vegetarianism and veganism is being promoted as part of Agenda 21 & Agenda 30 which, among other things, are threatening complete control of our health, lives and possessions by the state in the name of 'sustainable development', 'social justice' and 'community-based living' (all these phrases being buzzwords to alert us of these agendas). I am not saying being veggie is a bad thing just because it forms part of a corrupt agenda, but it is being promoted for the wrong reasons and could cause the health of many people who are not suited to going without meat to suffer. Rather than become distracted with Agenda 21, I will suggest you carry out some research on this for yourself to see how it will affect you and your family.

Vegetarian Health Issues – no I am not talking calcium!

There are real health issues for vegetarians.

From the new perspective of GNM, when our body is in a biological programme that is controlled by the old brain, and we are experiencing night sweats, it is very important that we eat a lot of proteins. This is because the night sweats indicate that TB bacteria are involved in our healing programme. TB bacteria require huge amount of protein, and when it is not available it will deplete our own protein stores, and this is the main cause of the 'wasting away' that we see in cancer patients. Ironically, this is the time when people begin promoting raw diets, juicing fasts and veganism as a 'cure' for the cancer or disease, but it is the worst thing we can do in this case!

Low zinc levels and high copper levels found in vegetarian proteins can cause copper toxicity. This has many nasty symptoms, but (interestingly) one symptom is feeling like you are dreamy – many people mistake this as feeling more spiritual since becoming veggie! If you are veggie and suspect you may have high copper levels, you may wish to try taking a zinc supplement. Vitamin C will also help to reduce copper levels. I have had a few clients with this problem.

Unhealthy vegetarians will substitute meat for extremely health-destroying meat alternatives like Quorn, soya and heavily processed

24

meat-free products (pass us the cardboard!). These certainly do not form part of a healthy diet! Soy is a xeno-oestrogen, mimicking oestrogen in the body and causing hormonal imbalance. In fact the soy will quite probably be GM, as over 93% of the world's soy is now GM (a time of writing). It is also high in glutamate, as well as is textured vegetable protein (TVP), which acts in the same way as MSG does in the body, binding with the glutamate receptors of our cells, including those across the blood-brain barrier.

Quorn is also a very unhealthful meat alternative, despite the company advertising to the contrary. It is made from a man-made fungus called fusarium venenatum, which has NEVER been tested or used as a human food before Quorn began using it (interestingly, venenatum in Latin means poisonous!). I have always naturally been repelled by Quorn and since researching its manufacture, I now know why! According to Dr Mercola it is linked to many unfavourable reactions, there have even been 2 deaths linked to Quorn consumption! Since its launch in 1985, several studies have raised concerns about its safety yet, as with many other harmful foods, it continues to be touted as healthy.

The healthy way to be vegetarian is to choose vegetarian dishes that comprise of a good variety of vegetables and pulses/beans. Man-made substitutes for any food, meat or otherwise, are manufactured rubbish!

Until recently, cheese was NOT naturally vegetarian. Cheese is traditionally made using rennet from calves, the main constitution of which is an enzyme called chymosin. However, according to the Soil Association, since 1987 all vegetarian cheese has used a genetically modified chymosin made by introducing a calf's gene into yeast. It is only very recently a very similar microbial enzyme has been discovered that can be used as a substitution. The Soil Association state they are strict in their non-GM policy, but only now that there is an alternative to the GM chymosin. However the Vegetarian Society appears to make exceptions to their non-GM rule when it comes to the GM chymosin. So if you eat cheese you need to bear this in mind.

Another issue is Vitamin B12. So many vegetarians are B12 deficient, and if this is unaddressed it can develop into pernicious anaemia which generally requires regular B12 injections. (which contain animal products and are tested on animals). B12 deficiency can cause many problems including migraine, hair loss, anxiety, low energy, repeated illness and more. You simply cannot get enough from any non-animal sources without supplementation, and the type of B12 found in supplements is not usually the most bio-available form. If you are a vegetarian, especially if your typing states you shouldn't be, I strongly recommend seeking a high quality B12 supplement. These will generally come from animal source, but it may just be a sacrifice you have to make if you are not prepared to change your diet.

In Conclusion

It is my opinion that we must eat what is right for our bodies FULL STOP. I would personally love to be vegetarian but I am now accepting of what I am. As a nutritional therapist and kinesiologist, I am discovering an increasing number of unhealthy vegetarians, surprisingly many more than meat-eaters, contrary to what many believe, and this really concerns me.

If you are currently a vegetarian and find you need to eat meat for your optimum well-being, you can always compromise by having a 'veggie day' per week as a personal protest to animal welfare, or your particular concerns. I know a few people who do this successfully. Likewise, if you are a meat eater and find out your metabolic typing can do without meat but you enjoy eating it, you could have meat only at weekends, special occasions or just for your Sunday roast, for example. So you see it is possible to compromise our wants with our needs!

26

If you are a vegetarian or vegan and your typing is suited to it then I salute you! I think if we can be vegetarian without negative health effects then I would definitely encourage it, as if you continue to eat meat then it would be through choice and not need. But all those veggie-wannabe-carnivores out there, please for your own sakes, take on board some of this information and do your own research if you feel the need. We are after all what we eat, and if we are not eating for our full potential it means we are not our full potential!

CHAPTER 6...Salt of the Earth

Himalayan Salt is basically pure salt that is mined in regions surrounding the Himalayas. It is believed to have been formed from ancient primal seas that were evaporated and pushed underground by the changing landscape. As it has been underground since these ancient times, it has been hidden away from modern-day pollutants in the atmosphere (such as carbon monoxide or nitrates). When the Himalayan massif rose approximately 250 million years ago, it broke up through the ancient sea beds generating much heat and pressure. It is believed that this heat and pressure could be what caused the salt to form with its unique crystalline structure. For over 3,000 years the salt has been harvested and used for its quality and health giving properties.

What Makes Himalayan Salt so Healthful?

It is believed that all life in the universe originated from a 'primal sea' and as Himalayan Salt is so untouched until it is harvested by hand, it has been found to contain (or rather have bound to its structure) almost all the natural trace minerals found in our bodies, and believed to be found in this primal sea. It is often promoted that it contains 84 of the 92 elements found on Earth. But what makes it more beneficial is that these elements are found in their own natural balance with each other, bound together in harmonious structure to the crystalline salt structure. They are found in a colloidal form, meaning the particles are so tiny they are easily absorbed by the body. Not only does it contain these essential elements (or more correctly, provides a transport system by 'carrying' the elements bound to its structure), it also holds the vibrations of the Earth energy within its crystal structure just like any other crystal would. There is more information on the energy of crystals in Chapter 65.

The benefits of natural Himalayan Salt are many. It is believed to:

- assist in maintaining a healthy pH balance in your cells.

- regulate the retention of water held by your body.

- help reduce signs of ageing.

- improve the health of blood sugar in the body.

- help with the absorption of food and nutrients through your intestines and digestive system.

- prevent muscle cramps.

- increase bone strength.

- help in the generation of hydroelectric energy in the cells of your body.

- support sinus and respiratory health.

- regulate your sleep pattern as it naturally promotes sleep.

- assist in a healthy libido.

- contribute to healthy blood vessels.

- help to regulate your blood pressure when taken with water.

- emit negative ions when heated which cancel harmful positive ions and promote healthy air

- contribute to your body's homeostasis (internal regulation of the necessary environment in which it can thrive)

Consuming Himalayan Salt is considered by many to be completely safe. Due to its structure and property of contributing to the body's homeostasis, including the maintenance of a natural balance of minerals, it is extremely difficult to absorb too much Himalayan Salt so it is considered safe to use quite freely. It is also considered not to contribute to high blood pressure, but rather as it helps the body's homeostasis it can have a regulating effect.

The Problem with Ordinary Salt

Typical table salt is salt that has been chemically cleaned and stripped of its minerals until we are left with sodium chloride. Chemicals such as free-flowing and anti-caking agents are then added. Our bodies tend to react to this salt as if it was a foreign body. We take in a lot of hidden salt from processed foods, so when we then consume more salt our body can get overloaded to the point that it cannot eliminate all the salt. The excess of salt is held in our tissues, attracting fluids. It has been stated that as much as 23g of fluid is required to break down just 1g of common salt, causing the tissues of the body to retain water. This fluid is taken from other cells, dehydrating them and can even cause them to die. In addition to water retention and dehydration, excessive salt consumption can also worsen conditions such as cellulite, rheumatism, arthritis, gout, kidney stones and gallbladder stones.

People are told to go on low sodium diets and avoid salt, and yet there are essential minerals that our bodies need in salt when it is pure, and this is therefore causing more problems in mineral deficiencies. In addition, low sodium intake can result in insufficient hydrochloric acid (stomach acid) as our body utilises the chloride from salt in order to manufacture the stomach acid. This will affect the correct processing of nutrients causing many digestive problems and further deficiencies as I have seen in many hair mineral tests I have analysed.

Sea Salt and Rock Salt

It is believed by many that sea salt is a healthy alternative to table salt, but sadly this is no longer the case. Toxic pollutants such as PCBs, mercury and dioxin can now be found at alarming levels in some areas, and oil spills polluting the sea are becoming more frequent. In particular, after the Deep Water Horizon disaster caused by BP in the Gulf of Mexico, thousands of tons of Correxit oil dispersant (believed to be 10 times more toxic than oil itself) was sprayed and dumped into the ocean along with GM algae to eat away the oil. Residents of Florida have been suffering from many unusual rashes, skin problems, breathing problems and aborted pregnancies since the disaster (but you will not hear of this in the mainstream media due to its destructive effect on the tourism industry). Due to the Gulf Stream, this concoction of dangerous chemicals will be carried around the world!

Another concern is the radiation from the Japanese Tsunami of 2011 which, despite being thought of as old news, many sources claim it continues to spew tons of radiation into the seas. Of course this radiation is (and will continue to be) carried all over the world with the currents.

Many people are avoiding eating fish and seafood due to these issues, but these foods are so nutritious that I believe this is not the answer and throws the baby out with the bathwater. If you are concerned, you could take zeolite when you eat fish as this will help to remove toxins and radiation. More information on zeolite can be found in Chapter 25.

It is estimated that 89% of sea salt producers are now refining their salt due to the presence of pollutants which means they will also be stripping essential minerals from it, so much of today's sea salt is no longer a healthy alternative.

Lloyd recently carried out a comparison of the Himalayan Salt we sell and Celtic Sea Salt. This was due to continuous attacks on Himalayan Salt by a particular seller of Celtic Sea Salt who even claimed it was toxic. Lloyd found that the sea salt contained 10 times more lead as our Himalayan Salt as well as a whopping 5.6 parts per million of fluoride!

In addition, if you were to look at sea salt and rock salt in a microscope, you would see that their structure is irregular and the elements it contains are not connected to its structure, making the elements not so readily available to the body. So your body needs to exert energy to process any elements in the salt, making the body's gain quite small compared to the loss of energy.

Consuming Himalayan Salt

Himalayan Salt is suitable for consumption as long as it has been handled as food grade during packaging and is supplied in food grade bags or tubs. It is usually available in extra-fine granules which are easy to dissolve and very convenient, granules which are slightly larger granules ideal for use in the bath or salt shaker, coarse granules which can be placed in a salt grinder or bath and salt rocks ideal for making sole (* see below) and for in the bath, or for placing around candles or a heat source to ionise the air. I believe it is good practice to replace all your culinary salt for Himalayan Salt, on the table and in cooking, and due to its excellent balanced mineral and vibrational content it is excellent for re-mineralising distilled water.

Sole (Pronounced so-lay)

Put a few Himalayan salt rocks or about an inch of salt granules into a glass of pure spring water. Leave it for at least 24 hours. If the salt completely dissolves, add more. Keep doing this until the salt rocks or granules remain in the water. This means the salt has dissolved into the water at a maximum natural strength of solution. At this stage Sole is created. Keep your sole in a container with a lid to prevent evaporation and make sure salt crystals always stay in the water, ascertaining the optimum solution strength. Add more water and crystals as required. It needs no refrigeration and will last forever! One tablespoon of sole is taken in a glass of spring water each morning. This replenishes electrolytes in the body, as well as the benefits mentioned in this article.

Himalayan Salt for Bathing and Body Cleansing

Place a handful or 2 in the bath and Himalayan Salt can help you to relax, it will absorb into your system and may at the same time help ease any skin conditions such as psoriasis and eczema! You can also enjoy the benefits of extra fine Himalayan Salt by using it in your Neti Pot (for nasal cleansing) as described in Chapter 22.

Himalayan Salt Lighting products

You will also find lamps and candle holders made from chunks of Himalayan Salt. These work as natural ionisers and air purifiers. Salt attracts moisture from the air (we know this as if you have a Himalayan Salt lamp and do not switch it on, it will get wet and a pool will form underneath it – a reason you must always keep them on!). As the salt lamp de-humidifies the air to some extent, airborne pathogens such as mould which require humidity to remain airborne and thrive will also be reduced, creating cleaner more healthy air. Additionally, when the bulb or candle inside the salt warms the salt up, it will attract more moisture which dissolves some of the salt before evaporating. It is the evaporation of this mineral-rich moisture that causes a release of negative ions into the air.

There are many positive ions in the air from electromagnetic smog, caused by electrical equipment especially those like portable and mobile phones, televisions, microwaves, etc.; also magnetic pollutants such as geopathic stress from underground pipework, leylines, overhead cables, mobile phone masts, etc. These positive ions can cause a general state of poor health and energy. By emitting negative ions into the air, we are combating the positive ions and promoting healthy air. Think of how healthy and cleansed you feel standing at the seaside or next to a waterfall where there are millions of negative ions in the air!

From an article in the Mail Online:

> *"In fresh country air we find up to 4,000 negative ions per cm^3 (the size of a sugar cube). Waterfalls and sea water contain up to 10,000 negative ions, whereas the number of negative ions in major capital cities at rush hour does not even reach 100."*

So, bearing all this in mind, it appears that Himalayan Salt really is the Salt of the Earth!

CHAPTER 7...Acid/Alkaline Balance

There is much information regarding alkalising the body and eating alkalising foods on the internet. It is very often claimed that the body is usually in an acidic state due to the highly acidic diet and environment that most people in the UK are used to. It is claimed that an acidic body will hold on to toxins, reduce our energy and absorption and create an unhealthy environment that disease and cancer cells can thrive in. It is claimed that when our body becomes more alkaline, toxins can no longer be held in our systems and they are therefore eliminated.

I would like to cut through the misunderstandings and myths that have been created by unqualified people who have taken this theory to extremes as I understand it. I do not believe that 'Alkalising the Body' is as simple as it sounds, or that it is the ultimate answer, and I previously had a feeling that this is a fad based upon a lot of assumptions and misunderstandings. After studying German New Medicine, and learning of the beneficial role that microbes have in our healing of biological programmes, it appears I was right!

First of all, an acidic environment is found in the vicinity of cancer tumours and disease, and it has been assumed that the acidic environment is a cause of the disease. However, the microbes that are activated to assist in our healing actually require an acidic environment in which to thrive and carry to their task efficiently. Therefore, to attempt to alkalise the body during the healing phase of a biological programme will actually hinder or even prevent our healing.

Secondly, our body's optimum pH is 7.35-7.45. I have heard some people trying desperately to get their entire bodies to the aforementioned pH of 8.4, causing their bodies extreme stress. Our body's homeostasis (its process that regulates and maintains a healthy environment throughout) ensures that our internal pH is maintained at the optimum level. Therefore I believe that the parts of our body involved in it's homeostasis are under the greatest pressure when our bodies are being forced to be acidic by unhealthy living, or too alkaline for health concerns. So extreme care must be taken not only to avoid foods lacking minerals but also in attempting to buffer the system towards alkalinity.

Alkalising through Diet

It is dubious calling a food an alkalising or acidifying food as when you learn about the metabolic typing, you will realise that some foods are alkalising to some people while being acidic to others. A prime example of this is red meat, generally regarded as acidic, but it is alkalising to protein types. However it is proven that it is essential nutrients and minerals are naturally alkalising. Take water for example. Water lacking essential mineral content (such as that which has been distilled) will become acidic. Adding Himalayan Salt with its trace minerals will naturally alkalise it. Additionally, when a food hits your stomach acid I cannot see how any physical alkalising effects will survive and it does seem that most success using an alkalising method has been either externally or intravenously, both methods avoiding the stomach acid.

Studying the pH of foods is very confusing as lemon juice and apple cider vinegar, deemed as two of the most alkalising foods, are extremely acidic! This proves that measuring a food's pH is not indicative of its acidifying/alkalising effect on the body, and this could be easily misunderstood by those who are new to natural health and holistic nutrition. In fact, the pH of food is measured by the alkalinity of the 'ash' it produces after it is burned for energy by the body. So it is wrong to call it the pH of food, but better to call it the pH *effect* of food.

Propaganda

There is a lot of propaganda on the acid/alkaline subject especially by those selling alkalising equipment such as water filters and pH kits, but there is also research that has proven that consuming alkalised water, etc. in the long term can have a detrimental affect on our health. Many people are known to have become extremely ill by trying to fight or prevent disease by over-alkalising the body. Not only is over-alkalising just as detrimental to health as over-acidifying, but I believe that some systems have used unnatural methods for alkalising and this has probably been their downfall.

I believe the most important aspect to consider is this: it is not just the pH that is important, but what is causing the pH level. Going back to water – if the water is unnaturally alkalised, it will not be beneficial to the health as it does not have the essential minerals that would otherwise make it naturally alkaline, despite possibly having a short term effect on acidic conditions. So it appears that many people have tried to apply the alkalising theory to foods and water without a true understanding (maybe even sometimes for deliberate misguidance and profit). If you follow the advice in this book on drinking water and eating for your metabolic type then you are on the right track in my opinion without the need to know the acid/alkaline science behind it all!

Sodium Bicarbonate

Sodium bicarbonate is used by many for alkalising the body as it is so alkaline. This can be taken orally, in the bath or sometimes by injection into affected tissues. It has been used to successfully treat many acidic diseases, but understanding GNM, as I explained, are these actually 'acidic conditions' or is this a misrepresentation due to the acidic environment required by the microbes assisting healing?

I do not use sodium bicarb for 'alkalising', and do not believe in this at all. Although, I use it for many other things as there are literally hundreds of uses for sodium bicarbonate, health and otherwise, but this would warrant another book! However I have listed some that may be interest here:

- Can be effective in whitening teeth, an alternative to toothpaste

- Can regulate stomach acid (mix with milk – really effective!)

- Softens the skin and neutralises acidic skin conditions by putting a handful in the bath

- Treats bee stings, make into a paste and apply to the sting

- Neutralises odour (try sprinkling in trainers!)

- Along with citric acid it is excellent for cleaning sinks when sprinkled into hot water! Also great for other bathroom and kitchen cleaning including scouring

- Whitens clothes and terry nappies

- Place a bowl of sodium bicarb in the fridge to eliminate odours

- Sprinkle on carpets, leave overnight then vacuum to neutralise odours without harsh chemicals

Italian oncologist, Dr. Simoncini, originally discovered the connection between fungal infections such as candida, and cancerous tumours. He also discovered that when cancer cells were directly soaked with or injected with sodium bicarbonate they died within days. However, with a knowledge of GNM, the discovery of candida fungus surrounding cancer is not surprising as candida fungus has the important job of breaking down tumours that are controlled by the old brain, assisting their removal from the body. But Simoncini made the incorrect assumption that the fungus he saw was the actual cause of the cancer. By using Sodium Bicarbonate, the fungus would be eradicated and symptoms abated therefore appearing to be healed. But, in fact, because the Biological Special Programme would simply have been forced back into the conflict-active phase where there are very few symptoms, and because healing had not completed on the psyche/brain levels, the programme would re-run its course once again, and this would typically be considered a relapse.

CHAPTER 8...Cholesterol & Fats

I do not know how mainstream can get it so wrong sometimes! Actually, I can take a good guess and I think it is either or both of these:

1.   They listen to the propaganda advertising of corporations who manufacture so-called healthy foods and pharmaceutical drugs.

2.   They are in cahoots with the corporations as these are the same corporations that will profit off us if we are ill.

I will just deal with the main misunderstandings or misconceptions.

Myth: Cholesterol is bad for you – it must be lowered at all costs and low cholesterol is much better than high.   Saturated fats cause cholesterol and we must use cholesterol reducing spreads and low fat products to lower our cholesterol or protect against high cholesterol.

Reality: Cholesterol is not bad for you.   Firstly there are 2 types of cholesterol, HDL is High Density Lipoproteins and is considered to be useful and good cholesterol. This can be increased by taking regular exercise and may actually help prevent heart problems. LDL is Low Density Lipoproteins and is considered to be bad cholesterol. It is only needed by the body in small amounts and excessive levels can cause health problems such as furring of the arteries. Cholesterol is found in the presence of particular heart attacks, and a hypothesis has been made to link the heart attacks with the cholesterol. However there are 2 points to consider:

1. according to the new perspective, cholesterol is instrumental in healing our blood vessels during the healing phase of certain biological programmes, and so it would be found where there is a heart attack (in the Epi Crisis of certain programmes)

2. the biggest cause of artery furring is calcium deposits often caused by magnesium deficiency (see Chapter 15).

So having a high cholesterol could just mean that either we are in the healing phase of a biological programme, or that we have high level of HDL cholesterol.

If you are too low in cholesterol it can cause many problems as our body needs cholesterol for its proper function. A healthy cholesterol is said to be no higher than 6.5 and no lower than 5. There is great danger with statins, as these can not only lower your cholesterol too much but also invite a plethora of other problems into your body. Statins act by blocking the enzyme in your liver that produces cholesterol. But according to Dr Mercola more than 900 studies have directly linked statin drugs to many problems, likely caused by the stress of the medication and the disruption to our healing, causing chronic conditions due to hanging healing.

So if you would still like to lower your cholesterol, I would strongly recommend this is done through diet and lifestyle modification.

Saturated fats and mono-unsaturated fats are actually the easiest forms of fat for our bodies to process. How much fat you can eat healthily will depend on your metabolic typing, or other aspects of your diet, as combinations of foods can have a different impact. I am a protein type and eat a lot of coconut oil and pure organic butter, I fry everything in them and eat them raw. I have previously followed a ketogenic diet

41

with 80% fat (see chapter 11), yet my cholesterol was low, it could do with increasing to be ideal!

So-called 'healthy' spreads and margarine are highly processed hydrogenated fats that not only have been damaged beyond healthy, but also have had many other chemicals added to them to give them their colour and flavour. Hydrogenation means that the oil is blasted with hydrogen to turn it semi-solid and translucent turning it into a trans fat. (No thank you, I think I will stick with my pure, unpasteurised organic butter!)

Cooking Oils

Which brings me on to cooking with oils and fats. I use butter and coconut oil as mentioned above. The two types of coconut oil I use are minimally refined (as I don't want everything to taste and smell of coconut) and virgin, both being organic food grade. My butter is organic. I also sometimes use organic sustainable palm oil for frying.

Healthful oils such as nut oils, hemp oil and olive oil should not be used for cooking as it destroys their properties, so they do not become healthful any longer – what a waste! Use them in dressings, pesto, salads, etc., or you can warm them gently, but don't fry them at high heat! Not only that, but the temperature at which they will turn to trans fat is still reachable in normal cooking. When an oil is heated beyond a certain temperature (usually when it starts to smoke), it turns into a trans fat which is very unhealthy. Olive oil and avocado oil has the highest turning points of approximately 185-200degC and 204degC respectively, rapeseed oil and other vegetable oils, even healthful oils like flaxseed can be as low as 120degC. Besides, rapeseed is from the canola plant of which most of the world's supply is now genetically modified.

Coconut Oil

In comparison, butter and coconut oil in particular are very stable. Butter is suitable for slow frying and can truly enhance the flavour of the fried food. Coconut oil is suitable for higher heat frying such as stir fry and is believed to be the most stable oil to cook with. In addition, many fantastic claims have been made about coconut oil, particularly virgin organic coconut oil, due to its lauric acid content. However, this research is based upon the hypothesis that microbes are not beneficial to us, and that diseases such as Alzheimer's are a malfunction. But GNM proves they are not malfunctions but meaningful biological programmes.

An advantage of using coconut oil that is claimed by many – excess amounts eaten do not add to the body's fat stores as with the consumption of other fats and it is also claimed to have a positive impact on the body's cholesterol levels (if you still believe that cholesterol is a problem!).

Omegas

Omega Oils are essential fatty acids that the body requires us to consume daily as most it cannot produce for itself. Omega 3 and 6 are required at a ratio between 1:1 and 1:5 respectively. There are also other omega oils such as 7 and 9. Suggested levels for these have not yet been established.

Omega 3 is found in oily fish. We need daily doses of omega 3 as it is essential for cholesterol regulation, heart health and brain function. It contains EPA (eicosapentaenoic acid) and DHA (docosahexaenoic acid). A healthy intake is considered to be 1.1g – 1.5g of omega 3.

Omega 6 complements omega 3 by boosting its effects on the brain. It is also helpful for hot flushes in menopause. It is found in nuts and seeds.

We generally consume plenty of omega 6 in our regular every-day diets.

Omega 7 is a rare omega oil and is found to be beneficial for weight and cholesterol maintenance and healthy skin. It is found in sea buckthorn berries and dairy products.

Omega 9 improves our blood sugar balance, improves our cholesterol by increasing HDL and lowering LDL and supports a healthy cardiovascular system. It is different to the other omegas as our body can actually produce it. It is found in some nuts such as almonds, pecans and cashews.

Krill Oil

Krill oil is believed to be the best source of omega 3 as it contains the highest levels of omega 3. Krill is a tiny shrimp-like marine crustacean. There have been no conclusive studies other than those by manufacturers of krill oil to substantiate this, however it is still recommended by many leading names in the alternative health field, and I consider this to be an excellent source from my own experience.

Hemp Oil

Hemp oil is made from the seed. Pure cold-pressed hemp oil has many claimed health benefits. It is rich in Omega 3 and 6 at an optimum ratio (usually around 1 omega 3 to 3 omega 6). However, as we generally are getting plenty of Omega 6 through our diets, you may wish to seek an oil higher in Omega 3 to bring the ratio back into a healthy balance.

Cannabis Oil – (Mentioned here to differentiate between the two). When the oil is made from the leaves and bud of the plant, it is claimed to have many other wonderful benefits. This is due to its natural THC and CBD content. It has been discovered that we have cannabinoid receptors all over our bodies, and we produce endocannabinoids for the

44

correct function and communication of our cells. In addition, cannabis in any form is highly supportive of the vagatonic state of healing, and due to its many properties such as pain relieving, anti-nausea, anti-convulsion, etc., it can be very useful. See Chapter 44 for more information.

Back to Omega 3, it is important to eat a source of omega 3 everyday, or to supplement with omega 3. It is found in oily fish, flaxseed oil and walnuts to name a few.

CHAPTER 9...*Sugar is not so Sweet*

Sugar is generally considered to be a natural substance and therefore, apart from being bad for our teeth and fattening, is OK to consume. But this could not be further from the truth.

Sugar is bad for us in many ways, although I would consider it the lesser evil compared to substances such as aspartame and sucralose!

It is highly addictive – some believe it is more addictive than cocaine, and excessive fructose is actually stored in our body as FAT!

Sugar is very stimulating, can hinder the healing phase of biological programmes and enhance the conflict-active phase, causing more intensive symptoms in the healing phase. In the conventional paradigm, symptoms are disease, but understanding the new perspective we know that symptoms are our healing. So this could be why the following is shown to be linked to excess sugar:

- high blood pressure
- cholesterol imbalances – decreases HDL, increases LDL, elevates triglycerides, elevates blood sugar
- heart disease
- diabetes

Different Sugars

Sugar comes in many forms, natural and processed, fructose is actually being discovered as much worse for your health than sucrose or glucose. Dextrose is the same as glucose but many companies have changed the name due to bad press about glucose!

Basically anything ending in -ose is a sugar. In my opinion only honey is actually beneficial to our body, and active manuka honey of a strength of 10 or above is believed to be very beneficial due to its many healthful properties and is claimed not to burden the body like sugar, including being safe for diabetics. Also, pure organic maple syrup can be beneficial.

Fruits

Despite containing fructose, whole fruits are extremely good if eaten in moderation. The fructose comes packaged with the fibre and the nutrients of the whole fruit and so the fructose has less of an impact on our bodies. The fibre found in fruit is valuable food source for our gut bacteria and our GI tract. In addition, dark coloured fruits, particularly berries, contain many healthful phytochemicals such as flavinoids, resveratrol and other polyphenols, serving important roles such as regulation of other nutrients consumed and offering valuable support for our health. The science of epigenetics and nutrigenomics has found many of these phytochemicals to favourably alter how our genes express themselves, however this research has been carried out in a petri dish, removing the cells from their psyche/brain/organ correlation, and therefore any reactions to the cells are based upon an assumption that the cells act the same when inside the body and a part of the psyche/brain/organ.

Juices

Juicing fruit leaves behind a high concentration of fructose without the bulk of the fruit to aid in its digestion so drinking pure juice is not recommended as a healthful practice (unless as a part of a complete holistic therapeutic nutrition programme such as the Gerson therapy). Supermarket juices made from concentrate are particularly unhealthful as they do not contain the enzymes found in freshly squeezed juice. Fruit juices impart such a huge sugar hit to the body especially when consumed alone. If you wish to continue drinking pure fruit juice, the most healthful way is to drink it with food, preferably meals, and dilute it 50/50 with water. Drinking juice or milk at mealtime is considered better than drinking a clear fluid as it does not dilute the stomach acid as much and so the negative effect on our digestion from drinking with meals is reduced. Vegetable juices are fine, although not quite as tasty (if you can stomach them at all!), as vegetables contain less fructose. Vegetable juicing can be handy if you want to load up on nutrients and for therapeutic doses of nutrients. However, I would still prefer to eat vegetables whole. Juicing with a slow or masticating juicer is the best option as it keeps the enzymes and nutrients intact. You can pop an apple or pear in to sweeten, if you need to!

Alternatives

Here are some substances that are often used as sugar substitutes but I would not recommend they are used:

Agave Syrup: This is incorrectly labelled as 'natural' when in fact it is typically highly processed and is generally 80% fructose.

Sucralose: Although marketed to be made from sugar, it is a chlorinated artificial sweetener that bears no resemblance to sugar and should be avoided as much as you would avoid aspartame!

High Fructose Corn Syrup: HFCS is particularly bad as its glucose content (45%) accelerates the consumption of its fructose content (55%).

And here are some healthy alternatives:

Xylitol: Wood alcohol such as xylitol, maltitol and sorbitol are generally considered to be a healthier alternative to sugar. However, they are not completely digested and so may cause digestive disturbance if taken in excess. Xylitol is becoming known for many health benefits such as its support in healing and repairing tooth decay, and is safe for diabetics.

Stevia: Stevia is a natural herb that is claimed to be 500 times sweeter than sugar so only tiny amounts are used. It was banned from sale in the UK until 2012 due it not being proven safe despite thousands of years of traditional usage. It is virtually calorie free but it has a liquorice after taste. Please be aware that there are many marketed forms of artificial sweeteners that are based on Stevia but in the same way as Sucralose, they bear little resemblance to the natural form and should be avoided as they have been insufficiently tested and their long-term affects have therefore not been established.

CHAPTER 10..."Superfoods"

There are many foods that are classed as superfoods, and this is because they are extremely rich in nutrients. Some can also be very expensive. My take on most superfoods is that it is fine to include these in your diet, but too much of a good thing is just as bad as not enough in many cases! So I think the "everything in moderation" rule is what we are calling for!

The best way to look at it is this. We wouldn't normally eat some of these things, and maybe that is for a reason. Some nutrients, especially plant nutrients need a certain amount of processing before our digestive systems can efficiently process them, which is why it is sometimes better to eat them second hand (i.e. algae through seafood, grass through grass-fed animals, etc.).

The other thing to consider is that if you have an abundance of nutrients it will only cause imbalances in your body, as nutrients in your body will be antagonised by some of the nutrients you are taking in. If these nutrients are in extreme proportions to what our body would naturally take in with our regular diet, and more than what we need, it will cause our bodies and digestive system internal stress and use up valuable energy in processing these extra nutrients. This will place our liver and kidneys under extreme pressure and, as many superfoods have a detoxing effect, they can also cause a cleansing crisis if over-consumed.

I choose not to eat too many superfoods for this reason, although I use a lot of herbs and spices and always combine them with my cooking. I tried to grow wheatgrass to have a shot per day when I had the lump in my breast, but really didn't get on with it and when I muscle tested, it was not showing as beneficial. Listen to your body, or maybe you could learn how to do kinesiology muscle testing to test the food on you (more info in Chapter 68), and be wary if you intend to take a superfood everyday unless you are extremely deficient or need its nutrients therapeutically.

I have listed a few of the most common superfoods (in my opinion). There are many more, and I have not included any I have covered in other sections.

Spirulina & Chlorella

Spirulina is a micro-algae that is rich in vitamins and minerals. It is also believed to be good at chelating heavy metals from the body. It can come in tablet form or a very fine blue-green powder and can be sprinkled into cooking (after cooking), or salads, etc. It tastes like pond water and will turn your cooking dark green with only a small amount! It is said to provide pre-digested protein, which is beneficial as it is easier to digest than the many undigested proteins that we consume. It is also a good source of Iodine.

Chlorella is also a micro-algae, renowned for its ability to chelate mercury and help to remove it from the body. It is also rich in nutrients and minerals and like spirulina, comes in tablet form or powder.

People make huge health claims over chlorella and spirulina including that they have reversed cancer, asthma, depression, obesity, diabetes and arthritis. While it may be supportive to healing, GNM proves that there cannot be any cures for these diseases (as they are meaningful biological programmes). Like spirulina, it is also a good source of

Iodine. Care must be taken if you have PKU, as it is generally recommended not to consume algae based foods if this condition is present.

Goji Berries

Goji berries are renowned for their ultra high vitamin C content, it is commonly claimed that they contain by weight 500 times more vitamin C than oranges. But other sources will explain this is unlikely. They are also very high in vitamin A, however as this is a fat-soluble vitamin it is very easy to take too much (as it can accumulate in our body). Goji Berries also contain selenium and germanium which are both very supportive to our health. I would not recommend consuming juice due to the very high sugar content – it is always best to eat a food whole!

Cacao

Raw cacao beans are basically raw chocolate. They are high in potassium, protein and zinc and are widely used in raw recipes and raw chocolate. They are best bought in whole beans or nibs, and are extremely bitter to taste. They are rich in vitamins and minerals and can have an anti-depressant effect, increasing serotonin in the brain.

Wheatgrass

Wheatgrass is believed to have excellent benefits for the blood, circulation and thyroid. It is very rich in enzymes which are the essence of our healing. Dr. Yoshihide Hagiwara, president of the Hagiwara Institute of Health in Japan, believes that the chlorophyll is extremely similar to haemoglobin and he claims that as it is fat soluble, when it enters our bloodstream it actually turns into human blood! It is used on the outside of the body as a healer and soother and internally used it can also have sedative properties, aiding in returning a natural balance of sleep. It is also proven to reduce the effects of radiation on our bodies. It is rich in nutrients including a very high calcium content, however this can deplete our magnesium. Despite these claims, wheatgrass tested unfavourably for myself when I was in healing, as I previously mentioned.

Psyllium Husks

Psyllium husks are used in Ayurvedic medicine for colon cleansing and better blood circulation. They are indigestible for human beings, and are therefore used widely as a source of dietary fibre. In this way they can ease symptoms of diverticulitis, IBS, constipation and diarrhoea. They are also used to improve and maintain regular GI transit. The indigestible husks create a constant volume of solid material regardless of what food is eaten or the condition of the gut. Psyllium husks (especially in powdered form) can be used in gluten-free baking to bind the mixture, ending in a less crumbly cake or bread. They are great added to clay or other detox minerals to prevent constipation.

Essiac Tea

Essiac Tea is believed to have come from the native Canadian Ojibway Indians. The recipe was shared by them with nurse Rene Caisse, who went on to assist many patients in the healing of their cancers. The original recipe consists of 4 herbs: Sheep Sorrel, Slippery Elm, Rhubarb Root and Burdock Root in exact proportions and prepared in a specific way, as written in an affidavit by Mary McPherson, a nurse that Rene Caisse trusted to make the tea for her patients.

Recipe:

1lb sheep sorrel powder, ¼lb slippery elm bark powder and 1oz Turkish rhubarb root powder, 6½ cups (24oz) burdock root (cut). Dry ingredients are mixed thoroughly and made at a ratio of 1oz her mix to

32oz water.

The herbs and water are boiled fast for 10 minutes, then left to cool and stand for 8 hours, stir then leave for another 8 hours. Then the mix is boiled again, strained and decanted into a sterilised amber glass bottle.

The decoction is taken 4 tablespoons in 4 tablespoons boiling water each day.

The herbs act on assisting clearing of blocked lymphs and lymphatic flow, and is therefore supportive of a healing phase where metabolic waste can be eliminated by the body with ease.

Raw Milk

If you are able to source some organic raw (unpasteurised) milk in your area, I highly recommend moving over to consuming raw. It is full of enzymes and healthy bacteria, and contains lactase which helps in digesting lactose, so people who are lactose intolerant will often be able to consume raw milk. When you begin, it may cause some tummy upset as it is very healing and replenishing, so best to begin with small amounts and work up. Myself and my family now drink and use raw milk in place of regular milk daily. It is creamy, delicious and we have the added benefit that it is ethically sourced from a great small family farm where we collect it weekly. It stores well in the freezer, and the milk we dispense is fresh that day and lasts at least 5 days in the fridge!

Nature's 'Medicine Chest' in your Herb & Spice Rack

Curcumin, a component of Turmeric, has become well-known for its anti-inflammatory properties. Others to look out for are Ginger, Garlic, Coriander (cilantro), Moringa, Rosemary, Thyme, Cayenne, Peppermint – in fact almost all herbs and spices will have at least some health benefits that support the holistic balance of the body, so use these freely!

CHAPTER 11...The Ketogenic Diet

My recommendation for general eating is to eat a wide variety of foods in moderation as discussed in the rest of this section. Our bodies love variety and in doing this we can obtain all of the required nutrients abundantly!

However, even though some may see this as a fad, when there are specific needs such as weight loss, fat burn, diabetes, epilepsy, cancer, for example, the ketogenic diet has proved to be able to offer a powerful therapeutic approach to many conditions. Of course, I always recommend that the conflicts related to any condition you have are addressed as well as following any therapeutic eating plan!

The ketogenic diet trains your body to use ketones for food instead of glucose. Ketones are produced when our body burns fat for energy. Therefore, the diet consists of eating a high percentage of fat, moderate protein and low net carbs. This is very difficult to accept for many as it really goes against mainstream brainwashing and belief that all fats are bad for us. But, hopefully by now you are open to the fact that this is not really the case!

The diet is basically of the following nutrient breakdown: 75-80% healthy fat intake (which includes animal fats if you wish), 15-20% protein and 5% net carbs, all of which is explained in a moment.

Intermittent Fasting

Alongside keto, the healthiest way to eat (which is now being discovered for increased longevity) is by calorie restriction. This is best implemented by intermittent fasting as I mention in Chapter 3. This has been scientifically proven and there are many presentations and articles by doctors and researchers, my particular favourite being on Youtube called 'Cancer: A Metabolic Disease With Metabolic Solutions' by Thomas Seyfried. Whereas we know from GNM that cancer is NOT a metabolic disease, his research into intermittent fasting is very good. Along with a keto diet, it is easy to skip breakfast and only have a window of about 6 hours to eat in. The reason this is easy on keto is because the body reverts to your fat stores when there is no fat being eaten, ensuring there is no energy slump or uncomfortable hunger as found with fasting when you are reliant on glucose for energy.

The Benefits

Calorie restriction and keto combined are found in many longevity studies to be more successful than anything else that has been tested so far. Many health advocates are now promoting its benefits to support the healing and long term management of many so diseases including epilepsy/ seizures, diabetes, Alzheimer's and cancer. This goes far beyond the obvious, and increasingly common use of the keto diet for fat burn in the sports and fitness arena.

Getting 'Keto Adapted'

It can take a few weeks, or even a month or so, to get what is known as 'keto-adapted' which means your body primarily seeks ketones for energy instead of glucose. Until this time, any slip up or imbalance in what you are eating will stop ketones being produced. After this time, you can have a few very occasional carb treats (sensible ones, not sugary things!) without upsetting things too much. In fact, a day per week or fortnight of allowing yourself extra carb intake is actually good for a longer term approach. You will know when you are keto-adapted as you will feel great, your appetite will reduce and energy slumps will be a thing of the past and your ketone levels will be pretty steady and will not be greatly affected by a one-off increase in protein or carbs.

You can purchase urine test strips online which test for ketones in urine and I test mine most mornings to make sure I am on track. You can also test your blood as this is said to be more accurate, but I found this to be more confusing, more expensive, not so convenient and not really needed once the urine was being tested.

A Warning

I went too extreme on low carb thinking that was good, but the fibre and carbs are very important to eat even if this means less ketone production. I was seeing the urine strip go darker and darker thinking I was doing great, losing a lot of excess weight and feeling fabulous. But then the weight loss slowed and stopped and I began feeling less fabulous. After a month or so of frustration, I took a hair mineral test. I had a candida infection!

At the time I was so confused – I was not eating sugar or carbs so how could this be? So once I was over the initial feeling of being slammed against a brick wall, falling flat on my face, and thinking there was a huge universal conspiracy against me feeling and being healthy (!), I did some research and I found out the candida that exists in our gut flora can also become keto-adapted!

Since learning GNM, I realised how amazingly adaptive our bodies are. Candida was instrumental to my healing, and even this found a way of adapting to what I was doing. Aren't our bodies just amazing?

At the time, I took two weeks off eating keto (conveniently over Christmas), though still staying off sugar. My candida symptoms stopped almost within a day or so of eating some carbs again. Of course, with my new knowledge, I realise that I had prevented the healing. With this new wisdom, I realised I should have not resisted the symptoms, allowed the healing, and only slowed the process if the symptoms were severe and I couldn't cope.

Getting Started

I will lay out the basics of the diet here, but I also suggest you look around at what others are saying to gain a better all-round understanding. There is some conflicting advice, but I have put together what has worked the best for me, and the information I find most important.

It can help to begin with (although I found it very restrictive to do in the longer term) to use a tracker of some sort. The one I used is one that Dr. Mercola uses and recommends called Cronometer, which also has an app for your phone. The free version is adequate to show you what you are eating and the ratios between the nutrients, and if you do this for a week or so it will give you an idea on quantities and get you started for continuing by yourself. If you want to use this tracker, the link for it is https://cronometer.com/mercola/ - it is adapted by Dr. Mercola to measure the correct level for the keto diet, although there is an option to change these levels and set your own goals if you want to.

The Diet

Bear in mind, where I mention below amounts such as unlimited, these will be limited on Cronometer. I have simplified the diet below in a way that actually works and to be much easier to follow in the longer term. This is why I only recommend using the app for the first week or so only, just to get an idea of quantity so you are not having to weigh, measure and calculate yourself!

You may also want to tweak the percentages mentioned to your own metabolic typing (e.g. a carb type may do better on increasing the carb to say 10% and reducing the fat and protein by 5% each). It is all trial and error really, so the first few weeks will be adjusting things to suit you. Keep testing your urine every day and see what stops and starts the ketone production and you will soon learn what works for you and come up with a tailored plan!

So the following can be used as a basis for your plan. For the record, I am personally a mixed type bordering on protein type. I do really well on eating meat and therefore, these recommendations take this into account. But there is no reason why a vegetarian (who is doing well on a vegetarian diet) couldn't follow a keto diet too.

One more point to consider, for ultimate health and well-being I recommend that you aim for 1/3 of your daily intake to be raw (i.e. salads, etc). Lightly steam your veg, and slow cook your meat or fish to reduce your intake of non-healthful chemicals that are created in the burning/high temperature cooking processes.

Unlimited Vegetables

As with healthy eating in general, it is important to eat as much vegetables as you can, with as much variety as you can. Make sure you lightly steam or slow roast any vegetables that generally require cooking, and eat raw any vegetable you like and would generally not cook (e.g. salad). You can add other veg that you like raw such as carrots, mange tout, runner beans, etc into your salads too.

It can be difficult to eat a lot of vegetables, particularly if you don't already eat a variety but here are a few tips to help:

Steamed vegetable dinners with a small protein serving served with butter, or large varied salads with oil-rich dressing and seeds with a small protein serving are two of the easiest ways to stick to keto. Most of my meals consist of these, varying my veg/salad mix and protein and using herbs and spices such as garlic and parsley to make it more interesting. I use asparagus, brussels sprouts, carrots, broccoli, cauliflower, runner beans, french beans, cabbage (green, savoy, sweetheart, red), leeks (fried in butter), and I have 3-4 types of veg per meal. Salads consist of a variety of leaves, onion, cucumber, cherry tomatoes, peppers, radish, broccoli sprouts, pickled beetroot and shallots (both home-made in apple cider vinegar), home-made sauerkraut, olives, yoghurt dip, and oil-rich dressing. Another favourite of mine is making cauliflower rice. Simply whizz the florets in a processor and dry fry for a few minutes to warm through. Add broccoli for a bit of colour too! Invest in a spiraliser (around £25), a clever manual device that turns veg into noodles, pasta and more! Make spaghetti, pasta ribbons or noodles from beetroot, courgette, carrots, cucumbers, etc. I also use organic passatta as a base for curries, bolognese or sauces.

75% - 80% of calories consumed from Fats

You can basically eat unlimited amounts of fats and this is best to be a mix of saturated and mono-unsaturated fats which are more easily digested, with a smaller amount of polyunsaturated fats. Although I say unlimited, you will naturally find you cannot eat too much as they really increase satiety and will fill you up quickly! This is because they are, in effect, more dense than protein and carbs. Protein and carbs provide 4 kcalories of energy per gram, whereas fat provides 9 kcalories per gram. This is why it is OK to say unlimited! These include:

Organic butter, coconut oil, palm oil (a sustainable source is recommended), vegetable oils (cold), nuts (take care as these are also high protein), seeds, avocados, olives, olive oil, animal fats and full fat dairy (raw unpasteurised dairy is best as it contains the lactase enzyme to break down the lactose plus many other benefits, but otherwise avoid milk and limit mild cheese due to their lactose content – cheese is also high in protein, too).

Increasing Fat Intake

It can be very difficult to eat such a high amount of fat when you are not used to it. I have heard of people adding coconut oil, and even sometimes butter, to their ground coffee to increase fat intake. I did not like this and as I enjoy fats, I have no problem eating plenty! If you do have a problem eating enough fats, try increasing it in the way you cook your food such as gentle frying or slow roasting. You can drizzle oil on salads or make a dressing with apple cider vinegar, olive oil, wholegrain mustard and/or a dash of raw honey. Just take a spoonful of organic virgin coconut oil each morning, and melt butter onto your steamed veg instead of making gravy which is higher in carbs (melted butter is a favourite of mine), eat your fruit with double or clotted cream, eat a spoonful of nut butter as a snack, make some guacamole and use as a dip for with a small serving of organic tortilla chips. Make some poppadoms (lentil flour), fried in coconut oil, onion bhaji (made with only gram flour and spices) fried in coconut oil. Sprinkle seeds onto salads, mix a healthy oil such as olive into bolognese after cooking, or coconut oil or coconut cream into curry. Use coconut cream with some cacao powder and honey, maple syrup or stevia to make a chocolate desert. Use ground almonds instead of flour, the possibilities are endless and there are many recipes that can be found online.

15% - 20% of calories consumed from Protein

Protein needs to be carefully managed on keto because excess protein is turned into glycogen in the liver and therefore can be used as glucose.

This stops keto-adaptation and ketone production. So take care. A fair example of the amount of protein our bodies need is around 1g of protein per day per 1kg of of your lean body weight. Try this to begin with but if you are a carb type or find you do not get ketones with this, I would reduce this to 0.8g/Kg, likewise if you find this is not enough and are protein type, you could try to increase to 1.2g/Kg. So, if you weight 75Kg and have 30% body fat (measured by a fat analysing scales), then you have 70% lean body mass, so your lean body weight would be 70% x 75 = 52.5Kg. This is how to work out your protein intake per day (for the mathematically shy!):

daily protein in g = lean body weight in kg X g/kg

So if you are starting off with 1g/kg: 52.5 X 1 = 52.5g protein per day

If you are tweaking down to 0.8g/kg: 52.5 X 0.8 = 42g protein per day

While this may appear to be a far cry from the 8oz serving of steak we may be used to, we need to remember to take into account the fat and water content, too. If you use Cronometer to begin with, it takes all this into account automatically and will give you an idea of portion size, without you needing to do all these calculations! But here is the calculation for those who are curious, based upon a 250g cut of rib-eye steak with approx 20% fat (bearing in mind as I've already explained, that fat is 9kcal/g and protein is 4kcal/g):

grams of fat = 20% x 250g = 50g (therefore 200g is protein)

kcalories from fat = 9 x 50 = 450

kcalories from protein = 4 x 200 = 800

so even though the fat content is only 20% of the entire steak, the actual calories from fat is more than half of the calories of the raw protein:

450 (kcal from fat) divided by 1250 (total calories) = approx 36%

If you further take into account the water content of the steak, this percentage could increase greatly, further lowering the protein intake. Cronometer give the readings for an 8oz rib-eye steak as 567 kcal, 46% of this protein and 54% from fat, and giving **the protein eaten as being just 60g**. So you can see how this is completely different from the original raw weight and percentage!

A Simple Approach

So, what we can take from this is that eating meat and fish with a higher fat content can allow you to eat a larger portion, and you can just count somewhere between a quarter to a third of the total weight of your portion towards your protein, depending on the fat content and how much it reduces during cooking (which is a good indicator of its water content).

For this reason, fattier cuts of meat and oily fish are preferable such as lamb breast & chops, fattier cuts of beef, thigh and leg of chicken with the skin, salmon, sardines, with the skin. I tend to limit pork due to its risk of containing preservatives and parasites, however pork crackling, belly pork and occasional mini chorizo bites are very keto-friendly!

Do not worry too much if you are consuming some protein in your unlimited fats, just keep measuring the ketones in your urine and reduce your protein ratio accordingly if needed. I found that basically sticking to 1 serving of fatty meat/fish per day prevents me from worrying about calculations, as this allows me to keep my protein consumption in check. I may additionally have a small amount for my other meals such as cheese, an egg or pulses in which case I slightly reduce the protein in my main meal. This is rough and simplified, but seems to work so don't stress too much!

Vegetarians can try legumes, cheese, nuts and eggs for their protein, but steer away from quorn and soy as previously mentioned in the book.

So, a summary of proteins: beef, lamb, chicken, turkey, game, all fish (especially oily), cheese (preferably mature), pork (limited), pulses, eggs (not overcooked). Seafood is low in fat and high in protein so it is not ideal for keto, but it can be eaten as part of your protein intake, particularly if it is cooked in fat or oil.

5% of calories consumed from Net Carbs

Although this is a small part of the diet, it is a very important part. When I say carbs, I mean NET CARBS, not total carb intake. This is another commonly misunderstood concept of the diet.

Net carbs are basically the amount of a carbohydrate that is going to impact upon our bodies. As fibre does not get absorbed into our bodies, it is not counted. This is why fibre is good for our GI tract. It bulks up our stools, so as we can pass toxins and waste more efficiently, it brushes through our intestines, 'clearing up' along the way to an extent, and, most importantly it provides nourishment to our gut flora. But it doesn't get used and absorbed into our cells and so doesn't affect blood sugar levels, glycogen production, etc.

If you need to work out the net carb value of a packaged food (which you should minimise and obviously always read the labels for 'hidden forbiddens'), you find the net carb by taking the total carbohydrate value and taking away the value "of which fibre". This result is the carb value that we are concerned with. It is important to eat your net carbs as this will ensure you are getting adequate fibre.

So, the carbs you need to eat for maximum effect are those that are high in fibre. These include fruit (especially berries), organic oats, a few other grains (if you wish) and lots and lots of vegetables (but not potatoes or starches). A small amount of raw honey, organic maple syrup or xylitol is fine once you are adapted, you can try them before and see if they affect your ketone level. Go careful with grains.

FRUITS:

To make it easier to see the net carb intake, here are some examples of fruit portions as related to your carb intake per day. All these are based upon a 100g serving unless stated:

Whole daily intake: Banana, grapes, mango, whole pomegranate

Half of daily intake: pear, kiwi, apple, pineapple, blueberries, tangerine/orange, water/honeydew melon, peach/nectarine/apricot, cherries, blackberries, raspberries

Quarter of daily intake: Strawberries, papaya, other melon, grapefruit, fresh figs, guava

GRAINS:

Eat very few grains. The following are OK in very limited amounts (suggested portions mentioned). Make sure they are organic. I tended to have 2-3 grain servings per week primarily oats for porridge. On these days I wouldn't have fruit as these will take up your carb allowance, however fruits contain much more for your health than grains, so this is why I primarily focus upon using up my carb intake on fruits, in particular berries.

Whole daily intake: ½ cup oats (e.g. mixed with 1 cup water to make porridge), up to ½ cup brown basmati rice, amaranth, buckwheat, millet, corn

Make sure you eat fat with your carbs to lower the GI impact. e.g. cream with fruit, cooked grains fried in coconut oil, oil-rich dressings, cream on porridge, etc.

Drinks

Increase water intake, herbal teas, and clear liquids. Avoid alcohol and caffeine, all fruit juices, instant coffee and obviously sugared drinks. I have personally found that I can have a 250ml glass of organic no added sulphur red wine 1-2 times per week without negative impact on my ketones, when I am well-adapted I can have 2 glasses if I wish! I have also found that a cup of ground, organic (preferably) coffee in the morning with cream and xylitol is also within my tolerance of still producing ketones. I rarely had regular tea, if I did I used cream or full fat milk (like I said, only rarely!).

Further Advice

In some ways, this diet is similar to Paleo, however the fat and protein are reversed. Paleo still depends on glucose production, but may be a suitable middle-of-the-road alternative for many. In any case, always take your metabolic typing into account when putting your diet plan together and tweaking it to suit you.

Many people suggest that keto should only be followed in the short term. While I do not follow keto long term, I do not see why it cannot be followed for a longer term gain in health, physique and well-being if it is carefully managed. I have heard many people go back and forth keto with good results. For example, 3 months on keto at the levels I have stated here, reverting back to a high protein and higher carb diet for a month or so before going back to keto again for 3 months, etc. Alternately, you could try to take a gentler keto diet by increasing the net carbs to 10-15%, and reducing this percentage off the fat intake. If you are testing your urine and the indicator goes light purple it is working! Try to keep the ketone level lower though so as not to go too extreme. You could allow yourself a regular increased carb day, say once per week and see if this works for you. Some people do this, or even a 5 on 2 off each week as a maintenance. I am not convinced that this would not cause increased stress on the body, so just see if it suits you.

I believe keto and/or paleo are how we would have instinctively and naturally eaten in the past as they basically are based upon a hunter/gatherer principle. This is also reflected in the intermittent fasting/calorie restriction recommendation and discovery of how this appears to increase longevity, as we would have had feasts and famine depending on hunting success, gathering of vegetables/fruits and other natural ways in which the food supply was affected. We are basically going back to how our ancestors ate!

Intermittent fasting suits keto very well, and you will find you can easily manage with skipping breakfast and eating only between 12noon and 7pm for example. I found this a very convenient and easy way to eat, and was always full of energy.

Before embarking on a diet such as keto or paleo, or including intermittent fasting into your lifestyle, speak to a health professional and advise your GP if you are on medication. They may be resistant to the idea of the high fat content, but the decision needs to be your own, based upon your thorough research, intuition and ultimate responsibility of your own health.

SECTION II.....Nutrition & Supplementation

CHAPTERS:

From the GNM perspective:

Supplements can be very helpful when used wisely. We need the correct nutritional elements to recover and rebuild and to successfully complete the healing phase efficiently. So the more balanced, healthy and full of vitality we are, the better we will cope with a biological programme should we experience a conflict. Therefore, diet and supplements can greatly assist us.

However, taking supplements we do not need or in higher doses than we actually require can cause additional stress, so we need to be careful.

The World Health Organisation state that Malnutrition refers to deficiencies, excesses or imbalances in a person's intake of energy and/or nutrients. GNM's first biological law states that Malnutrition can cause symptoms without a conflict shock. However, please note that the list of signs of deficiency on each vitamin or mineral may be a healing symptom of a biological programme!

CHAPTER 12...
Supplementation: The Basics

It is definitely best practice to obtain the nutrients required by eating a well-balanced, healthy diet which is right for you. The reason for obtaining as much as possible from food is that all the nutrients exist in harmony and balance as nature intended. Therefore they are the most bio-available forms of nutrients as they will be in balance with their synergistic and antagonistic partners. For example, as previously mentioned, a vegetarian may suffer copper toxicity as the vegetable proteins do not contain copper and zinc in balance. Another example is vitamin C – it is very difficult for our bodies to absorb vitamin C if it is only present in ascorbic acid form without being in combination with bioflavinoids (sometimes referred to as Vitamin P) which make it able to be processed more easily by the body.

In the following summaries of nutrients, the RDA is the official government recommended daily allowances. Where I have discovered evidence to suggest a higher level is beneficial, it will be stated. The Upper Safety Limit is the highest dosage that is considered safe, but this is based upon daily and general usage and not therapeutic use. Where there is no Upper Safety Limit stated, there is no official limit set. I have only included the main nutrients. Also please bear in mind that the RDAs are set based upon what is deemed as an 'average' sized person, yet another attempt by the government and authorities to enforce their 'one-size-fits-all' philosophy. So you may wish to pro-rata your dosage if you are particularly big or small. All RDAs quoted are correct at the time of writing and may be subject to change.

Potencies are measured in mg (milligrams), mcg (micrograms) and iu (international units). International Units are a unit of measurement dependent on the biological effect or activity of the substance, and therefore it's equivalence in mcg or mg will differ for each substance. The iu values tend to be set so they appear to be very high dosage. But don't be afraid by this. A prime example is with vitamin D3. In the past, I've taken 15,000iu per day and 50,000iu as a therapeutic dosage when needed. This sounds a horrendous amount, but when you consider that our bodies will manufacture about 10,000iu after only a few minutes of optimum direct sunlight, it no longer seems so much!

Two Types of vitamins

There are two types of vitamins – fat soluble and water soluble. Fat soluble vitamins can be stored in our bodies and accumulate over time, so these vitamins can be taken in larger doses less often. Water soluble vitamins cannot be stored by the body and any excess is carried out through our body's elimination process and therefore these vitamins are best taken little and often for a constant supply. For this reason, many water-soluble vitamins are available in timed-release forms, but I would generally avoid these if there are unnecessary processing and additives used.

Supplementation

If you should suspect that you are deficient, or wish to supplement a mineral or vitamin that is lacking in your diet for some reason, it is important to choose your supplements carefully. Be sure to purchase from an ethical, reputable supplement company, preferably not pharmaceutically owned, and remember that you get what you pay for. Many mass produced synthetic supplements are not bio-available and are low potency so will have hardly any benefit for your well-being. These are often referred to as 'Me-Too' supplements. When you are choosing your supplements, it is better to opt for taking the least amount of capsules or pills as possible to avoid consuming excess 'capsule fillers'. There is some concern over fillers such as magnesium stearate, but in my opinion, **if there are no suitable alternatives** then the amount of goodness you are getting from say a 5,000iu vitamin D capsule far outweighs any possible effects from the tiny amount of magnesium stearate. Some people prefer to opt for liquids but these can be high in sugars or contain sweeteners. So it really is up to you – read the labels, do some research and realise, as with most things, there is a sensible happy medium to be found without needing to go to extremes.

You may wish to learn kinesiology muscle testing to see if a particular supplement is going to be beneficial for you. I have found this an invaluable tool to know. If you are interested in learning the basics of muscle testing, have a look at the kinesiology show we filmed on our Youtube channel "Holistic Show" as we have a tutorial on how to use muscle testing for yourself. I also run muscle testing workshops which will be detailed on my websites, and you can learn the basic technique in Chapter 68. You can also use dowsing with a pendulum.

Multis

I don't recommend multivitamin/mineral supplements for general use. It is much better to target deficiencies when needed with the required nutrient rather than taking a general multi. An exception is with B-vitamins which I find work better for clients in a B-complex rather than the individual B vitamins.

CHAPTER 13...Hair Mineral Analysis

Hair Mineral Analysis is non-invasive and a great way to show how well our body is functioning on an intracellular level. It is believed by many leading doctors in the nutrition field that your hair can reveal a lot about your inner health.

A sample of hair is generally taken from the back of the head (if possible) and sent to an analysis laboratory. It is important to find a laboratory that does not wash the sample prior to analysis. The service is usually offered by nutritional therapists or other natural and alternative health care professionals and some health shops. Some will give more detailed results than others so don't be afraid to ask what you will receive for your money!

Hair analysis is more accurate to the overall levels of minerals than other tests such as using urine or blood. This is because blood and urine levels will be influenced directly by food recently eaten, whereas the hair test shows average levels over the 2-3 month period of hair growth.

Benefits

The great thing about hair mineral analysis is that it can pick up imbalances, toxicities and deficiencies before they may even be manifesting as symptoms. Results will usually show a trend of conditions that your current levels may indicate in the future and give thorough dietary and supplementation and detox advice on correcting the imbalances before they become a problem. If you are currently experiencing symptoms, it is surprising just what may be happening inside your body and how a slight alteration in your diet can help. For example, a low sodium diet is often promoted, however if you are deficient in sodium it can cause low stomach acid and poor assimilation of nutrients causing other levels to be low too – something that may not be realised without a hair mineral analysis.

Removing the Guess-work

Supplementing blindly can lead us to further unbalancing our mineral levels as so many minerals are antagonists or synergists with others (i.e. they can work against or with them, causing depletion and toxicity). A prime example of this is quite a few years ago. I was reading about zinc and I thought that I would benefit from zinc supplements. So I took some supplements daily, just at the mainstream recommended level – nothing too extreme. My symptoms didn't improve and then I came across the hair mineral analysis service and thought I would try it out with the view to offering the service to my clients and shop customers (which I now do). My results revealed that I was extremely deficient in copper as the zinc I had taken had depleted my copper. The more hair tests I have analysed, the more I am learning about the extremely delicate balance of nutrients and why I generally do not advise supplementation unless there is a very good reason to determine that there is a deficiency, or for therapeutic use which would be as part of a complete programme. In my opinion it is so important to take the guess-work away if possible.

The other personal experience is my confirmation of how effective I was absorbing magnesium through magnesium chloride flakes in my bath. My levels had more than trebled (from 10.7 to 34.8 – see the image of an excerpt of my hair test of January 2013 – previous test results shown are from November 2011). This had happened over a year of having 2-4 magnesium chloride baths per week containing over 1Kg of flakes each bath. My level was at a stage where it was starting to deplete other minerals and in addition, if I had continued I may have been in danger of magnesium toxicity, although understand that I was having quite an extreme dosage and magnesium toxicity is very rare! But I am now comforted with the fact that my magnesium to calcium ratio is optimum at a healthy ratio of 1.5 calcium to 1 magnesium, however would probably be more optimum for my body at about 2:1 so as the magnesium didn't deplete other minerals.

Please note the chart is based upon official recommended values so it may appear that my magnesium is very high, but new studies prove otherwise!

Toxins

A hair analysis test will also show whether you have accumulated any toxic metals, for example mercury, arsenic, lead or aluminium. Some claim that inorganic mercury such as that found in fillings may not be detected, but any hidden toxicity can generally be recognised by assessing the levels of other related elements that are out of balance.

I would strongly recommend a mineral analysis, or another method that takes away the guesswork such as kinesiology, especially if you are considering supplementing your diet or are experiencing any unfavourable symptoms or conditions at present.

CHAPTER 14...*Summary of Vitamins*

VITAMIN A (Fat soluble)

Found in: chicken & turkey liver & giblets, spirulina, eggs, dairy, yellow, orange & dark leafy green vegetables.

There are 2 forms of vitamin A, retinol from animal source and pro-vitamin A carotenoids from vegetable source, the most popular being alpha-carotene and beta-carotene.   It is believed that vitamin A supplements containing retinoic acid may block vitamin D activity in the body so it is best to acquire your vitamin A from colourful vegetables. It is depleted by smoking cigarettes.

Signs of Deficiency: eyesight problems especially in the dark, blindness, dry eyes, dry scaly skin, weak or breaking hair and nails, dental problems, irritation or problems associated with digestive, respiratory or urinary tracts

RDA: 700mcg (2,333iu) women, 900mcg (3,000iu) men

Upper Safety Limit: 3,000mcg

B VITAMINS (Water Soluble)

There are many members of the vitamin B family. Here are the most common. Alcohol consumption, smoking and some medication depletes B vitamins.

Found in: meat, fish, poultry and eggs. These are prime sources of B vitamins as they are in balance in these foods. Additional vegetable sources are as detailed.

Signs of a General B Vitamin Deficiency: Low energy, fatigue, skin problems, slow metabolism, carbohydrate intolerance, adrenal fatigue

Vitamin B1 (thiamine)

Also found in: wholegrains, artichokes, corn, leeks, potatoes

Signs of Deficiency: complications in diabetes, irritability, sleep disturbances, abdominal discomfort, beriberi, acceleration in Alzheimer's, swollen legs, difficulty walking, poor stomach acid.

RDA: 1.1 to 1.2 mg

Vitamin B2 (riboflavin)

Also found in: cabbage, avocados, Brussels sprouts, spinach and mushrooms

Signs of Deficiency: sore mouth, cracking in corners of lips, dandruff, anaemia, B6 deficiency, poor red blood cell production, growth and development problems

RDA: 1.2 mg

Vitamin B3 (niacin)

Also found in: vegetables especially sweetcorn

Signs of Deficiency: diarrhoea, digestive problems, inflamed mucus membranes, mental confusion, scaly skin, cholesterol imbalance

RDA: 11 -12 mg

Vitamin B5 (pantothenic acid)

Also found in: cauliflower, broccoli, turnip

Signs of Deficiency: acne, increased sensitivity to insulin, poor red blood cell production, hormonal imbalance

RDA: 4 – 5 mg

Vitamin B6 (pyridoxine)

Also found in: cauliflower, broccoli, avocados, brussels sprouts, onions

Signs of Deficiency: anaemia, rash, dandruff, mood changes, decreased immunity due to poor antibody production

RDA: 1.3 – 1.7 mg (dependant on protein consumption – more is needed for increased protein intake)

Vitamin B7 (biotin)

Also found in: cauliflower, broccoli

Signs of Deficiency: recurring fungal infections, dry skin, rashes, brittle hair and nails, hair loss, abnormal facial fat distribution

RDA: 30 mg

Vitamin B9 Folic Acid (folate)

Also found in: spinach, asparagus, brussels sprouts

Signs of Deficiency: diarrhoea, greying hair, mouth ulcers, peptic ulcers, stunted growth, swollen tongue, irritability, weakness, birth defects

RDA: 300 – 400 mg, pregnant women 600 mg

Vitamin B12 (cobalamin)

Also found in: meat, fish, dairy, eggs. The body inefficiently absorbs B12 from plant foods, so if you are a vegetarian a supplement should be taken, plus a B6 supplement at the recommended daily allowance, to make sure there is a correct balance. Methylcobalamin is the form of B12 found in non-vegetarian foods and is the most bio-available.

Signs of Deficiency: hair loss, skin abnormalities/problems, fatigue, tingling hands and/or feet, pernicious anaemia, fainting, headaches, recurrent illness, blood problems, nerve & DNA damage

RDA: 2.4mcg

Other B Vitamins

There are many more B vitamins that are being discovered and investigated. Vitamin B17 is worth a mention as it is believed to kill cancer. Although according to the new perspective, we do not necessarily want to 'kill' cancer cells as they will be naturally removed! It is found in papaya, fruit seeds particularly kernels of apricot, apple, peach, orange, cherry & nectarine, lima beans, almonds, clover & sorghum (although the latter is often high in cyanide). The most common source is bitter apricot kernels. B17 is not strictly a vitamin but a cyanogen which means it breaks down into cyanide. Therefore it must be used with extreme caution, built up slowly and not over-prescribed! I took apricot kernels when I had the lump in my breast and muscle tested the amount every week, which started at 4 and built up 1 per week until I got to 17 which I only tested positively for a few weeks and have tested negatively for them ever since. Laetrile is a partially synthetic form and amygdalin is the natural form. TAKE CARE: Therapeutic doses of vitamin C taken alongside B17 can cause cyanide poisoning.

B-Complex: As mentioned in the introduction to this section, I find a B-complex is more beneficial for clients than a specific B vitamin. A very effective product I use is Zell Oxygen Plus by Dr Wolz. It is excellent as a tonic, for adrenal fatigue, thyroid support, B vitamin deficiency, balancing the blood sugar, digestion and so much more as it is a unique formula that works at cell level. I find it invaluable in my practice, and I also use Vitalkomplex which contains the B-complex along with a plethora of phytochemicals, ideal for anyone who does not eat plenty of fruit and vegetables.

VITAMIN C (Water soluble)

Found in: oranges, berries, broccoli, cabbage, potatoes, cauliflower, tomatoes and pineapple

Signs of Deficiency: swollen gums, joint pain, vision problems, low blood pressure, anaemia (helps the absorption of iron), free radical damage, wrinkles, poor collagen production, weight problems, furring of arteries

Vitamin C is best taken in bio-available form ideally from foods, make sure there is a balance of bioflavinoids. Ascorbic acid alone does not offer full spectrum of vitamin C and therefore it is difficult for our body to process it. Therefore if you are taking ascorbic acid, eat some foods rich in bioflavinoids along with it such as fresh berries.

RDA: 250-500mg

Safe Upper Limit: 3,000mg, although dosages of much higher have been given therapeutically, generally by IV injection. However high doses such as this have a stimulating effect and is therefore contra-indicative to the vagatonic healing state.

VITAMIN D (Fat soluble)

Vitamin D is actually a hormone and as such is essential to maintaining total body health, yet it is not found in many foods. It's needed daily to keep bones and teeth strong and to ensure the proper functioning of heart, muscles and nerves.

Vitamin D3, or cholecalciferol, is the same type of vitamin D your body makes when exposed to sunlight and it is also usually (but not always) the version used to fortify foods. It offers support for healthy bones by maintaining normal blood levels of calcium and phosphorus, thus promoting calcium absorption. It helps combat fatigue and supports healthy cells with cellular growth regulation. It is known to be effective in preventing S.A.D. (seasonal affective disorder). With an estimated 70%-80% of the population deficient in Vitamin D levels, I believe it can be a healthy addition to your home medicine chest!

It is widely claimed that Vitamin D helps our bodies to regress cancer and protects us from it. Understanding GNM, it is suffice to say that it is supportive to our biological programmes. When we expose ourselves to the sun, it is our body's manufacture of vitamin D that protects our skin from damage and yet this is being blocked by harmful chemicals in the sunscreens we are pressured into wearing (see chapter 35 for more information).

Signs of Deficiency: bow legs/knock knees, calcium deficiency symptoms, bone pain and frequent breaking, muscle weakness and aches, depression, sun sensitivity

Vitamin D2 is an unnatural form and not easily utilised by the body – in fact many believe it is toxic. It is important to check that foods are fortified with D3 and not D2.

RDA: 200iu – however I recommend at least 5,000iu per day, more for occasional therapeutic use. According to the Vitamin D council:

"As one of the safest substances known to man, vitamin D toxicity is very rare. In fact, people are at far greater risk of vitamin D deficiency than they are of vitamin D toxicity."

Prolonged therapeutic dosages of vitamin D3 can deplete calcium and magnesium, and Vitamin K2 is needed alongside higher doses.

VITAMIN E (Fat soluble)

Found in: healthful oils, nuts, seeds, fish, fortified cereals, mango, kiwi fruit, vegetables in varying proportions

Signs of Deficiency: increased susceptibility to illness, incontinence, loss of feeling to limbs, muscle weakness, blindness/vision problems

RDA: 15mg

VITAMIN K, K1 & K2 (Fat soluble)

Found in: broccoli, parsley, chard, kale, spinach, dried beans, pak choi, generally more vitamin K is released when cooked.

Signs of Deficiency: easily bruised, bleeding & clotting problems, heavy periods, blood in urine/stool

Vitamin K can interfere with anticoagulants such as warfarin. Vitamin K2 is believed to be safe for those on anticoagulants but please first check with your prescribing healthcare professional. It is important to supplement with vitamin K alongside vitamin D.

RDA: 90mcg women, 120mcg men

CHAPTER 15...Summary of Essential Minerals

CALCIUM

Found in: dairy, dark green leafy vegetables, seafood, enriched foods & drinks

Signs of Deficiency: weak/brittle bones, irregular heart rhythm, muscle spasms, numbness, seizures, teeth problems, weak nails

We more than often get enough calcium from our normal diets, however calcium requires magnesium, vitamin D, amino acids (found in protein), dietary silicon (you can obtain enough by eating whole foods) and Vitamin K2 to be processed and used efficiently by the body.

Depleted by: uncooked spinach, cabbage, sweet potatoes, rhubarb, beans, broccoli all contain oxalic acid which is destroyed once they are cooked. Also phytates in soy, wheatgrain, wholegrains, nuts, seeds, beans (can be removed by soaking overnight before cooking).

RDA: 1,000mg, rising to 1,200mg at age 50 (women) or age 70 (men)

IRON

Found in: red meat, dark green leafy vegetables, eggs, liver, poultry, fish. Heme iron (animal source) is absorbed much more easily than nonheme (vegetable source).

Iron needs vitamin C in order for it to be absorbed and utilised.

Signs of Deficiency: weakness, fatigue, headaches, dizziness, poor appetite, cold hands and feet, breathing difficulties, poor red blood cell function, growth and development problems

Depleted by: resveratrol (found in black fruit skin and pips especially grapes and organic sulphate-free red wine), calcium, bran, black tea

Too much iron causes the body to age more quickly and it is recommended that men and post-menopausal women take a resveratrol supplement or combine their foods to ensure that they do not absorb too much iron (such as organic sulphate-free red wine with steak).

RDA: 8mg (men), 18mg (women), 27mg (pregnancy)

COPPER & ZINC

Signs of Deficiency in Copper: nerve problems, weak/brittle bones sugar intolerance, zinc toxicity, poor red blood cell production

Copper is depleted by: prolonged diarrhoea, refined foods, fluoride, high zinc, molybdenum and cadmium intake

RDA: 900mcg

Signs of Deficiency in Zinc: diarrhoea, weight loss, poor smell and taste, poor night vision, 'dream-like' feeling, copper toxicity

Zinc is depleted by: onions & garlic

RDA: 15mcg

Copper & Zinc are together as it is important they are in balance. They are antagonists meaning more of one will cause the other to deplete

Best sources of copper & zinc in balance are: meat & animal proteins (meat, dairy, fish, molluscs).

Copper needs to be in balance with zinc, as found in animal proteins. Vegetarian proteins such as nuts, beans, legumes & seeds tend to be high in copper and low in zinc. Therefore vegetarians should consider taking a zinc supplement.

SELENIUM

Found in: brazil nuts, seaweed, seafood, meat, dairy

Signs of Deficiency: no particular symptoms but generally not feeling 100% and increased susceptibility to illness, cell damage and thyroid problems

Depleted by: Crohn's Disease, poor soil quality

RDA: 55mcg

Selenium is generally regarded as safe to take if you are in doubt as to whether you are deficient.

IODINE

Found in: seaweed, seafood, meat, dairy

Signs of Deficiency: low thyroid function, fatigue, depression, weight gain, poor concentration, constipation, dry skin, intolerant to cold

Depleted by: goitrogens in cauliflower, broccoli & cabbage. 90% of goitrogens are destroyed by cooking.

RDA: 150mcg

Iodine protects the thyroid from radiation damage. Most people are considered to be deficient in iodine and so I recommend taking a good quality supplement such as Nascent Iodine, taken orally or as I do, 1-2 drops painted onto the skin each morning (if the stain remains one morning, skip that day).

PHOSPHORUS

Found in: meat, dairy, fish, eggs

Signs of Deficiency: anaemia, muscle weakness, bone pain, rickets, seizures

Depleted by: medications

RDA: 700mcg

POTASSIUM

Found in: chicken & turkey, white meat, bananas, potatoes, oranges, avocados, celery, carrots, cantaloupe, broccoli, spinach, dairy, peanut butter

Signs of Deficiency: constipation, fatigue, muscle cramps, abnormal heartbeat, metabolism problems, depression (if sodium is also deficient)

Depleted by: medications especially water tablets, alcohol

RDA: 4.7g

COBALT

Found in: meat, eggs, dairy

Signs of Deficiency: Cobalt (cobalamin) is a component of vitamin B12, so deficiency symptoms are those of B12 deficiency

Depleted by: being vegan or vegetarian

RDA: none set

MANGANESE

Found in: cocoa, legumes such as chickpeas, berries, pineapple, leafy vegetables, Himalayan salt, herbal teas

Signs of Deficiency: poor fat and carbohydrate metabolism, bone demineralisation, infertility, seizures, weakness, dizziness, hearing loss, anaemia, weak hair and nails, convulsions

Depleted by: alcohol, antacids, oral contraception, phytic acid from grains, nuts and seeds (removed by soaking overnight)

RDA: 1.8mcg (women) 2.3mcg (men)

CHROMIUM

Found in: lean meats, cheese, organ meats, broccoli, mashed potato, grape juice, mushrooms, asparagus

Signs of Deficiency: poor blood sugar balance, sugar cravings, poor metabolism

Depleted by: alcohol, high carbohydrate foods

RDA: 20-25mg (women) 30-35mg (men)

SODIUM

Found in: soups, gravy, Himalayan salt, bacon, Marmite, pickles

Signs of Deficiency: low stomach acid, poor absorption of nutrients, muscle cramps, headaches, lethargy, confusion, decreased appetite, nausea, muscle weakness, heart/kidney/liver failure, depression

RDA: maximum of 2.3g (in basic table salt form – equivalent to approx 5.5g salt due to its chloride content). However, I recommend obtaining sodium from pink Himalayan Salt which is more bio-available as described in Chapter 6.

MOLYBDENUM

Found in: leafy veg, liver & kidneys

Signs of Deficiency: increased heart rate, increased breathing, reduced night vision, headaches

Depleted by: Crohn's disease

RDA: 45mcg

SULPHUR

Found in: proteins, garlic, cabbage, kale, kohl rabi, brussels sprouts, mustard greens, watercress, leeks, onion, radish, cauliflower, horseradish, fruits, breads, juices, beer, wine, cider, sausages

Signs of Deficiency: protein intolerance, muscles weakness, poor muscle mass, skin problems, arthritis

Depleted by: excess zinc, some medications

RDA: none established

BORON

Found in: almonds, walnuts, avocados, broccoli, potatoes, pears, prunes, honey, oranges, onions, chick peas, carrots, beans, bananas, red grapes, red apples and raisins.

Signs of Deficiency: worsening of arthritis, osteoporosis, osteoarthritis, poor calcium and magnesium metabolism, poor mental alertness, blood clots, weak bones, hormone imbalance

RDA: none established
Over-supplementing with boron can deplete vitamin B2

CHAPTER 16...
The Magnesium Deficiency Epidemic

During my extensive research on magnesium, which ultimately led to the addition of Magnesium Chloride Flakes to my shop's range, I have discovered that magnesium deficiency has fast become somewhat of an epidemic. This is due to it being depleted so easily by so much in our everyday lives including stress, pollution and eating incorrectly. As it is involved in over 600 processes within the body, it is no surprise that it is so crucial to our health, and is the reason I dedicate an entire chapter to it!

Unfortunately allopathic (conventional) doctors and allopathic medicine fail to recognise the many symptoms of magnesium deficiency and their insistence of covering up symptoms with prescribed drugs can do a lot more harm in the long term as the deficiency will fail to be addressed.

One reason magnesium is so important to our body is that it is needed for the efficient utilisation of calcium. When we are deficient in magnesium, calcium wanders around aimlessly and can end up leaving calcium deposits in our joints and a chalky deposit in our blood vessels.

Lack of the absorption of calcium can then have a negative impact on our teeth and bones. When we realise we are lacking in calcium, we take or are prescribed calcium supplements which then worsens the problem.

Calcification of the blood vessels is far more widespread than cholesterol, and the main cause of 'blood vessel furring'. We almost always get enough calcium in our diets, but rarely get enough magnesium, and if we do this is quickly and easily depleted by stress, prescribed medicines and the toxins we are exposed to in our everyday lives.

So it is extremely important that we supplement with magnesium for optimum health, especially if you are already experiencing some deficiency symptoms (such as calcium deposits, heart conditions, inability to relax, insomnia, muscle cramps and aches). Ideally I would recommend having a Hair Mineral Analysis test, as magnesium can antagonise other minerals directly and indirectly and so a test will take away any 'guess-work'. You can also visit a kinesiologist who will assess deficiencies, but since it is estimated that as much as 80% of the population may be magnesium deficient there is a high likelihood that you will find some benefit from magnesium supplementation. In my experience to date of analysing hair mineral tests over the past few years, this figure is more like 100%! In other words, I have yet to analyse an initial hair mineral test for someone other than myself who has not been deficient! More worryingly most are also much too high in calcium which is putting them at great risk of calculus (calcium depositing) and throwing many of their other mineral levels off balance, despite not being symptomatic at the time. Even more worryingly, many of these clients have been taking some form of oral magnesium, or bathing in Epsom Salts thinking they were obtaining magnesium from this. However, the magnesium form in Epsom Salts (magnesium sulphate) has a drawing effect, to supplement with magnesium transdermally, magnesium CHLORIDE is the most efficient.

I believe it to be most effective to supplement transdermally (through the skin) as it is estimated that we only absorb a maximum of 40% of magnesium taken orally, this is the net effect as our bodies will use magnesium to process it, turn it into the correct form, and deal with any excess. But transdermally, magnesium chloride which is already in the form used by the body, is delivered directly into the muscles and tissues where it is needed, and our body will absorb as much as it needs within 15-20 minutes. There is very little risk with this method as long as you don't really overdo it, but if you have a kidney or thyroid condition I advise you seek medical advice in the first instance.

There are 2 easy ways to get magnesium into your body:

1.   You can put magnesium flakes in your bath or foot spa (500g-750g into a bath, or approx. 250g in a foot spa). I suggest you do this at least weekly, or 2-3 times per week if you have signs of deficiency, and even more often if using a foot spa. I supplemented with magnesium baths adding magnesium to almost every bath I had for a year and in that time the magnesium levels in my hair sample more than trebled. This proves to me how effective a magnesium bath can be in increasing your magnesium. My new ratio of magnesium to calcium was 1.5:1 (it was 5:1), however there were some depletion in other levels suggesting my metabolism had decreased. So this told me that I needed to stop supplementing for a little while before going back to a general maintenance of a weekly bath.

2.   Make up some magnesium oil to spray onto the body, rub in, leave for 20 minutes then wash off. This is the most cost effective method, as if you make your own with magnesium flakes, 250ml oil should only cost you approximately £1! This can be done daily as you are not applying as much as what you would be in a bath.

To make your own oil is so easy! You will need a mister or spray bottle, magnesium flakes and pure water. I recommend distilled water or spring water is the best but tap water will be fine if your area is not fluoridated. You simply dissolve the salts into the water until no more will dissolve (you will know this as there will be a small amount of salts that stay in the bottom of the solution). That is it! No need for expensive preparations that others will so willingly sell you – be warned! I have been extremely shocked to find others selling ready made magnesium oil for £20-£30! I really cannot understand how people can cash-in on things like this. I would personally much prefer to offer products as inexpensive as possible so more people can benefit!

If the oil irritates your skin, it often means that you are extremely deficient. You may dilute it further until there is no reaction and build up the strength. Also rotate the areas of the body you spray on (arms 1 day, legs next day, etc). Otherwise a foot spa or bath may be best.

Excess Magnesium

As I discovered personally, excessive magnesium can reduce your metabolism which can cause depletion of other minerals. But it does take a lot to overdo it – in my case over 1Kg in the bath 2-4 times a week for a whole year (see my results on page 74) – and in addition it is much harder to overdo transdermal magnesium than if taken orally! So based upon this personal experience and the research I have carried out, the advice above can still be followed quite safely.

If you are not currently experiencing any symptoms of magnesium deficiency, I suggest you still follow this supplementation advice as this will help to bring your ratio up to the ideal of 2:1 – 1:1 (generally people are 8:1 – 20:1, although I have had some results with the ratio above 100:1!). After about 3 months, reduce to a maintenance level of a weekly bath, or use the spray just a few times a week instead of every day.

Although very rare, signs of excess magnesium in addition to those mentioned above are over-relaxation such as muscle weakness, low blood pressure, slow heart beat and diarrhoea

CHAPTER 17... *Probiotics*

There is much publicity and confusion over probiotics today. Many companies are misusing the information to mis-sell products. I believe that probiotics can be a vital supplement to a healthy body. This is especially important if you have had your appendix removed as recent research suggests that the appendix plays an important role in the maintenance of bacterial balance and the replenishment of bacteria in the gut.

What is High Count?

When you consider that there are an estimated 100 trillion bacteria in our bodies, commercial probiotics containing millions of bacteria become a mere drop in the ocean and are not as beneficial as many make out. In order to make a difference we need BILLIONS not MILLIONS!

Why take Probiotics?

The delicate balance of our bacteria is essential to a healthy body and for correct absorption of the nutrients into our bodies. This delicate balance can be upset by many factors in today's world such as pharmaceutical drugs like antibiotics, poor diet such as one high in refined carbohydrates, stress, hormonal changes, emotional issues, pregnancy, shock, operations, basically anything that disturbs our system. If the bacteria is out of balance, or depleted by overuse of antibiotics or pharmaceuticals, we will not have sufficient levels to assist us in healing.

Candida overgrowth is popularly believed to be invasive to our body and a precursor to cancer. However GNM proves that Candida fungi actually assist in the breaking down of tumours in the healing phase of a biological programme. Unfavourable symptoms accompany a candida infection such as lack of energy & fatigue, repeated episodes of fungal infections such as thrush and athlete's foot, poor digestion & bowel problems, bloating, food intolerances, brain fog, forgetfulness, the list goes on. However these are all healing symptoms. We can take the edge off these symptoms if they are severe but we are best to assist the healing and work through them, allowing our body to complete the healing phase it is experiencing.

Many people find probiotics beneficial to their symptoms. I have personally found benefit from using probiotics, but more recently have found huge benefit from replenishing bacteria and enzymes with raw unpasteurised organic milk. My family and I now consume this daily in place of pasteurised milk. I also make water kefir and sauerkraut and consider natural enzyme and bacteria rich foods to be healthier than taking a supplement.

If you take probiotics and find that multi strain is not working for you, it may be that you need a single strain. As the bacteria of probiotics are generally bound in chains, it can be difficult for a single bacteria to be replenished if it is bound to other bacteria. In this case you may need to seek help from a kinesiologist to ascertain which strain you actually need.

SECTION III.....Detox & Body Cleansing

CHAPTERS:

From a GNM perspective, detox and body cleansing are very helpful. Ensuring our exit pathways are clear will facilitate in the removal of metabolic waste that is produced in the breakdown of tumours in the healing phase of a biological programme.

Additionally, accumulation of toxins can rob us of our vitality and place stress upon our system, which is contraindicative to the vagatonic, non-stress state required for healing.

CHAPTER 18...General Detox Advice

Detox seems to have become somewhat of a buzzword or trend, but I take this subject seriously. We are exposed to thousands of toxic chemicals and heavy metals in our modern world which our bodies are not 'designed' to cope with or eliminate. So we need to give our bodies assistance in the best way we can. It is true that people thousands of years ago survived without thinking of detox, but they didn't have the constant toxic bombardment that we have today either! Even our parents and grandparents didn't – their food was naturally organic, artificial additives were very few, and radiation a thing of the future! If unaddressed, these toxins have a negative impact on our bodies and our health, not only from the individual effects but also from accumulative and synergistic effects of the stored toxins within our body.

So it is important that we address the subject of detox without the 'trend' or 'fad' mentality, but one of a serious health concern.

In this section you will find many different ways in which we can effectively detox our bodies, and each has its benefits. It is important that you do not overdo it and that only 1 method is introduced at a time. When one method is established, and your body is used to it, you can, if you wish, introduce another method. But I would only use one of each type of method. So, for example, if you began taking a detoxing mineral, you could then complement this with a weekly enema or Epsom salt bath – I would not introduce another detoxing mineral. Of course, whichever methods you use would always be accompanied by a 'clean' diet as this will help prevent unwanted side effects and prevent undoing your work by bringing new toxins into the body! By a clean diet I mean an organic, natural, wholefood diet. The path you choose is your own, so do what feels right for you!

Troubleshooting & Unfavourable Effects

Detoxing the body can produce unfavourable effects, however these are not usually persistent and nothing to worry about. You may experience some effects such as flu-type symptoms, IBS, swelling, fatigue and even a slight aggravation of your original symptoms (known as a Herxheimer reaction, commonly seen in holistic health methods).

This is perfectly normal and is a sign that your detox is working.

They are caused when toxins are agitated within the body, and if the detox is too severe it can cause what is known as a 'cleansing crisis'. The symptoms can be eased by increasing your water intake to help flush the toxins from your system. You may also want to take a high dose of vitamin C (3 x 1,000mg per day). Drink Rooibos tea or Green Tea for their antioxidant properties. Also you may wish to eat some rice or other carbohydrate that can absorb the toxins released. I find rice and salty foods (salty with Himalayan Salt) in particular are very good. If these are not part of your chosen detox regime, a one-off small portion will not hurt to ease your symptoms. In fact it will slow the detox down slightly and make it more tolerable for you.

If it becomes a problem reduce the dosage or frequency of your chosen detox method, but try not to stop it even if it means going down to the smallest dose possible.

If you experience constipation (which can be a problem if you choose a detoxing mineral such as zeolite or clay) then you may consider adding a teaspoon of psyllium husks (or psyllium husk powder) to your mix.

Results

I have displayed below my hair mineral analysis results from January 2013. It clearly shows how my holistic lifestyle and detox regime has had a favourable impact on my body as the results of the toxic elements in my body are negligent. I don't do anything that isn't in this book and to me it is proof itself that detoxing and then avoiding toxins in your everyday life is very beneficial!

Listed toxic elements in order are: Antimony, Uranium, Arsenic, Beryllium, Mercury, Cadmium, Lead and Aluminium.

Sb	U	As	Be	Hg	Cd	Pb	Al
Antimony	Uranium	Arsenic	Beryllium	Mercury	Cadmium	Lead	Aluminum
N/A	.0005	.003	.0010	0.02	.001	0.10	0.3
N/A	.0008	.005	.0010	0.02	.002	0.10	0.5

CHAPTER 19...Epsom Salt

Epsom Salt, or Magnesium Sulphate, is renowned for its health properties. It is named after the town of Epsom in Surrey where it was originally prepared from the town's mineral waters. Some of the many uses are listed here:

- Exfoliating & cleansing the skin
- Drawing of boils and abscesses
- Drawing toxins from the body
- Correcting magnesium deficiency in soil
- Stress relief
- Constipation relief
- Easing mosquito & insect bites, bee stings and Poison Ivy rash
- Easing sore muscles
- Raising the body's magnesium & sodium levels (not the best for magnesium though – see The Magnesium Deficiency Epidemic, Chapter 16)

Epsom Salt Bath

The most effective way to detox with an Epsom Salt Bath is to place 1 kg in a hot bath (as hot as you can comfortably stand, but do not burn yourself and be careful not to get giddy!). Soak for about 10 minutes. Then with a massage mitt rub yourself all over briskly in circular motions. You will get very hot very fast and the water will get quite cloudy. When you have rubbed yourself all over, try to stay in the bath for another 10 minutes, or at least 5. Then be careful when you get out, dab yourself dry and quickly wrap yourself in a hot towel or duvet and stay wrapped up for 2 hours to allow your body to sweat. After the detox period, shower off.

I personally find that an Epsom Salt bath can cause me to have a restless and sleepless night, and can cause my mind to also become restless. I have also heard of similar experiences from friends and clients. Some saying they felt drained after using them and others with similar unsettled feelings as I experience. When I use Epsom Salts in my bath it is usually for a purpose such as drawing a boil or bathing a wound, for example. I find it excellent as a drawing agent for boils and abscesses, however I tend to stick to magnesium chloride due to the 'side' effects I experience with the Epsom Salts.

Taking Epsom Salt Internally

It is not advised to take Epsom Salt internally on a regular basis due to connections with bleeding ulcers and hypermagnesemia (overload of magnesium levels in the body).

However a teaspoon (or less) on occasions is proven to provide excellent constipation relief, and flush the liver. The Salts are believed to open the bile duct and allow gall stones to pass more easily.

If you plan to take Epsom salt internally on occasions, it is essential that you obtain Food Grade Epsom Salt (BP or FCC grade).

CHAPTER 20...*Modern Cleansing with Ancient Wisdom*

(an excerpt from my article published in Health Freedom News Magazine, November 2011)

Each day people all over the world awake to their own personal cleansing routine, but quite often the cleanliness of the inside of the body is neglected. The ancient tradition of Yoga on the other hand has considered internal purification of the human body in great detail and offers cleansing practices called shuddhi-kriyas to help to achieve total purification of the body.

Yogis believe that organs which come into contact with external matter regularly, where there can therefore be a lot of impurities, require these cleansing practices to become purified. Some of these practices have been adapted for modern day use as they are especially effective in today's climate where there are many man-made chemicals that come into contact with our bodies and increase our toxic overload.

Body cleansing removes the waste materials and toxins held in our bodies which the normal elimination processes cannot remove. Toxins can drain the body of energy and make you more susceptible to disease and infections. Everyone is exposed to toxins, no matter how healthy they are, and everyone can benefit from a regular detox. Eastern

100

medicine claims that toxic accumulation can increase susceptibility to many degenerative diseases, and many conditions can and have been relieved with some of these practices. They have been adopted by thousands of people, including those in the medical profession all over the world who are finding great benefits from their practice, proving to be valuable additions to their regular routine for increased health and well-being.

ENEMA

The main practice which has entered our modern lives and is regularly used by medical professionals and hospitals is Vasti. Vasti is basically what we call today enema, the act of cleansing the bowel with a liquid solution which is taken in and expelled out through the anus. Usually water is used but prescribed herbs, supplements and remedies can also be added to the enema liquid. Traditionally in Yoga instead of using a bag or can to hold enema fluid and a tube to administer the fluid into the colon, the practitioner would suck water or even air in through anus to cleanse the colon (impossible as this may seem!). The benefits of removing putrefying faeces from the colon go way beyond relieving constipation. Also relieved are IBS, food intolerances, toxic overload in the body, low energy levels, even skin conditions are just some of the ailments that can benefit from taking occasional home enema or the more professional colon cleanse.

Please see Chapter 21 for more detailed information.

NETI

Neti is another extremely beneficial cleansing technique and one that is becoming more and more popular. The practice is called Jala Neti and is the act of cleansing the nose with a neti pot. It is known by satisfied users for its many physical and psychological benefits. The nose is the body's primary anti-pollution filter that cleans and warms the air we breathe into our delicate lungs. If the nose is not kept in clean working order then it will stop functioning properly, just as a vacuum cleaner ceases to perform when its filter is blocked or needs replacing. Blowing the nose is usually the only way we try to keep this vital life sustaining filter healthy, and many people have even picked up the habit of by-passing this filtration process completely by mouth-breathing! When cold, unfiltered air enters our lungs it will worsen conditions such as asthma and many other chronic chest and upper respiratory complaints. Our lungs find it difficult to expel toxins so it is of utmost importance that we use our nose properly!

Salt water is used for nasal cleansing, however in tradition, salt water was not the only liquid used. Milk (called Dugdha Neti) and even a dilution of one's own urine (Swamootra Neti) was used, both having their own benefits, especially the latter – believe it or not! Swamootra Neti works in a similar way to homeopathy, where "the ingestion of like cures like". As it passes the olfactory nerves in the nasal passage, waste products in the urine can educate the brain on the body's overall health gradually re-programming it to fine-tune the body's metabolism and making this a very potent healing process. This must only be practised in conjunction with a specialist diet so as not to harm the delicate nasal passages.

Further information can be found in Chapter 22 on Jala Neti.

Owning a natural health shop which specialises in body cleansing & detox, and being a Yoga teacher myself, I have found many benefits to my health, energies and spiritual growth in detoxing my body through some of these cleansing practices. Of course in holistic healing, health complaints are often brought out in order to be healed, making it a challenging but very rewarding journey that still continues for me.

CHAPTER 21...Home Enema

Bowel problems are nature's warning for serious health problems so it is important that our bowel is kept healthy. The colon is an important route for expelling toxins. When it does not work effectively, toxins can accumulate in the body which can result in the complication of many healing programmes, even apparently unrelated to bowel health and cleanliness such as stress, depression and premature ageing.

Our modern day lives, environment and diets place extraordinary burdens to the body and its elimination process. Our diets may contain many toxic additives and ingredients, GM and heavily processed foods. Even if we avoid these burdens, we may still tend to eat too many glutenous grains which can wreak havoc to our bowel health. It is likely that our colon struggles to eliminate this overload of toxic matter and much of it can remain in the gut, preventing the efficient absorption of nutrients.

Eastern medicine believes that toxins are a primary cause of unfavourable symptoms. When toxins, such as those contained in faeces, accumulate in our bodies they can disrupt our natural bacterial balance and inhibit healing which can cause leaky gut syndrome and as the toxins are reabsorbed into the blood, it can become poisoned.

The following is based upon an excerpt from the Holistic Valley Enema Booklet written by myself.

Introduction to Enemas

Colon cleansing, or enema, has been used for thousands of years where its ancient origins are found in the practice of Yoga and the Indian Medicine practice of AyurVeda. In these origins it is called 'Vasti' which literally means bag or container and in ancient times sterilized urinary bladders of animals were used to administer the enema.

Enema is basically an internal bath or douche for the colon. It is effective for the relief of many digestive disturbances such as IBS, constipation, distension of abdomen, flatulence and it is claimed that even problems resulting from bed ridden conditions like paralysis can also be relieved. Enema can also be used to give supplementation and herbal preparations to the body bypassing the stomach acid and digestive system.

In addition, enema is supportive to the healing phase of a biological programme as it clears the exit pathway for waste and toxins to be eliminated. In this way it can regulate our body weight and prevent premature ageing, promoting healthy longevity. It can help relieve backache, sciatica and other pains in the joints, sharpen the mind and give a welcome sense of well-being. It also improves the condition of the colon.

Enema will help cleanse the colon of poisons, gas and constipated waste, the accumulation of which can easily allow toxins to absorb back into the bloodstream and into our cells, accumulating and slowly poisoning the body. During colon cleansing, toxic material is broken down so it can no longer harm the body or inhibit assimilation of nutrients and elimination.

As enemas prevent the accumulation of constipated waste in the colon, and therefore the related absorption of toxins into the bloodstream, toxin levels will be reduced in the blood stream. The toxins that are concentrated in your tissues will then diffuse back into the blood where they will be eliminated by your liver and kidneys. These organs will no longer be overwhelmed by toxins as long as you control constipation and try to avoid pollution from other sources.

Who Should Avoid Enemas?

Do not take enema (unless medically advised) under the following circumstances:

- in pregnancy, especially before 7 months
- in extreme cases of piles or rectum ulcers
- severe intestinal obstructions
- weakness after other treatment/illness

How to prepare your Enema fluid

For general use, water that is body temperature is best for general enema. It is best to use boiled and cooled water or filtered water, but tap water is fine if the latter are inconvenient (and your water is not fluoridated).

A slightly colder enema is useful for dysentery, diarrhoea, haemorrhoids and colitis. A slightly warmer enema is helpful for pain due to constipation, gas, abdominal pain or painful haemorrhoids.

There are also ingredients that can be added to the enema water to benefit certain conditions.

Neem Leaf Powder – is known to help in the case of amoebic intestinal infections, ulcerated colitis and it conditions the colon.

Coffee – regular ground coffee should be used. It is thought helpful for dysmenorrhea, eczema, gout, IBS, psoriasis, rheumatoid arthritis, rosacea, chronic constipation, liver ailments, past or present drug abuse & AIDS. This is an excellent way to support the liver in eliminating toxins. For extra detox effects and support for your liver and kidneys you can use 1 mug of (ready made) filter coffee diluted in the enema water (usually 2 litres). Any organic ground coffee can be used, but it must be fresh not instant and it must be organic. It is good practice to do a cleansing water enema before the coffee enema as you will be able to hold the coffee enema for longer for more benefit.

Oil Solution – can help in the eliminative process. Sesame and Castor oils are particularly useful as they have a calming effect on the nervous system.

Fenugreek – 2 teaspoons of fenugreek seeds are soaked in 1 Litre of water overnight and then boiled it in the morning. Cool and strain before use for an anti-bacterial and anti-inflammatory effect, useful for colitis.

Honey – mix 50g honey to 500ml-1L of water. This has a moisturising effect and helps to loosen solid matter.

Herbal Solutions – there are also many herbal solutions that can be prepared for enema use such as bitter herbs to help parasites and bile, astringent herbs to help haemorrhoids, Spicy herbs to help digestion and aid circulation and calming herbs for their calming effect. It is suggested you seek the advice of a qualified herbalist if you wish to use herbs, preferably one who works with the principles of GNM so you can be assured the herbs are in harmony with the body's healing.

A Summary on the Technique

Enema should be given four to six hours after a meal or preferably in the morning before breakfast. Bowels and bladder should be evacuated prior to treatment if possible. Otherwise a brief clear fluid enema can be administered as a 'clean out'.

Make sure you will not be disturbed, and create a pleasant atmosphere by lighting some incense and playing relaxing music. You need not be in the bathroom, but make sure a toilet is nearby. There are several positions that are used for administering enema, including some Yoga postures however it is most important to be comfortable.

An enema bag or can is used. The nozzle or catheter if using one is lubricated and inserted into the anus. The tap or clip is then released to let the enema fluid enter the bowel. Massaging the lower abdomen gently counter clockwise while the solution is flowing in can help loosen hardened faecal material.

You will begin to feel an increased sense of urgency, sometimes almost straight away. Use your breath to help you relax and ease this feeling. When you feel you cannot take any more, stop the fluid and try to retain the water for as long as possible.

When you are ready, go to the toilet! It is expected that there may be several episodes of elimination after enema.

After enema a light diet should be taken for one day.

If you purchase an enema kit from a reputable supplier you should receive full instructions with your kit.

How often should I take Enema?

Some believe your colon would become lazy if enema is over-practised, however there is no real proof of this provided common sense is applied. It is best to let your body be your guide as to how often you take enema. Many people take enemas once a week, some once a month, others whenever they feel they need to. During severe episodes of constipation or aggravation of your condition you may wish to take enema daily in the short term, but do not rely on this in the long term. I consider the most important advice is not to replace your natural evacuation with enema.

CHAPTER 22...
Jala Neti: Nasal Cleansing

Why Cleanse the nostrils?

We have looked at Jala Neti nasal cleansing in the previous chapter, Modern Cleansing with Ancient Wisdom. But here we will go into it in a little more detail.

The nasal cavities contain many features which are extremely important to physical and mental health, such as the olfactory nerves which have the most direct link from our external environment to the brain out of all the nerves in the body. Correct nasal breathing is required to keep this network functioning properly. It is considered by many that cleansing the nasal cavities to restore a healthy nasal environment can lead to better health that reaches far beyond the nose.

I have been selling neti pots in my shop since it began in 2004, having used one since around 1998. It was one of the first items I wanted to offer as I had previously found it extremely difficult to source a neti pot in the UK. Now there are many places selling neti pots as the demand is growing from personal recommendations from satisfied users and even recommendations from some doctors and ENT surgeons!

The Method

A device called a "Neti Pot" is filled with warm water (roughly body temperature), about 1/4 teaspoon salt is added, dependent on the size of neti pot, and the spout of the pot is inserted into one nostril. While leaning over a sink with the head horizontal and turned to the side, the water will begin to flow in and around the sinuses and out of the other nostril. Sometimes a little adjustment is needed if the water is felt at the back of the throat. When the neti pot is empty care is needed in blowing the nose very gently one side at a time into the sink. The blowing is repeated, increasing in force each time, before using the neti pot on the other side.

Once both nostrils are completed, a drying process is required. The head is dangled upside down for about 30 seconds to drain any excess water from the sinuses. It is also helpful to turn the head from side to side in this position. Each side is then blown once more and only then are both nostrils blown together. To dry the nasal passage, a quick and forceful breath is practised in and out 10 times, blow drying the inside of the nose.

The technique is surprisingly extremely comfortable and you will feel the refreshing benefits straight away! It may take a bit of getting used to but with a little patience the process will quickly become second nature, and can be performed in less than a couple of minutes.

What are the Benefits?

Due to the direct links to the nasal passages, nasal cleansing can help upper respiratory disorders such as sore throats, sinusitis and coughs.

It can also provide symptomatic relief to allergy sufferers such as hay fever and dust as it washes away trapped particles of the offending substance.

It can benefit conditions like asthma and bronchitis by reducing the tendency to 'mouth-breathe' which chills the lungs and worsens the condition.

It is believed to have a cooling, soothing effect on the brain, relieving headache, migraine, depression and general mental tension. Regular use is also believed to be beneficial for those suffering from epilepsy, tantrums and panic.

Problems associated with the eyes can be helped and it can promote general eye health as it cleanses the tear ducts, and it is especially helpful for contact lens wearers (like me). I am often complimented by my optician on the health of my eyes despite wearing contacts since age 12 and now using continuous wear lenses!

It cleanses the eustachian tubes which lead from the nose to the ear, and so can benefit some ear problems such as glue ear, middle ear infections and tinnitus.

It can have a beneficial and cleansing effect on the Ajna Chakra that helps in awakening higher states of meditation.

If you smoke, it is claimed that it can sensitise the nose to the actual smell of nicotine and stale smoke, and in effect can naturally turn you away from the habit! This happened to me during pregnancy as I was completely turned off smoking and felt nauseous at the slightest smell of cigarettes. However I am not entirely convinced it was only due to the nasal cleansing, as it could have also been due to hormonal changes!

CHAPTER 23...Ear Candles & Cones

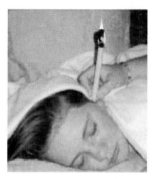

Ear candles or cones are commonly known to be the holistic alternative to syringing the ears, but their benefits reach much further than the ears and head as they affect most of our whole physical and non-physical bodies. Ear candles do not require a prescription nor do they require specialist administration. If the instructions supplied with your ear candles are followed closely, this is a safe, painless way to treat many common ailments and promote complete well-being of body, mind and spirit.

Background History

The history of ear candling is surrounded by mythical and colourful tales. Despite many claims to the contrary, they were NOT used by the Hopi Indians of America. This was first misrepresented by Biosun, who manufacture ear candles, and this misconception has been adopted throughout the industry, despite many requests by the Hopi Indians to stop using their name incorrectly.

Many still believe that ear candling or ear coning is an ancient practice used by the Egyptians, Indians, Tibetans and many ancient tribes thousands of years ago. There is also a belief that it is an ancient Atlantean practice and that the Ancient Greeks used ear candles for cleansing the spirit and healing the soul. As much as we would like this information to be true, there is little or no evidence to support any of this ancient history. However it is proved that ear candling has been practised since the early 20th century.

How They Work

There is much debate as to the exact way that ear candling works, but thousands swear to its effectiveness. Some common theories such as using a chimney effect to draw out wax has since been disproved by medical research. What has been proved is that the effects of ear candling reach far beyond that of the ENT (Ear, Nose and Throat) and head.

What we know from studies and research is the burning flame produces a vibrational effect on the inner ear and ear drum encouraging impurities, residue and toxins to be released. This also encourages secretion of the frontal and para-nasal sinuses.

It stimulates important acupuncture and reflex points. On a spiritual level, the Chakras are cleansed and balanced and the Kundalini is stimulated.

Despite many courses and therapists believing and promoting that ear candles actually draw out ear wax from the ear using a chimney action, it is a common misconception that has been scientifically disproved. The residue in the candle after treatment is simply the wax from the candle and not ear wax! We have personally proved this by burning several varieties of ear candles without an ear attached to the end. Still there is the same residue! However, as ear wax is encouraged to naturally disperse during and after ear candling it remains an effective alternative to syringing the ear despite the misconception of how this happens!

How they are used

The candles vary in length, but average at about 22cm long and have a burning time of 10-12 minutes. The recipient will usually be lying down on their side. The candles/cone is placed at the entrance to the ear, and lit at the other end. It is important that you have help in performing this for safety reasons. You should keep your eyes closed for maximum effect, and have a relaxing atmosphere in a draught-free room. You will usually receive full instructions with your ear candles when you buy them, and it is important you follow these instructions carefully for safety reasons. You can visit a thermo-auricular therapist to have your ears candled professionally, however it is a very easy practice that can be practised at home for a more cost-effective option.

The Benefits

Ear candles are recommended for symptomatic relief of almost all ear, nose and throat conditions, and are especially good for:

Excessive wax; pressure regulation in cases of sinusitis, rhinitis, glue ear, colds, flu etc.; migraine and headaches; TMJ (clicking jaw) pain; otis externia /tropical ear; tinnitus and noises in the ears; hearing impairment.

Further benefits include:

Revitalisation; Chakra balancing; stress and tension relief; stimulation of energy in the meridians (directly affects the stomach, small intestine, triple burner, gall bladder, liver and the bladder meridians and the governing and conception vessels); balancing Yin and Yang energies; stimulation of Kundalini energies.

They are not recommended for people with perforated eardrum, or tympanostomy tube implants. Also not recommended if you have skin disease in or around the ear. If you have a current ear infection, you need to wait until this has cleared up before using ear candles.

What are they Made From?

Ear candles and cones are generally made from a pure natural material such as cotton or hemp dipped in beeswax. Some have added ingredients such as bee propolis or essential oils. Some have added safety features for your reassurance such as flame retardant discs and filters.

Ear candles are available widely on the internet and in good health shops, and prices can range from under £3 per pair up to £10 per pair. There are many hand-made varieties on the market, but I would definitely recommend that you only purchase those that hold the CE certification due to the obvious safety risks with this type of product.

CHAPTER 24...Diatomaceous Earth

Diatomaceous Earth is becoming increasingly popular due to its excellent parasite control and detoxifying properties. It is being widely used in farms, gardens, around the home and for human and pet health. It presents itself as a fine white or off-white powder and is completely natural.

Diatomaceous is pronounced di-at-om-ay-shus (I am often asked this!!), and its name is derived from the fact that it contains the skeletal fossilised remains of diatoms. Diatoms are an ancient phytoplankton which were the primary food source for marine life millions of years ago. It is very rich in silica and has extremely high porosity, making it very lightweight.

Which source?

There are many sources of Diatomaceous Earth, most deposits being from salt water sources. However these are not considered to be as pure as the fresh water source, which are generally harvested from dried up lake beds. DE from a fresh water source is recommended for food use due to its exceptional purity and low heavy metal content. DE will be sold as 'Food Grade' if it is suitable for human use.

DE as an Anti-Parasite Treatment

If you look at DE under a microscope, you will see it has many razor sharp edges which are the remnants of the diatoms' hard shells and skeletal remains. When sprinkled onto bugs, insects or parasites such as fleas, bed bugs, etc., the particles of DE get into the joints of their exoskeleton and its razor-like edges basically pierce through it. As DE is very porous, once it gets through the parasite's exoskeleton it will effectively dehydrate the parasite. As this is a purely physical process there is no danger of any parasites building up an immunity to the treatment as it can with those preparations that poison the parasite.

Silica & Other Nutrients

As DE is very rich in silica, generally about 85%-95%, it provides the body with this essential mineral. Silica is used for cartilage, bones, teeth, hair, nails and the production of collagen which is the substance that holds all our cells together, our connective tissue. Silica is well-known and widely reported to be excellent for ageing muscles and joints and gives our skin more elasticity, the latter property being why both artificial and natural collagen is often added to, or the basis of, anti-ageing products.

Along with silica, DE also contains approximately 20 other minerals including calcium, magnesium, sodium and iron and is believed to assist the re-mineralisation of the body.

How Diatomaceous Earth can be Used:

Home, Pets & Garden

DE can be used around the home, on pets and livestock animals and in the garden as well as being used for human consumption (providing it is food grade). When it is sprinkled onto surfaces and in crevices such as around skirting boards it acts as a barrier to prevent infestation of parasites. When rubbed into carpets and bedding it can prevent and kill fleas, bed bugs and more. However care needs to be taken when vacuuming as it can clog the filter of the cleaner. You must also take care if you are using it in large quantities to wear a face mask as the plumes of DE can be irritative to the chest if breathed in.

It can be used on animals fur to kill parasites such as fleas, by simply rubbing into the fur. It can be left on, or it can be washed off after a few hours. When I used to treat my dog, as she was very old her skin was quite thin so it tended to dehydrate her skin if I didn't wash it off after a few hours. However my cats are fine if I just leave it on them. As they clean themselves they will take some internally for added benefits!

It can be added to animal's feed to prevent worms and internal parasites. I give my cats and our young medium-sized dog about a teaspoon each day. Obviously the dose would need to be adjusted for different sized animals.

It can also be periodically sprinkled onto the lawn if it is suspected that there are fleas present (e.g. if your pets keep becoming re-infested this may indicate that your garden has outdoor fleas!). Many gardeners use it on and around their plants as a barrier to pests. It is also used as a growing medium for hydroponic gardens and is widely used in swimming pool and water filtration due to its ability to absorb tiny particles that would not be caught by filtration.

Human Use

It is essential that you make sure the DE you buy is food grade. There are many industrial grade cheaper alternatives around, but these generally lack purity so are not suitable for human consumption.

If you wish to take DE, it is recommended you take approximately 1 tablespoon a day mixed into some water. You may wish to start off with less and build the dosage up. I tend to take it at night as it can then get to work on my body while my digestive system is at rest. If it is taken on an empty stomach it allows for the DE to absorb toxins without interfering with or absorbing the nutrients from foods. For this reason, I would not recommend it is added to smoothies, or taken at the same time as other supplements or medication.

Benefits

We have already looked at the benefits of the silica and mineral content of DE, but its properties do not stop there! Here are some more:

Detox – DE absorbs heavy metals and other toxins from the body as it passes through our system. It is also claimed to remove pesticides and drug residues.

Parasites – DE is active against internal parasites it will therefore help alleviate symptoms caused by parasites. I regularly use it successfully in my kinesiology practice for clients who are experiencing parasite infection.

Inflammation, wounds & lesions – DE can be mixed into a paste and applied to the area held in place with a gauze. This will supply the area with essential silica to assist in the healing process and prevent infection.

General increased well-being and resistance - as DE will help to keep your body free of parasites and reduce toxins which can aid the efficient assimilation of nutrients and therefore improve your energy and give an increased sense of well-being.

Sourcing Diatomaceous Earth

When you are looking to buy DE, you must make sure it is food grade and that it is sold in food grade containers. The purest source is from Peru. It needs to be freshwater sourced. There are many places selling inferior grades of DE, many of these are only suitable for animal use and many are not very pure.

In my shop we sell our own brand (Holistic Valley) High Quality Food Grade DE for £2.50 per 75g tub (standard sized coleslaw tub), £6.50 for 300g (fits in a 1 Litre tub) - prices correct at the time of writing! It is a very light powder so the weight is very light for the volume you get. You should not have to pay more than this and if you find cheaper, make sure it is the proper grade and purity.

CHAPTER 25...Zeolite

Zeolites are porous minerals with a crystalline structure that consists of 4 oxygen atoms surrounding metal ions (generally aluminium or silicon). The zeolite's atoms are stacked in such a way that microscopic channels and cavities are formed which gives the zeolite its cage-like absorbent properties. Clinoptilolite is considered to be the most abundant member of the 45 natural types of zeolite and is formed by the alteration of fine-grained volcanic deposits by underground water. Since 1950, there have been 100s of synthetic types of zeolite manufactured but for health concerns it is recommended to stick with natural Zeolite Clinoptilolite.

The crystalline structure of zeolite has a strong negative charge due to an unpaired electron allowing the attraction and absorption of positively charged heavy and radioactive metals and numerous positively charged toxins. Unlike other silicates, zeolites are 20-50% void enabling them to harness these toxins and metals within their structure. Once these toxins are harnessed by the zeolite, they remain extremely stable as the zeolite ionic bond is so strong that in order to release the trapped compounds it needs to be heated in acid to approximately 1,000 degC! Yet there is also evidence that zeolite has a clever 'ionic exchange' property which allows it to release ions without breaking the structure and can also selectively absorb ions that fit into its cavities acting as a molecular sieve. It will also hold larger particles to break them down into smaller particles known as catalytic cracking. According to the British Zeolite Association:

"The shape-selective properties of zeolites are the basis for their use in molecular adsorption. The ability preferentially to adsorb certain molecules, while excluding others, has opened up a wide range of molecular sieving applications."

Zeolite has been used to remove radioactive metals like strontium and caesium from radioactive waste and to clean sewage. It is widely used in industry in many different ways, and also in water softeners and air purifiers. It was used in the Chernobyl disaster to decontaminate the people and the area, and it was thrown into the reactors to absorb the radioactive metals.

Uses for the Body

Due to its ability to remove radioactive metals, zeolite clinoptilolite is extensively used nowadays by the military forces.

Due to zeolite's strong absorbency properties, it would likely contain many of, if not most of, the elements of the Periodic Table. According to Dr. Karl Hecht it can provide essential elements and minerals to the body thanks to their ion exchange property.

The British Zeolite Association explain zeolite's ion exchange property thus:

"The loosely-bound nature of extra-framework metal ions means that they are often readily exchanged for other types of metal when in aqueous solution."

In the US and in Russia, Zeolite Clinoptilolite is used in the production of food supplements. In other countries it has also been used to produce anti-diarrhoeal medicine for the treatment of dysentery, food poisoning and other gastrointestinal disorders.

Zeolite for Detox

When zeolite is taken internally it will trap and harness heavy metal toxins and radioactive metals as it travels through the body, offering an excellent detoxification supplement.

Using zeolite to detox is extremely beneficial, as due to the way in which the heavy metals and toxins are held in the structure, it ensures they are carried out of the body completely and not deposited anywhere else in the body. When using zeolite for detox, it is believed the strongest attraction is to the primary heavy metal toxins such as lead, mercury, arsenic, etc. Once these are removed the next strongest attraction is to toxins such as those found in pesticides and herbicides. As the body reacts to the reduced toxic overload, the increased liver function assists in the elimination of further toxins and impurities.

Other properties

Zeolite attracts and absorbs pre-virus components. Unlike heavy metals and toxins which are attracted into the cage structure, these viral components are absorbed into the zeolite aggregate itself.

Zeolite acts as a complement to traditional antioxidants as it attracts and captures free radicals which have a positive charge. These free radicals cause havoc inside our cells, dashing around like a wild fireball causing damage to the cells. Unlike zeolite, traditional antioxidants will work on an ionic level by effectively neutralising the molecule.

Additionally, zeolite is believed to assist the regulation of the body's pH level to between 7.35 to 7.45, which is the optimum pH for the human body.

As the body balances and regulates itself, and in conjunction with a good balance of nutrients through correct diet, the body's well-being and resistance to disease will increase. It will help to maintain healthy cell membranes and cleanses and helps to maintain intestinal health. Energy levels will be beneficially affected and many find relief from symptoms of depression and anxiety.

Suggested Intake

Clinoptilolite is not approved as a food supplement in the EU, so you will not find a legal food grade zeolite product in the UK at present. However there are zeolite-based products available in some EU countries. It is yet to be determined what impact the UK exiting the EU will have on any health claims or food graded products, hopefully it will be less restrictive. It is on the Generally Regarded As Safe (GRAS) list issued by the FDA. Therefore, at the moment, you need to make your own decision whether you want to consume it!

Should you choose to take it internally, most people find benefit from taking 1 teaspoonful per day mixed into water or suspended in a smoothie (however it will absorb some of the nutrients of a smoothie so it is recommended that the smoothie is classed as only for the purpose of taking zeolite and not for nutrition!). It is advisable to take it away from food, supplements or medication so it does not interfere with absorption.

If you currently have amalgam (silver coloured) fillings or any other metal dental work, you may wish to put the zeolite into empty capsules to take. This will avoid the potential of the zeolite reacting with the metalwork in your mouth. Some people have told us that their fillings and areas around the metalwork get very sensitive when they have taken zeolite in water.

If you find unfavourable detox effects as previously mentioned, reduce your dosage to ½ or even ¼ teaspoon and build up slowly.

It is important to drink plenty of water during a detox programme.

Particle Size

Zeolite particles are measured in 'microns' which are 1/1000th of a millimetre. The smaller the particle size or microns, the easier it is to suspend in water, but also the cost will escalate as the particle size decreases. Most zeolite is available between 10 micron and 300 micron size, up to granules, the size indicating the largest sized particle you would find in that batch. However most of it would be of smaller particle size, for example my shop supplies 40 and 300 micron zeolite - in the 300 micron size, 75% is below 100 microns, 50% being below 30 microns. Finer grade zeolite is often more expensive than the coarser, so if you want to keep costs down, you could get the 300 micron, and if you do not wish to drink the small amount of unsuspended larger particles you can mix more than you need in a glass so the sediment that settles can be discarded. The 40 micron will mix easily with water without sediment. Either way, please do not be ripped off as there are many sellers offering zeolite at extortionate prices!

MYTHS

"Zeolites are poisonous as they contain heavy metals"

FACT: They contain heavy metals? Of course they do – they are such strong magnets of heavy metals that they will absorb heavy metals from the environment around them! But this will not pose a threat to health, as we have seen that unless our bodies can heat our stomach acid to almost 1,000degC, then the heavy metals held within the cages will be extremely stable and there is no fear of escape.

"Zeolite must be purified for internal consumption"

This is a common myth promoted by the pyramid selling companies who market liquid zeolite. They claim to have destroyed the crystalline structure in order to remove the heavy metals toxins. But as they have destroyed the crystalline structure, it would not really be much use in absorbing and trapping toxins when passing through our bodies. In addition, if they have failed to remove all the heavy metal toxins encased in its structure, it leaves potential for them to leak out into our bodies as the structure is now damaged!

"You should only consume activated zeolite"

Yet another myth promoted by the liquid zeolite 'salesmen' based upon fake science. Zeolite is already actively absorbent – there is no need for any such activation! If it was not actively absorbent, it wouldn't have absorbed the toxins held in its structure in the first place!

"Liquid zeolite is far superior"

What the pyramid sellers have done, is given a load of scientific facts based upon the use of unprocessed zeolite powder, then made up fanciful reasons for processing it to create a 'patented' product which they can profit from (big time!). They cannot patent pure zeolite powder so they have to alter it to do so. To make matters worse, when you buy liquid zeolite, you are buying such a tiny amount of zeolite dissolved in purified water, potassium sorbate and citric acid, padded out with a plethora of micro and macro nutrients. For this you will be charged in the region of £35-£60 for a 30ml bottle! In comparison, if you obtain your trace minerals from Himalayan Salt, you can purchase powdered zeolite for only £5.00 for 250g at my shop. That's 50 doses!

CHAPTER 26...Bentonite Clay

Bentonite clay is formed from volcanic ash. There are different types that have varying content, but in general they are mainly composed of montmorillonite, illite or other smectite minerals. Clay is extremely porous and many variants have a high pH, generally around 9-10, making them very alkaline. As previously mentioned in this book, fungus and microbes that assist our healing thrive in an acidic environment and die in alkaline. Bentonite is therefore beneficial to neutralise acidic conditions where symptoms are severe, however it needs to be used wisely so as not to prevent healing.

Similar to zeolite, bentonite clay has a negative charge as it's protons are not equal to its electrons. It therefore acts as a magnet for attracting positively charged toxins and organic metabolic toxic waste such as lactic acid and is therefore very supportive in the healing phase of a biological programme that involves cell removal in healing. Due to its nature, as with zeolite, bentonite will have a presence of heavy metal toxins upon analysis. However, as with zeolite, these remain within the clay due to its strong bond and will not be harmful to the body.

Sodium & Calcium Bentonite

The 2 types of bentonite I have researched are sodium bentonite from Wyoming and calcium bentonite from Spain. Sodium bentonite has a

127

higher pH of 9-10 and has greater porosity with an amazing swelling capacity. For this reason some people find sodium bentonite too harsh for internal usage. In this case they therefore choose calcium bentonite. Both clays are extremely similar in make-up and are generally over 50% silica. Both will contain calcium and sodium, but the sodium bentonite will have slightly more sodium than calcium, and likewise the calcium bentonite will have slightly more calcium than sodium.

Important notes:

- Never use metal utensils when mixing or measuring clay

- Do not force yourself to take a certain amount, you must listen to your body, and practice moderation

- For most applications, clay is best hydrated.

Using Clay Internally

Clay is commonly mixed with water to be taken internally. If you find the clay difficult to mix, or if taking it is causing you discomfort, you may wish to hydrate it first (info below). It is not unpleasant to consume as it has a pleasant fairly sweet taste, however if it is hydrated you may wish to further mix water in to make its consistency suitable for drinking. It is best to start with 1/2 a teaspoonful mixed into a glass of water, once a day and it is better taken on an empty stomach. You may increase the dosage and frequency if you wish. Everyone's body is unique, so listen to what your body is telling you. If you experience discomfort, reduce the dosage or make a break for a week and start with a smaller dose again, or you could try taking hydrated clay as previously mentioned.

You may also wish to include psyllium husks along with the clay for added cleansing benefits and constipation relief.

Hydrating Clay

Clay can be used as powder, but many applications of clay require it to be hydrated. This is done by simply adding your required dosage of clay to water and letting it swell until it becomes almost like a consistency of wallpaper paste. You can leave it for a few hours or, as many do, leave it overnight. It can be made up in this way in larger quantities and stored in a covered container for future use, which is really handy if you don't want to be planning your applications in advance!

Using Clay Externally

The cosmetics industry uses clay in many products. It works well as a poultice, compress, body wrap or face mask, and simply as a powder. Most applications will require hydrated clay.

A compress is effective for achy joints and muscles, and is made by diluting some hydrated clay to make it quite runny, then spreading this onto a flannel or towel and wrapping the affected area with it. Warm or chilled water can be used to dilute the clay depending on whether you wish to have a warm or cold compress! You may also wish to wrap it further with greaseproof paper and a warm or cold towel to maintain the chosen temperature.

A poultice is similar to a compress but the hydrated clay is not diluted. It is applied directly to the affected area, wrapped in greaseproof paper or a waterproof dressing, and left in place to dry out. This has a stronger effect than a compress.

I used this on my grandmother's suspected skin cancer growth, removing the dressing each day to cleanse, apply some colloidal silver, and leave to dry for 30 minutes before applying more clay poultice and redressing again. It actually fell off without scarring within a few days!

For a home body wrap, take some hydrated clay and dilute if necessary as you will need it to be spreadable. Apply it to the areas you wish, and wrap them in cling film and a warm blanket or towel. For a whole body application, it is best to use warm blankets or towels with a plastic sheet. Keep the wrapped area/s warm and covered for about 30 minutes before washing off – and take care not to block your plug hole!

A face mask is applied in the same way (but do not wrap your face in cling film!!). Just leave it to dry and rinse off. Make sure you use a gentle toner such as rose or lavender water or witch hazel and then a natural moisturiser such as an aromatherapy cream. Natural pampering at its best!!

Some people use clay in the bath – however I have no experience of this as I would be afraid of drainage problems as it is suggested to use 1-2Kg of clay in a bath!!

You can use clay as a body powder, as it is great for any rash or wound that needs healing.

Sourcing Bentonite Clays

Clays are not recognised as food in the EU so you will not find bentonite clay that is legally labelled as food grade at present. Although, this may soon change now we have opted to leave the EU. However, you can still check it is handled hygienically and supplied in food grade containers. I can supply high quality clays with prices from £5 for 200g, so use this as a guide when you shop around.

SECTION IV...... *Avoiding Toxins in Everyday Life*

CHAPTERS:

According to GNM:

Toxins cannot cause cancer due to the nature of cancer being a meaningful biological programme triggered by a conflict shock, originating in the psyche. However, the toxins mentioned in this section are poisonous. They slowly poison our system, cause mineral depletion, loss of vitality and energy, cell damage and cause systematic stress. They will, therefore, greatly hinder healing causing a prolonged healing phase. I believe the links they may have to disease are misinterpreted as being a 'cause', but they are actually prolonging the healing of a biological programme which may have otherwise gone unnoticed.

CHAPTER 27...Foods to Avoid

I hope you like (or rather dislike) this picture of a potential supermarket of the future – if the corporatists have their way!

As you may already know from reading the foreword, I am passionate about good ethics, and educating people on harmful food additives enabling them to choose their family's food wisely. Sadly much of this information is not covered by mainstream media.

There is no doubt that the food chain has become controlled by faceless and ruthless corporations who put profit before health so we need to educate ourselves on whether we are eating anything that is harming us.

The main dangerous ingredients I suggest you avoid in foods are (by no means an exclusive list and some are detailed further in this section!):

ARTIFICIAL SWEETENERS: Aspartame, Acesulfame K, Sucralose (Splenda), Nutrasweet, Saccharin, etc., even the new stevia-based sweetener, Truvia, is very bad news. These are insufficiently tested, and where testing has been performed, it is often biased as it is carried out by the manufacturer and based upon junk science. These have been linked to tumours, weight gain and even death. There are 92 FDA-documented reactions to Aspartame alone!

MONOSODIUM GLUTAMATE (MSG): A flavour enhancer found in many foods especially crisps and snacks, that attacks your brain cells. It works by neurologically causing people to experience a more intense flavour from the foods that they eat rather than just flavouring foods, and has been linked to many symptoms and ethical issues. Alternative glutamates may be used (E numbers 620-625) and those such as glutamic acid, yeast extract, hydrolysed protein, and many more.

FLUORIDE: I mention in a further article about the dangers of this toxic substance found in almost all mainstream dental care, and in some water supplies.

SODIUM NITRATE & NITRITE: Found in deli meats, such as bacon and ham.

HYDROGENATED FATS: Fats that have been blasted with hydrogen to make them semi-solid such as in 'healthy' spreads. Fats that have been altered in any way are extremely bad for us. Hydrogenated fats chemically resemble plastics more than food, possessing no healthy properties of oils or fats once processed.

GM FOODS: Genetic modification, or engineering, is completely unethical and untested, no-one has any idea how these foods will react to our bodies. The argument against GM is too lengthy to cover here but please see Chapter 29 for some more information.

SOY: Despite soy (or soya as it is sometimes referred to) being labelled as a health food, it is very high in destructive glutamates and has disastrous effects on the hormones. Not only this but over 93% of the world's soy is now genetically modified! Soy is classed as a xenoestrogen. These act in the same way as oestrogen in our bodies as they bind to oestrogen receptors and trigger a hormonal response, while blocking the body's oestrogen from binding to the receptors, thus causing hormonal imbalance. According to Livestrong:

> *"Consuming soy foods may disrupt lactation, interfere with the normal onset of puberty, inhibit your ability to produce fertile and viable offspring, compromise your fertility and alter sex-specific behaviour, according to research published in the October 2010 issue of "Front Neuroendocrinology."*

Along with the similar hormone-altering effects of BPA as previously discussed in Chapter 1, I wonder could it be having a negative effect on today's pubescent youth? There seems to be an increasing trend of angst and despair over the years, and it appears to me this is often over their physical development or sexuality, both of which would be directly affected by hormone disruptors as described by the research above.

CHAPTER 28...
The Innocent Poisoning of Our Children

published in Health Freedom News Magazine in 2011

NOTE: *this was written before I studied German New Medicine. From a GNM perspective, cancer and disease originate in the psyche and therefore cannot be caused by toxic food ingredients, however artificial sweeteners are poisonous and can cause symptoms without a conflict shock.*

People are generally so trusting of the food chain that they do not even read the labels of the foods and drinks they consume. Many people are of the opinion that "it wouldn't be allowed in food if it was bad for you", but large corrupt corporations, biased research, bought-out organisations that claim to be regulating the products for our good and mass-marketing have enabled this not to be the case.

We have often heard that artificial sweeteners and certain food additives such as Monosodium Glutamate (MSG) are bad for our health but has much of this information actually made a difference to how we feed our children? Sadly this does not seem so in many cases.

Specifically in this chapter I want to draw your attention to artificial sweeteners. The truth of the matter is that there is (to date) **NO artificial sweetener that is actually proven to be safe to consume.** In fact many have been linked to tumours and cancer with prolonged usage. The dangers of small amounts of these additives used in controlled amounts may be considered safe by the FDA, but the fact that sweeteners are now included in the ingredients of so many foods including health foods and drinks means that it will accumulate in our system and build up to levels that are harmful, especially to children, pregnant and nursing Mums and those with compromised health.

Sucralose has been linked to obesity, aborted pregnancies, anaemia, increased sugar cravings, digestive problems and conditions, migraines and seizures. Acesulfame K has been linked to kidney tumours, although is usually not found on its own but part of a toxic sweetener blend. However the most dangerous sweetener of all and the one I will concentrate on is Aspartame.

This deadly chemical is widely available in unlimited amounts in many food and drink products – including products that are specifically aimed at children, and more importantly are very widely used by playgroups, parents, schools and nurseries under the false belief that it is actually good for children.

To first understand why Aspartame is on the market and in our foods, it is necessary to understand who it got there in the first place.

It was discovered by accident in 1965 when James Schlatter, a chemist of G.D. Searle Company, was testing an anti-ulcer drug.

Aspartame was approved for dry goods in 1981 and for carbonated beverages in 1983. It was originally approved for dry goods on July 26, 1974, but objections filed by neuroscience researcher Dr John W. Olney and Consumer attorney James Turner in August 1974 as well as investigations of G.D. Searle's research practices caused the U.S. Food and Drug Administration (FDA) to put approval of aspartame on hold (December 5, 1974).

On January 21, 1981, the day after Ronald Reagan's inauguration, Donald Rumsfeld, the CEO of Searle and the main financier to Ronald Reagan's election campaign, re-applied to the FDA for approval to use aspartame as a food sweetener. Reagan's new FDA commissioner, Arthur Hayes Hull, Jr., saw that it became approved. In 1985, Monsanto purchased G.D. Searle and made Searle Pharmaceuticals and The NutraSweet Company separate subsidiaries.

Aspartame accounts for over 75 percent of the adverse reactions to food additives reported to the FDA. Many of these reactions are very serious including seizures and death and are detailed further on in this chapter.

With the backing of such a large and powerful (and corrupt) corporation such as Monsanto, there is very little we can do to take this dangerous substance off the market. However what we can do is spread awareness to people so they can decide whether to keep buying and feeding this to themselves and their families. The more these items are left on the shelf of supermarkets, maybe the message will get through that we do not want to have this poison in our food chain.

I fool it is imperative that products containing sweetener and especially aspartame are not given to our children by establishments such as schools, nurseries and playgroups where the parents have no control over what is given to their children during the times when they are there. So if you want to take action, write a letter to your school or education authority. The more people that write in, the more they will listen!

Ingredients of Aspartame

Phenylalanine (50% of aspartame) – Phenylalanine is an amino acid normally found in the brain. People with the genetic disorder phenylketonuria (PKU) cannot metabolize phenylalanine. This leads to dangerously high levels of phenylalanine in the brain (sometimes lethal). It has been shown that ingesting aspartame, especially along with carbohydrates, can lead to excess levels of phenylalanine in the brain even in persons who do not have PKU. Many people who have eaten large amounts of aspartame over a long period of time and do not have PKU have been shown to have excessive levels of phenylalanine in the blood. Excessive levels of phenylalanine in the brain can cause the levels of serotonin in the brain to decrease, leading to emotional disorders such as depression. It was shown in human testing that phenylalanine levels of the blood were increased significantly in human subjects who chronically used aspartame.

Aspartic Acid (40% of Aspartame) – Dr. Russell L. Blaylock, a professor of neurosurgery at the Medical University of Mississippi, recently published a book thoroughly detailing the damage that is caused by the ingestion of excessive aspartic acid from aspartame. Blaylock makes use of almost 500 scientific references to show how excess free excitatory amino acids such as aspartic acid and glutamic acid (about 99 percent of mono-sodium glutamate (MSG) is glutamic acid) in our food supply are causing serious chronic neurological disorders and a plethora of other acute symptoms.

138

Methanol (aka wood alcohol/poison) (10% of aspartame) – Methanol/ wood alcohol is a deadly poison. It is the poison that has caused some "skid row" alcoholics to end up blind or dead. Methanol is gradually released in the small intestine when the methyl group of aspartame encounter the enzyme chymotrypsin.

The absorption of methanol into the body is sped up considerably when free methanol is ingested. Free methanol is created from aspartame when it is heated to above 86 Fahrenheit (30 Centigrade). This would occur when an aspartame-containing product is improperly stored or when it is heated (e.g., as part of a "food" product such as Jelly).

Due to the lack of a couple of key enzymes, humans are many times more sensitive to the toxic effects of methanol than animals. Therefore, tests of aspartame or methanol on animals do not accurately reflect the danger for humans. As pointed out by Dr. Woodrow C. Monte, director of the food science and nutrition laboratory at Arizona State University,

> *"There are no human or mammalian studies to evaluate the possible mutagenic, teratogenic or carcinogenic effects of chronic administration of methyl alcohol".*

Diketopiperazine (DKP) – DKP is a by-product of aspartame metabolism. DKP has been implicated in the occurrence of brain tumours. Dr. Olney (the original neuroscientist who objected to aspartame) noticed that DKP, when nitrosated in the gut, produced a compound that was similar to N-nitrosourea, a powerful brain tumour causing chemical. Some authors have said that DKP is produced after aspartame ingestion. I am not sure if that is correct myself as I am no scientist, however it is true that DKP is formed in liquid aspartame-containing products during prolonged storage.

G.D. Searle conducted animal experiments on the safety of DKP. The FDA found numerous experimental errors occurred, including "clerical errors, mixed-up animals, animals not getting drugs they were supposed to get, pathological specimens lost because of improper handling," and many other errors. These sloppy laboratory procedures may explain why both the test and control animals had sixteen times more brain tumours than would be expected in experiments of this length. In an ironic twist, shortly after these experimental errors were discovered, the FDA used guidelines recommended by G.D. Searle to develop the industry-wide FDA standards for good laboratory practices!

Symptoms caused by Aspartame Consumption

Aspartame accounts for over 75% of the adverse reactions to food additives reported to the FDA. Many of these reactions are very serious including seizures and death.

According to researchers and physicians studying the adverse effects of aspartame, the following chronic illnesses can be triggered or worsened by ingesting of aspartame: Brain tumours, multiple sclerosis, epilepsy, chronic fatigue syndrome, Parkinson's disease, Alzheimer's, mental retardation, lymphoma, birth defects, fibromyalgia, and diabetes.

Here are the 92 documented and officially confirmed side effects of aspartame consumption held by the FDA. However, there are many more in a 1038 page medical text called Aspartame Disease: An Ignored Epidemic by H. J. Roberts, M.D.:

Headache	Seizures and Convulsions
Dizziness or Problems with Balance	Memory Loss
Change in Mood Quality or Level	Fatigue, weakness
Vomiting and Nausea	Other neurological
Abdominal Pain and Cramps	Rash
Change in Vision	Sleep problems
Diarrhoea	Hives

Change in Heart Rate

Itching

Change in Sensation (Numbness, Tingling)

Grand Mal

Local Swelling

Change in Activity Level

Difficulty Breathing

Oral Sensory Changes

Change in Menstrual Pattern

Other Skin

Other Localized Pain and Tenderness

Other Urogenital Change in Body Temperature

Difficulty Swallowing

Other Metabolic Joint and Bone Pain

Speech Impairment

Other Gastrointestinal

Chest Pain

Other Musculo-Skeletal

Fainting

Sore Throat

Other Cardiovascular

Change in Taste

Difficulty with Urination

Other Respiratory

Edema

Change in Hearing

Abdominal Swelling

Change in Saliva Output

Change in Urine Volume

Change in Perspiration Pattern

Change in smell

Eye Irritation

Unspecified

Muscle Tremors

Petit Mal

Change in Appetite

Change in Body Weight

Nocturnal

Change in Thirst or Water Intake

Unconsciousness and Coma

Wheezing

Constipation

Other Extremity

Pain

Problems with Bleeding

Unsteady Gait

Coughing Blood

Glucose Disorders

Blood Pressure Changes

Changes in Skin and Nail Coloration

Change in hair or nails

Excessive phlegm Production

Sinus Problems

Simple Hallucinations

Any Lumps Present

Shortness of Breath on Exertion

Evidence of Blood in Stool or Vomit

Dysmenorrhea

Dental Problems	Retardation
DEATH	Change in Breast Size or
Other Blood and Lymphatic	Tenderness
Eczema	Anaemia
Complex Partial Seizures	Change in Sexual Function
Swollen Lymph Nodes	Shock
Hematuria	Conjunctivitis
Shortness of Breath Due to Position	Dilating Eyes
Difficulties with Pregnancy	Febrile Convulsions
(Children Only) Developmental	

By law, additives must be inert or non-reactive. But surely this list of 92 documented symptoms including seizures, coma and death, are not indicative of an inert or non-reactive additive? Additionally, neurosurgeon Russell Blaylock, M.D. has written an entire book entitled "What To Do If You Have Used Aspartame" giving advice on detox after aspartame consumption!

Even if you do not believe this yourself – please don't feed it to your children. They have no choice in this and they will pay the price dearly. Remember, we have only been subject to this since the early 80s, whereas our children have had them in their diets since birth!

School Dinners

Despite some of the exposure that Jamie Oliver has given to the unhealthy school meals our children are faced with, it still remains a problem that schools have a typically mainstream idea of healthy food and drink. Even if we send in packed lunches they still offer tuck shops. In state schools, the mainstream idea of healthy eating is sugar-free, artificially sweetened drinks and 'low-fat' foods. In our children's old schools there were NO alternatives to artificially sweetened drinks. Sadly this is also the case in most nurseries, creches and youth groups.

So you may wish to take this up with your school to ensure that suitable alternatives are offered to your child. There is a template letter available for contacting your children's school in the Blog on the Shop website for your convenience, under the 'Taking Action' section.

CHAPTER 29...Genetic Modification

Genetic modification is when an organism is genetically altered, usually by introducing a gene from another species. It is also known as genetic engineering. The result of genetic modification is a GMO (genetically modified organism).

The argument against GM including the many ethical, health and moral reasoning is much too great to go into in this book, however I will offer a summary outline of the potential of the folly introduction of this grossly under-tested phenomenon into our foods and lives.

GMOs are mainly developed by huge biotechnical corporations such as Monsanto (now Bayer). We have previously heard how such a corporation really does not have humankind's best interest at heart. What appears to be happening on a huge scale is that crops are being subject to conditions (natural or otherwise) such as extremely high levels of aluminium in the soil, harsh chemical pesticides and herbicides and changeable climates. Then the corporations conveniently produce a GMO that is resistant to the threat that is preventing the natural growth of that crop.

Not only is this immoral, but also I believe this could be an attempt to monopolise and control our available food. When the same, or sister corporation is also responsible for the manufacture of pharmaceutical drugs, it makes you wonder if their intentions are for our well-being, or

144

their profits and the profits of their partner.

Threat to the Environment

In addition to this immorality, the simple idea of playing God and messing with nature is just completely alien to anything that I (and many others) feel is good and true. This is showing a huge impact on the honey bee population which you may think is not that important. However some estimate that human life will not survive more than a few years without bees, and the true extent of the impact on human life is still unknown. It is because two thirds of the world's crops are used for food production and these crops rely on insect (particularly bee) pollination.

There have been many theories for the reason of the massive decline in the bee population such as Wi-Fi and mobile phone signals, unknown virus or illness, climate change, etc. But most researchers agree that it is most likely down to the crops that have been genetically modified to have in-built pesticides and also those which are genetically modified to withstand heavy spraying with Round Up herbicide, so much that it is killing the wildlife and insects. Of course this is not mentioned in the mainstream media (who are the biggest corporation propaganda tool), and I suspect that there will be some GM 'saviour' crop that can germinate itself so we just don't need bees any more – that is providing we buy and use the patented seeds! To the masses who listen to the propaganda, of course GM will then seem like a saviour as is being promoted by certain corporate sponsors (or puppets) who are claiming GM crops will cure world hunger and poverty (despite third world countries like Africa standing up and declaring they do not want GM crops).

In the USA the honey bee decline has been such an epidemic that it has even been named, Colony Collapse Disorder (CCD). Since 2006 bee keepers have reported there has been an average loss of between 30-45% per year despite having increased the number of hives. But really speaking this negative effect of GM crops is only the tip of the iceberg.

Threat to Organic Farming

It is a simple fact that when a GM crop is introduced to a country, through nature's process of germination the crop will fertilise other crops in the country. This will give new and future generations of crops the GM gene and will therefore eradicate organic farming, as organic standards do not allow the use of GMOs. In addition, and as has already happened in the U.S., the corporation who developed the GM crop will have a patent for its use and can then sue the local farmer for growing their patented crops without permission! Look up the case of Percy Schmeiser V Monsanto. This only shows their thirst for global food control, in my opinion.

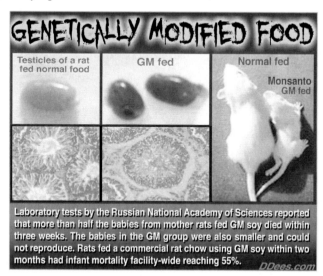

GENETICALLY MODIFIED FOOD

Testicles of a rat fed normal food	GM fed	Normal fed
		Monsanto GM fed

Laboratory tests by the Russian National Academy of Sciences reported that more than half the babies from mother rats fed GM soy died within three weeks. The babies in the GM group were also smaller and could not reproduce. Rats fed a commercial rat chow using GM soy within two months had infant mortality facility-wide reaching 55%.

DDees.com

Threat to our Health

There are so many scientists and doctors speaking out about the unknown dangers and insufficient testing of GMOs and the impact that introducing a genetically altered food into our systems may have. Already they have been found to alter DNA patterns and behaviour and cause havoc to our bodily functions.

More recent studies on GM foods given to rats have conclusively shown horrendous tumours and abnormal growth!

The Extent of GM

The most popular crops that are genetically modified are soy, cotton, wheat, canola (rapeseed), corn and rice. According to the USDA, in 2009, 93% of soy, 93% of cotton, and 86% of corn grown in the U.S. were GMO and it is estimated that over 90% of canola grown is GMO. There are also GM varieties of sugar beets and it is estimated that up to 80% of processed and packaged foods available in the supermarkets in the U.S. & Canada now contain GMOs. Maybe not surprisingly, more up-to-date figures are hard to find.

According to DEFRA (Department for Environmental And Rural Affairs):

> *"No GM crops are being grown commercially in the UK, but imported GM commodities, especially soya, are being used mainly for animal feed, and to a lesser extent in some food products."*

For this reason alone I choose to buy organic!

At the time of writing (December 2019) as far as I am aware, Waitrose are the only UK supermarket to have upheld their ban on GMOs in their own products and as food for animals used for their own label meat and dairy. You may wish to check with your regular supermarket.

CHAPTER 30...
Is Fluoride Something to Smile About?

Written by myself and my husband Lloyd in 2010

NOTE: this was written before we studied GNM. *From the new perspective, cancer and disease originate in the psyche and therefore cannot be caused by fluoride. However, fluoride is a poison and can cause symptoms without a conflict shock.*

There is such a fanaticism about this toxic chemical being good for teeth, it is almost impossible to find a dentist that will say anything bad about Fluoride. But there is a reason. They are governed by a code of practice that prohibits them from saying anything bad about it.

There is no dispute that Fluoride is toxic. But how toxic is it? A quick look at the MSDS (Material Data Safety Sheet) reveals the LD50 (Median Lethal dose at which 50% of subjects die) is 52mg/kg in rats which borders the level between Moderately Toxic and Highly Toxic (Ref: CCOHS). Here is an excerpt from the MSDS mentioned above:

Special Remarks on other Toxic Effects on Humans:

Acute Potential Health Effects: *Skin: Causes skin irritation and possible burns, especially if skin is wet or moist. Eyes: Causes eye irritation and*

148

burns. May cause chemical conjunctivitis and corneal damage. Ingestion: Harmful if swallowed. Causes digestive (gastrointestinal) tract irritation and burns. May cause severe and permanent damage to the digestive. Ingestion of large amounts may cause salivation, thirst, nausea, vomiting, hypermotility, diarrhoea, and abdominal pain. May affect behaviour / central nervous system/nervous system (headache, nervousness, dizziness, seizures, convulsions, tremor, muscle weakness, somnolence), respiration (respiratory depression, dyspnea), cardiovascular system (weak pulse, hypotension, dysrhythmias, cardiac arrest), liver, urinary system (polyuria, polydypsia) brain, metabolism (loss of appetite, hypercalcemia, hyperkalemia, hypomagnesia), teeth, bones, and blood (changes in red and white blood cell count, interference in blood coagulation) Inhalation: Causes irritation and chemical burns of the respiratory tract with coughing, breathing difficulty and possibly nasal septum perforation and coma. May affect bones. Chronic Potential Heath Effects: Chronic ingestion may cause fluorosis.

Effects of fluorosis may include joint pain, weakness, limited joint mobility, brittle bones, ossifications on x-ray, thickening of long bone cortices, calcification of ligaments, osteomalacia, osteosclerosis (skeletal (bone and teeth) abnormalities) and mottled tooth enamel. Other symptoms may include anaemia, nausea, vomiting, diarrhoea or constipation, kidney damage and weight loss/anorexia. Chronic inhalation may cause bronchitis to develop with cough, phlegm, and/or shortness of breath. liver (hepatic enzymes increased, jaundice).

But perhaps we don't need to delve too deeply into the science – let's see what the 'experts' say. Reported in the Independent:

> *"What we do know is that fluoride is toxic – so toxic, in fact, that in 1984, the makers of Colgate, Procter & Gamble, reportedly admitted that a small tube of their toothpaste "theoretically at least*

contains enough fluoride to kill a small child"

So what are the sources of Fluoride?

1. Fluoridated Water Supplies

2. Dental Care

3. Foods manufactured using fluoridated water sources

1. Fluoridated Water Supplies

Please note that the following information is true at time of writing (January 2013 and updated with relevant information in 2016).

Currently in the UK, only England has significant amounts of water fluoridation (fluoride added to the water supplies). Everywhere has trace amounts of fluoride naturally found in the water supply but these levels tend to be relatively low and as such are not generally considered to be a  great risk to health. This is also generally a naturally occurring fluoride which exists in balance as found in nature along with other minerals and therefore our bodies can cope with it. Naturally fluoridated water which also contains calcium or magnesium should not cause a health problem in the long-term provided there is no surplus of fluoride in the water. The unnatural fluoridation of water is another story and it is unnatural ADDED fluoride we are concerned with. In addition to the negative effects of fluoride as mentioned above, the fluoridating acid – hydrofluorosilicic acid – contains contaminants in minute quantities. We are told that 5.36mg of the acid is added to 1 litre of treated tap water in order to achieve 1mg fluoride per litre, the acid being a 20% solution. Many of the contaminants which are heavy metals or substances such as arsenic, are bio-accumulative so in the long-term, our health is bound to become increasingly challenged.

Northern Ireland & Ireland

Northern Ireland is not currently fluoridated, however it is rumoured that there are plans to do so and there are campaigns already in place to try to stop it from happening.

The Republic of Ireland is the most heavily fluoridated country in Europe. See NHF Ireland at www.thenhfireland.com for more details about the long-term damage of water fluoridation and their campaign to get it removed, which is one of many in Ireland.

Scotland

There are currently no plans to fluoridate water supplies in Scotland. However Scotland's 'Childsmile' dental health programme includes painting children's milk teeth with a fluoride varnish to stop decay.

Wales

We have had confirmation from the Welsh Assembly that there are no plans to introduce water fluoridation to Wales. They advised that there is a scheme called "Designed To Smile" which targets schoolchildren and encourages the use of fluoridated toothpaste in schools. This scheme is currently being piloted around Wales and includes the dental varnish applications as in Scotland. Our initial impression of this scheme is that the guidelines and warnings about Fluoride ingestion are insufficient and that although the scheme requires parental consent, there are no fluoride-free options within the scheme. Additionally, it appears that the teachers are to be trained to supervise the children brushing themselves. We have yet to see how this would be practicable with a class full of 25-30 children. Despite positive short term results of this scheme in Scotland, it appears that the long term effects of the promotion of using fluoridated toothpaste and dental varnish have not been considered at all as there is no mention whatsoever in the reports.

England

In England, the decision of whether or not to fluoridate fell into the hands of the County Councils and Unitary Authorities in April 2013. They, in turn, are obliged to honour decisions of their Directors of Public Health, most of whom are known to be pro-fluoridation. This is likely to eliminate the public consultation stage that was necessary when the decision was in the hands of the Local Health Authority. In the case of currently fluoridated populations, the possibility of successfully using the democratic process in order to stop fluoridation is very much in doubt because fluoridating councils will probably defer to the opinion of their pro-fluoridation DPH's. This pessimism is perhaps justified when we review the situation in Southampton, where 72% of those people who took part in the fluoridation consultation in 2009 voted against fluoridation, but were ignored due to the presence of pro-fluoridation 'officers' working for the local health authority who ensured that residents' democratic rights were overridden.

Currently, at time of writing, only a few areas in England have fluoridated water supplies. For example, the North East of England and West Midlands already have extensively fluoridated areas. See www.wmaf.org.uk for more information.

In February 2009, the Board of South Central Strategic Health Authority agreed the request from NHS Southampton City to fluoridate the water in Southampton and parts of South Hampshire despite the extensive continuing protests and opposition. The Strategic Health Authority disbanded in April 2013 and the decision moved to the City Council, however it took until October 2014 for the announcement that the plans to fluoridate had thankfully been scrapped.

This is great news as it could have set the precedence for other areas of the UK. The advice in this book on drinking water will help if fluoridation becomes more widespread in the future.

In addition to ingestion of fluoridated water from drinking and cooking, we must consider the absorption of fluoride through the skin while bathing. If a whole-house filtration system, or a filter for your bath tap is not a feasible option, then it is advisable to take other precautions. Our friends in Ireland prefer short showers to baths for this reason, keeping the water at a lower temperature so as not to inhale much steam.

2. Dental Health

Fluoridated toothpastes and dental varnishes etc.

Over the counter fluoride toothpastes range from about 500ppm (Parts Per Million) Fluoride to 1450ppm. Prescription toothpaste contains 5000ppm. This equates to 0.5% Fluoride. Some dental varnishes have over 20,000ppm Fluoride which is 2%!

Fluoride in this concentration represents a huge potential risk to individual health. Although toothpaste cartons carry a warning "do not swallow" or similar on the box, we are not told what the risks are. Indeed often the only risk acknowledged by the dental profession is the risk of dental fluorosis, which they incorrectly state as being merely cosmetic! By the time a child has ingested enough fluoride to manifest itself on their teeth in the form of dental fluorosis, you can be pretty sure

153

they will have a toxic build up of fluoride in their system. A spokesperson for the UK Government in 1999, Baroness Hayman is on record as saying that "We accept that dental fluorosis is a manifestation of systemic toxicity". Hansard, 20 April 1999: WA 158. As for the varnishes and other dental preparations, these will eventually be swallowed as they are eroded from the teeth while eating and therefore pose an additional burden to the accumulative build up of fluoride in the body.

Dental Health Without Fluoride

It is important not to be deficient in magnesium. Please see "Magnesium Deficiency Epidemic" Chapter 15.

Other beneficial vitamins and minerals for teeth and bone health include Vitamin D3, Boron and Vitamin K.

So why is it then that these beneficial vitamins and nutrients are practically ignored by mainstream medicine?

There are many fluoride-free toothpastes on the market, due to the ethical values of the companies, and the absence of other harmful chemicals like SLS & parabens, I recommend Urtekram or Weleda. It is noted that Weleda Ratanhia toothpaste contains 0.2ppm of naturally occurring fluoride so is not in essence completely 'fluoride-free' but contains 'no added fluoride'.

3. Foods That Use Fluoridated Water in their Manufacture

Another consideration that we must address are manufactured foods and drinks that may contain fluoride. Most definitely, foods and drinks manufactured in fluoridated areas that use the tap water in their production will contain fluoride, and if this product is cooked or heated, the fluoride will be more concentrated. A prime example is Pepsi Max which is made in fluoridated Rugby. The concentrate is made up with fluoridated water containing 1mg/litre of water.

Food manufacturers do not have to legally declare the level of fluoride which they add to their foods and drinks if the fluoride is contained in the product water and is not deliberately added as an ingredient. The same holds true for Indian and China tea which contain a lot of fluoride. Fluoride has been found in Irish cheeses, butters and other Irish products too. Some companies even add fluoride to their bottled water however these are not generally available in the UK. This must not be confused with natural fluoride content which should not cause any health problems. I have read recently of a trial scheme in Blackpool where school children are being given fluoridated milk in their breakfast clubs to try to improve dental health. This is absolutely absurd and an extreme violation to our children's health and our rights! It is forced medication without consent!

In many cases, people are overdosing on fluoride to levels above the maximum of 1.5ppm fluoride per litre of water or equivalent due to the accumulative dosages they are receiving through all these combined sources and the more this can be reduced, the better it is for your health.

CHAPTER 31...Dangers of Fluoride

By my daughter Beth Bryant (date of interview 28th November 2011)

As part of a personal investigation on adding fluoride to water supplies (fluoridation) I conducted this interview with Scott Tips, president of the National Health Federation. By publishing this interview I hope this will give an insight into the dangers on using fluoride in your dental care and water supplies.

BETH: What, to you, is the most worrying fact about fluoride that people may not know when putting it in their bodies?

SCOTT: That fluoride not only harms their physical health but their mental health as well. In certain sub-populations that are especially susceptible to fluoride's effects, fluoride can make those people more docile. It blunts their ambitions and drive.

BETH: Why do you think Dentists promote the use of fluoride?

SCOTT: It's their training. They were educated in schools that taught the conventional – but very wrong – belief that fluoride will strengthen one's teeth. This is reinforced once those students graduate from dental school and become dentists by both peer pressure and by corporate interests that continue to market and sell fluoride-based dental products such as toothpastes and mouth rinses. The inertia of continuing with what they "know" is extremely easy, and it is very difficult to swim

156

against the tide of conventional thinking even though we now know that there are far better and safer ways of strengthening teeth such as taking supplements like magnesium citrate, boron, Vitamin D3, and Vitamin K. Most U.K. diets are more than adequate in calcium so no need to supplement with calcium.

BETH: What effects could the fluoridation of water have on communities and future generations?

SCOTT: It will weaken our overall health and that of our children. Fluoride is an acknowledged toxin and contaminant, but couple it with all of the other toxins and contaminants that we are exposed to in our environment such as pesticides, herbicides, plasticizers, endocrine disruptors, petroleum by-products, xenoestrogens, etc. and the deleterious effects of fluoride are *multiplied*! We already have a major problem with fertility. With each successive generation exposed to these kinds of toxins, that kind of fertility problem will increase. Eventually, there might not even be any future generations if we keep medicating ourselves so unwisely as this!

BETH: Do you know what a persons average daily intake of fluoride is in the UK and Ireland and is this dangerous?

SCOTT: Yes, it is very dangerous and negatively impacts consumers' health (see above). In the UK the mean daily fluoride intake, when including tea but excluding water, amounts to 1.2 mg/day for the adult population. A new UK Fluoridation Study (2011) showed that fluoride intake exceeds the recommended safe maximum in nearly two thirds of consumers receiving Fluoridated Water (0.8ppm). The recently published paper on fluoride consumption is by Dr. Mansfield, MA, MB, Bchir, FRSA, a retired medical practitioner.

BETH: Excluding dental care, are there any other products that contain fluoride and what is your advice on avoiding them?

SCOTT: Most food products that are made with fluoridated water will contain elevated levels of fluoride. This would of course include beverages made with such water.

BETH: How do you feel about governments fluoridating their waters without a public vote?

SCOTT: A more appropriate question might be: How would I feel about governments fluoridating water even with a majority vote? I wouldn't like it at all – with or without a vote. No government has the right to medicate me without my own personal, informed consent! The fact that a majority vote has been held does not add even one iota of legitimacy to the act . . .I am still entitled to opt out and you simply cannot opt out from public fluoridated water without a lot of cost and trouble. With or without a vote, the government has no right to mass medicate society with any drug.

BETH: Do you have anything we haven't covered that you would like to add about fluoride?

SCOTT: Yes, unlike in North America, the soils of the British Isles are very selenium deficient. Yet, fluoride displaces selenium in the body! So, anyone trying to get adequate selenium intake from eating any kind of British diet, while drinking fluoridated water, is asking for trouble. Selenium is a strong antioxidant, with proven benefits. To deplete our bodies of this scarce and very necessary nutrient through mass dosage of the populace with fluoridated water is a double insult to our health!

CHAPTER 32...Mouth of Metal

The metal fillings in our mouths are known as amalgam fillings. They have been used for over 150 years to fill tooth cavities and are still widely used today. They are made from a mixture of metals, and are approximately 50% (43-54%) mercury, the rest being an alloy mainly of tin, silver and copper. There is much increasing controversy over their use due to the extreme toxicity of mercury to the body. In fact the World Health Organisation states that there is NO SAFE LIMIT of mercury in the human body. It is so toxic that if you put the amount of mercury contained in an average filling into an average-sized lake the water would be rendered too poisonous for human consumption!

So to have such a toxic metal compressed permanently into our mouths is both worrying and disturbing to say the very least! Many dentists will justify using mercury as they say it is stable once in the filling, but there has been much research to prove otherwise and that mercury gas is being constantly released (search for "The Smoking Tooth" on Youtube!). Even if this were not the case and the dentist was right, the extreme danger still lies in the wearing down of old fillings and the breaking of current fillings whereby an extreme release of mercury gas will be experienced. There is also the potential of systematic poisoning as many traditions believe that the teeth are linked to and can therefore affect our organs.

The fact is that mercury is so toxic that extreme measures need to be taken in the removal of amalgam fillings such as a throat bung, a detoxification programme both before and after removal, specialist equipment and an air filter in the room. So doesn't this suggest that it would be extremely toxic for your body if a filling were to break down in your mouth either from eating something hard or from wear and tear? What if (as many do) your filling came out during eating and was swallowed?

HEALTH CONCERNS

So let's look at the toxic effects of mercury on the body.

According to the Environmental Protection Agency:

Health effects caused by short-term exposure to high levels of mercury vapours: Cough, Sore throat, Shortness of breath, Chest pain, Nausea, Vomiting, Diarrhoea, Increase in blood pressure or heart rate, A metallic taste in the mouth, Eye irritation, Headache, Vision problems.

Health effects caused by long-term exposure to mercury vapours: Anxiety, Excessive shyness, Anorexia, Sleeping problems, Loss of appetite, Irritability, Fatigue, Forgetfulness, Tremors, Changes in vision, Changes in hearing.

This is just the official story. When we look at unbiased independent research, we see a much more worrying picture.

Holistic dentist, Paul Gilbert states that there are certain links to amalgam fillings and many neurological conditions. Dr. Hal Huggins is an expert in mercury removal dentistry, and he reports on numerous psychological disorders that appear to be the effect of mercury in amalgams.

Mercury exposure will also affect the gut and especially the internal flora balance which will hinder any healing programme and may cause

160

symptoms similar to IBS, Chronic Fatigue, Fibromyalgia, Leaky Gut Syndrome, Rheumatoid Arthritis and much, much more.

Have you ever had electrical shock type feelings in your teeth when you have introduced another metal such as tin foil into your mouth? This is called "oral galvanism" and is a type of allergic reaction to the amalgam fillings. The metal in the filling becomes like a battery when it reacts with saliva and then when a different metal is introduced it causes an electric current.

Safe Removal of Amalgam Fillings

So there is no question in my eyes that amalgam fillings are a definite no-no, and it greatly disturbs me that they are still even being fitted into children's mouths. But if you have these fillings, what can you do about it?

Most dentists will not touch amalgam filling removal (I wonder why!) but they will use the excuse that they are "better left alone" - well not in MY mouth, thank you!!

First you need to seek a Holistic Dentist who appreciates the dangers of the mercury removal. At the very least there should be a special suction fitting that encases the tooth, an air filter in the room to remove mercury gas released, a bung in the throat or at least a protection to stop particles of mercury being swallowed, a nose mask or cover for the nose to prevent breathing in the mercury gas released and you should also be advised on an appropriate detoxification programme to follow before and after the removal.

I personally had 7 amalgam fillings removed in 2011, plus a crown removed and the tooth extracted as it was full of amalgam and I could not afford the work to have a crown re-fitted! Lloyd had 6 plus a root canal removed (they are also very bad news – just do an internet search for "root canal effects").

Detox

As we have already carried out a lot of research in detox, we decided to follow our own detox protocol. Daily, for 2 weeks leading up to removal we took 1 teaspoon of zeolite plus twice the recommended amount of chlorella. On the day we also took charcoal tablets which were provided by our dentist. Then we continued with the zeolite and chlorella for about 1 month afterwards.

There is much discussion on the amount of fillings that should be removed at a time. Our dentist suggested one side of the mouth at a time with a maximum of 3 fillings each visit as some were only small.

We never felt any negative effects from the removal.

Cost

It is very comforting to know that our mouths are not poisoning our bodies any more and we are really happy we had them done. It can cost a lot, the average price is £60-£80 per filling – but this was spread over a couple of months. You may find it more expensive in the city so it may be worth looking for an out-of-town dentist.

I was quoted £75 per filling at a cosmetic dentist but when I emailed to ask what protocols they used to ensure the safe removal of the amalgam and negate the negative effects of mercury exposure they did not answer my query. So not surprisingly I did not go there!

You may also find out about a dental plan which can give you a good discount off the work done (it was worth it for us as the discount we received was greater than a year's subscription!)

Lastly – know that you have a choice – if you or your children need a filling – do not settle for the amalgam, even if you have to contribute towards the cost, it is well worth it as there is no price when it comes to our health and the health of our children!

It is reassuring that the EU have recently agreed to a phasing down of the use of mercury containing amalgam fillings (although it seems by their reasoning that they are more concerned with the environment as opposed to our health!). Whether this will follow through to UK policy now we have chosen to leave the EU remains to be seen, but we can hope! They are already banned in some countries such as Sweden and Denmark, and have been since 2008. According to Dr Mercola:

> *"The momentum toward mercury-free dentistry is gaining speed and, it appears, may be set to become a reality in the 21st century.*
>
> *The final mercury treaty session took place in Geneva, Switzerland in January 2013. There the mercury treaty was finalized, and included important provisions to reduce and eliminate mercury pollution, one of them being a requirement for countries to phase down the use of dental amalgam (mercury fillings)."*

CHAPTER 33...Vaccines:
What Doctors Don't Tell You!

I have compiled 10 brief points you need to consider before deciding on vaccinating yourself or your children. These points are based upon unbiased studies and independent research:

1. Vaccines have many serious side effects such as paralysis, brain damage, infertility, they can even kill. Many of these can be explained by the science of GNM. In addition, the risks can be greatly multiplied if given to someone who is unwell or has a medical condition (that may not even be known) at the time.

2. Vaccines contain toxic ingredients:

Formaldehyde: an extremely toxic substance and a known neurotoxin

Mercury (Thiomersal – US spelling Thimerosal): Mercury is one of the most toxic substances known to man. According to the World Health Organisation there is no safe level for mercury in the human body.

Aborted foetal cells: human or animal cells are used to grow the live virus on. Some such as the flu vaccine uses chicken eggs which can cause problems for egg allergy sufferers.

Aluminium: is an extremely poisonous neurotoxic.

Monosodium Glutamate (MSG): toxic preservative used as a stabilizer in vaccines (and also found in many foods).

3. Many vaccines are inadequately tested, if at all (usually just the ingredients are tested but not once put together in a vaccine), and many have proved to cause sterility, although these findings are kept from the public. Testing is carried out cruelly on animals which has been proved many times to not always correlate to the effects on humans.

4. Many vaccination programmes involve giving multiple vaccines at one time which are rarely tested alongside with each other creating further unknown risks.

5. Vaccines are a very profitable business:

Pharmaceutical corporations make a lot of money from vaccine programmes, this is a multi-billion dollar industry for them.

Doctors receive funding to vaccinate us and our children which increases when targets are met, making them mere sales reps for the pharmaceutical companies.

6. Many diseases were already extinct or dying out BEFORE the vaccine was introduced. In addition many vaccines are now created for minor illnesses such as flu and measles, the vaccine side effects greatly outweigh the actual effects of the disease. The only reason we think otherwise is down to fear-mongering advertising campaigns that concentrate on rare, extreme cases.

7. Vaccines don't work! 20% – 50% of people who are vaccinated don't get a resistance to the disease against which they have been immunised. From a GNM perspective, diseases originate in the psyche, including those caused by apparent 'viruses' and therefore vaccines are useless!

8. Vaccines actually REDUCE our resistance and ability to heal as they cause us physical and emotional stress.

9. As the number of children being vaccinated increases, so does the

number of children diagnosed with Autism. This is true in the UK and all countries where children are vaccinated. This can be explained from the new perspective, by what's known as an "Autistic Constellation" which is caused when 2 specific conflicts are active involving both brain hemispheres. One of both of these conflicts could be caused by the vaccine itself or how it was administered (such as being forcefully restrained). Drug companies have even applied for an injunction to stop research to establish a link between vaccination and autism. There are only a small number of doctors and other medical professionals such as Dr. Andrew Wakefield who are prepared to take the moral path and sacrifice their jobs when they discover the dangers.

10. The 'Cervical Cancer' vaccine (HPV) is very dangerous and calling by this name is very misleading. In tests, every lab rat became sterile from one of the ingredients (polysorbate 80). It has caused many deaths and serious side effects since its introduction.

What to do if your Doctor or school wants to vaccinate:

1. KNOW YOUR RIGHTS – it is NOT compulsory to have vaccinations, despite much correspondence from GPs and schools that give the impression otherwise. If you wish you may even write a letter to your child's school informing them that you forbid your child to receive a vaccination, or better still, keep them home on vaccine days as often they may take your child's attendance as 'uninformed consent'.

2. SEEK THE FACTS – look at other sources of information and if you are not happy or have any concerns it is best not to do it. Once these ingredients get into the bloodstream there is no going back.

3. DON'T BE BULLIED – do not let your GP or Health Visitor make you feel that you are a bad parent for not vaccinating (this can be common practice, not maliciously but simply as they may just believe it is right to vaccinate through the biased information they receive in their

profession). It is also common for family members or friends to try to persuade you otherwise if they do not realise the facts. It is YOU that must be happy – listen to your heart and stick to your decision!

4. LOOK AT VACCINE ADVERTISING LOGICALLY – don't be fooled by the propaganda and fear-mongering. Just think – it was not long ago that we built up our child's 'resistance' by going to visit friends with childhood illnesses so they would catch them young and become 'immune' naturally (however according to GNM diseases are not even contagious as they originate in the psyche!). The number of vulnerable people such as children and the elderly receiving the flu jab is very worrying as their natural ability to heal is being attacked further every year. They almost always get flu symptoms from the vaccine (if they are lucky enough not to have a more serious reaction), but they may not get flu if they don't have the vaccine, so there is a greater risk of being ill with the vaccine than without. We often hear people say since they have

been having the flu jab they have not caught flu – just ask them if they got flu BEFORE having the vaccine every year? Our guess is the answer will probably be "no, not really!"

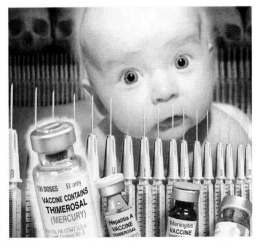

Regarding 'Herd Immunity' that is so often pedalled, this has been repeatedly disproven for many reasons. The increasing number of apparent outbreaks of disease in vaccinated children only prove this is a myth, regardless of GNM which blows the entire vaccine concept out the window in any case!

CHAPTER 34...*Vaccine Propaganda Analysed & Exposed!*

To Vaccinate or Not To Vaccinate – THAT is the Question! It certainly is a question that only YOU can answer whether it is immunising your baby or having the flu vaccine.

I am hoping that this analysis of and insight into the propaganda surrounding the vaccine drives by local health authorities will help you to see how your logical thoughts are manipulated to make you afraid NOT TO vaccinate. This is mainly achieved by the use of fallacies which are tricks that can stop you thinking logically, and can therefore alter your decisions and even beliefs!

From every September onwards, when vaccine season is certainly upon us, we begin to see many distasteful "advert" banners outside doctor's surgeries stating things like **"ROLL UP ROLL UP FOR YOUR FLU JAB"** – like it's some sort of circus! What a clever way to try to make the vaccine seem that it is not a serious issue – no big deal! But then maybe this should also tell us that we shouldn't be taking the advertising and scaremongering seriously!

Sadly, though it really IS a serious issue, especially to those who have been harmed by the vaccine, or the family members of those who have died soon after having the vaccine.

The chant "Roll Up Roll Up" also puts me in mind of a snake oil salesman – is this REALLY what our doctors are becoming? If I were a doctor I would be insulted by this approach to advertising one of my services and I think it is appalling that the government feel they can treat our health so trivially and non-seriously! They think it's a circus? And what are we? The monkeys? Yes – that would be test monkeys held in our cages of fear!

The vaccination campaigns are almost all based upon a fallacy that appeals to our emotions and the emotion they most commonly use is fear. When we are afraid, especially for our health and the health of our children, we will do anything to help ourselves, but in truth this is just making us more vulnerable to misinformation.

More recently, they have been appealing to pity as well. There have apparently been pleas from parents of children with cancer or other immune compromising conditions that mean they cannot have vaccines, and we have been told that we must vaccinate for the sake of their children. But I say apparently, as what we are not told, is that this is untrue. How can it be true when the families of these children are given exemption from vaccines and told their child must stay away from recently vaccinated children so they won't come into contact with the live virus that they shed as this would be dangerous to a so-called 'immuno-compromised' child?

They also encourage us to make an assumption. The assumption that if something is believed to do something good then it isn't bad (or at least can't be THAT bad).

169

You can see by the NHS poster opposite how much they use fear to promote the jabs. Fear is induced not only by the exaggerated and inaccurate imagery, but also stating that we do not know all the facts about flu, making us think there is a lot more to it and scaring us into the jab. But what they don't do is state the fact that we do not know all the facts about the jab EITHER!

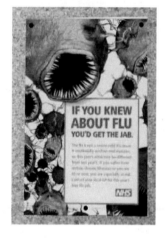

The wording states that the flu virus is clever as it "continually evolves and mutates". This makes us think of something alien or disgusting, further adding to fear. **But if you read between the lines, what this ALSO states is that the vaccines cannot possibly help!** The vaccine you have in your arm was developed (at least) months previously – so this means that the virus the vaccine apparently protects against has now surely mutated and evolved into a different strain!

It also states "if you suffer from certain chronic illness or are 65 or over you are especially at risk" – yet this is also true of being at risk from side effects from the jab (but they hide this information from you).

In 2008 there was an advert shown on T.V. for the 'HPV' vaccine. It is a shame I cannot play it in this book, but I have captured a still of it. The link for it on Youtube is underneath. This advert is clearly trying to

170

belittle the HPV vaccine, trying to demonstrate that it is a matter-of-fact everyday thing. Also in this way putting the message across that it is not serious.

But the truth is that it IS serious and the decision to have a vaccine that contains an ingredient that made EVERY rat tested on STERILE should not be taken lightly at all!

Here is a list of fallacies that I have found in this very short advert (after only a short while):

Fallacy 1: Appeal to Common Practice – if everyone does it then it is OK for me to do. This is shown by all the pupils going about their day and having the vaccine.

Fallacy 2: Appeal to Popularity – most people approve of this so it must be OK.

Fallacy 3: Bandwagon – everyone else does it so I will too or otherwise I may not be accepted. This is shown by linking arms with her friend, both getting the vaccine together (i.e. 'herd mentality').

Fallacy 4: Questionable cause – HPV and cervical cancer sometimes occur together so HPV must cause cervical cancer (this has been proved NOT to be the case by the FDA without the presence of an infection). In the words of the FDA:

> *"Based on new scientific information published in the past 15 years, it is now generally agreed that identifying and typing HPV infection does not bear a direct relationship to stratification of the risk for cervical cancer. Most acute infections caused by HPV are self-limiting [1, 4-7]. ...Repeated sequential transient HPV infections, even when caused by 'high-risk' HPVs, are characteristically not associated with high risk of developing squamous intraepithelial lesions, a precursor of cervical cancer.*

> *A woman found to be positive for the same strain (genotype) of HPV on repeated testing is highly likely suffering from a persistent HPV infection and is considered to be at high risk of developing precancerous intraepithelial lesions in the cervix. **It is the persistent infection, not the virus, that determines the cancer risk.**"*

Fallacy 5: Appeal to Authority – the NHS are passing on information given to them by pharmaceutical salesmen, but making us think they are the experts in this, and so we trust them.

Fallacy 6 (double): Appeal to Emotion (fear) & Slippery Slope – HPV MAY occur and IF it does Cervical Cancer WILL be inevitable (jut read that again.....this is how it makes us think – but it is not logical!!) and this invokes our fear to be scared into having the vaccine.

And finally...calling the vaccine the "Cervical Cancer Vaccine" is extremely misleading as it does NOT protect from cancer at all. There are still many strains of HPV not covered by the vaccine and, according to GNM, HPV does not even cause cervical cancer, or any cancer, anyway. But calling it this lures people into a false sense of security and gives them false information just from the name.

What makes things worse about obtaining information about vaccines is that we trust what our GPs tell us, and they generally tell us there is nothing to worry about and the vaccines 'save lives'. But as we have discovered, the fact is they are given increasing funding for the number of patients they vaccinate. As many surgeries/doctors come to rely on this funding their advice inevitably may become more profit-related than health-related.

More information on fallacies including an explanation of the most commonly used fallacies can be found in Chapter 80 and some more information on the flu vaccine in Chapter 49.

CHAPTER 35...*Safety in the Sun*

We all know that sunshine is good for us – it is vital for our health and life and is the best and most natural source of Vitamin D. But did you realise that its benefits go further than this? For example, it is supportive for the healing phase of biological programmes, and is very helpful for easing depression, which is the main reason why people suffer more depression in the winter months and feel so good and positive in spring!

Even though we need regular sun exposure, there are occasions where it is possible you may overdose causing sunburn and this is when it leads to damage to your skin. The threat of this skin damage is what the pharmaceutical and cosmetic industries have been pushing, making us fearful of exposing ourselves to any sun at all.

From the new perspective, we understand that the sun does not cause skin cancer. Melanoma affects the corium (under) skin and is triggered by an attack conflict, and skin cancers such as carcinoma effecting the epidermis are triggered by a separation conflict. However, extreme repeated skin damage may be subconsciously perceived as an attack upon the skin, thus triggering an attack conflict, and this can explain the link between skin damage though sun exposure and melanoma.

Time in the Sun

We basically need to have some common sense and be careful. It is all too easy to overdose on sunshine especially for children and fun-loving adults during the summer months. Hours in the pool or at the beach can interfere with monitoring our time in the sun on holidays and it's easy to lose track of our "fun in the sun" weekend time – especially for those of us spend most of our working week indoors. So make sure you only stay in direct sunshine for short periods.

Sunscreens

Sold by the propaganda from the pharmaceutical and cosmetic industries, we opt for the safe not sorry option of slapping on the sunscreen. But most commercial sunscreens are extremely damaging to our health and interfere with vitamin D absorption. According to recent research many sunscreens actually stop our bodies from producing and obtaining vitamin D completely. In addition they contain a cocktail of toxic ingredients which are absorbed into our bloodstream.

The fact is that our bodies produce its own vitamin D using the UV-B sunlight, so it is essential to expose your skin to the sun without sunscreen.

We need to wean ourselves off the over-use of sunscreen that we have been frightened into, then we will naturally build up our own defences again, and may even correct deficiencies in Vitamin D. After using the 24-hour once-a-day sunscreens for quite a few years I ended up suffering terrible prickly heat rash and had trouble tanning at all, it was almost like I had become allergic to sunshine! Now after having weaned myself and my family off sunscreens by decreasing their use over a couple of years, I have found that I am able to stay out in the sun so much more than I could a few years ago and I now tan very easily with hardly any burning if I am careful!

174

Types of Sunscreen

There are two kinds of sunscreens: chemical and physical. Chemical sunscreens protect you from the sun by absorbing the ultraviolet (UV) and visible sun rays, while physical sunscreens reflect, scatter or block these rays. If it is required, I believe the physical sunscreen to be the lesser evil of these.

The Toxicity of Sunscreens

Sunscreen contains 'active' ingredients and so it is regulated by the FDA as an over-the-counter drug. However the safety of these ingredients is extremely controversial, and so are the 'corporate' FDA's intentions.

According to Dr. Mercola, one study found that the main chemical used in sun lotions to filter out ultraviolet light may be toxic – and the chemical's toxicity doubled when exposed to sunlight. Octyl methoxycinnamate (OMC), which is present in 90 percent of sunscreen brands, was found to kill mouse cells even at low doses in a study by Norwegian scientists. When researchers shone a lamp for two hours to simulate midday sunshine, even more cells died.

Sunscreens significantly penetrate the skin according to a study in the April 2004 Journal of Chromatography. Many consider absorbing poisonous chemicals through the skin more dangerous than ingestion because they are carried directly to the bloodstream. So, when you use sunscreen your whole body is absorbing poisonous, cell-damaging chemicals. To make matters worse, sunscreens carry the instructions to apply liberally every few hours! That's it, make sure plenty of toxins get in there – Oops you missed a spot!

Safer Sunscreens

Titanium dioxide acts as a physical barrier that reflects UV rays, and is generally considered the least absorbing. Paba Ester (Padimate O) is one of the most natural active ingredients found in sunscreens.

However, after much research, including our own experience of giving up wearing sunscreens, it is my opinion that using sunscreen should be avoided. But I recognise that when we visit countries that our bodies are not used to, we need to be extra careful.

What About Vitamin D?

Ultraviolet B, or UV-B, is known as the "burning ray" because it is the primary cause of sunburn caused by overexposure to sunlight. However, UV-B sunlight on the skin produces vitamin D, and stimulates the production of MSH – an important hormone in weight loss, energy production, and in giving you that wonderful tanned appearance. It has also been claimed by some health experts that Vitamin D deficiency could lead to improper brain development.

According to the Vitamin D Council, we can produce 10,000iu of vitamin D in a few minutes of sunshine. Prolonged sun exposure will not increase vitamin D production above 20,000iu, but it will increase the danger of skin damage. There are several things to consider when exposing yourself to UV-B rays:

- Latitude and altitude of location – The further north you are the less there is; the higher up you are the more UV-B reaches you.
- Your skin pigmentation – The darker your pigmentation or more tanned your skin, the less UV-B penetrates.
- Weather conditions and air quality – Both clouds and pollution (smog and ozone) can block UV-B
- Time of year – Virtually no UV-B is available in winter months in the U.K.

Sunscreen will block you from producing Vitamin D on the skin, so I recommend using them cautiously. I recommend taking a good quality vitamin D3 supplement, at least 2,000iu per day in summer increasing to 5,000iu in winter months, though it is good to get this confirmed through muscle testing or similar. In an interview with Dr. Mercola, Dr. Robert Heaney (considered to be one of the leading vitamin D experts in the world) states that your body requires 4,000iu daily just to maintain its current vitamin D level.

Other More Natural Ways to Protect You & Your Family

1. Take a higher dose vitamin D3 supplement the morning before exposure to the sun. This will help increase the skins natural protection.

2. Apply organic virgin coconut oil liberally. Coconut oil protects our skin but still allows us to manufacture vitamin D. It is believed to protect to around an SPF of 15. However this is not very accurate as it works in a different way – with our body instead of against it! We use this with excellent results, and its really nourishing for the skin, too!

3. Wear a hat and cover up regularly.

4. During the summer, limit exposure when the sun is most potent – from 11am to 1pm. UV-B rays are only generally present between the times of 11am and 3pm, so it is important to get a little exposure, and there is more harm from exposing your skin to the UV-A rays found after 3pm. So it is strongly recommended that you cover up after this time. In my experience I get burned a lot quicker after 3pm than I do the rest of the day so I always go for siesta or cool off in the shade from 3pm when on holiday.

5. At the beginning of the season limit your exposure to the sun. Progressively increase the time in the sun so that in a few weeks, you will be able to have normal sun exposure with less risk of skin damage.

6. DO NOT SHOWER WITH SOAP as it takes 48hrs for the vitamin d3 that is formed on the surface of your skin to penetrate into your

bloodstream. Washing with soap simply washes it away. It is OK to wash the groin and underarm areas but just rinse the rest of your body!

Tips for Natural Relief of Sunburn

No matter how careful we are, sunburn can happen. Overexposure to the sun could result in a mild first-degree burn. If it's severely painful or covered with blisters, seek medical help.

Here's what you can do if you or your child suffers from mild sunburn:

1. If you've been in a chlorinated swimming pool, rinse the pool water off thoroughly, don't rub or use a cloth. Pat yourself dry.

2. Take a cool (not cold) bath.

3. Apply fresh aloe vera gel. Avoid expensive manufactured after sun lotions and gels- they are not as effective and they lose their potency over time.

4. Pat cool, sugarless tea over the area – this works very well for sensitive areas around the eyes. The theanine in tea provides an active soothing ingredient.

5. **OUR FAVOURITE AND MOST EFFECTIVE TREATMENT** – Keep some fresh tomatoes (preferably beef tomatoes) in the fridge while on holiday. Cut a tomato in half and rub over the burnt area, allowing the juice and pips to stay on the skin (this will feel very cold and may sting a little as it draws out the discomfort). Let the juice dry, then it can be showered off with a cool shower. Fantastic for reducing pain – you can even slap it afterwards!! Then apply aloe vera gel or juice to the area to moisturise and assist healing.

The best remedy for sunburn is and has always been prevention. And if you think you might be in the sun longer than is good for you – please be safe, not sorry!

178

CHAPTER 36...Radiation & Environmental Concerns

It seems a common theme that many people simply fail to see danger in something they cannot see. X-rays, scans, microwaves, Wi-Fi, mobile phone signals, to name but a few are all constantly bombarding our energetic and physical bodies, and yet just because we fail to see them, doesn't mean they don't exist. We cannot see radio waves, but we can hear the radio and the signal somehow gets into the radio – so it must be there in the ether around us – it MUST exist! This is just one frequency, a very low frequency. As the frequency increases so does the risks to our health. Do you remember basic physics and the electromagnetic spectrum? Yes these waves and fields exist! It is estimated that we can only perceive 0.0035% of the entire electromagnetic spectrum!

I have mentioned only a few pointers here, but I suggest you do a little bit of research yourself regarding these issues.

Mobile Phones, 5g & Wireless

There are many dangers of the radiation from mobile phone devices, Wi-Fi signals and antennae. I personally know of a sadly increasing number of people who have had tumours which have been admittedly believed to be caused by mobile phone usage.

179

Children are especially susceptible to the radiation as their skulls are not yet formed properly and so are much thinner than the adult skull. This enables harmful radiation to penetrate into their brain a lot easier.

Here are some tips for you to consider to make your mobile phone usage safer:

AT&Tumor

1. Please make sure you use your mobile devices wisely, not excessively.
2. Talk on hands-free whenever possible or use a separate earpiece or handset.
3. Do not carry phones or portable devices next to your body, especially vulnerable parts such as the near the reproductive organs or breasts (i.e. in front trouser pockets or bra!).
4. Do not let children use bluetooth devices.
5. Keep phones and wireless devices away from your bedside at night.
6. Do not put mobiles near babies or use them while holding a baby.
7. Smart phones can be particularly harmful as they have an internal antennae so other smart phone users in their vicinity may obtain a signal from your device instead of a mast. In most phones this antennae may be switched off, but on some phones it remains permanently on.

If that isn't enough, there is an impending threat of 5g looming at the time of writing. So many professionals are speaking out at the folly of unleashing this into our environment when it has never been tested with regard to safety and any effects upon our health. Where 5g has been rolled out there are already signs that it is negatively affecting vegetation in proximity of the masts. It is not just the 'next generation' of 4g, but an order of magnitude stronger, and more intrusive due to the requirement of having antennae in close proximity of each other. This means that we will never be more than a stone's throw away from an antenna and be constantly bathed in radiation! We can only inform MPs and councillors in the hope that our towns will follow some of those that have placed a moratorium on the roll out of 5g pending further safety testing.

3D TV & Films

I do not like all this 3D craze at all. I have seen very few 3D films – a few features and 1 film in fact – and I have felt ill afterwards each time. There is not much information on the health effects, and especially the effects of the mind, however Samsung have issued health warnings on their website and the effects are believed by many to have an extraordinary impact on the brainwaves. Unnatural rapid eye movement, flashing scenes and unnatural frequencies can have extremely negative effects and 3D has already been linked to attacks of epilepsy, stroke and altered vision. I would not like to think of the impact it can have on our mental state, emotions and spiritual health let alone the potential of hidden uses of NLP techniques and subliminal messaging by advertising or anyone wanting to alter our way of thinking.

Smart Meters

Smart meters monitor, control (in the future) and communicate utility usage to the utility providers. They do this by using a 'smart grid' of wireless signals which you will be subject to 24 hours a day if you agree to have one installed. More than 5,000 studies have shown that the electromagnetic radiation such as that caused by smart meters is harmful to all living creatures.

According to Dr David Carpenter, Director of the Institute of Health and Environment, University of Albany, New York and ex-head of the New York Department of Public Health:

> *"We have evidence that exposure to RF radiation increases damage to the nervous system, causes electro-sensitivity, has adverse effects and a variety of other effects on different organ systems. There is NO justification for the statement that 'smart' meters have no adverse health effects."*

Besides this, the smart meters are able to monitor and communicate with (and control) modern appliances as they have a compatible chip inside them – this is a violation of your privacy!

It is NOT compulsory by law to have smart meters installed (at the time of writing) however there was a law passed preventing the removal of smart meters once fitted, so it's important to refuse them! Also beware when changing energy providers as some may offer cheaper prices but have compulsory installation of a smart meter in their terms and conditions! If you have one fitted, or move to a house where there is a smart meter, you can try changing to a supplier who does not use smart meters, and they may change the meter for you. If not you can ask to be changed to a pay meter, and then later change back to a regular meter.

Electromagnetic Stress

We have such a large amount of electrical appliances and equipment in our lives today, but many people maybe do not realise the impact this is having on our health. Electrical items have electrical fields which are constantly vibrating with alternating magnetic and electrical energy. This is known as an electromagnetic field or EMF.

EMFs are strongest nearer the emitting item so if you spend time close to an electrical appliance all day, it is recommended you look into some sort of protection.

Effects on our Health

It is scientifically proven that EMF affects us, and at the right frequency can even alter DNA! The main effects that have been measured are:

- Interference with cell growth
- detrimental effects on the unborn foetus
- Increased stress levels
- detrimental effects on our nervous system

These are the proven facts, but there is potentially much more that is still as yet 'officially' unproven. Some claim to experience increased joint pain, digestive problems, depression, insomnia, anxiety, skin, ear and eye problems, sweating, tingling sensations and much more. If you read Chapter 63 on vibrational healing and energy you will maybe get more of a picture of the unseen effects too.

Protection

There are many ways to protect yourself against EMF.

- Laptops should never be placed on your lap, but on radiation protecting cushions or a table.
- Avoid using electric blankets and electrically adjustable beds.
- Sit as far away as possible to TVs and monitors.
- Avoid or minimise the use of personal electrical appliances such as hair styling products.

Geopathic Stress

Geopathic Stress is when a blockage or disruption in the Earth's energies cause an interference in our well-being. For example, a building that has been built in an area of geopathic stress may possess certain characteristics, such as a theme of regular flooding without a definitive cause, or a recurrence of illness with a particular theme in the people who work or reside there.

These areas of geopathic stress are generally caused by geographic features such as underground channels and waterways, leylines (energy channels of the earth), underground crystal or mineral caves, overhead cables, underground pipework and even the residual energies of these features that were there in the past.

Another cause of area-specific problems is residual energies of past occurrences at the site which may lead to similar happenings in a particular theme to keep occurring. It may seem strange, but if you think of the Earth as a living being (which she is) then it is quite easy to understand that there are energies that are unbalanced or require healing.

Does my home suffer geopathic stress?

The best way to answer this is to see how you feel. Do you or your family have recurring symptoms with a similar theme? Has something not been right since you moved in? Do things happen in the house that are linked with, or affecting, yours or your family's emotions?

If you suspect, or are worried about, whether you are living in a 'sick house', you can call in a professional dowser who will assess your home, or you can look up dowsing yourself and give it a go. It is quite simple to learn and very inexpensive to buy the tools needed, and you can even make your own!

If you decide to dowse yourself, you need to be extremely respectful of the Earth's energies and set firm and positive intentions before dowsing. I will not go into dowsing here as you need to read properly about it so you do not do more damage to these powerful energies!

Remedies for both Electromagnetic and Geopathic Stress

The following advice is effective in healing your home and creating a brighter and more pleasant atmosphere which can also benefit your health holistically:

- Plants are excellent cleansers and can be placed near your most used appliances.
- Crystals can also help to protect our bodies from the effects of EMF radiation.
- Orgone energy pendants can be helpful in protecting yourself. You can buy ready made ones (but watch for expensive pyramid sellers) or simply make your own from metallic shavings and crystal chips set in polyester resin.
- You may wish to move your furniture around so you are generally not sitting in close proximity to electrical items, and try sitting in different directions and different areas.
- Himalayan Salt Lamps are excellent at emitting negative ions into the air to combat the potentially harmful positive ions in EMF.
- Consider Shamanic or spiritual healing for your home, or taking the advice of a Feng Shui consultant (or read about it yourself!)
- By placing crystals, metals, etc. around the home you are in effect creating your own positive protective grid of energy!
- Cats seem to favour negative geopathic stress and EMF. Do not choose to sit or sleep in your cat's favourite settling spot! Dogs on the other hand tend to prefer positive geopathic energy, so the opposite applies!

Earthing

We have become accustomed to insulating ourselves from connecting with the earth's energy by wearing rubber soled shoes, and covering our beautiful land with concrete and decking! This is bad for 2 reasons:

1. it prevents us from discharging electromagnetism and positive ions within the body which will then accumulate and cause imbalances and poor well-being.

2. It prevents us from receiving the pure, healing energies from the Earth.

As much as possible, and preferably daily, stand outside with bare feet directly onto the earth to discharge built up negative energies and reconnect with the nurturing of the earth's energies. If this is not possible, most radiators are earthed but be careful to make sure it is not hot! There is a lot of information on the internet about the profound effects of this simple treatment and many people have found relief from chronic illnesses just by taking off their shoes regularly!

I personally take regular trips to the beach and walk barefoot on the sand, even in winter! I will also often paddle in the sea, especially in the summer! I also visit the local forests and either walk barefoot (if I am brave enough!) or just connect with the trees there. I often feel a build up of static in my hair when I know I need to 'discharge' and connect with the earth, and sometimes I feel like my mind is too busy.

It is now stated that gardening is an 'anti-depressant'. Gardening will connect us with the earth and discharge our energies. Try not to wear gloves, and really feel the earth. You can always wash mud off, so don't be afraid to get your hands and feet a little dirty!!

CHAPTER 37...
Toxic Stripes (Geo-engineering)

There are 2 types of trails left by aeroplanes.

One type are called contrails. These dissipate quite quickly and are caused by the condensation from the engine.

The second stay in the sky, polluting our air with toxic chemicals such as

huge amounts of aluminium, along with barium, mould spores and strontium. These are commonly called Chemtrails due to their toxic chemical make-up, which has been measured and scientifically proved despite being labelled a "conspiracy theory".

This spraying is more technically known as atmospheric aerosol dispersal/injection, geo engineering to name a few. The majority believe it to be linked to weather control and manipulation. By admission, the military spray along flight paths to enhance radio signals.

It has been observed that the chemical mix is sprayed by adding it to the jet fuel, and it can also be sprayed from separate nozzles to the engine jets which usually produce the fumes and condensation trails.

There are many other controversial theories as to why these chemtrails are being sprayed into our air but 2 things are for certain:

1. They are NOT the normal functioning of the jet engine – they are purposefully sprayed. We know this as there are many more lines left than there are flight paths, and many planes that spray these trails perform strange manoeuvres such as circles or U-turns, just like they are crop-spraying.

2. The substance being sprayed is toxic. There have been many studies done on both the substance in the trails, the soil content on the ground after spraying and the precipitation caused by the chemically enhanced clouds.

Many governments officials, whistle-blowers, airline and military officials (those who do not deny their existence) have admitted that these trails are purposefully sprayed and given many different reasons for it when asked by the public. But whether it is vaporised toxic waste, radiation protection to block 'harmful' sun rays, weather control experiments or something else, the simple fact is they are harming our health, polluting the air we breathe, altering our natural weather system and climate and shielding valuable vitamin D from the sun.

As more and more people are waking up to this spraying, the mainstream media have began to run stories about how the Earth's climate needs to be manipulated and the temperature cooled to prevent global warming. So it appears that they are beginning to admit these trails exist but are making them appear to be for our and the Earth's benefits. I believe the truth is far from this portrayal, and there is proof that they have been carrying out these operations without our knowledge or consent since the 90s, many believe since WWII.

There are many companies online advertising aerosol spraying services in particular relating to weather manipulation and modification programmes including the spraying of aerosols to seed clouds. Could this be the real reason for our changing climate? It brings a new meaning to "Man-made Climate Change" doesn't it? They are even telling us they are doing it, just twisting the meaning!

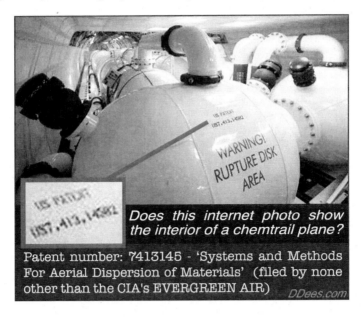

Does this internet photo show the interior of a chemtrail plane?

Patent number: 7413145 - 'Systems and Methods For Aerial Dispersion of Materials' (filed by none other than the CIA's EVERGREEN AIR)

DDees.com

Threats to Our Health

Breathing fresh clean air is our birthright. When toxic waste including aluminium is pumped into our sky, it is destroying our clean air and denying us our right to breathe pure air. Aluminium is hugely toxic to the body and is a neurotoxin. This is why it is also advisable to not use aluminium cookware.

Not only does this global operation have a huge impact on our clean air but it will have impact on our soil and environment, and therefore our food chain. Aluminium in soil is turning the soil alkaline which is not suitable for growing many crops, and farmers are finding it increasingly difficult to grow their crops, some even resorting to GM crops which will withstand high alkaline and high levels of aluminium (mmm...do I detect an agenda here?).

Protection

Our best protection against this invasion of our health is to support our health by eating correctly, taking appropriate supplements and avoiding any additives, vaccines, etc that stress our body. You may also want to look into building a chembuster, which are orgone energy generators that purify your air and dissipate the chemtrails above them and in the vicinity (instructions are available on my blog website as Lloyd and I have made some, and run some workshops. You will find lots of instructions on the internet).

But to stop this happening, we must spread the word to others to make them aware, and inform those who may be able to help such as our MPs (be sure to be armed with evidence such as patent applications as otherwise they will probably dismiss it as a 'conspiracy theory'!). There are many excellent websites that provide well-researched and scientific information regarding chemtrails such as carnicominstitute.org, and a directive to stop the spraying with downloadable evidence at www.chemtrailsprojectuk.com. Many groups and protests are now coming together in an effort to stop this violation.

CHAPTER 38...Smoking: Advice from a Quitter!

Since I was 16 years old I smoked between 10 and 20 cigarettes per day, only giving up during pregnancy and early breast feeding (I suffered terrible morning (all-day) sickness and was turned off cigarettes anyway!). When it came to my 30th birthday I decided enough was enough!

Getting Ready

Many smokers wanting to quit will say that it's not the right time for them to quit at the moment. Non-smokers will reply there's never a right time, and no time like the present. Of course they're both right, but the factor that can decide whether you succeed or fail is whether you feel ready because if you are not ready you will be bound to fail. If you try anyway, it could leave you disheartened and frustrated and probably smoking more than before for comfort. If you think you are ready and would like to give it a go, don't take it too seriously, and just let it be that you are just "giving it a go". If it turns out you weren't ready, the disappointment and frustration will be less if you take it as matter of fact. I don't mean to say take it light-heartedly, you need to strike a balance in the middle somewhere.

If you would really like to give up but don't feel ready, be patient. I wanted to give up for 10 years. I'd tried and tried to quit but always failed, and this made me feel like I was weak, which brought down my self-confidence, which made me smoke more and feel more guilty for smoking more....it goes on! (Sound familiar?) It so happened that even though I didn't realise it at the time, I wasn't happy for most of that time for another reason. Once the cause for this unhappiness had gone, something just clicked inside.

What I'm trying to say is look at the WHOLE picture. If you keep failing but really want to give up and can't understand why you can't, it may be something else is wrong. I believe in treating everything holistically, treating the whole not the part, and the same applies here.

You may also wish to ask yourself, do you really want to give up? You can only do it for yourself!

The Next Step

Decide how. I needed people to support me, understand me, guide me and just be there for me. I didn't want gimmicks or gum! Everyone is different, though. I also wanted to tell the world – a feeling I'd never felt before. I think if you feel like telling the world – you're ready. If you want to tell the world but are afraid to in case you fail – maybe take a little longer in your preparations. Remember it is time well spent. You are building foundations upon which your success will stand. Weak foundations will send it tumbling down! I used to get frustrated if I'd decided to quit on a whim and then been advised to plan and prepare – I couldn't be bothered with all that it's just wasting time! That's one reason why I always failed! However, if the whim is strong enough, it can work. Sometimes these 'whims' are when something just clicks inside, so if you feel that has happened just go for it!

192

How I Did It

My husband was a member of a forum which I'd never really been interested in (a kind of computer enthusiast forum!). I'd met one of his friends who also wanted to quit so I suggested starting a thread for members who wanted to quit – a sort of support thread. We had a good response from wannabe quitters and ex-smokers with oodles of advice for quitters. We went 'live' and I've never looked back.

If I was feeling weak, I'd log in to the forum. There would nearly always be someone else who'd posted a message, feeling just as weak as me or sometimes even worse. I'd then offer loads of tips and advice to them and before I got to posting my SOS message, my craving had passed! My fingers were busy and my mind was diverted. If things were really bad for me or one of the others, we'd have a live chat. I'm not saying it was easy, but I really believe I couldn't have done it on my own. The best bit was, after a while I could look back at my old messages and I'd realise how well I'd done. It was all there in front of me. I'd even saved some of my live chats which I still looked at for a few years after!

That was 18 years ago at time of writing! I can't believe I've finally done it! Believe it or not I still had hard times up to 3 years after quitting. If something triggered me off, I would feel like I was quitting all over again, but just for a little while. But I will NEVER go back. It would feel like I was letting all my forum pals down as well if I did! It's great to detox and know I'm not counter-acting it with tar and nicotine infusions!

If you think this method may work for you too, why not find, or start up, a Facebook group? Just a thought...

CHAPTER 39...
Health is More Than Skin Deep

When you consider how many harmful chemicals are in our food, it may come as no surprise that there are even more in our toiletries and cosmetics. The problem with this is most people just don't realise that our skin is a semi-permeable membrane so it will absorb anything you put on it, and these harmful chemicals will end up in your bloodstream, adding to your body's toxic overload, and damaging your cells.

If you don't really believe me then ask yourself why your fingers go all crinkly when you have been in water for too long. Or why your make-up fades during the day/evening. Have you thought that it may not just be wearing off, but also being sucked into your skin?

This applies to anything that comes into contact to your skin, including household chemicals (quick get the Marigolds out!), and it is really shocking that many companies will create toxic concoctions that they make to purposefully penetrate the skin such as anti-wrinkling and ageing preparations.

Chemicals to Avoid like the Plague!

The main chemicals to avoid which are found in most commercial mainstream cosmetics are Parabens, SLS/SLES and Aluminium. These are officially reported to be carcinogens (they cause cancer). Even though from the GNM perspective, cancer cannot be caused by toxins, I have quoted this to emphasise what little regard to health these companies actually must have to use known 'carcinogens' in the manufacture of something that will absorb into the body! In addition to this, please heed the harmful chemicals found in sunscreens as detailed in Chapter 35, and also understand that these are just the main toxic ingredients – there are many more! A great book is "What's Really in Your Basket?" by Bill Statham which covers additives in foods and cosmetics in a handy reference guide.

Parabens

There are many types of parabens: methyl, isobutyl, ethyl, propyl & butyl. They are sometimes listed as these names, or sometimes tagged with the word 'paraben' such as butylparaben. These are used as preservatives in cosmetics and are synthetically produced from esters of hydroxybenzoic acid.

There is much controversy over the harmful properties of parabens, with the cosmetic and mainstream industries insisting on their safety, however this is conducted with their own laboratories and is therefore easy to be biased towards their own requirements and wishes. Even if they are correct, official potential effects are 'allergic' reactions, endocrine disruption (control of the body's homeostasis process – i.e. keeping everything healthily regulated through hormonal release and reaction to stimuli), contact dermatitis, toxic by ingestion. From the GNM perspective, contact dermatitis is triggered by a separation conflict, the separation can be wanting to separate from something, or missing something you are separate from. In this case, it would be triggered by wanting to separate from the chemicals! More worryingly parabens are also found in some processed foods!

SLS

Sodium Lauryl Sulphate can be natural or synthetically sourced by sulfation of lauryl alcohol with sodium carbonate. It is used for 3 properties:

> 1. Denaturant – according to Bill Statham's book, the definition of denaturant is "a poisonous substance added to alcoholic cosmetics to prevent them being ingested. It is also a substance that changes the natural qualities or characteristics of other substances."
>
> 2. Surfactant – a wetting agent, that lowers the surface tension, allowing it to penetrate and spread more easily.
>
> 3. Emulsifier – to stabilise and ensure consistency.

But number 2 worries me the most. "Allowing it to penetrate more easily" - do we really want soap with parabens, bubble bath, toothpaste with fluoride, etc. to absorb into our body more easily?

Again, there is much controversy with official sources claiming its safety, however official potential effects are listed as: eye, skin & mucous membrane irritation, mouth ulcers, liver & gastrointestinal toxicity, teratogenic (capable of affecting a growing foetus) and in addition is listed on the National Institute of Health's hazardous list!

And again, SLS is found in foods too, especially cake mixes, dried egg products and marshmallows!

SLES

It seems that the cosmetic industries have recognised the adverse effects of SLS as they preceded to replace this with SLES in products for sensitive skin or where they wanted to minimise the impact of SLS. SLES (Sodium Laureth Sulphate or Sodium Laryl Ether Sulphate) is basically SLS which has been processed further to substitute ethoxy (ether) molecules onto the lauryl chain thereby reducing the negative effects, but these effects still remain despite it being milder, In addition, SLES may cause the formation of nitrosamines which can easily penetrate the skin. Nitrosamines are toxic compounds caused when nitrites and nitrates combine with amines. These nitrosamines can cause much physical stress on the body.

Aluminium

Aluminium salts are found in antiperspirants and deodorants and this can accumulate in our lymphatic system. The aluminium salts not only kill the bacteria which causes body odour but also 'plugs' the pores of the skin preventing sweat from leaving the body. Now when you understand that the reason the body sweats is to eliminate toxins, you will realise that not only are you contributing to the body's toxic overload by plugging the pores, but also by allowing it to absorb aluminium.

I know that aluminium from deodorants (that I stopped wearing over 10 years previously) was a previous issue for me. My lymphs had shown up as blocked under my armpits and down into my breasts on a thermal imaging scan I had in 2016, and when I began to detox with Essiac tea and diet, my kinesiologist discovered an aluminium toxicity emerging, which could only have been explained by the deodorant I had previously worn! This was just a temporary toxicity caused by the removal of the toxin, and was clear within a couple of months.

To this end, the statement I would suggest is "why gamble with your health?" - if unbiased studies have found these substances to be detrimental to the body's health & well-being, in my opinion they should always be avoided!

ALTERNATIVES

The easiest way to avoid these chemicals is to find natural alternatives, of which there are many good quality products on the market. A great alternative is to purchase a plain SLS & paraben free cosmetic base from an aromatherapy supplier and either use plain or add some essential oils. There are some great ethical ready made products on the market such as Faith in Nature, Clearspring & Suma. But really we do not need most of these cosmetics and toiletries and cleaning products. A few choice essential oils and other products such as salts and vinegar are all we need to keep ourselves and our homes clean and hygienic!

Hair

Hair does not actually require shampooing, in fact shampoo strips the hair of its natural oils and can destroy the colour pigments. It is believed that hair will self-clean in 3-6 weeks of being only washed in water and/or Epsom Salts, Sodium Bicarbonate or vinegar. There is a lot of information on the internet regarding the non-washing of hair including the amazing results that have been found. Hair becomes thicker and healthier and natural colouring has even been known to return after greying! Many believe that the hair has mystical properties and do not shampoo for this reason.

I followed a 6-week hair detox regime of non-shampooing and then returned to using just organic aloe vera shampoo. It has really made a difference as my hair is thicker than it used to be and doesn't require washing as often. For the detox I put sodium bicarbonate and Epsom Salts in water and just soaked my hair in it to wash it every 2-3 days. I also rinsed with dilute apple cider vinegar occasionally. I found a fine-tooth comb helped it to look softer and less greasy during the day. Every couple of weeks I put a mix of natural black and red henna to cover greys, which is excellent in drying the greasiness out! Lloyd lasted

198

over 6 months, just rinsing in Epsom salts, and you would never know he didn't use shampoo at all! He only went back to washing with organic shampoo as he grew his hair longer.

Natural Dye and Grey Coverage

Natural henna is a great way for covering greys, especially if you have darker hair. I use red henna mixed with lemon oil or redbush tea in the summer to make it more vibrant, and a varying mix of black (also called Indigo) and red mixed with black tea for the winter to deepen the colour. Henna is quite messy to use but very effective and conditioning. It is mixed with boiling water, allowed to cool to a temperature that it will not burn and applied to the hair while still hot. Then cover with a cap or plastic bag and leave for anything from 30 minutes to 2hrs+. Then wash off and shampoo as normal. The henna makes the greys deep and vibrant and they only need touching up every month or so. There are recipes and further information on my blog website.

From the GNM perspective, grey hair is related to vitiligo, caused by a prolonged conflict active phase of a separation conflict, which makes the hair/skin lose pigment. When I first stop washing my hair on a detox, my head becomes quite itchy and flaky, indicating a healing phase has began. This tells me that the separation is 'wanting to separate from the shampoo/conditioner'. As we wash regularly, it could be that we are basically in continued conflict active phase (with no symptoms), therefore this could explain the loss of hair colour when we age!

Skin

Just some bath salts and if you feel necessary, a little bit of natural soap is all we need to keep ourselves clean and fresh. Some natural aromatherapy moisturiser or oil to correct any dryness, and a natural deodorant stone or crystal of ammonium alum or potassium alum for all day freshness without body odour, applied with a little floral water if you would like a little scent. Dry lips can be corrected with some natural beeswax lip balm, which also acts as a lip gloss for evenings out! Castor Oil brushed onto the eyelashes will look like you are wearing mascara and as a bonus it will feed them and not destroy them like chemical mascara does! This simple but very effective beauty routine along with drinking plenty of clean water and eating correctly for our metabolic type will allow our skin to return to its natural radiant beauty and very soon you will be wondering how and why you ever wore make up and used all the cosmetics you did!

Personally, I hardly ever wear make-up. All I use on my face is aromatherapy cream (which I make) and occasional natural collagen cream and I am quite often complimented on my skin. If you feel you need to use make-up, ask yourself if there are any emotional issues behind your wearing of a 'mask'. If you choose to use make-up, try to source some organic or natural products.

Cleaning

Household cleaning can be done easily and cheaply with essential oils and floral waters. Sodium Bicarbonate, vinegar and salts are a must to have in your cleaning cupboard, along with a microfibre cloth that works excellently at cleaning without the addition of any chemicals at all!

Soap nuts or laundry balls are a great way of laundering your clothes free of chemicals, or alternatively you could purchase an ethical, natural laundry liquid and unscented fabric conditioner such as Bio-D with some essential oils to clean and freshen the clothes.

Further information, ideas and recipes for choosing the natural option without having to resort to more expensive ready-made toiletries and cleaning agents can be found in Chapter 42.

200

SECTION V...Natural Remedies

CHAPTERS:

From the GNM Perspective:

Natural remedies work very well within the principles of German New Medicine, however, they need to be used with care. The knowledge of GNM needs to be applied while considering the properties of the remedy to make sure it will be acting in harmony with the phase of any programme the body may be in at the time. On the whole, you do not want to interfere with the body's healing process by killing or attacking microbes as they are involved in the healing process. However intense healing symptoms may be lessened by using some of the remedies wisely.

Modalities such as homeopathy and flower remedies work in natural harmony with our body's life force, and can be very complimentary to the natural healing process.

CHAPTER 40...*Silver*

written by myself and Lloyd

The use of silver as a dietary supplement or first aid treatment is not regulated by the Food and Drug Administration (FDA), therefore the direct health benefits cannot be detailed by manufacturers and retailers of silver products (who are mainly in the US). Due to the restrictions also now in the UK for selling natural health products, and offering advice and information alongside, it can be extremely confusing for consumers to obtain information on non-mainstream health products, especially those with huge potential which are seemingly being kept out of public knowledge. While this can protect us from the 'snake oil salesmen' making false claims in their sales spiel, it has prevented people selling products to offer sound advice based upon research, experience and even scientific studies.

I am very careful not to make huge statements or promises on any particular product, as even if I have personally had a very positive experience, it does not mean someone else will or that other factors were not involved. So rather than making claims about silver, I have simply outlined the proven facts of silver and its use in this chapter and continued to explain the pros and cons of the different types of silver available on the market.

History

Silver used to be widely used before antibiotics were readily available to fight microbial infections, whether they be viral, bacterial or fungal due to its ability to kill microbes on contact. It is used today in wound dressings to draw out impurities, fight infection, aid healing and disinfect the wound.

It is most commonly used in the alternative health arena as colloidal silver. There is much controversy and confusion, information and disinformation on the internet around the use of silver as an anti-microbial and healing health supplement. So here are some well-researched facts that I have put together that encompass our years of research into the silver products available.

Our research has led us to talk to many people for first-hand advice into which silver product is the safest and most effective including Jay Newman, inventor of Opti-Silver complex and Scott Tips, president of the National Health Federation – both members of the Silver Safety Council.

Silver Facts

- Silver is a proven non-toxic disinfectant and healing agent.

- In the old days cowboys would fill their canteens with water and flip a silver coin in to purify it.

- Silver is odourless, tasteless (although can have a slight metallic after-taste), virtually non-stinging, harmless to eyes & ears, is completely pure and has no known contra-indications or reactions with other medications.

- In tests, it has been known to kill every virus/bacteria or other pathogen it was presented with.

- Most silver is absorbed by the body before reaching the gut, so it is believed to have very little effect on the population of friendly gut bacteria. However, it is always recommended that a high count, multi strain probiotic supplement is taken in conjunction with taking silver (but at a different time of day).

- As silver works by killing organisms through physical means (it is believed to paralyse the 'lung' of the microbe), there will never be a resistance to it as with other antibiotics.

Silver Safety

Silver can be used safely by all ages, and is safe to use anywhere inside or outside the body. However, excess silver can cause a permanent skin discolouration call Argyria in extreme cases where the silver deposits itself under the skin. This has lead to much controversy over the use of colloidal silver and the pharmaceutical corporations and media have been very quick to publicise these rare cases to discredit the use of silver in the mainstream. It would just not be profitable to them to offer something so effective as they need your repeat business! It is worth noting though, that people reported to have this condition such as the infamous 'blue man' generally report having great health apart from the discolouration!! This actually is testament to the fact that silver is non-toxic, as these people must have consumed vast amounts of silver to have such a discolouration. Although this discolouration is not common, it may be under-reported due to the stigma, so you should seriously consider this when deciding to take any type of silver on a long term basis. More frequent is minor discolouration on certain parts of the body such as around the fingernails.

About Colloidal Silver

Colloidal Silver has historical usage of over 100 years and so it is no surprise that it is often stated as the proven form of silver. Colloidal Silver is itself tiny particles of silver suspended in purified water. Most manufacturers of Colloidal Silver agree that the smaller the particles, the better the colloidal silver. In fact, this appears to be true but is only part of the story. The more important fact by far is that only a very small amount of the silver in colloidal silver is the bio-active form of silver, which is silver ions. And the little bit of silver ions that does exist in colloidal silver is in the form of silver oxide, which is not soluble and therefore only releases a small amount of its silver ions into the body. Therefore, larger doses are required of colloidal silver in order to get the ionic particles needed.

PPM (Parts Per Million)

Colloidal Silver is sold in many different PPM (parts per million) and the higher PPM, the higher amount or "concentration" of silver present. However, it does not necessarily mean a better product. In fact the opposite may be true. This is because the higher concentration of silver or PPM, the more likely it is that larger particles will have formed. Only a certain PPM can be maintained in a colloid before this occurs. In general, PPM is not an important factor at all in comparing colloidal silver since you can just adjust the usage amount to compensate for the concentration level – at which point the only variables are cost per microgram of silver and how much water is coming along for the ride. While you will find varying reports of the best PPM for colloidal silver, there really is little difference when it comes to PPM. What does matter is the "form" of the silver – the actual chemical make-up of the silver. This will depend somewhat on the sizes of the silver particles in the first place, but that's not even remotely as important as the amount of bio-active ingredient – silver ions – and the way they're delivered into the body.

Home Made Colloidal Silver

Many people make their own colloidal silver which is done simply by placing 2 thin rods (or thick wires) of silver into a glass of distilled water with the ends sticking out and running a low voltage electricity current through them, causing particles of silver to break off into the water. This is by far the cheapest method of using silver, so it may be worth investing in equipment to make your own. However, there is no control at all over the quality or chemical make-up of the silver particles (as already mentioned), which can cause difficulty in deciding on dosage levels. Also bear in mind that a TDS meter does not give accurate PPM of silver, as much of the silver may be silver oxide which our bodies cannot use. Certainly, home-made colloidal silver falls into the category to be concerned about if you want to use silver for regular long term usage, although in an emergency, or for someone with a long-term need and limited budget, the benefit may outweigh any associated risk.

It is my opinion that colloidal silver, whether bought from a reputable company or home made, is excellent for help with warding off illness at the onset, for short term use internally, external use and first aid measures and for using around the house. Rather than take it long term, I am a believer that an overall general health is key through correct diet and detox. Having researched this thoroughly I would not consider taking colloidal silver regularly in the long term, simply as a precautionary measure, especially as microbes are essential in our natural healing process. I would only use silver in the case of reducing severe symptoms and infections.

Ionic Silver

Only a few years ago, many of the major colloidal silver manufacturers were proud to announce that their silver had maximum silver particles with minimal silver ions. More recently, they have changed their tune to state that they have minimal silver particles and maximum silver ions!! The reason for this is that today, with a modern understanding of chemistry, it is increasingly well known that the only bio-active form of silver is silver ions! In fact, there have been a number of patents that range from medical devices and surgical equipment to washing machines that rely on the fact that the bio-active form (the type that kills pathogens or germs) of silver is IONIC! So what you actually want from colloidal silver is as much of it as possible to be silver ions rather than particles. Whether it be from a crudely made colloidal silver or from a silver quarter in a jug of milk, you will get a small amount of Ionic Silver being released off the larger silver particles.

The challenge with silver Ions (in basic terms)

So we have a bio-active silver ion ready to neutralize a pathogen. However, it will react with and bind up with a chloride ion if it's in the vicinity, and if the silver ion is available or "unattached". Once silver chloride is formed it remains intact and thus renders the silver ions inert or neutralized. So the amount of benefit that people find from Colloidal Silver or from any silver product is therefore proportional to the sheer amount of silver ions delivered to the target area after getting past the chlorides in the body, and in the case of colloidal silver it entails taking in a sufficient amount to get enough silver ions that can then find their way to a target pathogen.

Ideally, what is needed in a silver product for human use is, first, that all of the silver be in the ionic state and, second, that it be delivered through a timed release mechanism to get it past the chlorides in the system and then released at the desired target.

Timed-Release Ionic Silver

At the moment, there is a novel product that overcomes this limitation by providing a delivery mechanism for the silver Ions into the body. It holds the silver in an equilibrium complex that can carry it into the body before releasing a silver ion. This technique is found in the Opti Silver Complex, which is the ingredient in the timed release ionic silver preparation, Silver100. So what you get is a vastly higher percentage of the Silver actually being made available in its useful form to different parts of the body compared to anything else currently available. Timed release ionic silver is by far the safest type of silver product out there as so little is needed to get great results and we can precisely measure and control how much bio-active silver we're taking, which is only about 25% of the EPA (Environmental Protection Agency) recommended limits for daily consumption of silver.

While this may appear to be a perfect silver product, its future at the time of writing is under threat. The owner of Invision International who manufacture Silver 100, Jay Newman, has (admirably) refused to sell out to pharmaceutical companies and to accept funding or investments from unethical sources, and it seems that the support from smaller ethical companies carrying this product, like my shop, Shop Holistic, are not enough to meet the cost of manufacturing and research involved for producing Silver 100. Sadly, this is typical of the natural health market, the struggle of smaller ethical companies with innovative products against billion-dollar corporations who have long forgotten the meaning of the word ethical. Without this product, and until another comes along, the true potential of silver may not be recognised, although some benefit can still be found with other forms of silver in the meantime.

I believe Silver 100 is the best silver product currently available that I am aware of. It is the silver that we have always taken when needed with great results. However, as its availability continues to be threatened, we have currently switched to colloidal silver for external use and hydrosol silver for internal use. Hydrosol silver contains a new technology called Silversol which has nano silver particles in solution. Despite this being a silver oxide, this formula muscle-tested as more beneficial than colloidal silver, though not quite as strong as the Opti-silver 100. So in the absence of Silver100 we are happy to go with this.

In summary, some points to consider when choosing a silver product:

• Although colloidal silver is proven to be beneficial, you must be careful if considering this for prolonged use.

• Many brands of colloidal silver are not specific about dosage amounts and where a dosage is recommended it is usually many times the recommended daily limits set by the EPA.

• Research the company you are buying from, as mentioned there are many that have lied in the past about their silver content (so can you really trust them?). We have also heard of people making home-made colloidal silver in their homes and selling this as a branded product.

• If you are considering making your own, be sure to do your research thoroughly and purchase the correct equipment for testing the resulting product. You want to know the PPM of silver in what you're taking!

• If you decide to use colloidal silver, and get any skin discolouration anywhere (particularly noticeable around the fingernails), discontinue use immediately as this condition is irreversible and will only get worse.

More information on the safety of silver can be found at the Silver Safety Council website at www.silversafety.org

CHAPTER 41...Dead Sea Salt

Dead Sea Salt and Dead Sea Mud have long been considered as a source of health and beauty. The Dead Sea is so-called as there is no life at all in or around it – no plants, seaweed or fish and this is due to its extremely high concentration of salts and minerals. It is toxic to fish, so much that any that accidentally swim into the waters from one of the feeding streams are killed instantly. Their bodies are washed to the shore, coated with a preserving layer of salt crystals. However deadly it is to fish and sea life, it is these minerals that give the water its curative powers.

The Dead Sea has ten times the concentration of salt compared to the regular sea, that is 33% compared to only 3%. The extremely high concentration of mineral salts make it very dense and when a person bathes in the Dead Sea they are more buoyant, so much so that it is difficult to swim!

The Dead Sea is completely landlocked, and its salinity increases the deeper you go. At about 130 feet (40 metres), the seawater comprises of about 300g of salt per kg of seawater. Below 300 feet, though, the sea has 332g of salt per kg of water, and at this point it is completely saturated. As the water evaporates, the excess salt piles up on the bottom of the sea and collects on the shores.

The salts found in the Dead Sea are mineral salts, uniquely comprising of magnesium, potassium and calcium chlorides, in addition to a high concentration of bromides.

People from all over the world travel to the Dead Sea seeking relief from skin and rheumatic disorders or simply relaxation. The therapeutic reputation of the Dead Sea dates back over 2000 years with many stating that the salt water eased the symptoms of arthritis, eczema, muscular pain and also to relieve tension, aid relaxation, and develop smooth silky skin.

The efficacy of Dead Sea minerals on conditions like acne, psoriasis and rheumatism, have since been proven by medical research and studies. Due to its extreme mineral salt content it is not suitable for consumption, only for bathing.

Dead Sea Minerals

Listed are some of the minerals contained in Dead Sea Salts which are beneficial to the body.

Magnesium – concentrations found in the Dead Sea are fifteen times higher than salts in other seas. See Chapter 15. The Magnesium Chloride flakes that I offer are of Dead Sea origin and it is considered a very good quality source.

Sodium - improves the skin's permeability and suppleness and is ideal for very dry skin.

Potassium - asthma sufferers have achieved good results from inhaling the salt vapours.

Bromine - has a deeply relaxing effect and its concentration is 50 times higher in Dead Sea Salt than in common salts.

Bitumen - acts as an anti-inflammatory agent.

Chlorine – vital for cell metabolism and necessary to maintain the correct balance of alkaline and acid in the body. Although when it is used to form artificial chemicals it becomes detrimental to our health.

Iodine – vital for the production of the hormone thyroxine, it supports the thyroid and is vital for both energy and cell metabolism.

Calcium – vital for the formation and maintenance of healthy teeth and bones, and also necessary in strengthening cell membranes and cleansing the pores.

Zinc – plays a role in enzymatic regulation of cell proliferation and the regulation of copper.

Using Dead Sea Salts

Dead Sea Salts can be used in the bath by placing 1-2 good handfuls, up to 1Kg, in a warm bath. Soak in the bath for about 20 minutes to allow for optimum mineral absorption. A Dead Sea Salt bath can be very relaxing and beneficial and is an ideal relaxing bedtime bath for babies and children due to its magnesium content.

They can also be used in a foot bath (in a lesser amount). You can use Dead Sea Salts to make a body scrub or you can dissolve some in water and use it to soak some cloth for a compress.

CHAPTER 42...Aromatherapy

Aromatherapy is the medical use of the therapeutic and aromatic properties of plants. The oils are believed to carry the vibrational healing properties of the plant and are therefore very effective in healing us on all levels, physical, emotional & spiritual. Please see Section VII for more information on vibrational healing and Aromatherapy as a therapy.

Aromatherapy is very powerful. Its essential oils are so concentrate it is quoted that 1 drop has 40,000 molecules for each cell in our bodies! Due to its high concentration, the oils can be used as powerful cleaners, disinfectants and have many other uses around the house and in our environment. But how aromatherapy works upon our holistic bodies is another matter. The scent of the concentrated oil (which is caused by tiny molecules of the oil being suspended in the air) enters our nose and are detected by the olfactory nerves. These nerves have a direct link to the brain and are the closest to external stimulus than any other in the body. This is believed to be why our 'aroma' memories outlast our regular memory. Have you ever smelt something and immediately it has conjured up feelings of reminiscence, or other emotions, and you can't quite remember why? The tiny molecules of the oils act upon our olfactory nerves, triggering memories and associations and bringing the past to the surface to heal, while the vibrational properties held in the tiny molecules heal us with their vibrational properties.

213

I love using Aromatherapy oils and discovering new ways in which to use them. I really enjoy creating my own toiletries such as shampoo, anti-bacterial hand wash, anti-wrinkle cream, pain reliever to name but a few, some are available on my shop website. I find great satisfaction in discarding and replacing chemicals with natural substances!

It is so comforting knowing that whatever way plants are used, they are benefiting yours and your family's health and well-being. It is in my discovery of how much we can use the properties of plants, and instinctively do to some extent, that has made me realise that my existence is so much more in harmony with Mother Earth than I once thought!

Essential Oils

Essential Oils come from liquid found in tiny sacs on plants and this can be extracted by methods such as distillation, cold pressing or by using a solvent such as pure alcohol.

Usually blended together and sometimes in a carrier, Essential Oils can be used on the face and body, in the bath, around the home and as an insect repellent.

Essential Oils are associated with colours and can be used in relation to the 7 Chakras. Oils are used with an associated colour that corresponds to the colour of the Chakra you wish to focus on. See Chapter 84 for more information.

Safety

Essential oils are extremely potent and need to be used with care. Please use sparingly, and NEVER more than the suggested dosage, especially if you have a medical condition. They should only be used undiluted when specifically instructed to do so. Essential oils are diluted using

Carrier oils, water or plain bases such as shampoo and bubble bath.

You need to consider these points:

- Never use undiluted essential oils directly on the skin – apart from lavender and tea tree which can be used just one drop undiluted

- Essential Oils are not recommended for internal consumption in the UK however many European countries prescribe internal usage. Unless you know exactly what you are doing or have been advised by a qualified aromatherapist, do not take them internally, the exception being 1 drop organic peppermint oil in warm water for relieving wind and indigestion. I also use a couple of drops of organic food grade orange, lemon and lime in cooking.

- Never increase the dosage as some oils can be toxic in large quantities

- Take care when choosing carrier oils if you are allergic to nuts

- If you are in a biological programme, make sure you do not use stimulating oils as these could accelerate the conflict active phase, and hinder the non-stress of the healing phase

First Aid Measures

Eye exposure: Essential oils in the eye: Flush with copious amounts of MILK for at least 15 minutes and seek medical advice if symptoms persist. Ingestion: Rinse mouth with MILK, drink plenty of water and seek urgent medical attention.

Pregnancy

As with all products, particular care should be taken while pregnant and breastfeeding.

The following essential oils are only a few that should be avoided during pregnancy:

Angelica, Basil, Cedarwood, Citronella, Fennel, Juniper, Jasmin, Lovage, Katafray, Laurel, Marjoram, Myrrh, Rosemary, Sage, Tarragon, Thyme, Yarrow.

Cancer

Lavender promotes the growth of cells, in this way it can be excellent for healing, but for this reason I would tend to avoid use in cancer patients. There are many other essential oils that have been found to be beneficial in a cancer protocol. For example, Frankincense and Myrrh have been found to have a positive effect on switching on apoptosis (programmed cell death) and reducing proliferation (multiplying) of cancer cells, and grapefruit has been found to have a positive effect on the reduction of proliferation of breast cancer cells. However, this research is carried out outside the body. Whether the cells will act in the same way inside the body and part of the psyche / brain / organ connection, is another story.

Carrier Oils & Bases

Carrier oils are extracted from the oily parts of the plant such as the nuts & seeds. There are also infused oils which is when the plant is infused in an oil such as sunflower. Carrier Oils have certain properties and can contain many good quality vitamins and omega oils which are taken into the skin and feed our skin and bodies. More than one carrier oil can be used if you want the additional properties, however, I would not suggest blending more than 2 or 3. Bases are plain cosmetic bases such as cream, shampoo, lotion, etc. to which essential oils can be added to make a purposefully therapeutic or simply scented product. If you have a nut allergy or sensitivity, please be aware that many carrier oils are

216

derived from nuts, and also check the ingredients of cosmetic bases.

Carrier Oils for Internal Consumption

Carrier Oils are generally pure and natural and many can be used internally as long as they are from a good quality source. However many aromatherapy suppliers do not bottle oils in a food-grade bottle or a food grade environment so if you intend to ingest a carrier oil, then it is best to check with the supplier.

Preserving a Blended Massage Oil

When essential oils are added to carrier oils to make a massage oil the blend will generally last only 3-5 days. To preserve the blend you need to use an oil which has a good vitamin E content. So either make the blend with sweet almond oil, or you may simply add a small amount of natural vitamin E oil, rice bran oil or wheatgerm oil (about a ratio of 1 part vitamin E or wheatgerm to 6-8 parts your chosen carrier). There is no need to be exact. – I think of it as the same ratio that I would mix squash to water for the children!

Choosing Essential Oils

Below are some of the most popular oils and their properties:

Uplifting Oils – Basil, Bay, Bergamot, Cinnamon, Frankincense, Geranium, Jasmin, Melissa, Neroli, Patchouli

Energising Oils – Bergamot, Cinnamon, all citrus, Black Pepper, Peppermint, Rosemary

Relaxing Oils – Benzoin, Bergamot (depending on what its mixed with), Chamomile, Geranium, Lavender, Mandarin, Sweet Marjoram, Melissa, Neroli, Orange, Ylang Ylang

Antiseptic Oils – Bay, Benzoin, Comfy, Eucalyptus, Juniper Berry, Lemon, Lemongrass, Orange, Pine, Thyme, Tea Tree

Sensual Oils – Cedarwood, Cardamom, Cinnamon, Clary Sage, Jasmine, Lavender, Patchouli, Rose, Sandalwood, Ylang Ylang

Tension/stress – Basil, Clary Sage, Cypress, Geranium, Juniper Berry, Marjoram, Melissa, Neroli, Patchouli (in larger doses), Rose, Sandalwood, Thyme, Ylang Ylang

Headaches – Chamomile, Lavender, Lemongrass, Marjoram, Melissa, Neroli, Peppermint, Rosemary

Blending Essential Oils

Essential Oils can be mixed together to give added benefits and individual blends. Some oils will adapt their properties when blended with others to form a 'synergy'. Therefore you may find some oils repeated in contradicting recipes!

Even though there are many recipes to be found in most aromatherapy literature, and you can buy ready-mixed blends, there is nothing like creating your own unique blend. This gives you the freedom to invent a blend that will be totally relevant for what you need, and to your own taste.

Essential Oils can cancel each other out and clash with each other. You will learn with experimentation, but a few basic tips are:

- Strong smelling essences tend to be unpleasant when combined.

- Lavender and Jasmin will mix well with all other Essential Oils.

Keep your blends simple, using no more than 3-4 different oils (although some blends can take up to 5 oils). To test the combination before mixing, place a drop of each oil onto separate tissues, hold together in a fan shape and gently wave under your nose, inhaling.

218

The top Essential Oils for mixing are:

Bergamot, Cedarwood, Chamomile, Frankincense, Geranium, Jasmin, Lavender, Lemon, Neroli, Sweet Orange, Patchouli, Rose, Sandalwood and Ylang Ylang.

Neroli, Rose and Jasmin are precious oils and are very expensive, however most aromatherapy suppliers will sell them diluted in jojoba oil. As they are very potent, there is usually no need to increase the drops you use if you use a dilution.

Perfumery Note Values

Essential Oils all have a different note value, Top, Middle or Bottom, depending on the rate at which they evaporate and therefore how long the fragrance and effects last.

The **Top Note** oils give immediate and noticeable effects and tend to have a lighter fragrance, e.g. you will notice Eucalyptus clearing your head, or Lemon refreshing you.

They are the shortest lasting oils, their fragrance and effect lasting between 3-24 hours. They are usually the most uplifting and stimulating of essential oils.

The **Middle Notes** are the second lasting oils in fragrance and effect, lasting between 2-3 days. They affect the bodily functions and are less potent than the Top notes.

Base Notes are mellower fragrances and have a deeper, less immediate effect on you. e.g. you will eventually feel less stress and relaxed when using Patchouli, although this may not make as noticeable a difference as a Top note oil as it takes time to take affect and calm the mind. These are the longest lasting oils, lasting up to 1 week. These essential oils affect the mind and emotions.

It is always a good idea to have one Base Note Oil in your blend with a mix of Top and Middle Notes. A blend consisting entirely of Top notes may clash and lack depth, and more than one Base Note may be too overpowering and clash.

There is a lot to consider when wanting to try out different blends but you may like to break the rules and experiment. We all have individual tastes and this information is only intended as a guide. Be bold and brave and let your imagination run wild!

Mixing Ratios

It depends on how the finished product is being used as to how much you dilute it. If you are making larger amounts of blends it is handy to know that approximately 20 drops of essential oil is equivalent to 1ml. The maximum ratio to use is 3% essential oil. Therefore you would add no more than 3ml (or 60 drops) essential oil to 100ml of base or carrier oil. Although it maybe easier when blending smaller amounts to half the number of mls to get the number of drops to use and this way you will ensure the ratio is below the maximum strength (e.g. 25 drops for 50ml base, or 1 drop per 2ml carrier). This is the ratio I use. The general rule for facial use is half the strength or 1 drop per 5ml carrier (the latter being better for sensitive skin). If only using 1 essential oil you will not need to use as much. It may not seem much, but as I previously stated, it is believed that there are 40,000 molecules for each cell in the average body per drop of essential oil as they are so tiny. Despite these molecules being so tiny they will still hold the vibrational energy of the plant, which is what is required for healing.

Body Use

Bathing & Soaking: I recommend using 8-10 drops placed directly into the bath water, or 3-5 drops per bowl for soaking your feet or hands. To

220

disperse the essential oils more effectively in the water they can first be added to Dead Sea Salts, Magnesium Chloride Flakes, Epsom Salts or Himalayan Salts and left to infuse before adding to the bath. Alternatively, you can add them to castor oil which some recommend as an oil dispersant.

The following oils are great for body use. The oils in brackets are blends that I have previously used and/or devised and so can be used together as a recipe.

Insomnia and tension – Chamomile, (Lavender & Marjoram)

Colds – (Eucalyptus, Niaouli & Peppermint)

Invigorate & Refresh – Peppermint, Lemon, (Geranium & Lime)

Headache – Rosemary

PMT, depression – (Bergamot, Clary Sage & Geranium)

Sedative – Sandalwood, (Lavender & Marjoram)

Deodorising (such as on feet) – Lemongrass

Other good oils for use on the body are:

Cedarwood, Neroli, Orange, Rose, Ylang Ylang

Some Suggested Carrier oils to use are:

Normal/Itchy/Sensitive – Sweet Almond

Dry or rough skin – Hemp

Oily skin – Apricot kernel

Scars – Wheatgerm, Rosehip Seed

Stretch Marks – Calendula, Rosehip Seed, Sesame

Wrinkles – Apricot Kernel & Evening Primrose

Facial Use

Some essential oils for particular use (again, recipes are in brackets):

Rashes and Itching – (Lavender & Chamomile)

Acne/ oily skin – Juniper Berry

Open Pores – Lemongrass

Scars & slack skin – Mandarin, Frankincense

Sensitive skin – Chamomile

Wrinkles – Orange, Frankincense, Neroli

Mature skin – Rose, Palmarosa

Some Suggested Carrier oils to use are:

Normal/Combination skin – Sweet Almond Oil

Mature skin – Wheatgerm Oil

Sensitive skin – Peach Kernel

Dry skin – Apricot Kernel

Greasy/irritated skin – Jojoba Oil

A combination of carrier oils can be used, especially if one carrier is heavier such as wheatgerm or jojoba.

As a Room Fragrance

Essential oils make lovely room fragrance. They lose some of their properties when heated to a high temperature, but they have been traditionally burnt to disinfect the atmosphere and create the perfect ambience.

In Oil Burners – 8 drops in hot water

On a Wood Fire – 12 drops on 3 pieces of wood, 15mins before lighting

Room Spray – 10 drops in 50ml water, shake before use

Pot Pourri – To make your own, simply dry out 6 cups of your favourite flowers, herbs and leaves from the garden, add 12 drops of essential oil and 2 tablespoon of talc and store an airtight container for 2 weeks agitating daily. Then place in an open bowl.

Other Household Uses

Essential Oils have many uses around the house. Here are some suggestions:

Kitchen Cleaner – Lemon, Geranium, Tea Tree. Add 8 drops to a bowl of warm water or into a spray bottle.

Bathroom Cleaning – Lemon, Lavender, Tea tree. Add 3 drops to a damp cloth.

Washing-up – Geranium, Lavender. Add 2 drops to the rinsing water.

In Laundry

Ideal for freshening and scenting your laundry, here are some ideas:

In your washing machine – Add 20 drops in the softener compartment with a fragrance free fabric conditioner if you prefer.

For Hand-washing – Add 5 drops to the final rinse water.

In the Tumble Dryer – put a few drops on a hankie and add to the drier with the clothes.

Ironing – Add a few drops to the iron water.

Storage – Place a few drops on some cotton wool balls in your drawers.

To freshen shoes – Mix 2 drops of essential oil to 2 teaspoons of bicarbonate of soda, sprinkle in the shoes and leave overnight.

Some suggestions:

Lavender, marjoram, chamomile or orange for bedsheets and nightwear.

Fragrances for laundry are may chang, or lemongrass for deodorising.

Insect Repellent

Essential oils can be very effective and kind insect repellents:

Moths – Camphor, Few drops hung in the wardrobe on a hankie.

Mosquitoes – Citronella, few drops on your pillow or 6 drops in 30ml Carrier Oil applied to the skin.

Most Flying Insects – Lemongrass, 15 drops in 1 pint water.

Ants and most crawling insects – 8 Tea Tree and 7 Thyme in 30ml water, spray where they walk.

Pet Fleas – 6 Geranium, 5 Lavender, 4 Tea Tree in 30ml water, comb fur back and spray at roots. Alternatively use Diatomaceous Earth. For a repellent, 6 drops each of rosemary, peppermint, eucalyptus, tea tree, and citronella in a water spray bottle, apply to the coat every other day (not for cats).

Spiders – A 1:1 mix of Clove Bud and Cedarwood essential oils, dilute with spring water and spray where the spiders come in to the house.

CHAPTER 43...*Hydrolats or Floral Waters*

Hydrolats or floral waters are generally the by-product of the distillation process to produce essential oils. However due to their versatility and increasingly wide usage, many are now purposely produced. True hydrolats contain tiny droplets of essential oils suspended in the water and therefore possess similar properties to the essential oil. They are very different from water which has had essential oil and a dispersant added. Many true hydrolats do not smell like the plant they originally came from or the essential oil which may arise from the distillation of that plant, despite the name of 'floral water' suggesting otherwise. Their smell can be pungent and earthy, but usually they are not unpleasant. Some hydrolats have no smell at all, but this does not detract from the sometimes very useful therapeutic properties. As Hydrolats are mainly water they are gentle and safe to use, they are easily applied, absorbed and ingested and can be used on babies, pets and the elderly.

The most popular hydrolats are Rose Water, Orange Flower Water, Lavender and Witch Hazel but there are many more on the market.

Suggestions on how to use Hydrolats

Hydrolats can be used around the house as an anti-bacterial cleaner and also they can be used as an alternative to cosmetics. They make excellent natural facial toners, an effective wound wash and some (such as rose water) are even used in cooking!

You can also use them as an ironing spray to give your clothes a light scent, and can be used in the final rinse of your hair.

Hydrolats are sometimes used in creams and lotions and even as a refreshing skin or face spray.

Witch Hazel

Witch hazel (Hamamelis virginiana) has long been used by the North American Indians as an excellent astringent when the bark, leaves and twigs are distilled and mixed with alcohol and water. It is also used to soothe pain or stiffness, as an eyewash, symptomatic relief for haemorrhoids, internal haemorrhages especially involving the lungs and excessive menstrual flow.

It has anti-inflammatory, hydrating, and barrier-stabilizing effects and also has antioxidant and anti-microbial properties. It has widely been used in mainstream preparations to treat haemorrhoids, irritations, minor pain, and itching.

Witch hazel has been said to treat vaginal dryness and menstrual problems. Witch hazel was used traditionally as a general household remedy for burns, scalds, and inflammatory conditions of the skin. It is also claimed that it can be used as protection against UV radiation.

Witch hazel has a long history of use in herbal medicine. Today, it is approved by the FDA, which provides additional merit to its usefulness.

This herb is most often found in the form of distilled Witch Hazel in most households. It is the most applicable and easy to use. As with all astringents, this herb may be used wherever there has been bleeding, both internally or externally. It is especially useful in the easing of varicose veins and has been used in the past to control diarrhoea and aid in the easing of dysentery.

Witch Hazel can be used on its own, or combined with an essential oil such as tea tree or lavender (as long as you are not planning to use it internally). Take care when applying to broken skin as it can sting!

CHAPTER 44...Cannabis

Despite its controversial background, no one can deny that cannabis, marijuana, or whatever you want to call it is an amazing plant. It has so many uses from clothing, paper, medicine, food, fuel, you can even make an entire house from it! Henry Ford made his first car entirely from hemp, and Levi jeans were also made originally from hemp due to its durability.

Hemp and cannabis are just different varieties of the cannabis plant, the name is dependant on the plants properties, cultivation and intended use. Strains that contain less than 0.3% THC (5-tetrahydrocannabinoid – the component of cannabis that gives the 'high') are known as Hemp. It is grown and cultivated for industrial use such as biofuel, food, clothing, rope and paper. Varieties that contain more than 0.3% and up to 30% THC are generally known as Cannabis. These are also cultivated differently. Hemp is grown for maximum yield and size, while cannabis is grown with careful consideration to its environment to nurture its desired properties.

The name "Marijuana" was not heard of when cannabis was widely used before its prohibition in the 1920s. It was a term used by the Mexicans, and as such was introduced to the public as a 'new drug' that had come from Mexico and was causing many problems. Fear of 'Reefer Madness ' caused the public to protest and demand that Marijuana was outlawed, not realising that they were protesting against their much loved cannabis which was used for leisure, medicine and industry. Of course the instigators of this propaganda stood to lose their investments in their industries that were threatened by cannabis, namely the paper (tabloid), pharmaceutical and oil industries, and their political henchmen were happy to bow to their sponsors' demands.

As I write it is still illegal in the UK to grow and possess more than a personal supply. This is despite there being no deaths in history from using cannabis. Many US states have now legalised cannabis, and it is hoped that these will set a precedence for legalisation around the world, as it should be!

Varieties and Strains of Cannabis

There are 3 main varieties of cannabis:

Cannabis Sativa is known for its energising and uplifting properties. In fact Sativa is linked to the Sanskrit word for daytime.

Cannabis Indica is known for its relaxing and sedating properties, with Indica being linked to the Sanskrit word for night time.

Cannabis Ruderalis is not a common variety as it is a small variety which does not have psychotropic effects, but due to its fast growth and its ability to grow in colder climates it is often used for hybridisation to give these properties to other varieties.

You will find hundreds if not thousands of cannabis strains, the majority of which are hybridised to produce specific ratios of CBD to THC, and easy to grow conditions such as auto-flowering and female only strains.

Cannabinoids

There are around 120 different components of the cannabis plant and these are called cannabinoids. The most common useful ones known at the time of writing are cannabidiol (CBD) and THC (already mentioned). CBD is almost like the antagonist of THC in many ways and so a balance of the two in certain ratios will give different properties that are useful in different circumstances. There are other components of Cannabis such as Terpenes which are also receiving much favourable attention in health studies.

Safety of Cannabis

Cannabis usage, by whatever means, is considered safe and there have never been any deaths directly attributed to cannabis. In fact, in an attempt to justify the continued prohibition of cannabis, Dr Donald Tashkin of UCLA received a large grant by the National Institute of Drug Abuse to show that Cannabis smoking was causing lung cancer. Dr Tashkin says:

> "We hypothesized that there would be a positive association between marijuana use and lung cancer, and that the association would be more positive with heavier use. What we found instead was no association at all, and even a suggestion of some protective effect."

But I will add that I have heard of many people suffering psychosis and mental instability after prolonged regular cannabis use. My research and instincts regarding this tell me that this is mostly due to the hybridisation of cannabis strains with street growers attempting to increase the THC to CBD ratio as high as possible. This causes the psychotic THC and anti-psychotic CBD to fall out of their delicate balance with each other, and in my opinion this destabilises the properties. Therefore, it is best to find original strains, or at least those with a good balance of CBD to THC. I would also check that the strain has not been genetically modified, as I have read that female only varieties can be a GMO.

Cannabis in Harmony with our Body

The very interesting thing to note is that our body has its own endocannabinoid system with cannabinoid receptors that literally fit the cannabinoids in cannabis like a lock and key. This is why it is believed to have such a positive impact on our health while working in perfect harmony with our body. In fact, cannabis is extremely supportive to our healing. Its anti-stress and relaxing properties encourage and assist healing, and if there is THC content we are able to see our conflicts from a new, non-stressful perspective which may assist in their resolution or downgrade.

Rick Simpson Oil (High THC Cannabis Oil)

I have heard many good experiences of using pure / high THC oil as made by Rick Simpson, especially in the cases of advance cancers. From our new perspective, healing must be completed on the psyche level in order to fully heal, so should anyone wish to take this oil for part of a treatment protocol of a cancer, it is important not to ignore the healing from the psyche level.

During my research I came across information that high THC oil caused hormone receptive cancer tumours to grow and increase in number., the ideal ratio of CBD to THC for hormone-driven cancers being quoted as between 3:1 to 5:1. According to GNM, the presence of hormones in a tumour is only relevant to the stage of growth of the tumour in the biological programme, and any tumours that appeared to accelerate in growth or spread would have more likely been due to new conflicts or conflict relapses, as explained in the initial GNM chapter. However, I would muscle test to see what is most beneficial for me and if my body preferred an oil with a balance of THC and CBD, I would supplement with additional CBD oil to make up this ratio if need be.

CBD Oil

Due to the THC still being illegal in the UK, CBD Oil and Extract is becoming extremely popular. CBD has many properties such as pain relief, relaxant, anti-nausea, anti-inflammatory, anti-spasmodic, the list goes on. It has become widely used with great effects by adults, children and even pets. I have researched, assessed and energy-tested many different types of CBD oils and extracts for my shop. Here are some tips I have put together on sourcing quality and legal CBD products based on what I learnt from this research:

- Hemp CBD is better than Cannabis CBD because Cannabis strains have higher THC content which has to be extracted to reduce the THC in the extract/oil to the legal level, thus denaturing the product.

- Due to its high CBD content, the best strain for CBD is Cannabis Sativa L. Other strains of industrial hemp have very little CBD content and the more plants that are used, the increased likelihood of contamination, as hemp plants absorb pollutants from the soil.

- Undiluted CBD extract, or diluted into the 'mother' hemp seed oil has better bio-availability.

- Extraction processes should be safe and not use petrochemicals or other harsh chemicals which leave behind toxic residue in the extract. The oils and extracts I have energy tested that are 'Super critical CO_2 extraction' have been the most favourable.

- Organically grown plants should be used. It is important when creating an extract to have plants without toxic contaminants.

The extract is highly concentrated and so will be any added toxins that come along for the ride!

However you choose to take your cannabis, and whether you choose to take it at all, there is no doubt in my mind that it has been unfairly demonised, and the only problem with its use is the stigma that is attached to it! I have a car sticker that describes this beautifully:

Man made Booze, God made Weed – who do you trust?

CHAPTER 45...Homeopathy

Homeopathic remedies are a system of medicine based on the theory that "Like Cures Like". A complete profile of your mental, emotional, symptomatic and physical conditions is taken during a session to assess which remedy is suited to your current situation. Homeopathy is extremely effective and supportive to the body's natural healing process. When the correct remedy is taken, results can be rapid, complete and permanent when the healing is also completed at the psyche level. They provide a completely safe holistic treatment without side effects. However due to the way that the remedies work you may experience an initial temporary aggravation of the symptoms, known as the Herxheimer Reaction.

Homeopathic remedies can be taken alongside other medication without producing unwanted side effects, and even by pregnant or nursing mothers and babies.

Homeopathy is completely natural and the remedies are based upon natural ingredients. Homeopathy works in harmony with your body unlike some conventional medicines which are non-supportive of our body's natural healing process.

Homeopathy treats the cause and not the symptoms – the opposite to conventional medicine which is mainly symptom based, however full emotional healing must also be completed for complete healing to take place.

A full session will assess every aspect of your condition and state of mind. The chosen remedy has to be matched to you in particular so how your condition is experienced, what aggravates it, what makes it feel better and what other symptoms you are experiencing will all be assessed.

You can purchase self-prescribing and first aid homeopathy kits online, however for chronic or persistent problems, or those with a deep emotional link, you are best to seek the advice from a qualified homeopath.

Professional Homeopathic Sessions

Sessions will generally last up to an hour, the first session may be longer, and the costs generally includes whichever remedy is required. A lot of information will be required about you, your likes and dislikes, family and medical history. It is crucial that this information is full and accurate as this will be the information your prescription is based upon. The remedy may be given at the first consultation, or if it is not held in stock, or the homeopath needs to do further research it will be given at your next session.

Potencies

Homeopathic remedies are available in various potencies, the most common being 6x, 6c, 30c & 200c. The X denotes a decimal scale which means the remedy is diluted 10 times at each succussion (process of vigorous shaking to obtain and enhance the vibrational properties of the original substance). So a 6x would be succussed 6 times, and the substance diluted 10 times at each succussion. The C denotes the centisimal scale which means each remedy has been diluted 100 times at each succussion.

Lower potencies are best for physical symptoms, and emotional or deeper more chronic issues are best treated with the higher potencies, at 30c or above.

The 6x or 6c and 30c are probably the most versatile potency to have. In fact the 30c can be used successfully for most physical, emotional and mental characteristics and most home remedy kits contain the 30c potency, and this is my go-to potency.

There is also a 'plussing method' which is generally only prescribed by a qualified homeopath. This involves beginning with a fairly low potency, dissolving the remedy into water, and shaking and sipping it regularly (often daily). This is sometimes referred to as 'shake and sip' method. The effect is that the potency increases by 1 succussion at every dose. This is often prescribed for chronic and serious conditions, and constitutional remedies, and taken for a longer period of time with regular check-ups.

Taking Remedies

Apart from the Plussing Method as mentioned, lower potencies are generally taken hourly until a change or improvement in symptoms then stopped. Higher potencies are taken once. They can be repeated daily or morning and night for up to 3 days. A qualified homeopath may prescribe differently, but for self-prescribing, no more than 3 doses is suggested, and only if needed. The remedies will work like a key in a car ignition. Once they have triggered a response you must not take any more and let the body's healing process take over, just like you do not keep turning the key once the engine has started. This may be after only 1 dose!

Remedies must be taken on a clean mouth. That is, no food or drink 20 minutes before or after, and strong flavours such as coffee or toothpaste must not be within an hour either side of taking a remedy. This is because foods and drink will interfere with the vibrational effect of the remedy.

Remedies must not be handled as the actual vibrational properties are on the outside of the pill. They must be tipped into the lid of the container or a clean spoon and tipped directly under your tongue as it is the closest and most direct route into your bloodstream. Then left there to dissolve.

Remedies come in sugar pills, lactose pills, tablets, liquid, and more. I find the best to use are sugar pills or lactose pills as they dissolve most quickly and easily.

Some Suggested Essential Remedies

Because there are so many different aspects to consider in remedy selection, it is difficult to give a list of general remedies. However the following appear to have marked effects on the symptoms listed.

Aconite – shock, fright, if taken within 12 hours of an illness presenting itself the illness will not usually progress

Arnica – any injury, bruising or bleeding

Silica – removal of foreign bodies such as splinters (take care as it can also remove piercings and pacemakers * see below)

Mag Phos – any pain especially if it is right sided

Gelsemium – great for traditional flu symptoms

Hypericum – nerve pain, or trapped nerves, or any crushing injury like trapped fingers

Apis Mel – insect stings & bites, or similar symptoms

Belladonna – illnesses or conditions presenting hot, red, flushed, violent symptoms

Cantharis – cystitis, burning itching symptoms

Chamomila – teething, calming, bedtime for babies, colic

Nux Vom – hangovers, overindulgence of rich foods, tobacco, alcohol, drugs etc.

Rhus Tox – muscular problems, better for movement

Bryonia – muscular problems, better for keeping still, coughs

Merc Sol – nerve pain in the tooth, radiating to face, ears, etc.

* I have personal experience of this. I gave my daughter some silica to help to remove a glass splinter from her foot. A week later her recent belly-button piercing was literally pushed completely out of her body! The tissue in front of the body bar became thinner and thinner over the course of the week until it just fell out. It literally grew out as if the body had naturally rejected it, as it left behind no open wound! (I will add that this was much to her chagrin as she had saved up for this piercing and we had not long agreed for her to have it done!!)

See Chapter 59 for instructions on how to make your own allergy remedy!

CHAPTER 46...Bach Flower Remedies

Flower remedies or essences were created by Dr Edward Bach. They work by addressing emotional imbalances. Dr Bach understood ahead of his time how emotional states affect physical conditions and he came to realise that our emotions can be affected by various plants and trees. He further discovered that many flowers and plants offered a nemesis to our emotional states, and could therefore balance these emotions.

There are 38 different flower remedies which can be blended together or used singly. Individual blends are usually made up by choosing remedies that are associated with the current emotions and unbalanced (or unhealthy) character traits of the individual.

The Bach Flower Remedies are generally preserved in alcohol but as they are only used in such small quantity, they are considered 100% safe and natural and work in conjunction with herbs, homeopathy and medications. They are safe for everyone, including children, pregnant women, pets, the elderly and even plants.

There are some ready-mixed blends available in health shops such as the Rescue and Recovery remedies for times of stress and shock, but the most effective is a blend created especially for the individual.

The Remedies

Dr Bach arranged his flower remedy system into seven emotional groupings.

FEAR

Rock Rose – emergency, panic, alarm, pain

Mimulus – fear of unfamiliar things, nervous, shy, timid

Cherry Plum – fear of being violent or losing control

Aspen – anxiety, apprehension, fear of unknown origin

Red Chestnut – over-caring & worrying for others

UNCERTAINTY

Cerato – indecision, easily led, doubting own judgement, looking for others opinions

Scleranthus – indecision, quiet, keep themselves to themselves, fluctuating moods

Gentian – easily discouraged, self-doubt, feeling dejected

Gorse – hopeless, apathetic, utter despair

Hornbeam – tiredness, weary, mental & physical fatigue, Monday morning feeling

Wild Oat – unfulfilled, no direction, indecisive

LONELINESS

Water Violet – reserved, withdrawn, independent, like to be left to themselves, aloof

Impatiens – impatient, tense, irritated, needs everything done in a hurry, will not tolerate others' slowness

Heather – needs company, talkative, self-interested, talk to anyone about problems

LACK OF INTEREST IN THE PRESENT

Clematis – dreamy, out of it, absent, in their own world, want to escape

Wild Rose – apathetic, resigned, drifting along, no effort to improve

White Chestnut – spiralling thoughts, cannot be free from unwanted thought

Chestnut Bud – failing to learn from experience

Honeysuckle – living in the past

Olive – exhausted, burnt out, drained of energy, everything an effort

Mustard – moodiness, gloom, all-of-a-sudden depression for no obvious reason

OVER SENSITIVE

Agrimony – inner torment, hidden worry, remain cheery despite enduring considerable torture, may drink too much

Walnut – sensitive to change, bound to the past/family tradition, need help coming to terms with life changes

Centaury – weak, kind, over-obliging, difficulty saying no, let people walk over them

Holly – revenge, hate, jealousy, suspicion, anger

DESPAIR

Larch – expects failure, lacking confidence

Pine – blames themselves for everything, guilt

Elm – overwhelmed by responsibility, feeling inadequate

Sweet Chestnut – welcomes death, anguish, as if limits of endurance have been passed and only oblivion left

Star of Bethlehem – grief, fright, shock of serious news, fright after accident, bereavement

Willow – resentment, anger, feeling sorry for themselves

Oak – persevering, over-achieving, struggle bravely in the face of adversity, angry if illness interferes with duties

Crab Apple – self-disgust, ashamed, unclean feeling

OVER CARE OF OTHERS

Chicory – manipulative, clingy, want others to conform to their standards, make martyrs of themselves, feign or exaggerate illness

Vervain – fanatical, stressed, perfectionist, never change views, want to convert others, incensed by seeming injustice

Vine – dictatorial, arrogant, ruthless, tyrannical

Beech – criticism, intolerance, arrogance

Rock Water – self-denial, too hard on themselves, overwork, deny themselves break/lunch

The Seven Helpers

These remedies allow as to see our ways and free us from old conditioning and habits:

Gorse, Heather, Oak, Olive, Rock Water, Vine & Wild Oat

The Twelve Healers

For assisting and integrating our personality:

Agrimony, Cerato, Centaury, Chicory, Clematis, Gentian, Impatiens, Mimulus, Rock Rose, Scleranthus, Vervain & Water Violet

The other 19 remedies are for everyday emotional stresses.

Taking Remedies

To take remedies you may have 2 drops neat as a one-off dose.

You can mix 2 drops in 30ml spring water and place 4 drops onto the tongue 4 times daily until improvement.

You may use up to 6 remedies in one go and make them into a blend.

CHAPTER 47...MMS:
Master Mineral Solution

I have decided to explain about MMS as it is extremely controversial, with many misconceptions and misunderstandings. So I wanted to say it as it is, as I believe it to be. I am probably in a good position to provide a balanced view of the truth of MMS after studying the Health Minister home study course and having experience of it myself. There are dozens of other remedies that are just as effective for a variety of conditions, some of which work in a similar way, but in comparison to MMS you will find a lot of positive information about these methods and they do not appear to have the same negative fear-mongering propaganda surrounding them as MMS does.

What is MMS?

MMS is Sodium Chlorite, which when activated (using a suitable acid) forms Chlorine Dioxide gas, a natural compound found in the body containing atoms of chlorine and oxygen. It is the chlorine dioxide gas that is useful to us in killing all kinds of pathogens and micro parasites, and restoring damaged cells, encouraging heavy metal detox and bringing balance back into the entire body system. It is the oxygen from the gas that is utilised in these processes, and when the Chlorine Dioxide gas releases the pure oxygen from it's structure, the only component that is left is a few granules of sodium chloride, which is such a tiny quantity there is no negative impact on the body and it is just eliminated from the body in the natural way. Chlorine Dioxide gas can be condensed into distilled water and this is called CDS (or Chlorine Dioxide Solution) which has recently been found to be more effective for most conditions and less problematic (i.e. better tasting, easier to take and less nausea effects) than using MMS in its activated state.

Chlorine Dioxide has a very low oxidation potential. It is enough to attack the cell walls of pathogens whilst leaving the body's cells unharmed due to the fact that the pathogen's cell walls are considerably thinner than the body's cell walls. In fact the body's cell walls are much too thick for the MMS to even come close to harming. This makes MMS extremely safe to use when used as directed. Long standing pathogens may have built up a resistant layer around them called a biofilm, making them extremely resistant to both general alternative and conventional methods of attack. However MMS has been found to be successful in breaking through the biofilm, although a different protocol and longer treatment time may be required. Due to the extremely low oxidation potential of MMS, it would be my preference over other types of oxygen based therapy such as ozone and hydrogen peroxide. These therapies may yield results, but as they have a much higher oxidation potential they also have a much higher risk of damaging the body's cell walls during their oxidation process. Chlorine Dioxide is one of the few substances to kill viruses and it does this by preventing the proteins that generally develop around the virus from forming and this ultimately kills it.

With my new understanding, I believe Oxygen Therapy is beneficial to the healing phase of a biological programme, as it provides the cells with oxygen to assist them to work in their optimum state. It is also very effective against parasitic infections which can rob the body of energy. However, if you are in the first phase of healing where there are beneficial microbes present, you would not be wanting to use it to kill the microbes as this would disrupt the healing process. However, it could be used wisely to slow the healing in an intensive programme. So as with everything, we need to support the process our body is going through.

Jim Humble & the MMS Controversy

Chlorine Dioxide gas has been used widely since 1947, but it was first discovered for use in the body by Jim Humble, who firstly named it "Miracle Mineral Supplement" due to his increasing discoveries that it appeared to cure so many ills. He later changed this name to "Master Mineral Solution" to fall more in line with FDA legislation. Before releasing it to the wider public in 2006, Jim claims to have treated over 75,000 willing people over 5 years in non-US countries to understand its best usage and its efficacy. He has received both adoration and attack, the latter being mainly from mainstream conventional sources, or those in the alternative field who have taken notice of the fear-mongering.

What Jim did that frustrated the pharmaceutical industries and conventional medicine so much is he took a very open and unselfish approach to getting MMS out to people. He released instructions and protocols freely giving detailed information of everything he has done and discovered, rather than trying to patent and sell it. He has also made a legal testimony that upon his death the MMS product, information and all his work will become public property and will be exempt from patent and copyright. This means that no person, or more importantly corporation, could patent the formula and research as it is public domain. It is so unbelievably inexpensive that it would not generate any profit for them in any case, and as MMS actually provides a cure for most diseases (according to testimonies), this is also contra-indicatory to their mission of creating long term customers reliant on their drugs and preparations. If their products actually cured people they would lose regular dependent customers and could eventually go out of business! Even though MMS would be of no interest to them to sell, protecting it in this way has prevented the pharmaceuticals from exploiting it, or the potential of patenting it just to stop others making it and obtaining it.

As the attack on Jim, MMS and extending to those who had become involved in MMS became more progressive, Jim had to take action. In his continued attempt to protect MMS and it's use he set up the Genesis II Church of Health & Healing, himself being Archbishop. He has since trained Health Ministers all over the world and there are 'churches' now in many different countries. Becoming a member of this non-religious church states that using MMS, obtaining high potency supplements, herbs and anything deemed necessary for maintaining one's own health becomes a part of your religious right. It also states that mainstream procedures such as vaccines and x-rays etc. are 'against' the member's religion. More information and I.D. Cards stipulating these 'religious' rights can be found at www.genesis2church.is.

The Misleading Facts of MMS

Because of the name (chlorine) it is mistakenly labelled as an industrial bleach. This is further confirmed to sceptics by the smell and the fact that it is approved for food use in the cleaning of fresh food produce. Many mainstream sceptics have jumped onto these 'facts' creating many myths and fallacies to scare people away from benefiting from MMS's amazing potential. No matter what sceptics say, you cannot ignore the thousands of testimonials claiming the successful use of MMS in treating all manner of complaints, including advanced life-threatening conditions. However these results are not considered by mainstream due to the lack of expensive and extensive pharmaceutical testing, and those controlled by the pharmaceutical companies who's fear campaigns are threatened by MMS's existence continue to spread their fear campaign. Unfortunately the mainstream have done such a great job of poisoning the well of MMS it appears to have spread into the arena of alternative health as well.

Making MMS

You can purchase MMS ready made but it can be expensive which is probably due to the risks involved in selling it. If you are a little savvy you can make your own. The substance needed to make MMS is extremely cheap (about 1Kg is about £15-£20 making enough MMS for thousands of doses). There is public information available including everything you need to know, all protocols for its use in different circumstances and many testimonials on Jim's many websites such as mmsnews.is, genesis2church,is, jimhumble.is, and many more (they all link with each other).

Safety

It is extremely important to follow the protocols as instructed by Jim Humble. MMS is very potent and must be used with caution. However I will add that there have been absolutely no deaths from the correct use of MMS, and neither have there been any conditions caused by the use of MMS according to Jim Humble and all the research available. Overuse of MMS has simply caused a vomiting or diarrhoea reaction in order for the body to rid itself of the MMS. There are a couple of claims of deaths linked to the misuse of MMS but this has not been officially proven to have been the actual cause of death. In comparison, hundreds of thousands of deaths worldwide each year are linked directly to prescribed pharmaceuticals.

MMS is taken at the relevant protocol until nausea (or sometimes diarrhoea) occurs, then the dosage is reduced back to the next step. This ascertains the optimum dosage required by the body and the disease. It is possible in treatment of chronic or aggressive disease that the body will have quite severe reactions due to the MMS working on the disease or pathogens and this is called Herxheimer Reaction. But it is important that the treatment is not stopped, even if reduced to the smallest possible dosage. As previously mentioned, long standing conditions will generally require longer treatment and possibly a more potent protocol.

My Experience with MMS

As I mentioned, I have personally completed Jim Humble's home study Health Minister course. I have taken MMS for various ailments, however I was greatly put off by the taste. I have also taken capsules and found these much better (except when they burst on the way down – urgh!). I have also used MMS for cleaning my teeth and treating dental problems. I regularly bathed my dog by adding CDS to bath water which helped her chronic skin condition above all other products I have tried, and also successfully treated her when she had temporal lobe disease. She fully recovered after the vet had warned us that she may not pull through and if she did there was likely to be permanent damage.

In my opinion there are other more user-friendly products available that offer similar potential to that of MMS. However, I find CDS just as easy to take as any other product. A full day's dosage in ready-to-drink solution can be made up in the morning and taken regularly throughout the day. As an extremely inexpensive and effective treatment I have no hesitation in using it for myself and my family, providing it is practical at the time to keep up with the hourly dosage required.

SECTION VI.....Common Conditions & Diseases

CHAPTERS:

These chapters have now all been re-written from my new perspective, while acknowledging the additional steps we can take to ascertain that we are in an optimum state of health to support our healing from the conflicts that are causing these symptoms.

CHAPTER 48...A GNM Perspective on Disease Prevention & Assisting Healing

Causes of 'Disease'

Understanding the meaningful biological programmes of diseases, we can see that a poor diet, toxins, smoking, and so on cannot in themselves cause disease, but that is not to say that they can't damage our organs. Malnutrition causing deficiencies, toxicities and injuries can all cause symptoms in absence of a conflict shock.

So what can we do to prevent disease?

We will experience conflicts which will lead to 'disease', so we cannot really prevent them. But we can help ourselves in the following ways:

- Eat healthily and ensuring we are in balance without deficiencies, toxicities, etc., so our body is able to optimally heal.

- Keep a positive mindset and see the positive in situations to minimise the effect of a conflict shock

- Recognise when you have had a conflict shock so you can work quickly to resolve the conflict. As the healing phase is directly proportional in length and intensity to the length and intensity of the conflict-active phase, this really is true prevention of a

251

more serious condition.

- Reduce every day stress so as not to hinder the healing of any minor conflicts we may be healing from, and to be emotionally stronger for when a conflict may occur

- Heal past emotions when they present themselves to bring emotional strength (it is not advised to dig up old trauma unless these present themselves to be resolved and are prohibiting a happy life, as you may trigger new conflicts)

Assisting Healing

Conventionally, we want to stop our symptoms and move away from them. True healing exists when we embrace our symptoms as the healing they are, feeling relief that our conflict has been resolved. Moving through our symptoms, and therefore through the healing, and understanding what to expect removes any fear or concern over what is happening. Working with our symptoms to allow healing to progress is paramount. Stiffness and pain cause immobility, and is our body's way of saying "don't move in that particular fashion as I need to heal this area", fatigue is our body's way of saying "rest as I need to use the energy to heal", and so on. We can learn to listen to what our symptoms are telling us and prevent self-devaluation by having positive thoughts and attitude. This is essential as negative thinking can trigger new conflicts such as self-devaluation or existence conflicts, and exacerbate the situation.

Supporting our health with a well-balanced, healthful diet will facilitate our ability to heal efficiently and effectively. Purposefully selected foods, supplements, herbs and remedies that work in harmony with the phase we are experiencing will also support the healing process. An excellent way of assessing what the body needs is through an energetic testing method such as kinesiology muscle testing (as explained in

Chapter 68), or simply knowing the properties of different substances, and avoiding the stimulants throughout the healing phase so as not to disrupt the vagatonic state.

Most important is a true understanding of the conflict and learning from the experience so we do not suffer a similar conflict in the future. Understanding the reasons for our symptoms is paramount to facilitate the healing process.

There is a lot more detailed information on assisting healing in the Candida & Parasites Chapter 58.

Tracks

Recurrences, allergies and chronic conditions are generally caused by a 'track' which is a subconscious link to the original conflict which triggers the biological programme to run again, even if the original substance or is not involved. This is explained in a lot more detail in the Eczema, Asthma and Allergies chapters.

Conditions involving the Temporal Lobe

Some of the conditions in this chapter are controlled in the temporal lobe area of the brain. This is a very complex brain layer and the conflicts that it controls are dependant on gender, laterality (left/right handed), and hormone status. Further complications to determining the conflicts that can occur for an individual are also affected by whether there is, or are, already active conflicts in one or both hemispheres. I have briefly explained this as best I can in the relevant sections without it getting too confusing. However, if any of these conditions are relevant to you, I would recommend watching the tutorial videos and researching on the learninggnm.com website to understand GNM further. You can then use the A-Z index and search function to research into your issues with a deeper understanding.

Cures?

With a true understanding of GNM, we also understand that we cannot 'cure' disease, as all disease originates at the psyche level from a conflict shock or trauma, and because we understand that diseases are meaningful biological programmes.

Also as I've already mentioned in this book, the research that has been done on apparent 'cures' is carried out in laboratories, mainly bringing the cells outside of the body and out of the psyche-brain-organ connection which is detailed in Dr Hamer's First Biological Law. There is no guarantee that these cells will act the same way out of the body and without the connection with the brain and psyche, so anything that presents as a cure is based upon assumption / hypothesis and not necessarily proven as is often claimed.

CHAPTER 49...Flu

Every Autumn we are told over and over again by the media that it is flu season. But does it make you wonder why flu is such a big deal this last few years? Is this just sales propaganda by the pharmaceutical companies and medical profession to induce fear and promote the extremely profitable flu vaccine? Maybe I need to let you decide on that for yourself!

The biggest issue regarding flu is the vaccine, so I will focus on that in the first instance. Please see Chapter 33 for a list of effects and facts of vaccines, and further information in Chapter 34, but here is some information regarding the flu vaccine in particular. Make an informed decision – it is your body and you have a right to!!

1. The risks of the flu vaccine can be greatly multiplied if given to someone who is unwell or has a medical condition (that may not even be known at the time). Bear in mind too, that those with a higher risk of complications from flu will also be more at risk from complications from the flu vaccine (that is common sense when you think of it!)

2. Flu Vaccines contain toxic ingredients: Flu vaccines in particular contain Mercury (Thimerosal). Mercury is one of the most toxic substances known to man. According to the World Health Organisation there is no safe level for mercury in the body.

Human or animal cells are used to grow the live virus on. Flu vaccines generally use chicken eggs which will cause reactions to those who are allergic to eggs. Also vaccines contain aluminium which is extremely toxic to our body.

3. Vaccines are a very profitable business: Pharmaceutical corporations make a lot of money from vaccine programmes, this is a multi-billion dollar industry for them, and a big earner for our GPs.   In April 2012, the Daily Mail ran an article stating:

> *"Doctors get £7.73 per vaccination for the seasonal flu jab. If the same price is agreed for swine flu, this could add up to a payment of more than £10,000 for a GP with an average practice list."*

In addition GPs are demanding further funding for better premises and more staff to cope with the 'increased uptake' that they are cajoling into the vaccines! So it sadly appears that doctors have become mere sales reps for the pharmaceutical companies, and I believe this is the REAL reason they tend to bully us into having them without informing us of the negative effects.

4. Flu Vaccines actually WEAKEN our body's support system and healing abilities as they interfere with our natural healing process. It is claimed by the NHS that the flu virus is constantly mutating, so how can a vaccine produced months, or even years ago in a lab still be viable today? In addition, the flu vaccine contains around 3 strains of flu, yet there are hundreds if not thousands of strains of flu.

The GNM Perspective

Dr Hamer found no scientific evidence ever showing that viruses even exist, and as such this leaves a huge question surrounding viruses such as the Flu. Here is how a 'flu' may play out:

The symptoms of flu are caused by a Stink conflict (if there is a head cold) and a 'Territorial Fear' Conflict affecting the bronchial mucosa and/or a 'Scare-fright' Conflict affecting the laryngeal mucosa. These are controlled from the temporal lobe.

Conflicts can occur when we constantly hear that it is 'flu season' along with a fear of the 'flu virus' invading your territory (body or home – causing a territorial fear conflict), the scare of hearing someone has 'caught' the flu near to you (causing a scare-fright conflict), and not wanting to breathe in the 'germs' (causing a smell or stink conflict).

A combination of any or all of these conflicts will cause a healing phase that is full of the symptoms we commonly associate with flu – first the stink conflict which affects the sinuses resolves, giving a head cold and fever, still conflict active with the territorial fear (affecting the bronchi) and/or scare-fright (affecting the throat) we will get hot and cold spells as we go between conflict active in one conflict, to healing in the other. Then the shivers subside as the other conflict/s resolve and we are full into healing with fever, fatigue, muscle aches, and the sore throat (if scare-fright conflict) and cough (territorial fear conflict) will begin. The fever 'breaks' at the Epi crisis and we begin to recover, left with a nasty cough to bring up the metabolic waste produced during healing.

Reducing Susceptibility and Supporting the Healing

Just understanding that we cannot catch a 'virus' which may not even exist is all we really need to reduce our susceptibility to experiencing conflict shock/s leading to flu symptoms. Should we succumb to it (as the understanding has to be on a subconscious level which is what triggers the biological programme to run), then we can support our healing to ensure the healing phase is over as efficiently as possible. The following advice will not only support our health in general during the season associated with flu, but also support the healing phase:

1. Take a good quality high potency Vitamin D3: 5,000iu per day – this will ensure you are not deficient due to the lack of sunlight experienced during the winter season.

2. Take a natural anti-microbial preparation such as colloidal or ionic silver if you are in the healing phase with intense symptoms. Just a small amount (as recommended on the instructions).

3. Take a high quality bio-available Vitamin C supplement at 1,000mg-3,000mg per day at equal intervals. Do not take extreme high doses we this has a stimulating effect and can inhibit the healing vagatonic phase.

4. Eat plenty of oily fish, or take a good Omega 3 supplement such as Krill Oil.

5. Eat plenty of fresh, organic vegetables and foods and eat right for your metabolic type.

6. **If you are in a healing phase,** you can support the process by avoiding stress, resting as much as possible, keeping yourself hydrated and nourished as much as possible and allowing the healing to complete with the least intervention and without fear, and with the reassurance that your body is healing and not malfunctioning, and knows what it is doing.

CHAPTER 50...
Real Cancer Awareness

It breaks my heart to see so many lovely, honest people thinking they are really doing good by supporting cancer research charities, but little do they realise the truth of just what they are promoting.

I just wanted to let you know what I have found out through my extensive research into cancer and why I will never give to a cancer charity again. This all came as such a shock to us as we had been giving to cancer charities in the past and thought we were doing good by it. I generally feel like I have to hold back from telling people about this as I do not want to upset anyone, but the truth must come out.

I already know of many natural substances that are supportive to the healing phase of a biological programme that may be diagnosed as cancer – however due to restrictions imposed by the pharmaceutical industry I am unable to promote these!

The cancer industry is created and controlled by pharmaceutical industries who refuse to acknowledge or publicise studies of potential natural cures which they cannot patent and profit from. If they cared about finding a 'cure for cancer' they would not lobby to arrest and imprison people who are actually using natural methods. There have even been stories in the media of parents being accused of child abuse as they are not willing for their child to undergo the harsh conventional procedures, or have chosen a natural supportive route!

Many research charities are owned by pharmaceutical corporations who use the campaigns as huge money generating machines, most of it used to subject unnecessary torture to innocent animals in their testing procedures. One such charity came to our door previously and Lloyd asked if they were looking at 'natural cures' yet (this was before we learnt about GNM - now our questioning would follow a different line altogether!). They said natural cures are not scientifically proven so all their money was going to stem cell research which is 'showing some promise' (yet this was scientifically unproven at the time too!). But why dismiss something that is producing results, when they could be proving it scientifically? As it happens, the stem cell research is showing how chemotherapy doesn't kill the stem cells, surgery rarely removes them and radiotherapy actually enhances them! Along with not understanding that cancer originates in the psyche and therefore requires healing at the psyche level, this is why it nearly always 'comes back' more aggressive.

The same corporations that sell cancer 'cures' (which as we see are actually poisoning us) are ultimately owned by or partnered with the same corporations that patent and sell the extremely harmful food additives, drugs, vaccines and cosmetics that reduce our energy and ability to heal from biological programmes. (Mmm...do I sense a pattern?)

These corrupt corporations have even made it illegal for anyone to state that a particular product can assist the healing and help cancer patients! If they really cared they would want people to have all the information they need to empower themselves and try any way they wanted to heal themselves, rather than have all the control, and withhold or restrict information. This is due to the Cancer Act of 1939. This act has (in effect) 'copyrighted' the 'treatment for cancer' which cannot be made as

260

a claim against any product or service that is not pharmaceutically approved.

Another instance that causes me to question their intentions is when I was asked a few years ago to give a Yoga and Meditation demonstration at a Cancer Charity event. My guided meditation script had to be 'approved' beforehand so I emailed them a copy. The meditation was a heart meditation in which the love and light from your heart is visualised to flow throughout your whole body 'healing and relaxing' as it went. I was told that my services were no longer required and when I asked why I was told that my meditation gave people hope and that

'cancer patients can not be given hope or the idea that they can heal themselves'

That was (pretty much) their exact wording! I was absolutely gob-smacked. This was one of the moments that introduced me to the concept that the cancer 'industry' was not what I had thought it was.

Taboo

The mainstream have made cancer such a taboo subject that by speaking out like this I am deemed to have no compassion and have lots of abuse thrown at me. In addition, cancer campaigns such as "Race for Life" are built around an appeal to emotion - "Who are you racing for?" - so if I dare speak out to someone who has been a victim, or has lost someone close to cancer, I am deemed disrespectful and heartless. The truth is, I have also lost people who are close to me to cancer and have had a my own journey too, so this could be no further from the truth. What I am trying to do is to spread awareness so as this monster can stop being fed and our energies can be put to use in our own education to protect ourselves from the conflict shocks caused by the fear propaganda in the first place and help our bodies to heal themselves naturally.

Breast Cancer Awareness?

In line with this, is it just me, or is Breast Cancer Awareness Month (and all the other 'Awareness' events) a bit of a scam? I mean no disrespect to those who have suffered, as I have too, but what I mean is – what are they actually making us aware of? We all know it exists – it is not like a rare disease that needs to be learned about. So all they are REALLY doing is promoting FEAR! There have been an increasing number of women recently who have had their breasts removed IN CASE they had cancer in the future (probably influenced by Angelina Jolie and the misinformation regarding the BRCA gene)! I know I am sticking my neck out here, but seriously, this fear-mongering has gone FAR ENOUGH!

To me, 'cancer awareness' should be 'health awareness' - educating people on the actual TRUE NATURE OF CANCER AND DISEASE by learning about GNM, so they can prevent themselves from falling victim to fear, and educating people on what they can do to support their healing, be this natural or otherwise (and NOT suppressing those substances that cannot be patented by a corporation to earn profit and power as they are doing now).

BRCA Gene

Despite the hype, having the BRCA gene does not mean you are going to get cancer. The very idea that mutated genes can cause cancer to grow is built upon the mainstream hypothesis that cancer is a malignant disease, or an error of nature. According to GNM, cancer is not caused by genetics. How can a conflict shock be in our genetics? However, the way we perceive different traumas can be influenced by our upbringing, beliefs, cultures, etc which ARE passed on through our generations. This can cause us to experience similar conflict shocks, and therefore, 'diseases', to our family before us. Understanding this is true prevention, not the barbaric actions of removing parts of our bodies.

As I have stated many times in this book, our power is in not seeing cancer as we have been conditioned to, that it is something to fight and something to fear. It is a natural process that requires only our allowing and support to facilitate its healing.

The most empowering aspect for us was understanding the true nature of cancer, most importantly the fact that metastasis is built upon a mere hypothesis that has never been proved. Our bodies are not out to harm us, but are hard-wired for Survival, Procreation and Life.

Dr Hamer, discoverer of German New Medicine, made the following quote which puts this beautifully:

> *"All so-called diseases have a special biological meaning.*
> *While we used to regard Mother Nature as fallible and had*
> *the audacity to believe that She constantly made mistakes*
> *and caused breakdowns (malignant, senseless, degenerative*
> *cancerous growths, etc.) we can now see, as the scales fall*
> *from our eyes, that it was our ignorance and pride that*
> *were and are the only foolishness in our cosmos. Blinded,*
> *we brought upon ourselves this senseless, soulless and*
> *brutal medicine. Full of wonder, we can now understand*
> *for the first time that Nature is orderly and that every*
> *occurrence in Nature is meaningful, even in the framework*
> *of the whole. Nothing in Nature is meaningless, malignant*
> *or diseased."*

CHAPTER 51...
My 'Breast Cancer' Journey

Since I began studying German New Medicine, I realise the actual cause of my breast cancer, how it played out for me and why the way I treated it worked in some ways, and delayed the healing process in others. Below is the original chapter I wrote from the old fear-based perspective that I had at the time. I have reassessed my journey with my new understanding of GNM, and explained the inaccuracies I had previously made in italics, followed by a section explaining my interpretation of the whole journey from the new perspective.

2016 – I have spent my summer coming to terms with a the probability of early breast cancer. It was a huge shock to me, as I lead a pretty healthy and fairly-toxin-free lifestyle. But this proved to me that this had been coming on for some time regardless and there were things I may have been missing. It was so ironic that I discovered this no more than a month after hosting an event I called "Cancer is not a Death Sentence", with a showing of the Highlights from The Truth About Cancer documentary series. Yet I now feel that I was purposefully led to this series, and to study it and put on the event, in order to deal with my 'diagnosis' in a positive and constructive way.

With knowledge of GNM, finding a lump as I did no longer needs to be feared. I highly recommend that you learn German New Medicine before you might experience a scare such as this! Also see the lymph drainage info at the end of this chapter!

I won't lie, I have had moments of being very scared and feeling very alone, including having panic attacks especially at the beginning, as naturally can be expected with our years of considering cancer to be a death sentence. Despite everything I know and have learned, it is still a big thing when it happens to you! I also had lots of fear to the extent of a few panic attacks of how I was going to tell my children, my parents and family, and how I was going to convince them that not going to the GP, or for conventional treatment was right for me without them being scared!

This is why it is important to share the knowledge with your family and friends so anyone in your 'pack' who experiences a shock such as this can have the necessary support. A practitioner with a thorough knowledge of GNM will help you to understand the process so that you are no longer scared.

It all began when I found a rather large lump in my breast while spending a few days away on a break. Looking back, I realise I'd had an inkling, as when I studied the 'Cancer' documentary series, every time someone would mention Breast Cancer I would have butterflies in my tummy and something was telling me to listen.

Had I known GNM at the time, I would immediately have thought "Oh, I have experienced some sort of Nest-worry or Separation conflict related to my mother/child or being a Mum (as I am right-handed). I wonder what that could be?" instead of "OMG look at that huge lump I have CANCER!" – I would have realised my conflict early, understood the process my body was now going to go through and allowed the healing to take place, supporting it in any way I could.

I had decided to start some preventative measures such as taking Essiac Tea, turmeric and making sure my magnesium and iodine levels were good. So, upon discovering the lump, I did not need a diagnosis, I just knew. But in order to confirm, I knew I needed to check it out. I decided on thermography and managed to get an appointment within 2 weeks, which confirmed that I most likely had early stages of breast cancer with tumours (possibly encapsulated as they weren't showing activity in themselves, but in surrounding tissues there was activity) in both breasts, and evidence of angiogenesis and blocked lymphs (actually this was a relief as I feared worse – that it was invasive and had entered the lymphs as I had armpit lumps).

While studying GNM, I discovered that the 'theory' of metastasis is based upon assumption. The GNM understanding of what appears to be cancer 'spreading' are actually new tumours caused by new conflict shocks, often from the shock of diagnosis. Had I understood this I would not have been scared, or at least not half as scared!

Now, had I gone for a mammogram, I would have:

1. risked the encapsulated tumour bursting under the pressure of the apparatus causing metastasis (spreading),

2. risked carcinogenic radiation which can make the tumours active and aggressive, and

3. would only have been told I had lumps and not seen the angiogenesis (extra blood supply) confirming that it was most likely early stages cancer, or the blocked lymphs that could well be the primary cause.

From a GNM perspective, encapsulated tumours are the result of a lack of fungi and bacteria to break down and dispose of a tumour during the healing phase because, for example, of an overuse of antibiotics. One of

266

the reasons of the apparent increase in cancer rates is due to old encapsulated tumours being discovered and treated as if they were current cancer – with the potential of causing more conflicts, and therefore new cancers, in addition to unnecessary treatment!

So I found myself on a natural path to healing myself!

My healing path changed week by week as I used kinesiology muscle testing to see what I needed that week. My protocol basically consisted of a Ketogenic Diet, Essiac Tea, Apricot Kernels (vitamin B17), Krill Oil, Magnesium Chloride Baths, Spreading my breasts with Nascent Iodine every day, Curcumin Extract, using Organic Turmeric in cooking, increasing vegetable intake, increasing fluid intake especially green and matcha tea, regular lymph drainage self massage, EFT (Emotional Freedom Technique), Meditation, Reflexology, and Yoga. But the biggest thing is to remain hopeful and positive. I had more energy and am feeling healthier than I have done in a long time. In fact I completed a Nutrition course specialising in Cancer Prevention and Longevity during this time which is based upon the new sciences of epigenetics and nutrigenomics. It was very interesting.

With knowledge of GNM, we understand that we need to be careful with taking supplements, medications and remedies as many are contra-indicative to the healing phase. By using kinesiology muscle testing to select supportive supplements, remedies and actions, which included working through my emotions, I ensured that my choices were in harmony with the process that my body was going through at the time. It is important to note that according to GNM, healing can only be completed when healing is completed on the emotional level.

4 mutations = cancerous cells – One of the most interesting experiences recently is that I had embarked upon a herbal detox after discovering from a Hair Mineral Analysis that I was toxic in Copper and Lead. So we had the council test the tap water (fed from a spring) at my old house and found it did, in fact, have toxic levels of copper and lead. After having completed the detox, I returned to my kinesiologist as I had by that time received the cancer 'diagnosis'. He decided to put me onto his Asyra bio-energy testing machine which picked up a toxicity – but this time in Aluminium. This didn't appear on the hair test, which means it was not what I call an 'active' acute toxicity (which is something that has been taken in recently and is flowing through the body like the copper and lead was). Furthermore, the remedy the bio-energetic results showed for this was not herbs (as these are effective on acute toxicity/conditions), but homeopathic, which work on deep down, hidden or dormant past issues. Having not worn aluminium containing deodorants or used aluminium cookware, etc. for at least 10 years, this toxicity that was now being released must have been from the copious amounts of deodorant I used from my teenage years up to early 30s! Looking back at my thermography imaging, the blocked lymphs were concentrated around the armpits and into the breasts. So it goes to show just how long this underlying condition has been going on, and that things we do can have a huge impact on us in the longer term!

Another discovery is due to becoming extremely sensitive to radiation/EMFs since my 'diagnosis'. One morning I was reading emails on my phone and my breasts became red hot. As I looked, the base of my phone was resting across the 2 areas where the tumours are! I am studying epigenetics on my new course, and it stated that the DNA or protein in cells require 4 mutations in order for the cell to become cancerous. So I have 2 – radiation and aluminium toxicity – and if the copper and lead had anything to do with it, that's 4, plus the lymph blockage, that's 5 issues that could each have caused a mutation!

From a GNM perspective, while toxic substances and radiation cannot in themselves cause cancer, heavy metal toxins can poison us and bring the body out of balance and therefore impede the biological programme. Physical blockages of lymphs prevent both toxic substances and the waste created from the breakdown of the tumour from leaving the breasts, which potentially slows down the healing process. Radiation physically damages our cells.

RESULTS – In November, I had my second thermography appointment (3 months apart). I really could not believe my eyes! The tumours were hardly visible and the activity in the lymphs has died right down!

Even without actual labelling of cancer, any breast with lumps are not healthy (cancerous or not), any breasts with abnormal activity like mine, are not healthy. As I have previously mentioned, without thermography I may possibly have gone for a mammogram or biopsy, both of which could easily have caused the cancer to spread. So I really do believe thermography, and of course my lifestyle changes, have saved my life!

As previously explained, the 'spreading' of cancer is a medical theory based upon assumption. However, a new cancer can be caused by a biopsy from a new conflict such as an attack conflict. Aside from the radiation, the real danger of a mammogram, in my opinion, is the discovery of an encapsulated tumour. It is already documented in the mainstream that there is a large number of cases of over-diagnosis and misdiagnosis of cancers using mammograms and other routine screening methods. Since thermography is also based on mainstream fear-based medicine, I can no longer recommend it, or any other method for 'early detection' which is peddled so much recently, as early detection also has the potential to cause unnecessary fear and conflict shocks. Understanding GNM, we see that tumours do not take years to grow as is claimed. However, when viewing thermography results from a GNM perspective, a new layer of understanding is revealed without the fear so it can still be a useful tool. I also realize that my life would not have been in danger from breast cancer itself as the breasts are non-critical organs, and this fear was based upon the belief of metastasis. However, had I chosen to take another route, unnecessary treatment or further conflict shocks that affected other organs could have been potentially life-threatening.

The following is 'part 2' and has been written with the knowledge of GNM. First I will explain the circumstances that are relevant.

September 2016, we had a Trading Standards visit and then a very popular product that we sold on Amazon was pulled from sale with no explanation (we suspected that the Trading Standards officer did this) which caused us much financial loss, and we had to move from our farmhouse.

2017, I was mainly distracted with planning my daughter's wedding which was in July 2017. I had also began practising kinesiology professionally after opening my therapy room in January 2017. I continued to eat a sugar-free and wheat-free diet very strictly, and was enjoying getting a little back to normal (though always with a degree of awareness, which I now realise was actually fear disguised as awareness!). I continued to work through past issues and emotions using EFT and kinesiology techniques and had began to feel more human. The lump had reduced by about a quarter, and was now about the size of a peanut in its shell (whereas before it was like a golf ball, though this was puffy so I realise this was surrounded in inflammation).

In August, we had a raid by Trading Standards, and I was accused of Fraud and contravening the Cancer Act as I had my breast cancer journey article on my therapy website. At the same time, I was targeted by numerous journalists posing as mothers of autistic sons who wanted to use CDS to 'cure' the autism, and subsequently appeared in hit pieces

270

in several mainstream tabloid newspapers. A few weeks later we had a further raid by Trading Standards and the MHRA which was very stressful, however by this time we began questioning their motives and began standing up for ourselves, as scary as that was! This was followed by a report the size of a phone book detailing over 50 products and full product ranges that we had to remove from sale. This would have been the destruction of our family business, so we did not remove most of the items from sale as we realised by now that our rights had been violated and the officer was basically trying to shut us down.

Then, in October, the inflammation came back and had become quite large. I began feeling a lot of anxiety and travelled to an emergency thermography appointment, however they confirmed that there was no further activity around the tumour. I was still classed as a '2' risk (on a scale of 1-5, 5 being worst). So I returned with a big sense of relief.

I buried myself in my work, redesigning labels, removing potential health claims from all the literature and websites, and researching into our rights and building a case against the officer who was later dismissed from her duties due to her victimisation of us (which we received the news of just before Christmas shutdown on 23rd December).

From then, and throughout early 2018, my breasts began getting very sore and painful, and increased in size, the left being more extreme than the right. This happened gradually so it didn't really alarm me at first, though I was getting anxiety attacks. The anxiety was based around "what if this was all wrong and I really had cancer growing", "what if my body is telling me what I want to hear and not the truth" (as I had even used muscle testing to ask if anything was happening in my body that I needed to be concerned about). I was having sweats, particularly at night, and feeling very tired all the time.

I remained buried in my work as my client base was growing. Then in

May I received the beautiful news that my daughter was pregnant, which was a big distraction to the anxiety from the fear of the symptoms I was still experiencing in my breasts and body. I continued with the lymph drainage massage throughout this time, and around June I noticed that the lump could no longer be felt (well, nothing that was not symmetrical to the other breast – symmetry usually indicates normal pathology). In August, I decided to have a thermography check, so I booked in with a different thermography company, expecting to receive excellent news as the lump was gone! I received my report and basically my heart stopped! In 9 months I had gone from a 2 to a 5 in my left breast and from a 2 to a 3 in my right breast!! The anxiety came back with a huge blow and I was thrown into a big black cloud. I could hardly function with worry of heading towards what I considered my imminent death, and I even distanced myself from loved ones so they wouldn't miss me as much when I was gone.

I muscle tested for what I needed to do. I tested for bioidentical progesterone cream, sea cucumber extract (works to stop angiogenesis), iodine, magnesium, a diet high in phytoestrogens, D.I.M. (diindolylmethane) and vitamin D3. I spent my time working, meditating with Joe Dispenza's Changing Beliefs and Perceptions meditation (the only time I didn't feel anxiety was in meditation), listening to Alan Watts, Wayne Dyer etc, and researching into cannabis oil, as I felt this was what I needed. As the supplements I had muscle tested for showed an obvious hormone imbalance, I read that pure THC would likely not be beneficial, and felt guided that I needed a 3:1 ratio of CBD to THC. Not knowing how or where I would obtain this, I simply put the thought of this into one of my meditations.

After a few weeks I went for a small break to Glastonbury where I just happened to be generously gifted some cannabis oil, and to my astonishment this was in the 3:1 ratio that I needed! Had I really manifest this? WOW!

I returned home and my muscle testing revealed that the cannabis oil plus DIM, iodine and magnesium baths was all I needed. I followed this protocol for 2 months and in that time I also had some sound bath sessions and Reiki which really helped the anxiety. I began feeling the anxiety leave my mind and body, I lost 2 stone in weight and felt better and better each day. The symptoms in my breasts had disappeared, and I felt that this had been resolved. During this time, I felt guided to ask a dear friend of mine who had completed her homeopathy training, if she wanted me as a case study, and she agreed. We had an appointment set mid November after my follow-up thermography scan.

In the meantime I had shared my story briefly with followers of my shop newsletter, and had received an anonymous email with some links to articles on German New Medicine. Being in the anxious state I was in, I couldn't focus on much of the information, but read enough to determine the conflict relevant to my breast.

My follow-up scan results showed I was still a 5! I was absolutely devastated at first, but then began to question it. I thought "no, I am feeling great, this is not right!" I refused to go back as asked in 3 months, and booked instead for 6 months as a lot of the anxiety was due to giving all my power over to the scan result, so I didn't want that to be my focus.

I was coming to the end of my cannabis oil supply and couldn't source any more. I had the last dose on the morning of my homeopathy consultation. My friend put me on a homeopathic remedy, which I was to take using a 'plussing' method, meaning the pill is dissolved into water, shaken and sipped every day (increasing the potency each time it is shaken). When I muscle tested on the remedy, I was strong, when I added the cannabis oil I weakened. This told me that my time for cannabis oil was over and I now needed to move to the homeopathy only. On the very day I ran out of oil – the synchronicity bowled me over!

I continued on the homeopathy and after the anxiety had quietened down enough for me to think rationally, I came back to the German New Medicine information I had been sent. I watched the lecture on Five Biological Laws (on LearningGNM.com) and it completely blew me away. I began the process of unlearning everything I thought I knew, and realising all the conflicts that I had experienced in my past!

I returned for a thermography scan in June 2019 – still showing a 5. But I actually questioned this as the lump had gone. I was told that I am only a 5 as this score is always given when there is a +1degC difference in temperature between the nipples, and that it could be my normal pathology so I may never get a lower score. In any case, I know from my GNM studies that it is nothing to worry about anyway! So much for that, then!

The Entire Journey from the GNM Perspective

So, now I can assess the entire journey, based on the GNM principles. This involves information that may not be mentioned in my original account, but I now understand its relevance.

In January 2015 I suffered a Nest Worry Conflict (which I determined by my symptoms) when we sold our family home, and in the process of selling I could not find another suitable home until 2 days before we moved. The process was very rushed and traumatic and I remember the exact moment the conflict shock occurred (and this is important in determining conflicts, as it is not just a period of emotion or stress that causes conflict shocks, it is the actual moment of shock). It was when I realised I really did not want to move, that I was giving up the home our family had grown up in, and I believed it was too late to pull out of the sale. This conflict was resolved when we moved to a beautiful farmhouse/small holding (which was my dream!) in November 2015. I began feeling ill around Christmas-time, firstly with fatigue.

In July 2016 I found the lump in my breast (it was deep in the centre which is why I it went unnoticed for a while). Coupled with the symptoms I was experiencing, this was a clear indication that I was now in the healing phase, though it was hindered by the financial stress and moving house, and the heavy metal toxicities I experienced.

In December 2016 I had a bad candida infection which I thought at the time was brought on by being too extreme on the ketogenic diet (as I researched that candida can adapt to ketosis). I understand now that this candida overgrowth was instrumental in the healing. However not realising this, I took an invasive treatment to get rid of the candida (a chitin inhibitor called Lufenuron). This greatly would have hindered any healing.

Additionally, I was under a lot of stress the entire year – particularly the stress with the Trading Standards victimisation issue, so this would have slowed the healing phase down which relies on vagatonia (non-stress).

The resolution of the Trading Standards issue was just before Christmas. The symptoms that began afterwards indicated that I was progressing through the healing phase.

As I had many other distractions such as working with clients, still trawling through the amendments required of Trading Standards (thought the fear was now removed as the new officer was nice), and in May 2018, the news that we were expecting our first grandchild, my breasts were basically left alone to get on with what they needed to do! (the news of my daughter's pregnancy appeared to trigger temporary anxiety of whether I would be here to see him born – likely this was the 'epi crisis').

This led to the 'disappearance' of the lump around June 2018. The high activity in my thermography scan was the scarring process (the second phase of healing).

So at the time of writing, I have no lump, no symptoms, and no anxiety! I have also not returned for any more thermography scans!

If you Find a Lump in Your Breast

When we find lumps in our breast it is easy to panic, even with a knowledge of GNM. This is because we have had so many years of fear. However, sometimes lumps can be caused by simple blockages that can be unblocked and drained. This simple procedure can help to reduce lumps in the breast that are caused by lymph blockage, and help lymph drainage around tumours. The breasts are energetically linked to the large intestine, and this energetic link is what we are using in this technique. The points we are massaging are the neurolymphatic points of the large intestine.

Step 1 – activating the lymph nodes:

- lightly smooth downwards on the back of the neck on odd number of times (e.g. 5, 7)

- lightly smooth downwards each side of the neck just between the throat and neck muscles, when you get to the bottom release with a 'flick'

- press into the left armpit while moving the left arm back and forth 15 times, repeat on the right

Step 2 – clearing the lymph blockage:

Gently touch the lump in your breast as shown in the image over the page, do not press just lightly touch, and keeping in contact with the lump, use the other hand to massage the neurolymphatic reflex of the large intestine on the SAME SIDE as the lump:

276

- start just below the side of the knee and move upwards to the hip, following where a trouser seam would be
- use small circular movements, with enough pressure to move the skin
- stay on each point for 10 seconds, more if the reflex is painful
- keep moving up a point at a time until the entire reflex has been massaged
- if there are several lumps, repeat the process with each lump

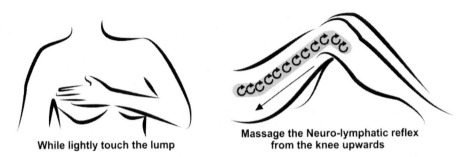

While lightly touch the lump

Massage the Neuro-lymphatic reflex from the knee upwards

You may find that the lump reduces or changes shape or firmness, even after the first time you do this. You may even find the lump completely disappears! Unless it does, this advice does not replace the need for getting lumps in the breast checked out!

Daily Lymph Practice:

After the Using a skin brush (or paint brush), brush the skin around the breast from centre outwards (avoiding breast tissue), first over the top to the armpit, then underneath to the side of the body. And then up the side to the armpit (5 strokes each).

CHAPTER 52...Eczema

Eczema is an itchy skin rash that tends to affect anyone but is most common in children and babies. In chronic cases, the eczema can persist into adulthood. All too often, a GP will prescribe steroid cream and antihistamines to symptomatically treat the rash, while failing to address the actual cause. If the cause is not addressed the eczema can make the sufferer's life a misery.

In my experience with my daughter's eczema which she had for 10 years since she had her baby vaccines (her only vaccines I must add!), I will detail the most probable cause and also detail some of the most effective natural treatments and remedies for easing eczema that I have found that do not interfere with healing.

Causes

From a GNM perspective, eczema is the healing phase of a biological programme triggered by a separation conflict, as with all conditions affecting the epidermis. Separation conflicts can be wanting to separate from something (such as a person, a substance, or something you associate with the area of the rash), or missing something or someone you have separated from or want to touch again. For example, a rash found on the inner elbows can be from wanting to hug someone you cannot hug any more. A rash that is triggered after using a product such

278

as washing up liquid is your body saying it wants to separate from that chemical or product. The rash appears after the conflict has been resolved, and this turns on its head our understanding of the cause. So if you are washing dishes, the rash will not appear while being in contact, as it is conflict active where there are no symptoms. When you wash/dry your hands, removing the product from your skin and therefore resolving the conflict, then the itchiness and rash occurs.

Recurring problems would be caused by a 'track' as explained in the Allergies chapter 59 of this section. It can also be caused by using cortisone cream which has a stimulating effect on the body. When it is applied to the rash in the healing phase, the stimulating effect puts it back into conflict active phase where there are no symptoms and it appears to have cleared up the rash. When the cream is not used, the body moves into healing again and tries to heal. But we stop the healing again, and so on.

From a physical level, and as far as I understand it, there are 3 main causes for eczema:

1. Allergies – this is explained above, as the GNM perspective on allergies is that they are 'tracks'!

2. Deficiency or Imbalance – an imbalance of, toxicity of or deficiency in essential minerals can cause eczema. Also high heavy metal toxin levels.

3. Emotional Stress – this needs careful consideration, especially as it may not be apparent what the cause of the emotional stress is. This, however is likely a track, so number 1 would apply

How to Support Healing

We can break the cycle by allowing the healing to occur, not scratching the rash (i.e. not scratching the wound), and not applying any steroid creams that will create the 'hanging healing'. Then identify the original conflict. If this cannot be fully resolved, then mentally resolve the conflict by changing your perception of it, creating a positive association, etc. Simply understanding GNM and allowing the healing can resolve the condition.

Once the programme has completed, if a relapse occurs, you will need to support the healing again as above, but also identify the track or trigger. The track can be neutralised by creating a positive association with the track, and by changing your perception of the situation.

To identify any tracks/triggers, assess what happened just before the rash appeared, and see if anything relates or reminds you of the original conflict. It could be anything from a person, to a colour, to a feeling, to a substance or food. If you are having no luck, you may want to try a process of elimination starting with the most probable first down to the least probable as follows:

1. Remove all Chemical-based Toiletries

My first advice would be to remove all chemical-based toiletries. The main cosmetic ingredients to watch out for are parabens and SLS. These harmful chemicals are know to cause reactions and aggravate eczema due to the physical stress they can cause. Go natural, use natural brands such as Faith in Nature, make your own with aromatherapy, or research into how the body will self cleanse so you don't need to use products like shampoo!

2. Bed linen and clothes

Next look at products that come into direct contact with the skin. Change from a chemical-based laundry detergent and fabric conditioner to a natural one like Bio-D or Ecover and you could even add some essential oils like chamomile and lavender to the wash.

280

3. Eliminate artificial additives from the diet

This is followed by elimination of artificial additives in foods especially aspartame, other sweeteners and MSG. These have all been linked to skin reactions such as eczema and psoriasis (not to mention the other more severe side effects!)

4. Assess vitamin and mineral deficiencies

Deficiencies in vitamins A, B, C & E, magnesium and zinc can trigger eczema. Ideally a hair mineral analysis could be taken to ascertain this rather than guessing, however taking the metabolic typing test in the first instance may be sufficient especially to correct vitamin deficiency.

Dead Sea Salts, Himalayan Salt or Epsom Salt can help to correct minerals deficiencies. Dead Sea Salt is particularly rich in Magnesium so adding these salts to the bath can correct deficiency and create a lovely soothing effect on the rash.

Also known helpful for eczema is omega oils, so consider trying a supplement or eating plenty of oily fish or other omega 3 rich foods.

5. Consider emotional causes

We've dealt with the conflict shock side, but additional emotional stress (which may not appear so obvious at first) may hinder the healing programme. For example if it is your child, are they getting enough attention/getting bullied/etc. If an adult is there something in your life causing stress such as a job you hate/relationship problems/emotional baggage from the past?

You may wish to seek emotional therapy, but another answer may lie in homeopathy. Homeopathy will assist healing on the physical emotional and spiritual levels. An excellent place for an online remedy prescriber is www.abchomeopathy.com/go.php. It takes a little while but it is very thorough and will prescribe you the remedy you require which you can them purchase from a health shop or online homeopathic pharmacy such as Ainsworths (who also have an advice pharmacy to help you choose the right potency). Of course the ideal would be to visit a qualified homeopath who can assess all your needs first hand, but self prescribing can be a cost-effective alternative to try first.

Natural Treatments

As well as homeopathy, I have found the following remedies to be the most effective at easing the symptoms when there is a flare up without hindering the healing programme:

- Dead Sea Salts or Himalayan Salts (added to the bath, and Himalayan Salt used with food)
- Aromatherapy Skin Calm Cream (plain cream base no parabens etc. with chamomile, lavender and melissa)
- Sodium Bicarbonate (in the bath can be added with above salts)
- Calendula cream can support healing
- Reducing all sugars in the diet and drinks high in sugar such as fruit juice
- Avoiding refined carbohydrates like white rice, white flour, white bread, etc.
- Eating plenty of meat and/or a higher protein diet
- Increasing Omega 3 rich foods or taking an omega 3 supplement

If you have been applying Steroid Cream

Consider taking a glucose test as long term or excessive use of steroid creams has been linked to interference with insulin, and can also worsen the eczema. It is claimed that the cream can cause diabetes, but diabetes is actually triggered by a fear-disgust or resistance conflict. This may be a new conflict, or can be related to the original conflict.

I would recommend that you stop applying steroid cream due to its stimulating effect as mentioned. But you will need to speak with your prescribing doctor before stopping a medication.

How I Eased my Daughter's Eczema

This was before I studied kinesiology and German New Medicine, so it is written from the old perspective and understanding of allergies!

I learned the concept of muscle testing for allergies while doing my Holistic Diagnosis diploma. I used this method to find out if my daughter was 'allergic' to anything. I included all foods and also environmental substances such as dust and dog and cat fur. I found she was allergic to dog and cat fur, and then went on to find she was also reacting to cut grass and sea water. You can learn muscle testing for yourself in our tutorial on The Holistic Show, and further in this section in the Kinesiology Chapter 68!

I then made a homeopathic remedy (like an antidote) out of the offending substances, assessed her dosage and potency by dowsing, and guess what – it worked!!

For further information, go to the Allergies Chapter 59, where are step by step instructions of how I made her remedies for dog and cat fur, cut grass and the seaside!

CHAPTER 53...Asthma

Asthma is a very common chronic inflammatory condition that effects the airways. It is estimated that over 5.4 million people are treated for asthma in the UK and this is rising. There are many different triggers, but according to GNM, only one cause. And yet, thanks to the allopathic approach of one-size-fits-all, the treatment is the same – inhalers, inhalers, inhalers (and maybe a nebuliser if it is particularly bad)!

The holistic approach from the GNM perspective is very different. Find the conflict and resolve it, or if that is not possible provide natural relief.

The symptoms of asthma are wheezing, shortness of breath, sweating, coughing, excess mucous and chest tightness and possibly pain. It can be very restrictive and miserable for sufferers of asthma, but maybe there is light at the end of the tunnel.

Let's look at the usual causes and some possible solutions.

According to GNM, there are 2 types of asthma. Both are triggered by 2 conflicts that are active involving both hemispheres of the brain. These are controlled from the temporal lobe area of the brain, more information can be found in the first chapter of this section, and also in the allergies chapter, for recurring conditions (tracks).

Despite asthma being a complex subject in GNM, I will list the associated conflicts, and you may know from this what situation or trauma triggered your conflicts.

Asthma is caused by a combination of either a Scare-fright or a Territorial Fear conflict, along with a territorial loss conflict or sexual conflict, territorial anger conflict or identity conflict, male territorial marking conflict or female marking conflict, or a territorial fear conflict or scare-fright conflict (i.e. one of both) – all this depending on a person's gender, laterality, and hormone status.

You may know your trauma, even if you are unable to work out the exact conflicts involved. The trauma causing the conflict shocks would have happened before the asthma began, by days, weeks or even months. If you know this, then the conflicts may not need to be worked out.

If you are able to work out the trauma that triggered the conflicts, this in itself may assist in your healing. You need to resolve at least one of the conflicts (i.e. heal emotionally from the trauma) and identify any tracks/triggers which may be causing relapses, as explained in the Eczema and Allergies chapters.

Food 'Allergies'

According to GNM, an allergy would be a track. But we can ascertain the track by looking at what is triggering. It may be that during the process of identifying your conflicts and tracks, that avoiding any offending substance temporarily would be beneficial.

It is recommended to go on an elimination diet. Basically everything that you could be 'allergic' to is cut out for about 2-3 weeks then re-introduce one food at a time per week after that, keeping a food diary and noting any triggers. This may result in a pattern (quite often dairy or eggs) that shows up the trigger.

If that seems too harsh you can also detect food allergies with a rotation diet. This involves not eating the same foods for 4 days. So you have milk on day 1 and you don't have it again until day 5. A food diary must be kept for this too.

If you want to take the easy way out, you could just cut out the most likely cause for about 3-4 weeks to see if there is any improvement, or a trigger on re-introducing the food. The main foods associated with asthma are: dairy, eggs, wheat, soy, fish. However remember to cut out all artificial additives too! This approach is kinder for children.

Environmental Triggers

These could be dust, pollen, mould, or any other airborne particles. A great natural remedy for washing these pollutants out of your body is nasal cleansing as detailed in Chapter 22.

Severe Heartburn

Gastro-oesophageal reflux disease (GORD) is commonly linked with asthma. You may wish to take apple cider vinegar or sodium bicarbonate to assist in regulating your stomach acid.

Medications

Asthma can be a side-effect of many medications so check out any long term medications you may be taking and consider changing them.

Possible Methods for Long Term Symptomatic Relief

For long-term relief I would advice the following:

Have a hair mineral analysis to ascertain whether there are any deficiencies worsening your asthma and to ensure the body is balanced in an optimum state for healing.

Magnesium Supplementation. A common deficiency is magnesium and you may wish to supplement trans-dermally with magnesium in the meantime to see if this helps. More information on magnesium is in Chapter 15.

Use a Salt Pipe. Many customers from my shop have reported excellent results from using a salt pipe, and I know 2 people who do not use inhalers any more! Salt pipes are devices with a spout that contain air-holes and salt. Air is inhaled using normal breath through the spout of the pot. The airflow passes through the salt, picking up salt ions and these exert a cleansing, clearing and healing effect on the lungs.

Nasal cleansing will help the upper respiratory tract to work efficiently and effectively and discourage mouth-breathing which can be a common cause of asthma.

Try some Yogic breathing exercises as described in Chapter 76.

Make sure there are no emotional issues that may be causing physical symptoms. It is surprising what stored emotions can cause! These can worsen conditions such as asthma due to the stress they cause in our body.

Traditional Chinese Medicine teaches that grief is an emotion that weakens the lungs. I have experienced this in action with one of my clients who had extreme chronic asthma and was taking many medications including a daily nebuliser. Through kinesiology, we discovered trapped grief from the death of a close family member in childhood. Upon energetically releasing the emotion with kinesiology techniques, and a few dietary tweaks and magnesium baths, the asthma was quickly relieved and mediation greatly reduced within only one month! Despite my obvious belief in kinesiology, this result continues to blow me away!

CHAPTER 54...
Arthritis & Rheumatism

The difference between arthritis and rheumatism:

According to Medilexicon's medical dictionary:

Rheumatism is:

1. An obsolete term for rheumatic fever.
2. Indefinite term applied to various conditions with pain or other symptoms of articular origin or related to other elements of the musculoskeletal system.

Arthritis is:

Inflammation of a joint or a state characterized by inflammation of the joints.

Rheumatoid Arthritis is:

a generalized disease, occurring more often in women, which primarily affects connective tissue; arthritis is the dominant clinical manifestation, involving many joints, especially those of the hands and feet, accompanied by thickening of articular soft tissue, with extension of synovial tissue over articular cartilages, which become eroded; the

288

course is variable but often is chronic and progressive, leading to deformities and disability.

Cause

From a mainstream angle, it is often stated that the actual cause of this degenerative disease is unknown. However on a non-mainstream angle, many Eastern doctors agree that the accumulation of toxins in the body, especially heavy metal toxins, can cause symptoms. Mineral deficiencies such as magnesium can contribute to calcium depositing in the joints and lactic acid in the muscles causing discomfort.

From the GNM perspective, whether the pain and inflammation are rheumatism, arthritis, fibromyalgia, etc, they are all caused by a self-devaluation conflict.

Usually this would begin with either an injury, or a mental self devaluation where we tell ourselves, or are told, that something is not working right, that it will deteriorate with age, or that we are not supple enough or too old to do something, for example. The area affected is either generalised (whole body) so it affects us as a whole 'I'm getting worse with age', localised as in an injury, or something associated with an activity (e.g. the feet associated with walking, dancing, etc), or it can be involving a person or situation figuratively 'I was not quick enough to do this' etc.

Once the conflict is resolved, we will get the well-known symptoms of inflammation (as the body needs a fluid environment to heal), stiffness (to immobilise the area being healed) and pain (caused by the inflammation). These can cause further self-devaluation, with pain or stiffness being a track. So each time we go to pick something up and it hurts, we internally say 'ouch my stupid back', or 'I can't walk properly on this stupid leg' or 'I can't do my craft any more as my wrist hurts, stupid wrist, I'm getting old'. These negative thoughts will send the message to the brain saying 'this area needs more healing' and guess what we need for healing? More inflammation! So this gets worse. Then we take anti-inflammatories and pain killers so we can go about our day, and these disrupt the healing phase. New triggers of self devaluation keep us in the loop of the programme causing a hanging healing and a chronic condition.

Remedies

To fully heal from a chronic condition, we must identify the conflict, stop devaluing and allow the healing to take place. Be patient and kind to your body and appreciate it for what it does for you!

Additionally, there are many remedies available to help to ease the symptoms of these conditions, without affecting the healing, however we need to understand that our symptoms ARE our healing, so easing them may be slowing the healing process down.

Homeopathy is a great remedy for long lasting results, but it can be very tricky choosing the right remedy!

Cannabis is excellent for promoting the non-stress state required for healing, while taking your mind off the self devaluation and provided welcome pain relief. However, if we are using pain relief, even if it is supportive, we need to remember why our body is in pain in the first place and that is because it needs us to immobilise the area!

More ideas that may help without interfering with healing too much are:

1. Remove the toxins – Many people have found relief from detoxing with products such as zeolite, or in particular diatomaceous earth due to its high silica content. Silica helps the body to produce collagen, the body's connective tissue which can restore and support the joints and synovial fluid between them. Diatomaceous Earth will also address any parasite infection issues, as I have often found to be an issue in clients with arthritis, rheumatism and fibromyalgia. Note that heavy metal detox can produce an aggravation at first (known as Herxheimer reaction) so it may be preferable to build up the dose slowly.

2. Replenish Essential Minerals – Magnesium is excellent at easing symptoms of arthritis/rheumatism/etc. as not only does it greatly support bone and joint health, but these conditions can be a sign of a deficiency in magnesium. The best way to absorb magnesium is through the skin using Magnesium Chloride Flakes, or Dead Sea Salts in the bath. Also by exchanging your regular table and cooking salt with Himalayan Salt you are ensuring that you obtain much needed minerals! Boron deficiency is also a major cause of Arthritis, read more in "The Borax Conspiracy" www.health-science-spirit.com/borax.htm

If you are concerned it is advisable to take a hair mineral analysis test or visit a kinesiologist to take the guess-work out of your supplementation!

Omega 3 oil can also be beneficial for joints so try increasing your omega 3 oil intake or taking a supplement.

3. Diet – Forget the myths and the reports on 'one size for all' diets, by eating right for your own metabolic type you can ensure your body is receiving the correct balance of nutrients. It has been reported that a high protein low carbohydrate diet eases symptoms, and it is true that most of us do not eat enough protein, but this combination would be a disaster for a 'carb' type individual.

4. Exercise – Nothing too strenuous but gentle Yoga stretches will really help you to keep your joints supple, release toxins and relax the surrounding tissues. It is also very supportive of the 'vagatonic' non-stress healing phase.

CHAPTER 55...*Migraine*

Migraine is a chronic disorder of recurrent severe headaches. These headaches are rarely understood and can cause the sufferer misery when they attack.

Causes

Migraines can have links to problems with diet, either a deficiency, mineral toxicity, allergy, intolerance or simply not eating the correct foods or balance for your metabolic type. Another major cause is dehydration from not drinking enough clean water (see Chapter 4 for information on clean drinking water).

From a dietary perspective, poisoning from artificial food additives, especially neurotoxins which affect the brain like MSG, chocolate, nuts, beans, dairy foods, alcohol, caffeine and sugar. Deficiencies in Vitamin B12 (very common with vegetarians), Vitamin B2 and/or Vitamin D have all been known to trigger migraines, and the migraines have stopped once the deficiency was addressed.

Other common triggers are bright, flashing lights, stress, over-exercise, skipping meals causing low blood sugar and medication side effects or sensitivity.

From the GNM perspective, migraines are in the healing phase of a biological programme, and are at their most intense at the Epi Crisis. They are mainly involving conflicts controlled by the premotor-sensory cortex such as female powerless conflicts, male territorial fear conflicts, frontal-fear conflicts, female scare-fright conflicto, otink conflicts, male resistance conflicts or bite conflicts. This is part of the temporal lobe.

If you are able to think back to when the migraines first began, and any trauma or conflict that may have occurred before the first migraine, then you will likely know the possible conflict.

Healing would need to be carried out at the psyche level, and tracks would need to be identified to prevent relapses (more information in the Asthma, Eczema and Allergies chapters).

Other Remedies

Until healing is completed on the psyche level, full healing will not be completed. The correct homeopathic remedy will help and may even assist with permanent relief. The following are also worth considering:

1. Eat right for your metabolic type

2. Make sure you are drinking plenty of clean water – your urine should be very pale to clear.

3. Address mineral deficiencies – take a hair mineral test, and a good quality B12 supplement if you are vegetarian. Also, address the possibility of magnesium deficiency (Chapter 16), and Iodine deficiency (page 84) as these deficiencies are common in migraine.

4. Follow an elimination or rotation diet to find food triggers, as explained in the Asthma chapter.

5. Practice stress management such as mindfulness or meditation,

and consider taking up Yoga.

6. If you are on medications, especially hormonal ones such as the pill or HRT, discuss natural alternatives with your doctor.

7. Visit a kinesiologist who will be able to assess the root cause of your migraines (such as parasites, toxicity or energy imbalance).

8. Visit an osteopath, chiropractor or good massage therapist to check your alignment and release tension from your muscles.

9. Work with a therapist with a good understanding of GNM to help ascertain and resolve your conflicts.

CHAPTER 56...*Diabetes*

Diabetes is a condition whereby glucose cannot be metabolised by the body due to either a lack of insulin production, or 'faulty' insulin production by the pancreas. This causes a high glucose level in the blood, and when this becomes a problem it is called hyperglycaemia. Symptoms of hyperglycaemia are increased thirst, headaches, giddiness, increased urination, stomach pain and feeling sick. As your body cannot get energy from the glucose in the blood, it will break down fat for energy and this is called ketoacidosis. If this happens it will cause the breath to smell sweet, rather like pear drops.

If too much insulin is taken, or if there is an irregular eating pattern, the blood sugar level can drop too low and this is called hypoglycaemia. This can be more dangerous as it comes on more suddenly. The warning signs are dizziness, fatigue, sweating, increased hunger and confusion. This will progress quite quickly into paleness, weakness, increased heartbeat and disturbed vision. If a diabetic person does not recognise these symptoms they could begin convulsing and may lose consciousness. It is essential that they have some juice or sugar before they go into a coma. We tend to feel some of these symptoms even if we are not diabetic when we skip a meal. This is because we are generally reliant on glucose for energy and regular eating keeps our blood sugar from dropping (unless we are on a ketogenic diet).

There are many different types of diabetes the main types are type 1 and type 2, however type 1 is the only true diabetes.

The official explanation of type 1 diabetes is that it occurs when the body's 'immune system' attacks the cells that usually produce insulin. It is generally an inherited condition. Type 1 diabetics generally need to inject insulin to metabolise glucose in their blood.

Type 2 diabetes is also called Adult Onset Diabetes and is officially said to be caused by poor diet, obesity and lack of exercise. So generally correcting these will bring the body back into balance. People diagnosed with type 2 are generally on a plethora of drugs such as statins, beta-blockers, PPI inhibitors, diuretics and often more which were originally prescribed to alleviate the warnings the body was giving us that our lifestyles are not healthy. These drugs escalate the problem, and are possibly the cause in the first place.

From the GNM perspective, diabetes can be explained and proved to not only be caused by a conflict shock, but it is also curable, and therefore given the right careful therapy, the healing can complete.

The conflict that causes diabetes symptoms is a fear-disgust conflict (a scare that involved an element of disgust, such as being attacked by a drunk) or a resistance conflict (being strongly opposed to something you have to do, especially having to put up with a decision made over your head, or as a child having to go to nursery or school). Gender, hormone status and biological handedness will determine the conflict that can be experienced. These conflicts trigger a biological programme in the islet cells of the pancreas, and the cells will experience function loss when the conflict is active.

In the case of the alpha islet cells being affected, glucogen production is reduced causing low blood sugar with symptoms such as dizziness, sugar cravings, fluttering heartbeat and steady weight gain. In the

Healing phase the blood sugar returns to normal, however at epi crisis there will be a quick drop in blood sugar with a potential of hypoglycaemic shock. After this the blood sugar increases, above the usual range, giving the symptoms of diabetes, before returning to normal at the end of the programme. A hanging healing would cause what has been called insulin resistance, or type 2 'adult onset' diabetes.

If the beta islets cells are affected, there will be a reduced production of insulin causing high blood sugar in the conflict active phase. This causes extreme thirst which is the body's attempt to dilute the sugar. Ketoacidosis can be experienced when the liver responds to the lack of insulin by producing ketones for the cells to use as energy. In the healing phase the blood sugar returns to normal, and at epi crisis there is potential for a hyperglycaemic shock or diabetic coma. In the second phase of healing, the blood sugar drops to below normal before returning to normal. With recurring conflicts in the active phase, the diabetes is diagnosed as type 1 diabetes or insulin-dependent diabetes.

It is very complex, and it is best to find more information at LearningGNM.com. This gives comprehensive details, including the evolutionary reasons for the symptoms. Due to the potential of the serious consequences of the epi crisis, I strongly advise you only heal diabetes (type 1) with the help of a medical professional.

CHAPTER 57...Depression

Depression, in different forms, is actually becoming very widespread and it concerns me as I really feel that most people could be incorrectly diagnosed. I believe there are three reasons for this which I will cover in a moment.

I would first like to mention my own experience. I was diagnosed with Post Natal Depression after the birth of my first daughter. I was told to take anti-depressants, but I didn't want to as I knew this condition would only be temporary. This was over 20 years ago, and I didn't really know about any of these issues then, but I trusted my instinct. Lo and behold, it lasted less than a couple of months (the time I was told it would take for the anti-depressants to take an effect!) so I was pleased that I had refused. About 5 years later (I had since had my son) I went to the doctors as I was finding it difficult to lose weight. He told me I was 'clinically depressed' (what is now known as bi-polar/manic depression) and he put me on Prozac. I felt so uncomfortable taking these, and I had noticed that my feelings had merely 'flat-lined'. They may have stopped me feeling down, but I also found it difficult to experience happiness. After 6 months I took myself off them, slowly but surely. I felt so much better!

Ever since, I have realised when I look back that I still have ups and downs and difficult times – but isn't that life?? I also realised that much of these cycles of up and down coincide with my natural biorhythms and the cycles around me. One of the biggest things in my life that I realised – I was sad for a reason. I was actually very miserable on times due to my current circumstances as I now realise that I was being purposefully manipulated and held back from following my true path. I also realised that there was a lot happening at the time that I wasn't aware of but suspected, and my 'depression' was obviously a reaction to this.

Is Depression as widespread as it seems?

I think that it is not – and I believe that depression is very widely misdiagnosed as I previously mentioned. Now it is difficult to hear a diagnosis for depression, and when you come to terms with it, I understand that it is just as difficult to realise that you may not have it after all. Being diagnosed with depression is almost comforting, as it makes us feel that there is a reason for our unhappiness that can be cured with a pill, or at least give us an excuse to allow ourselves to be sad. But this latter mentality will further make us believe we are suffering from this condition and can then actually manifest the symptoms due to our beliefs. It also allows us to hand the responsibility and power of our happiness over to the condition, which prevents us from actually facing what it is that could be causing it.

I personally believe that depression is misdiagnosed for three reasons:

1. The doctor's inability or laziness in not getting to the bottom of the problem (which could be physical or emotional).

2. The pharmaceutical influence on the doctor's training to provide a long term (i.e. maximum profit) quick fix.

3. The individual's lack of understanding, patience or courage, or fooling unable to cope with the root cause.

After all, when you are feeling that low in depression, we feel we NEED a quick fix, we feel we NEED an excuse for our sadness and we feel we just cannot cope with anything else.

SSRIs

Anti-depressants fall into a category of pharmaceutical drugs called SSRIs. This stands for Selective Serotonin Re-uptake Inhibitor. They effectively block the signals from getting to the brain and triggering hormonal responses in the body. The problem with SSRIs is that they are highly addictive, they affect our behaviour and thought patterns, and they come with a huge string of side-effects alarmingly including 'suicidal tendencies, self-harm, violent behaviour' – but aren't these the more serious of the symptoms we are trying to treat?

It is stated that almost every mass killing has had a direct link to either the use of or the withdrawal from SSRIs. But surely our common sense would tell us that anything that alters our brain signals cannot be good! If you don't believe the extent of SSRI use and violence, just take a look at the information at following link: www.ssristories.com/index.php

So now we will look at the reasons for depression and what you can do to help yourself.

From a GNM perspective, depression originates in the right temporal lobe area of the brain. Depending on the person's gender, hormone status and whether right or left handed, depends on the conflict that triggered it.

Right handed male (normal hormone status) or right handed female (low oestrogen e.g. birth control, hysterectomy, post menopause, pregnant/breastfeeding, HRT, etc) would experience depression through territorial conflicts such as territorial fear, anger or loss.

Left handed women with normal hormone status, and left handed male with low testosterone (e.g. past a certain age, hormone drugs), will experience depression through a scare-fright, identity, sexual or marking conflict.

All other people would not suffer depression with these conflicts, but would suffer mania, as mania originates in the left side of the temporal lobe. The exception is when there are 2 conflicts active involving both hemispheres which could trigger manic depression. Whether the person presents as manic or depressive would depend on which conflict was most active at the time, and explains why someone can go from one to the other.

This is quite complex, so I advise you look this up on LearningGNM.com after having a good understanding of the basics of GNM to understand the conflicts that have triggered the depression. Then we can begin to understand why, and heal those issues.

Make sure you are Balanced to facilitate healing.

The main deficiencies associated with depression (but they are not a cause, as we understand from GNM!) are:

- **Vitamin D deficiency** – especially in the winter months, you may benefit from taking a vitamin D3 supplement.

- **Magnesium deficiency** - magnesium deficiency can inhibit healing of many mental health problems. According to George Eby Research:

    "Severe, suicidal depression, bipolar disorder (manic depression) and mania appear very rapidly curable with dietary magnesium treatment."

But in addition, calcium is an important mood regulator and when we are deficient in magnesium, calcium cannot be effectively used by the body.

- **B Vitamin deficiency** – B vitamins in balance are essential for effective energy metabolism and can cause imbalances when deficient.

- **Zinc deficiency** – this deficiency interferes with the absorption of copper which can lead to toxicity and further mineral imbalances, and also helps in the absorption of calcium. It is especially common in vegetarians.

- **Vitamin B12 deficiency** – also very common in vegetarians.

On an Emotional Level

- **Is it Unhappiness?** Are you *really* depressed? Reflecting on my experience, take a good, long, hard look at your life and see if there is anything at all that is causing you unhappiness or unnecessary stress. Be brave, deal with it – and always know that you are stronger than you can ever imagine!

- Take heed of the information in Symptoms or Messages Chapter 61 regarding the way we talk to our selves and our bodies.

- Learn EFT Tapping for relief (more info Chapter 70)

- Read about Earthing in Chapter 36.

CHAPTER 58...*Candida & Parasites*

Candida

Candida is so rife today, and it is believed to be an underlying factor in many chronic conditions and complaints. However, with an understanding of GNM, we now know that fungi such as candida are instrumental to our healing from biological programmes that are controlled by the 'old brain'. As a nutritional therapist, for years I thought that candida was our enemy, and if you have read a previous edition of this book, you will know that this chapter was originally 22 pages long and included a complete 'anti-candida' plan. What appears to be a chronic candida overgrowth infection is actually what's know as a 'hanging healing' whereby the healing phase of a biological programme is being interrupted. This could either by caused by 'tracks' which are re-triggering the conflict, or (as in my case of having chronic candida for quite a few years) our own intervention or interference in the healing process.

What is Candida?

Candida is a fungus that exists in a dormant state in our bodies, as part of our endodermal and some of our mesodermal germ layers. Biological programmes controlled by our 'old brain' involve cell proliferation (the creation of what we call a tumour) in the conflict active phase. The purpose of this is dependant on the organ or body part (e.g. in the case of an indigestible morsel conflict affecting the intestine, additional temporary cells will be grown to increase the surface area of the intestinal wall so it may secrete more digestive juices to 'digest the morsel'). These temporary cells are what are called 'cancer cells' as they differ from normal cells, but they are different for a reason. When the conflict is resolved, candida fungus, along with mycobacteria such as tubercular bacteria are activated by the brain to remove these temporary cells as they are no longer required. And they are easy to identify as they are different to our regular cells.

Candida overgrowth is actually this process in action. In the medical and alternative field it is also known as Candida Albicans (one of the strains, but there are many), Candidiasis, Dysbiosis, Yeast Overgrowth, Imbalance in Gut Flora and more.

Candida does produce unpleasant symptoms, but if we interfere with what the body is trying to do, we may cause a hanging healing and cause the symptoms to get worse. It is believed by many alternative health professionals and non-biased medical researchers that candida is a pre-cursor to serious conditions such as Chronic Fatigue Syndrome, ME, Fibromyalgia and even Cancer. Understanding GNM, we can see why this association is made, as the presence of candida means the body is healing and therefore will be experiencing these unpleasant conditions. You can also see why Dr Simoncini made the assumption that cancer is caused by fungus, and subsequently treated it with sodium bicarbonate. While he has a degree of success, we need to ask whether thus apparent success is actually just causing the programme to slow down so much that it appears to be resolved, and whether many of his patients then have relapses due to their body trying to heal again.

'Candida Symptoms'

What many call 'candida symptoms' are actually healing symptoms of the biological programmes in which candida play a part. If any of these symptoms are persistent or chronic, this may be the case for you:

Emotions/mentals – dizziness, foggy brain (confusion, dream-like, clumsy), forgetfulness, migraine, inability to concentrate, mood swings, depression symptoms, lethargy, no energy, autism, fatigue, insomnia, anxiety

Head – recurrent colds/flu, ear problems, oral thrush, white coated tongue, recurrent sore throat, eye problems, thyroid problems, bad breath, ulcers, dry mouth, receding gums

Respiratory - any respiratory problems, chronic cough

Digestion – food intolerances/allergies, gas, bloating (especially after eating), IBS, diarrhoea, recurrent nausea, constipation, stomach ulcers, heartburn, stomach pain, indigestion, sugar cravings, itchy anus

'Allergies' – foods (especially refined carbohydrates and sugars such as wheat, sugar, fruit, alcohol, etc.), hay fever, increased sensitivity to any substances

Body (muscles/joints, etc.) – painful/swollen joints, skin rash (especially involving the corium (under) skin), aching muscles, shivers/cold, athlete's foot, fungal infection, recurrent vaginal thrush, acne, dry skin, water retention, liver spots

Women's problems – menstrual problems, infertility, dryness, lack of sex drive, PMS, endometriosis, hormone imbalance

Other – weight problems (underweight or overweight), premature ageing

Supporting Healing

When candida is active, we are best to work through the symptoms. So, unless these symptoms are debilitating and severe, we need to support the healing process and allow the healing to continue, knowing that it means you are healing and not malfunctioning, and that it will get better!

Ideally, you would take time out and rest as much as you can. If you listen to your symptoms, you will see what your body is asking of you – fatigue = "I need you to rest", for example. The most important thing to do is reduce stress in any form as much as possible to support the healing 'vagatonic' state.

To further facilitate the process, you can ensure you are not adding to the body's stress-load by following the advice in this book regarding eating healthily, and avoiding everyday toxins which put stress on the body.

Emotional Healing

It is part of the healing to understand why. So I would advise you to look up any symptoms you may be experiencing on LearningGNM.com so you can ascertain your original conflict. However, if you are very fearful I would give a word of caution as it can be quite challenging at first to hear that your body is running the same programme as it would if you had something more serious (from the GNM perspective, the only different between a 'sickness bug' and a stomach cancer is the intensity of the programme). If it is mainly gut-related it could be that you have suffered an 'indigestible morsel' conflict, the morsel being literal or figurative (such as news or a situation you cannot digest). Though, there are many other 'biological programmes' that it could be. But you need to understand that the symptoms mean you have resolved the conflict. This means there is no more work to do in that sense, and just knowing what triggered it will be enough to move forward and prevent a hanging healing (which I know from experience can make the candida appear to be a chronic condition that is taking over your system!)

When you discover that you are healing from something, you can feel a little overwhelmed that something has been going on that you didn't realise. But that is the past, and we need to move forward, appreciating that you can now assist the healing and get yourself better. Once you have made this shift, you may feel a renewed determination to start putting positive changes into action, such as de-cluttering your home, only to find that you are quickly exhausted after the first burst of energy. This is normal as the fatigue that is required for healing can set in and make you feel that your to-do list, or your plan will never get done! The answer here is NOT to get stressed and frustrated, but to take a positive step in recognising that you have no deadlines and when your energy has improved as move through healing, you will then be able to action more of your plan! Be kind to yourself and realise that recognising the things causing you stress, and affirming that you will solve them, is an accomplishment in itself and a positive step in the right direction.

These thoughts and realisations helped me and I hope they help you too!

When Symptoms are Severe

If symptoms are particularly severe, we can ease them by slowing healing down. However, this will prolong the healing process, but it can help us to live with the healing symptoms so they do not impact too much on our lives. We have to find a balance here, though. We do not want to stop symptoms (as much as you want to), as otherwise we will be stopping our healing!

Here are some things you can do to slow the process (assuming you are following the good eating practices as previously discussed in this book):

- reduce intake of sugar (particularly refined sugar) and fruit. You can use xylitol or stevia for sweetening

- reduce intake of refined carbohydrates, and opt for wholemeal

- have 1-2 cups of organic ground coffee per day (not after 4pm)

- Take some Diatomaceous Earth at 1 teaspoon to 1 tablespoon per day. However if your symptoms disappear, then reduce this dose, as you don't want to stop healing.

- drink Rooibos tea or Green Tea for their antioxidant properties

- take 3 x 1000mcg vitamin C per day

- Take coffee enemas 1-2 times per week

When Symptoms are Long-lasting

When the candida symptoms have been particularly long lasting, you are likely to be in a 'hanging healing'. This means that there are likely to be something preventing your healing from completing such as imbalances, physical or emotional stresses, or conflict relapses. If you particularly have a lot of food intolerances or suffer from bad 'IBS' symptoms, it may mean you have what is called Leaky Gut Syndrome. This is caused by an extended 'hanging healing' which causes the candida to damage the intestinal walls.

Just understanding and supporting the healing can be what brings you out of the hanging healing. If you suspect you have leaky gut, along with the advice above for slowing the process for severe symptoms, you can follow a rotation diet. This will assist in putting as least stress on your gut as possible to facilitate healing. You need to eat as much of a variety of foods as possible while avoiding obvious sugars and sticking to the basic food rules in Chapter 2. The tricky part – you must not eat the same food for 4 days. So if you eat rice on Monday, do not eat it again until Friday. I found this quite difficult, and it helped to keep a food diary and make a meal plan for each week. It is best to stick to simple meals of 2 or 3 items rather than having meals made up of 10+ ingredients or components as this will give you a bit more flexibility in the coming 4 days!

To assist in the healing you may wish to take a good quality healing preparation/supplement like neem, aloe vera or ionic silver. I have used all of these, and also I used colostrum however this was more expensive. If you want to use an enema, these preparations can be added to the enema fluid. You can follow this until things begin calming down for you.

Other Ways that have helped me

In addition, when I was coping with a chronic candida infection (before understanding the GNM perspective of it) I also found the following therapies to help me on my path to well-being. As mentioned, it is absolutely essential that emotional issues are not ignored at this time.

Reflexology – I had regular (approximately monthly) treatments of reflexology to help stress levels, assist in the detoxing process and also correct any imbalances in my body.

Hypnotherapy – I had an 8-week course of hypnotherapy in order to help me release past issues that were holding me back. EFT has also greatly helped emotional releases (see chapter 70)

Meditation – simply practising being in the 'now' has greatly helped me stop worrying about the future. This has also had a huge impact on my tolerance and compassion. Seeing the good in everything (with wisdom of course), using the law of attraction and being grateful for everything has also helped a great deal. More information on this is in Chapter 63.

Kinesiology – played a major part in assessing my body's needs on a deeper level, and helped me not to over or under supplement.

Parasites

In my time as a kinesiologist, I have discovered so many symptoms being caused by parasite infection. From arthritis to IBS to skin conditions to mental health problems. While all these conditions can be explained from a GNM perspective as relating to conflict shocks, I have found they can also be caused by parasites. Whether there is an underlying biological programme that has been exacerbated by a parasite infection, or whether the parasite infection itself is causing symptoms that are similar to those experienced during the healing of a biological programme is maybe another topic of discovery. As Dr Hamer, discoverer of GNM, stated "malnutrition, poison and injury can all cause symptoms in absence of a conflict shock". In some ways parasites could be causing malnutrition, or acting as a poison to us. But, in any case, a parasite infection that is causing imbalance will be putting stress on our system and inhibiting healing from taking place.

If you have any symptoms that you cannot seem to shift, parasites may be a factor. I advise you have this confirmed by a kinesiologist. I always use diatomaceous earth for parasite infection as it consistently tests positively for my clients, and the dosage tests as most beneficial in the majority of cases is 1 tablespoon a day (build up to this over a week). As DE has many other positive benefits, it is something you could try in the first instance.

CHAPTER 59...Allergies:
Tracks, Reversals & Remedies

From the perspective of German New Medicine, allergies are actually 'tracks' or subconscious triggers that run a specific biological programme each time the 'track' is experienced. So the 'allergy' is originally caused by a conflict shock which triggers a biological programme. At the moment of the original conflict shock, the subconscious mind will create a subconscious association with something it is experiencing such as a smell, something being touched, eaten, seen, etc at the time. The reason it does this is to provide the mind with a warning sign for a possible future event, so if we come into contact with the same substance in the future, the body will run the biological programme in preparation for the conflict shock, should one occur.

An example would be that as a child you are petting your dog, and you get scared by loud voices such as parents aggressively arguing. This could cause a 'scare-fright' or 'territorial fear' conflict depending on gender/left or right handedness, both of which would trigger a biological programme that has symptoms of asthma. If a subconscious association, or track, is created linking the dog fur to the shock at the moment it happens, then each time that child would come into contact with dog fur in the future, it would trigger the same biological programme, the healing from which would include an asthma attack.

So the ideal 'allergy' reversal would be to identify the track or triggers, identify the original conflict and bring logic into the equation (which our subconscious mind is unable to do). So we must bring what is in the subconscious into the conscious. Past case studies have proven that this can be all that is needed!

This is the ultimate allergy 'cure', however it can also be very tricky to find the original conflict to the track (allergen). Before I learnt GNM, I remedied my daughter's eczema homeopathically as detailed below.

Making your own Homeopathic Allergy Remedy

Homeopathic remedies work on the basis that 'like treats like', so you are treating a condition with the poison that created it (or a substance that produces the same symptom pattern). Therefore, it got me thinking that if someone were allergic to something, then a remedy made from that substance will cure it, or at least ease it. 'Well obviously!' you may say, but my homeopathy diploma didn't go into making your own remedies, just how it works and the prescribing part of it, so I guess it took a little while for the penny to drop!

Curing My Daughter's Lifelong Eczema Problem

As my daughter has suffered terrible eczema ever since her first baby jab (boy do I regret agreeing to that!), I set about finding out what it was that was making her react.

As a nutritional therapist, my first instinct was cutting out dairy, which helped a little, cutting out wheat, sugar, etc – one by one to see the reaction or non-reaction. But it still flared up, although once some allergens were cut out from the diet the flare-ups were not so bad.

When I studied Holistic Diagnosis I learned how to do kinesiology allergy testing, so I set about trying to ascertain what foods or substances she was allergic to. During the test I also tested some substances that are common allergens by shaking them vigorously (succussing) in reverse osmosis filtered water (distilled is also good to use), then placing the essence in a capsule under her tongue while testing her. It turned out she had a strong reaction to our dog and cat fur! So I did some research and set about making her a remedy.

I dowsed her eczema with a pendulum asking it which potency to make, and how often she should take it to stop her reacting to the fur. I will explain all this in a bit. Then I made a 27C potency of cat & dog fur remedy which she took for 5 days, 3 times a day (as indicated by dowsing). After that treatment I dowsed again. This time it said another 3 days of 32C potency. So I made that remedy and she completed the course. Her eczema completely healed and she has not had a reaction to fur since (that was over 5 years ago at time of writing!).

Cut Grass

The following Spring her eczema flared up again really bad, and we realised that it was whenever someone was cutting grass. So next time we mowed the lawn I saved some cut grass along with some daisy and dandelion petals and grass flowers and let the energies infuse in filtered water again for a day or so. Then I made her a remedy (after dowsing) of 30C which she took for a week twice daily. She can now play barefoot on the grass while we are mowing it!!

The Seaside!

Hot weather came and we took a trip to the sea. She had always complained of her eczema stinging at the seaside, but we thought she would be OK as she didn't really have it any more. But she flared up big time at the beach and couldn't bend her legs or walk after 15 minutes! So I tried again. I collected seawater, sand and small amounts of different seaweed into a bottle and brought them home to make a remedy. This time I decided to make a blog so others may find use with this information (this is still available on my website and in my shop's blog – let this empowering information be free to all!).

My daughter helped me make her cut grass remedy as part of her home-school work, and she found making this one more interesting as she was a year older and so she understood more. I think this also has a very positive input into the remedy, as her desire and intention to cure herself also went in to the mix! Anyway, 2 years later, after many successful trips to the beach, running on freshly cut grass, we still have cats and a new puppy dog

Making your Remedy

Anyone can do this. It doesn't have to be exact but you must respect the energies. Always hold the intention that the remedy will work and will heal the condition. Always intend that any energies inside the bottles, pipettes and other equipment you are using are cleared leaving them completely empty and uncontaminated. Intention rather than accuracy and precision is key in my experience!!

Collecting Your Allergen

As I did, collect not just the potential allergen but things associated with it. For example I put petals of daisies and dandelions, and different types of grass including the feathery flowers into the grass remedy. I put a snip of each of my 3 cat's fur plus dog fur, plus a flea (dead) into my fur remedy, etc. Put the collected bits into distilled (or reverse osmosis filtered) water, let it stand for about 24 hours and then succuss it (shake it vigorously approx 30 times).

314

If the allergen is atmospheric or environmental, leave an open bowl of distilled water in the environment for 24 hours, as it will absorb particles from the air due to it being 'empty' water. Then use this as your master formula. You still need to succuss it once it is in the bottle.

Once you have made your master formula, label the bottle and date it. You can use it to make more in future, it just needs succussing to freshen it up. I use a urine sample bottle for mine, they are ideal. You can get them quite cheaply on Ebay (or from your GP!).

What you will need to make your remedy:

Master Formula in urine bottle (or similar sterile container)
1 x 3ml pipette
1 x bottle dropper (or pipette clearly marked to define it from the other)
2 x 5ml dark coloured glass bottles with screw caps (essential oil bottles are great but not after they have had oils in!)
1 x 10ml glass bottle with dropper top (for final remedy – or a 5ml bottle full of blank pills available from homeopathic pharmacies
labels, paper & pen
distilled water (or reverse osmosis water)
vodka or other edible alcohol
Dowsing Pendulum
Most of these can be supplied by Shop Holistic!

Find the Potency you Need:

Dowse the area affected (where the rash is, the tummy if that is affected, etc) or just the person, and while you are dowsing start to visualise the condition or problem. Let the pendulum swing back and forth and ask for 'yes' answer, it will usually spin around clockwise. Then swing the pendulum over the master formula, let the pendulum swing a few times then bring it back to the area. Keep the pendulum swinging and ask which potency of 'C' remedy is needed. Count up slowly 1, 2, 3, etc allowing the pendulum a few swings before moving onto the next number. When it circles for yes, go back a number and repeat to check it was correct.

Alternatively, you may prefer Kinesiology muscle testing to dowsing. Look for our tutorial on the Holistic Show on Youtube, or consult a Kinesiologist.

The 'C' remedy I have always found the easiest scale to work with. It means at each succussion the remedy is diluted 100 times. The number indicates the number of times it is diluted and succussed. Hopefully you will only need up to a 30 or so remedy!!

Then ask how many drops (or pills if using) for each dose so say slowly 1,2 etc. Then ask how many times per day, then for how many days in the same way.

Make Your Remedy:

* Use the dropper (which I will refer to as the remedy dropper) to draw up some of the master remedy and put 1 drop only into one of the 5ml bottles. (5ml is roughly 100 drops)

* Empty the remedy dropper and shake it well to empty and dry it, then set it aside with the master formula.

* Add 2 x 2.5ml of your clear water using the 3ml pipette (which I will refer to as the water pipette) – it doesn't have to be highly accurate!

* Put the lid on the bottle and succuss it 30 times.

* IMPORTANT – mark a tally on your paper (or you will quickly forget how many times you have diluted and succussed!!)

You have now made a 1C remedy.

* Use the remedy dropper to take 1 drop from the 1C remedy into the clean 5ml bottle.

316

* empty the 1C remedy bottle and shake to empty and dry it

* Empty the remedy dropper and shake it well to empty and dry it, then set it aside with the empty 5ml bottle.

* Add 2 x 2.5ml of your clear water using the water pipette

* Put the lid on the bottle and succuss it 30 times

* mark a tally on your paper

Now you have a 2C remedy!

Repeat until you reach the last-but-one succussion. Then, on the final succussion, add your drop to vodka or other plain alcohol. Succuss as normal. This is your medication remedy. Label and date it.

TIP – If you are making a remedy that is quite high in number, you can preserve and keep every 10th or 20th succussion in case you lose count or tip some to save going back to the start! But bear in mind you will then need more 5ml bottles!

Making & Taking Your Final Remedy:

To make your remedy for taking, put a few drops of your medication remedy into 20/80 vodka to water if you wish to take it as drops, or add 1-2 drops to a bottle and fill with blank pills. Shake the bottle vigorously a few times (not as much as succussing) to infuse the remedy onto the pills or into the alcohol solution.

Remedies should be taken in a clean mouth, at least 20 minutes either side of eating or drinking. Pills should not be touched but tipped into the lid of the bottle or onto a clean teaspoon and then tipped straight under the tongue to dissolve. Drops should be placed under the tongue.

Energy Mis-Match

As a kinesiologist, I have become trained in a very useful 'add-on' technique which corrects allergies, and also helps us with addictions. It is based upon the concept that when the energy of a substance enters our aura, it is categorised as either 'Beneficial' to the body, or 'Not Beneficial'. A mis-match occurs when our energetic body fails to categorise a substance correctly. So, something that would normally be healthy causes a reaction (allergy), something that is harmful, the body thinks it needs and therefore craves (addiction). This can also be a useful potential tool to assess possible diagnoses of disease, etc, as the one that the body is allowing to grow or exist in the body is likely to be the one that the body has a mis-match to. This would be a purposeful mis-match, created by our body to run a certain biological programme. Likewise, a mismatch to a pathogen that is contained in a vaccine may cause a reaction (is this one of the missing links in the vaccine debate?), and a match to a pathogen means the body recognises it as an enemy, therefore do we really need that particular vaccine? This certainly has potential. I have also used this method to assess whether a particular nutrient, mineral, or hormone for example, is being utilised properly by the body, and have experienced many clients (and including myself) whose deficiency or toxicity was due to this.

As well as testing, there is a technique that is performed to correct a mis-match, which is tapping certain meridians. This is a very thorough and non-invasive way of correcting the mis-match and also a potential alternative to chemical vaccinations, diagnostic testing and much more. Understanding GNM, it is very important to have energetic permission to perform this correction, as it may be that the mis-match has been triggered by the brain for the purpose of a biological programme.

Energy Mis-match is a specialised kinesiology process and you need to seek a kinesiologist who is trained in this technique if you wish to pursue this.

318

CHAPTER 60...Menopause
& Hormone Imbalance

Menopause happens to both men and women! Though with men it is often not as noticeable. German New Medicine teaches us that this is controlled by the temporal lobe area of the brain. The left side controls female conflicts (such as sexual, identity and scare-fright) and oestrogen, and the right controls male 'territorial' conflicts and testosterone.

Ordinarily, females with a normal hormone status will only suffer female conflicts, and men of normal hormone status will only suffer male conflicts. In later years, however, when the woman's oestrogen falls, she will move into the 'male' side and now experience male conflicts. And for the men, when their testosterone lowers as they reach later years, they will move into the female side and begin to experience female conflicts. This is why men tend to soften as they get older, and women tend to become the master of the house, so to speak!

In addition to this, as explained in the Depression chapter, when the left female side of the brain is active with a conflict, there is mania (hyperactivity, restlessness, anxiety) and when the right male side is active, we see depression (low mood, lethargy, complacency, etc). At the time in our lives when our hormones are naturally changing, the change then will also produce mood swings, from mania to depression and vice

319

versa. It also explains why women are more prone to depression at and after menopause, as it is at this time when women move over to the male depressive side.

As new conflicts begin to be experienced when hormonal changes move us over into the other brain hemisphere, we would naturally experience new symptoms as the conflicts are related to different biological programmes. Along with the obvious symptoms caused by the hormone changes, such as hot flushes and changes in menstruation, maybe these 'new' symptoms are also what could be seen as 'menopausal' as they have not before been experienced?

Women can suffer extremely with menopause, yet some breeze through it and simply 'realise' they have not had the past few periods! Typical symptoms are described as:

Hot flushes, night sweats, irregular / heavy / absent periods, migraine headaches, muscle aches and weakness, anxiety, depression, the list goes on and on. However many of these symptoms are also healing symptoms of biological programmes. I wonder how many of us 'put it down' to menopause just because of age?

Hormone Imbalance

With my understanding of GNM, hormone imbalance could be a natural change, or facilitating certain processes required for healing. Ideally it is best to leave our body do what it does best, and that is to survive and heal itself. But when symptoms are very uncomfortable and troublesome, many will want to 'balance' their hormones.

I would advise against forcing hormones onto or into the body, whether they be synthetic or bio-available, unless they had specifically been energy-tested as beneficial. This is invasive and could cause further imbalances.

However, you will be pleased to know that there are ways in which we can ease symptoms naturally, in a non-invasive way. Here are some tips that have helped myself and clients:

Eat a diet high in phystoestrogens

There are different strengths of oestrogen. The oestrogen our body produces is a fairly strong oestrogen. Strong oestrogens are also found in animal protein and xenoestrogens which act as very strong oestrogens are found in plastics, particularly bisphenol-A (BPA), and soy products. Weak oestrogens are found in plants, such as cruciferous and other vegetables, some fruit, grains and nuts. Eggs and milk (I recommend raw) are stronger than plant-based, but weaker than meat.

Due to the compound's similarities with estradiol, which is a precursor to oestrogen, consuming phytoestrogens will help to regulate oestrogen whether it is high or low.

Foods particularly high in weak phytoestrogens are:

bananas, cruciferous vegetables (broccoli, brussels sprouts, cauliflower, cabbage), peas, lentils, blueberries, cherries, oats, peanuts, barley, rye, brown rice, onions, garlic, sesame, pumpkin and poppy seeds.

Linseeds are often used however these, like soy, are extremely strong oestrogen and I would usually avoid them.

Supplements / Herbs that may help:

- **Diindolylmethane** (D.I.M.), derived from cruciferous veg
- **Maca Powder** – add this to smoothies
- **Black Cohosh** – good for hot flushes

CHAPTER 61...Symptoms
– or Messages?

Through my journey from the breast cancer scare to health, I have been keeping a journal of my journey, from day 1 of finding the lump to present. Primarily, I thought this was a good idea to record what I was doing and the effects of what I was doing, but also to get feelings and emotions out to clear my head before sleep, and as an aid to my emotional healing. Some things I have used Emotional Freedom Technique on, but mostly it helps just to get things out of my head and onto paper. It has been a very healing practice, and also is quite informative, so maybe one day I will put it into another book!

In the meantime, I would like to share an insight/realisation I had when I received my results from the second thermography appointment, showing the huge reduction in the activity surrounding the tumours (although since learning GNM, I realise that this was the healing process stopping due to the stress I was under at the time, but obviously as I did not know GNM at the time, I had thought this was positive!). Lloyd had seen the images at the session as he was facing the screen, but I had not seen the images so he told me what he'd seen. But, deep down, I didn't really believe what he'd told me, and waited for the doctor report and images to be sent to me. If I am honest, I was scared to believe him, as if

I had I would have had high expectations of the report and I was afraid I would be disappointed if it wasn't as good as I'd thought. This is what I wrote in my journal that day. I found it very emotional and quite profound, and I hope that it helps others who may have negative emotions about their health to see things from a different perspective. Much of this is actually a little along the lines of my more recent research into German New Medicine.

Tuesday 15th November 2016

I had the doctors report today. I am now classed as 'Low Risk of Cancer' and they don't want to see me for another year! The images confirm what Lloyd was saying, with the tumour areas being hardly noticeable and the lymphs having pretty-much normal activity! I took some of the images and made a comparison chart and I cannot believe it – mainly I cannot believe how it has happened so quickly!

While I rejoice, there is a part of me that is very sad to let my journey go, although I remind myself I am still on it – and will be for a long time. I am a little afraid that I won't feel 'myself' if I am not aching, or focused on some problem or aspect of my health – that I'll lose myself if there is not a constant reminder that my body is here and needs helping – that I'll take it for granted and forget to nurture myself. And also, I feel that I still don't know myself, and I was just getting to know certain things about myself through all this, like a journey of self discovery, uncovering all the things that have led to this moment. I am afraid that if I don't need to do all this, and the things I was getting around to do more of such as exercise and meditation, that I won't do them if I am not scared into it. That I will lose the impetus to look after myself if I do not have a life-threatening condition.

The truth is I have been loving my journey, and each layer of healing that emerges has made me appreciate myself and my body so much more. I would say I am closer to truly loving myself now than I have ever been. I really feel that I have this fairly unique position through my research, studies and now my experiences to follow a mission of spreading the truth about cancer and the choices that are available, yet hidden from mainstream views and sources. People need to know this:

"when it comes to health issues there are choices beyond fear and destruction, in fact, in the opposite of these – there is a choice in love and nurturing."

In spite of my little fears of not continuing on my journey and letting things slip, I am realising that it is through this mindset of not taking action unless something is driving me (such as illness or fear) that got me in this position in the first place. My lack of care for my body and my self, my weakness in being governed by food addictions and tastes, my lack of love for my body (especially being so self-critical about my weight), my non-acceptance, my taking for granted all the wonderful functions my body carries out every second of every day to keep me alive, my lack of nurturing, appreciation, gratitude.....This is what happens without these things, no matter how healthy we choose to live, how toxin-free our homes and toiletries are, how organic our diet is, how good our supplements are, etc.

My body has been calling me for attention so much over the last 8 years or so and now it has made this huge cry for help!

I feel so sad that my body had to grow this cancer just to get me to properly listen (note to self – I am SO SORRY!). I have been trying to look after myself physically with supplements, diets and various other things – even emotional work on past issues, etc – but completely neglected my relationship with my body! The thermographer told me that emotionally and energetically, a tumour on the left breast can indicate unresolved emotions or problems with a female (actually GNM proves it is mother/child if you are right-handed) – well, I understand

324

now that the female is ME!

I am not blaming myself, there is no blame here. What a negative emotion attached to guilt, anger, frustration, sadness, etc. No – blame would be of no benefit at all. This is a "Eureka" moment, where I discover the missing link to all the good I have been doing!

Everything I have done for my health, all my life, even emotionally and spiritually, has been to ease symptoms – in other words "Shut my body up" so I can continue with my life without being held back or interrupted by my body's calls for help and love (symptoms). Every intolerance has been a curse, every recurrent ache has been a negative obstacle, every symptom is something that has stopped me living my life to the fullest – all negatives! I am sure this sounds familiar to many. Now, all of a sudden, I am not thinking narcisistically like I used to, that these symptoms are to be angry or frustrated at – how selfish is that? If a baby was crying in the next room, should I go to it and help it, and give it whatever it needs so it is happy and content? Or should I ignore it and hope it goes away, or even shut the door so I can't hear it any more (i.e. treat it symptomatically) and carry on with my life the best I can – probably harbouring some negative emotions such as guilt and maybe even resentment that it has got in the way of my life and what I want? Is this baby I have been dealing with, my inner child/self/true nature (whatever you want to call it)?

In other words, do I have compassion for what is really going on in my body?

With this new mindset, the things I have been doing with pure intention have helped instead of being rejected like they have done in the past. I used to try loads of remedies, diets, supplements, and even though I truly believed in them as they had worked so well for others, and the research and evidence was there, they never really worked for me very well. All these remedies I have tried over the years being holistic (so

325

they work in harmony with our body, mind and spirit on many levels), and I have realised that energetically my body may have even been blocking these from working well, as I have not been listening properly, I have not been compassionate to myself and I was approaching my problems from the conditioned, conventional mindset of wanting to shut my body up!

Now all my babies have grown up, my body needs to be my baby to listen to, care for and love unconditionally, knowing that anything it does wrong, and any signs it gives me, are a cry for help to let me know I am not listening or giving it what it needs. It is like symptoms are our body's language, it's communication with us. We often get that little voice or feeling telling us to do or not do something. Well life (and our ego) has a tendency to drown out this little voice, and this gives our bodies no choice but to shout.

If any of this resonates with you, maybe it is time you began listening and loving, rather than declaring war on your body! Next time you experience a symptom, try asking yourself some questions:

Am I eating healthily? (Truly, honestly, our bodies do not lie!) Am I drinking enough water?

Am I moving around and exercising enough?

Am I getting enough magnesium? (a VERY common problem – if you are not using magnesium chloride, quite possibly you are deficient!)

Am I unhappy in any aspect of my life? Am I handling stress well? Am I doing too much?

Am I meditating, or taking some quiet time?

Is any aspect of my life toxic? Is something messing with my mind? (TV, news, someone, a job, a belief, etc)

Am I considering my body, mind & spirit equally? (Many 'spiritual' people forget to live in the physical, many physical people disregard

326

their spiritual side, many of us disregard our emotions and mind, etc) All 3 must have equal attention to be in balance!

Interpreting Our Body's Language

Here are some hints that may help to interpret what our bodies are trying to tell us.

Problems on the left tend to be linked to female, and the right linked to male. From the GNM perspective of assessing conflicts, biologically right handed people will generally experience conflicts relating to mother/child/nest/maternal on their left side, and everything/everyone else on the right. The opposite is true of left-handers.

Certain organs can be related to emotions through the elements in traditional Chinese medicine.

Heart – Joy (or lack of); Lungs – anxiety/grief; Large intestine – anxiety; Kidneys – fear/fright; Liver – anger; Stomach – anger; Spleen – anger/pensiveness/mental fatigue

Symptoms at the areas of the Chakras may also be relative to that chakra (See chapter 84).

Also look at the pattern of symptoms and what they could mean:

Trapped wind: are you feeling trapped? Anxious?

Nagging pains: is there a recurring problem, or something nagging you?

Thumping pains: do you feel like you are banging against a brick wall?

Tearing pains: are you feeling cut up, or separated from something?

Obviously, now with an understanding of German New Medicine, we can see the science behind the link between the symptoms of disease and conflicts or traumas. This takes the emotional link to a whole new level of understanding. But it proves that the compassion message, the appreciation and gratitude, and the positive mindset and relationship and language we speak with our bodies are so very important, as one of the biggest problems and causes of chronic disease is that of self-devaluation.

The Way We Speak to Our Bodies

Am I Handing over my Power to my symptom/condition?

We hand over our power to our condition/symptoms by blaming them for things we need to do, can't eat, or can't do. Do any of these sound similar?

"I can't eat that because of my IBS" or "I can't exercise because I look too fat" or "I don't want to go out as I am depressed"

What we are literally saying is "my condition/symptom is what is controlling my decisions, my life and I have no power to overcome it!"

Try changing these statements to:

"I choose to eat something different as my body prefers this at the moment" and "I enjoy exercise in a way that feels comfortable" and "I am choosing to stay at home and keep myself company today"

Am I Labelling myself?

We need to be very careful what we put after 'I am' as we are labelling ourselves and giving out a very strong affirmation. Stating and thinking "I am Depressed", "I am Diabetic", "I am fat" etc is removing our divine selves and making us the 'label'.

By changing our language to: "I am *experiencing* depression/diabetes/etc at the moment", not only retains our divine 'I am', but it also merely describes what we are experiencing, and also states that it is temporary. This can be a powerful way of disassociating with the condition or symptom, and in turn, makes it easier for our subconscious to let go of it.

328

Have I taken Ownership of the condition/symptom I am experiencing?

Do you think of it as "MY depression" or "MY IBS" or "MY dodgy knee" or "MY weak ankles"? By taking ownership of anything, we are subconsciously less willing to let it go! It is 'ours' why should we give it away?

Change this language to "the depression I am experiencing at the moment" etc, or simply "the way I am feeling at the moment".

All the 'wrong' statements I have detailed above are a form of self devaluation which Dr Hamer proved to be the conflict behind many chronic conditions.

Positive Affirmations

To offset any self devaluation we can practice positive affirmations. While these sound airy-fairy, we can see the negative effects of the self devaluation are caused in a similar way by giving ourselves negative speak and affirmations, so when this is turned around, we can stop the self devaluation. Positive affirmations that are frequently repeated act like subliminal messaging and in time can become a part of our deep beliefs.

You can create positive affirmations yourself that are relevant to you. They must be in the present (even if you do not believe them or they are not yet true!) and they must not contain anything negative (such as "I don't have pain").

Here are some examples:

"My body is strong and healthy"; "I am healing quickly"; "All is well in my world" (that last one is courtesy of Louise Hay!)

Blessing and Forgiveness

An ancient practice that I have introduced into my daily life is one of forgiveness, self love, compassion and gratitude. It is a very powerful Hawaiian blessing called Ho'oponopono.

Ho means 'to make' and pono mean 'right'. The pono is repeated as it means 'to make double right' or 'right with ourselves and with others (or even God)'. Use this as a mantra everyday, run it over in your mind like a catchy tune, and use it in meditation. You can direct it to yourself, a person, a situation or anything. And here it is:

I'm Sorry…..Please Forgive Me…..Thank You…..I Love You

Or you could try a daily Self Blessing I wrote for my Yoga class which is inspired by different techniques and meditations that helped me through a period of extreme anxiety. Try it first in your mind, then out loud. Once you are used to that, you can say it in the mirror for maximum benefit!

Daily Blessing for Self Love

Say, or read silently, the following while placing your left hand over your heart. Pause between each line and truly feel the blessing:

I Bless my Body – *that it is Healthy, Strong and free from suffering*

I Bless my Mind – *that it is Peaceful, Balanced and free from fear*

I Bless my Soul – *that I see and feel the Love within me and in all living things*

I Bless my Present – *that I notice the Beauty around me in every moment*

I Bless my Future – *that it is not a reflection of my past*

*I **Bless my Past** – that my challenges and lessons turn into Wisdom*

*I **Bless the Divine in me** – let it flow around me, and through me, and guide me on my path…and let it show me signs so that I know it is real*

***Now, I give gratitude** – for my life, and for **ME**…..(and add anything you are grateful for)*

And for all the times I have shown myself anger, frustration or fear….

I am Sorry, Please forgive me, Thank you, I love you…..

Namaste

Also see the information on Law of Attraction in Chapter 63.

SECTION VII.....Holistic Therapies & Healing

CHAPTERS:

CHAPTER 62...Introduction & Finding a Therapist

The therapies I am covering are certainly not an exhaustive list. There are many excellent effective therapies out there! However I have just written about the therapies I know from studying, or have had experience of and found extremely beneficial.

Therapies from a GNM Perspective

Understanding the GNM principles confirms that therapies themselves cannot alone offer a 'cure' for any disease. However there are many ways we can support the natural process with therapies, though we need to take into account the phase we are in. Some examples are Reiki Healing, which is useful in the healing phase to help to de-stress and relax, and a gentle, pampering massage can promote a feeling of relaxation and well-being during this phase. Mindfulness and meditation is useful throughout the biological programme when we need to change our perception of situations and relieve old patterns, and this can be assisted with hypnotherapy or sound therapy if need be. Kinesiology at each phase through the biological programme can assess what the body needs and wants at that time, addressing deficiencies and toxicities and bringing our body back into a balanced state to enable it to better cope with the healing process. Homeopathy works in harmony with the body's own healing so works well with GNM. Nutritional Therapy and Aromatherapy with a therapist who understands GNM principles, may be used effectively to facilitate the process. Although it is not going to necessarily resolve a conflict, EFT tapping may help manage stress and anxiety, and help to 'downgrade' an intense conflict. It is always advisable to seek a therapist who has a firm knowledge of GNM so their actions do not bring about a severe healing crisis, or are contra-indicatory to the phase you are experiencing. If you cannot find a therapist who knows GNM, why not enlighten them?

Before Thinking about Paying for Therapy

Consider that there are many ways in which you can help yourself before considering a therapist. Some of the information in this book is a good start! One way you may consider helping yourself is through a technique called Emotional Freedom Technique, or EFT Tapping. You can find information on this in Chapter70). Sometimes, however, it is difficult to see the wood for the trees when healing yourself, and it is often beneficial to have a consultation with someone who may be able to shed some light, and of course receive therapies which you are unable to give to yourself!

Tips on Finding a Therapist

It is important to choose the right holistic therapist for you. There are many people who are 'in it for the money' and this will reflect on their treatment. It is ideal if a therapist has been personally recommended to you, and I find most of my clients are from personal recommendations. I always feel put off by therapists who are too 'business-like' and I feel that this takes away from the holistic approach (rightly or wrongly this is how I feel). A therapist should allow time for extended treatments if required (i.e. if an area needs a little more work than anticipated), and enough time between appointments for each client to be able to relax after treatment with a glass of water, get dressed (if applicable) and have a chat to reflect on the treatment and for the therapist to offer any advice they may have picked up during the session. If after treatment the therapist is rushing, or clock-watching for the next client, it can be extremely off-putting and contraindicative to the therapy that has just been received. For this reason I take a maximum of 3 clients per day. I know some that take many more!

I also tend to choose a therapist who has studied their therapy in a single diploma, or as a combined complementary therapies degree at a university rather than one of these combined part-time 'Holistic Therapy' qualifications that are meant to qualify the therapist in up to 6 therapies in a part-time year. I can't see how it is possible for anyone to study a therapy in the same depth as someone taking a single therapy diploma in the same time. I also tend to be wary of beauty therapists and spas as some of these treat holistic therapies as pampering and not serious health promoting therapy. That is not to say that they are all the same at all as there are some excellent therapists who also offer beauty treatments and have studied combined diplomas, but it is best to check them out and go with your gut feeling.

Cost

Therapists tend to charge pretty much what they want, I know some therapists charging £30 per hour, and others charging up to £100 per hour. The average seems to be £30-£50. It will depend on where you live as some areas are more expensive, but I have found that the simpler 'no frills' therapists who are usually at the cheaper to mid end of the scale, are the ones who are doing it from the heart. There can be a lot of snobbery in the field but to me this is ego driven and not holistic at all! You do not necessarily get what you pay for in this field, though someone who is quite sought after because they are very good will often charge more too!

It obviously also depends on the therapists expenses. If they practice from home I would expect them to be cheaper than one who hires a room or has a premises. If they travel to you they must also allow extra time and cost for travelling.

Above all, it is important to listen to your feelings and your heart and choose a therapist who resonates with you. Try to meet the therapist beforehand if you can, chat to them on the phone (a good way to see if they have time for you!) or just book a taster treatment so you can try them out without committing to too much cost. You may wish to attend a few health shows or mind, body, spirit festivals as many therapists will offer free or very reasonable tasters at these shows so you can 'try before you buy'! However, be aware that there are a lot of varied energies at these shows and many therapists (including myself) often avoid trading at shows for this reason. If you want to attend a health show, you may wish to wear a protective crystal such as amethyst, or carry or wear some orgonite.

CHAPTER 63...*Vibrational Healing & Energy*

Most holistic therapies, including homeopathy and aromatherapy, work on vibrations. All things that exist possess a natural vibrational energy field or Aura. This energy exists in vibrational harmony with its natural surroundings. The Aura can affect energies or vibrations of anything that enters its energy field and likewise, the 'being' will be affected by other energies that enter its Aura. In aromatherapy for example, essential oils extracted from plants will possess the vibrational energies from the plants. By using aromatherapy oils we are using the plant's energies, vibrations, and therefore its properties. When used on our bodies, the vibrational energies of the oils alter and affect our own Aura. In the same way when crystals enter our aura we are letting their vibrational energy interact with our vibrational aura. This is also how homeopathy works, by capturing the vibrational essence of a substance and coating a sugar pill with this vibration.

With vibrational healing, imbalances and blockages in our Aura that are causing us problems can be healed and released. The energy centres of our Aura are called Chakras, each affecting different aspects of our physical health, personality, emotional health and being, with each Chakra having a colour associated with it. It is believed that the vibrational energy and frequency of the colours and associated colours of essential oils, crystals, substances etc. can restore harmony and balance, and release blockages within the relevant Chakras. There is a lot more information on the Chakras in Chapter 84.

To fully understand the effects of vibrations and vibrational healing, we need to look back to school and simple physics. When you study waves, you observe that when 2 different wave patterns interfere with each other, a new wave pattern is formed. This is the same with vibrations. If you are having trouble thinking of us having vibrations or being vibrational energy, then think scientifically. We have energy, energy is vibration. Vibration cannot be contained in an object (i.e. our body) just like sound is vibrational energy and we can hear things through walls. So this energy is in us and around us (hence our aura).

Our thoughts are not held in our brain as per common belief, but are a part of our vibrational energy, and therefore must be energy themselves. We know this as we sometimes have thoughts from our stomachs (the solar plexus area) which present as gut feelings, we sometimes have thoughts from our heart which present as realisations often accompanied by a sigh or a flutter. Buddha's teachings state "what we think, we become", our thoughts are energy so they can attract the circumstances which help to make us who we are.

The Law of Attraction

Speaking of which, have you ever noticed how you think of something and then it happens? This is the law of attraction at work. Now we are getting into quantum physics, but rather than blowing our minds with scientific theory at the moment (we will leave this until later!), in short our thoughts are believed by science to be "electromagnetic representations of neuronal information" according to Wikipedia. This electromagnetic energy attracts similar energies. We see this in life as we often meet like-minded people 'coincidentally', but it is because they are of a similar vibration to us and our energies were attracted to each other at the time.

The law of attraction states that energetically like attracts like, and like karma, what we give out we receive. It plays in our lives relentlessly without judgement, without a break. Additionally, it is believed that the electromagnetic energy of these thoughts are magnified exponentially when combined with our powerful heart energy so when these thoughts are accompanied with feelings and emotions they are much stronger. So we really must take care of the thoughts and feelings that we are emitting. A good example is when you wake up and realise the alarm has failed and you are late, you put out a negative thought accompanied with a panicky negative feeling, which is returned by another negative event, such as you tip your coffee over your clean blouse, then you think "It is going to be one of those days", and the universe will reflect these feelings and give you exactly that!!

There have been many books written on the Law of Attraction, so you can appreciate that this is explained in very simple terms but it is basically how I came to understand and accept it at first with my scientific mind demanding an understanding of 'how'!

Now to explain it differently in relation to how we see our world. We are energy and have vibration which resonates at a frequency – just like a radio wave. If we are tuned into the negative radio wave we will see the negative in everything. We cannot see the positive as we are tuned into the wrong station. But by realising that Radio 1 still exists even if we are listening to Radio 2, it is easier for us to see that likewise, the positive side of the events and circumstances we are experiencing exist alongside the negatives! We just have to tune into them to find them. In order to tune ourselves into the correct frequency for receiving the positive vibrations of our lives, we must be grateful for what we have and think more positively. When something happens, find the positives, even if it is just that you have learned a life's lesson! Nothing is hopeless (unless you think it is)! Doing this will raise your vibrations onto a higher frequency enabling you to tune in to the more positive side of life. The good thing about this is that when you are resonating at a higher frequency you will begin to fail to notice some of the negatives as they will no longer affect you, and I know this as it happens to me! And I know that if I begin to be affected by negative emotions, I need to raise my vibrations a little more!

One thing I do to raise my vibration is thinking or looking around for something I love. Even if this is just a colour. Biologically, when we are thinking of or looking at something we love we release endorphins, serotonin and oxytocin, the feel happy and love hormones. These not only help me to feel better, but can have a profound healing effect on the body and mind.

It is also through the law of attraction that we can attract and manifest illness and disease, upset and sorrow, by our continuing negative thought patterns. If you really feel like a victim the universe will present circumstances that will continue to make you a victim! It is OK to feel sorry for yourself once in a while but do not dwell on it. I have developed the habit of counteracting negative thoughts immediately with a positive one, even if it is just "all is well". In this way, if you have a health condition and you use it to make excuses, you are handing all your power over to your condition – and becoming the victim again (more information on this in Chapter 61). To take back your power is simple. Every time you think of your condition, stop, and think immediately of something that you are grateful for. This way you are offering your love and power to your health and not your lack of health.

As you are probably aware by now, I am an advocate of balance in all things. Some people have taken the law of attraction to the extreme and blocked out all negativity from their thoughts and lives. But this can leave people in a false delusion of happiness and in denial of reality, so practice in balance and with wisdom.

A Fresh Look at Time

Alan Watts, an inspirational philosopher, first introduced me to the concept that we view time backwards (our past is first, then our present and then our future). But he is right, as this does not make sense. As Alan explains, we first think of something we want to do (in the future), we then do it (the present) and then it becomes our past. This blew my mind! Then, when I was learning the Silva Method (explained in the Meditation chapter), Jose Silva explains that in our subconscious mind, the future is to the left, present in front and past to the right. Now I have always thought of the future being to the right in my mind, so this was a big turn around for me! I now visualise a conveyor belt moving from left to right, and anything I want to manifest I place to the left on the belt so it moves into my present!

How Trapped Emotions Affect Us

As I mentioned, we are of an energetic nature and are essentially at one with the invincible life force (I believe this to be what is referred to as God). Emotions and thoughts are energetic and will effect the body's energy/vibration (taking it from this pure ease state to dis-ease, in other words, lower its vibration away from life force). This will effect how it works, develops and deals with and accepts foreign substances, whether they be good or bad. This is proven by the placebo and nocebo effects – how our thoughts and beliefs can change our physical reality.

We are obviously hard-wired to generally process natural substances efficiently as they are natural to us and therefore cause us the least energy expenditure/stress in processing them. But if the body is already energetically compromised (has its vibration lowered) by trapped emotions and/or negative thoughts or conflicts, then it cannot cope with further depletion, and if the vibration dips low enough, a negative response occurs. If our body was completely at ease, we are able to offset/manage our response as our vibration is higher than the offending substance and it cannot therefore effect our frequency (not enough for us to worry in any case). It's like having a stress cup and everything that stresses us fills the cup a bit more, whether it be physical stress by eating toxic foods, or emotional stress or everyday chronic stress. If the cup is not very full we have room to cope with additional momentary stresses and biological conflict shocks in a calmer and more rational way, and this will help us to not have such an intense reaction. But if the cup is already full, we cannot cope with a conflict shock or additional stresses and the reaction is more intense.

One of the reasons why only some people have negative responses to substances and why they will never find definitive causes of disease is that our personal reactions are very subjective. So we all perceive situations differently and will therefore manifest as different shocks and biological reactions will also then be different. I do believe that if we are pure in thought and do not hold on to negative emotion that our bodies could potentially be fairly invincible as we would be vibrating at one with the life force and lower frequencies just wouldn't even touch us – we would have, in effect, risen above them. Maybe this is why we rarely hear of spiritual people such as Buddhist monks get cancer, etc. I also believe it is why there is such subversion to cause negative emotions and bring us down emotionally as this depletes our life force and brings us more into this chronically stresses state with a full 'stress cup' which makes us more susceptible to their physical and mental poisons.

So it is the holding on of emotion that causes damage where we would otherwise be able to cope with the conflict shocks, traumas and stressful situations that inevitably come our way once in a while. Proof of this is my client experience in the Asthma Chapter 53.

342

CHAPTER 64...Reiki Healing

Reiki is pronounced "ray – key", and is a healing system that works with the energy systems within the body. 'Rei' means 'universal' and 'Ki' means 'energy'. Universal Energy is channelled through a Reiki Practitioner to the client through the Practitioner's hands.

Reiki healing energy works on a purely holistic level, in harmony with the body's natural ability to heal itself. Quite often certain Reiki hand positions are used, but the nature of Reiki allows it to find its way to wherever it is needed. It works on releasing blocked energies within the aura whether these be physical, emotional, mental or spiritual, and its vibration encourages the release of toxins from the tissues of the body bringing it back into a state of balance.

Reiki can be useful to help with any illnesses, as it will promote the non-stress state that the body requires for healing. I find it especially good for physical conditions which have an emotional trigger and for conditions such as anxiety, IBS, depression, insomnia and lack of energy. It is very relaxing to receive Reiki, so relaxing you may even fall asleep! Some people actually have a spiritual experience during their Reiki session, or have vivid dreams and visuallsatlons.

Reiki is performed fully clothed and you will generally lie down on a massage couch. You can also receive it sitting on a chair, or even by distance through meditation. The practitioner may begin performing a body scan to assess the energy blockages in the body, and then proceed to place their hands on or just above certain points on your body. It is common practice to work from the top of the head down but many practitioners work instinctively and will do whatever they are guided to. Each hand position is held for a few minutes, sometimes longer if required.

During a Reiki treatment you will reach a deep state of relaxation. You will feel the energy from the practitioners hands as heat, cold, tingling or a kind of 'buzzing'. You may feel sensations in your body as the healing shifts energies within you. But on the other hand you may not feel anything at all, just relaxation. I always find benefit in having 3 Reiki treatments over a period of 3 or 6 weeks to gain the maximum benefit from Reiki.

Reiki is suitable for anyone regardless of their faith or beliefs, however it is believed that the healing will flow more freely and be more effective if the healing is approached positively and with an open mind. It is suitable for animals as well as humans, and they are very receptive to it.

The traditional and most common branch of Reiki that is practised is Usui Reiki (Usui Shiki Reiki Ryoho). There are many other styles of Reiki that enhance and assist in the healing process when invoked during sessions, if the Reiki practitioner is attuned to practice these too.

It is also possible to give Reiki Healing distantly and even to the past and future. Reiki works on the universal energy which, as perfectly explained by David Icke is "all that is and ever was and all that will be". In this level of consciousness, time, space and distance do not exist as these are, in effect, constructs of the limitations of our own minds. This has been explained beautifully by Jose Silva who describes this as

344

"going to your level" and teaches how to reach the 'alpha sate' in order to better connect with universal energy. Our spiritual minds are not restrained by these limitations and the universal consciousness that we are conditioned to reject as fact is very real. It makes sense to me, and understanding this, I can see how therapies like Reiki actually work.

Training

Reiki training is different from any other type of therapy. You do not need to study it or go to college for it. It is taught by a Reiki Master/teacher who will perform an attunement and give you teachings and guidance. An attunement is a kind of 'ritual' whereby your Chakras (or spiritual energy centres) are balanced and you are connected to the Reiki source. This connection will be permanent and will allow you to channel Reiki Healing in order to give healing to yourself and others. It is a little like giving you a key to unlock a door.

I have met some people who say they do not need an attunement and can already channel healing – well may be they can channel a form of healing but it is not Reiki! We all have natural healing abilities, but Reiki is a powerful 'extra'. Some even have the misunderstood belief that if they know the Reiki symbols they can use them. But reflecting back on the 'Radio Stations' analogy of our vibrational existence, if we are not attuned to their frequency we cannot access their power. There is much debate on whether these symbols should be kept sacred and secret until Reiki level 2. In my opinion, the only harm it does to know them without the attunement is this potential of the confusion of being able to use them without attunement, and therefore I tend to not reveal them until I am teaching them.

Reiki I is the first level of Reiki. It will enable you to channel healing energy to yourself and friends and family. You are unable to practice Reiki professionally at this point.

Reiki II is the second level of Reiki. At this level you will be attuned to work with symbols which will enable you to channel healing to the past, present and future, over distance and particularly into the emotional body. Along with insurance, you are able to practice professionally at this level.

Reiki Master/Teacher is the third level of Reiki. This level enables you to pass on all attunements to others, including the master/teacher level. You are attuned to an additional symbol with which to be able to do this.

Some teachers will tell you the Master/Teacher level is the fourth level, and there is an interim 3rd level called 'Master' level. This is not so. It is exactly the same attunement that is used and only the knowledge of how to pass the attunements on is held back at the so-called third level! In my opinion, Reiki Masters offer the Master-only level for one of two reasons: either to make more money, or to protect their catchment area. Both reasons I disagree with as I believe Reiki needs to be passed around with love and light and the more the merrier! Also I believe that people need to find their own teacher, the right one for them, and the more teachers that are about the more choice there is!

Even if you have no desire to be a professional Reiki Healer, it makes a wonderful, effective way to heal yourself, your family and friends. Many people are attuned to the first level of Reiki only, simply so it can enhance their lives and those around them. It really is a worthwhile home remedy to learn, and can be used for a multitude of ailments to bring back balance, relieve pain and our pets love it too! From the results I have seen and experienced with Reiki Healing, including the way it has helped in my spiritual development, it is my opinion that it would be of great benefit to be attuned at least to level 1, and I would highly recommend it!

CHAPTER 65...*Crystals*

How Crystals Heal Us

Crystals have been used for thousands of years for their vibrational healing properties. As I have mentioned, we are all made of energy and have a vibration, our energy field is called our Aura. Our Aura can become blocked with the accumulated energy from negative emotions and imbalances and these blockages can cause physical, emotional, mental and spiritual problems for us.

Many people believe crystals are actually living as they hold energy, whether this is the case or not, they DO hold energy and they all have a vibration (which is why quartz crystals are used to keep perfect time in clocks) and the different crystals have different vibrations. Their vibrational properties will depend on many aspects including their colour (which is also vibrational energy) and the energies and properties of their content or make-up. Remembering back to physics class in school – when 2 vibrations (or waves) interact they alter each other. Therefore, by bringing specific energies into our Aura, we may release the blockages held there and protect our Aura from further attack from negativity.

Crystals are easy to use as a home remedy but you can also visit a crystal therapist who will lay appropriate crystals onto your body while you are lying down and relaxing. The therapist may also combine other healing techniques such as Reiki Healing, dowsing and kinesiology. Crystals can also be used in conjunction with other therapies such a reflexology.

DIRECTORY

Here is an alphabetical list of some crystals along with some of their supportive properties.

AGATE, BLUE LACE – growth, composure, infections, fevers. Brings calmness when worn and removes irritation and anger.

AGATE, MOSS - meditation, identity, lungs, glands

AGATE TREE – stabilising, promotes safety & security, gives strength in challenging and unpleasant circumstances, connects with nature, so good for plants and trees, helps find the positive in negative situations.

AMAZONITE – clarity, insight, emotions, nerves, growth. Beneficial to students as it assists insight and clarity of thought.

AMETHYST – devotion, neuralgia, protection, insomnia, addictions, acne. It softens negative feelings bringing peace and tranquillity, and is ideal for protecting against EMF when placed near electrical appliances.

AQUAMARINE – love, growth, allergies. Gives insight and has a calming effect upon the nerves, it also assists in cleansing the body.

AVENTURINE – eyes, migraine, tension, insomnia. Promotes healthy growth and development, including the development of mental abilities. Enhances judgement and promotes calmness.

BLOODSTONE – blood, toxins, depression, spine. As the name suggests, Bloodstone is primarily associated with the bloodstream promoting healthy blood, circulation and associated organs. It also encourages acts of kindness. It is green quartz with red jasper specks.

348

CALLIGRAPHY STONE – assists in keeping your cool under pressure, promotes seeing the positives, and turning hopeless situations into positive ones.

CARNELIAN – focus, arthritis, rheumatism, passion, neuralgia. Linked to the Sacral Chakra, it enhances sexual energy. Assists concentration and motivation and promotes a healthy bloodstream.

CHALCEDONY – stamina, tiredness, depression, circulation. Agate, Carnelian and Jasper are part of the Chalcedony family and the properties of this stone therefore will include each of their qualities.

CHRYSOPRASE – passion, renewal, fertility. Brings passion back into physical love. This stone will fade in direct sunlight.

CITRINE – cleansing, skin, diabetes, circulation. Brings sun to any situation, and linked to the Solar Plexus Chakra will help anxiety, depression and stomach tension. It assists in finding a new direction and purpose to those who are 'lost'. Promotes pleasant dreams when placed under the pillow. Also fades in sunlight.

FLUORITE – caring, infections, inflammation, bones, strengthens teeth. Promotes restoration, caring and healing and can assist those in the caring and healing professions.

HEMATITE – activity, tiredness, travel stress, eyes, blood. Helps to alleviate travel tiredness and stress, including jetlag. Assists healthy blood and circulation. Helps painful joints and promotes endurance, energy and courage.

HOWLITE – resilience, competing, bones, teeth

JADE – benevolence, bladder, digestion, kidneys, eyes. Used in many traditions as a protective amulet against negative people and for safe travel. It also brings friends together and promotes prosperity and longevity.

JASPER – comforting, attraction, digestion, nerves, blood. Jasper works slowly to promote health and balance in all aspects. It exerts a calming, soothing and comforting effect. Best worn continuously.

JASPER, DALMATIAN – nurtures and protects, promotes health, grounding and detoxifying. Excellent for using in areas of geopathic stress.

JASPER, LEOPARDSKIN – glands, eyes, safety, focus.

JASPER, YELLOW – liver, stomach, endurance, protection.

LABRADORITE – assists relationships bringing harmony and dissipating arguments. Heals inhibitions and offers spiritual and energetic protection. It promotes attractiveness and reveals hidden qualities.

LAPIS LAZULI – spirituality, creativity, bones, heart, eyes. Enhances creativity and assists in communication as it is linked to the Throat Chakra. It is refreshing to the spirit and can fill its environment with its qualities.

MALACHITE – recovery, optimism, rheumatism, asthma, teeth. Malachite uplifts the spirit bringing renewed optimism and assists in clarifying problems. Encourages prosperity in business and trade especially when it is not going well.

MOONSTONE – dreams, PMT, femininity, devotion, promotes will power in dieting. Moonstone promotes faithfulness and attracts love & romance. It also assists in healthy longevity.

MUSCOVITE – assists connection to angels, and promotes the awareness of the higher self, it also banishes insecurities and promotes self confidence.

OPAL, ROSE – brings joy and uplifts, and is good for diabetes.

350

OBSIDIAN – stomach, digestion, stress. Assists in achieving goals and attracting positive influences to overcome obstacles. It encourages negative feelings to be revealed so they can be healed and eases stress.

PREHNITE, TOURMALINATED – properties of tourmaline & prehnite. PREHNITE: enhances spiritual clarity and visualisation. Assists connection with higher energies. It can relieve nightmares and assists in remembering dreams. See tourmaline too.

QUARTZ, CLEAR – when placed or used with other crystals, clear quartz will amplify their energy. It also helps to purify the soul and helps Vertigo and Dizziness. It is often used for scrying and helps to clear the mind.

QUARTZ, GREEN – in addition to quartz properties, is good for the Heart Chakra, it helps to turn negative to positive, and is also known as Prasiolite.

QUARTZ, ROSE – stone of unconditional love, it also assists forgiveness. Known to help migraine, headache and wounds. Promotes joy and happiness in all relationships. Linked to the Heart Chakra it will encourage self love and acceptance.

QUARTZ, RUBY – promotes a joyful, passionate outlook and raises the vibrations.

QUARTZ, SMOKY – depression, abdomen, spine. Used as a good luck charm, and gives hope to those suffering difficult times. Reawakens the spirit and raises energy levels.

QUARTZ, SNOW – stress, nerves, relaxation, peace. Promotes tranquillity and retreat. It is ideal for meditation. Also called Milky Quartz.

RHODONITE – restoration, recuperation, communication, hearing. Relieves amnesia and helps to rebuild life after disaster

SELENITE – calming, brings peace and serenity, promoting a peaceful atmosphere. It assists angelic connections and is excellent for meditation

SERPENTINE – assists meditation, helps the stomach, PMT

SODALITE – assists meditation, helps the wearer to be more assertive, blood pressure, sleep, chest problems. For communication and offers assistance to those in the spotlight such as speakers, teachers and performers. Absorbs EMF and is great for meditation.

SUNSTONE – brings sunshine and joy to the wearer's life, good for SAD (seasonal affective disorder), promotes individuality and encourages abundant good fortune.

TIGERS EYE – grounding, protection, integrity, insight, limbs, asthma. Encourages looking beneath the surface to reveal truth. It is lucky and encourages bravery.

TOURMALINE – success, confidence, luck.

TURQUOISE –- throat, creativity, communication, environment, comfort, respiration. This protective and expressive stone helps friendships to develop and protects the home. It can purify the atmosphere in a room and promote tranquillity.

UNAKITE – back ache, muscles, feet. Promotes mental and physical stability and strength through difficult times. Enhances the effect of other stones.

ZODIAC STONES

Different crystals are believed to be particularly suited to the different zodiac signs. But there are no solid rules as you may require a different stone at particular times in your life! Here are some of the stones that are commonly associated with each zodiac sign:

ARIES (Mar21 – Apr20): Aventurine, Citrine, Bloodstone, Agate, Jade

TAURUS (Apr21 – May21): Carnelian, Bloodstone, Jasper, Jade

GEMINI (May22 – Jun21): Unakite, Aventurine, Agate, Citrine

CANCER (Jun22 – Jul22): Chalcedony, Hematite, Sodalite, Moonstone

LEO (Jul23 – Aug23): Labradorite, Jasper, Amazonite, Bloodstone

VIRGO (Aug24 – Sep22): Carnelian, Amethyst, Jade, Amazonite, Jasper

LIBRA (Sep23 – Oct23): Chrysoprase, Moonstone, Amethyst, Blue lace Agate

SCORPIO (Oct24 – Nov22): Amethyst, Unakite, Tigers Eye, Jasper, Moonstone

SAGITTARIUS (Nov23 – Dec21): Turquoise, Sodalite, Obsidian, Smoky Quartz, Chalcedony

CAPRICORN (Dec22 – Jan20): Tigers Eye, Smoky Quartz, Amethyst

AQUARIUS (Jan21 – Feb18): Aventurine, Rhodonite, Amethyst

PISCES (Feb19 – Mar20): Blue Lace Agate, Carnelian, Turquoise, Amethyst

ALL SIGNS – Rose Quartz and Clear Quartz

CHAPTER 66...
Aromatherapy as a Therapy

I have already covered aromatherapy in depth in Chapter 42, and this becomes a therapy when combined with massage. The combination of the two can have a profound effect on the mind, body and spirit.

Aromatherapy sessions can be anything from 30 minutes to 2 hours long depending on which part of the body that is to be massaged. Aromatherapists will offer anything from facials to full body massage and many will combine aromatherapy massage with other massage techniques such as sports massage, Lomi Lomi massage, Shiatsu and others. Some also use Reiki Healing.

Massage itself gives us one of our primary needs and that is touch. Unless there are issues present, we all feel better after the touch of another person whether it be a hug, a pat on the shoulder or being held in the arms of someone special. Touch has always been a huge part of our happiness. Babies are soothed by their parent's touch, we may be holding emotions in until we are hugged and the profound effect of that touch will encourage the release of all the blockages holding back those emotions.

Touching offers security and reassurance, it connects us on a deep level and it allows our auras to be affected by each other. If we have a slight blockage in our auric field, another's aura can help rebalance, just the same as introducing a crystal or essential oil into the auric field.

Touch is soothing and invokes a feeling of love and worth. It is not to be underestimated at all. Psychological studies have shown that how we feel about ourselves and how we interact with the world has a direct connection to how much affectionate touch such as hugging that we were brought up with.

On a physical level, massage can release blockages and muscle knotting by manipulation and release muscle tension. This can have an immense affect on the body's mobility. Conditions such as Repetitive Strain Injury (RSI) and Frozen Shoulder can be relieved just by easing the muscle knotting surrounding the problem area. Muscle knots occur where muscle is repeatedly over-used, or not used correctly. They commonly develop around an injured joint as the muscle tries to compensate for the ineffective movement of the joint. The muscle fibres effectively knot up and fuse together, but when these areas of congestion are manipulated by massage they can be broken down and the fibres released. Sometimes they need to have extra pressure applied which briefly starves the fibres of oxygen causing them to spasm. When this happens they usually will return to their natural shape, releasing lactic acid and toxins into the bloodstream for removal from the body (why you should always drink plenty of water 24 hours after a massage). This can be quite uncomfortable but can provide long term, and sometimes permanent relief, as healing can continue unhindered when there is no further self devaluation causing a delay in healing.

So it is no surprise then that massage combined with the power of the vibrational healing of aromatherapy oils can produce profound effects on all levels of our holistic bodies.

You will obviously need to undress for an aromatherapy treatment, but you will have towels for covering those parts not being massaged.

CHAPTER 67...Reflexology

Reflexology is a particular massage that works upon reflexes in the feet and/or hands to release tension and relieve illness in the entire body.

History

Reflexology originated in many parts of the world and in different traditions, each having their own version of pressure therapy. However it is mainly believed that a pressure therapy related to acupuncture formed the basis for reflexology originating over 5,000 years ago in China. It is also believed that the Egyptians practised a form of reflexology approximately 4,300 years ago due to cave drawings which appear to show people practising something very much like reflexology. Tribes in various places have also practised their own traditional reflexology-type therapy.

In Europe there is evidence that a similar type of pressure and zone therapy has been practised since at least the 16th century as there is a book on the subject written at that time. The benefit of working on the feet and in particular extended treatments on tender parts was discovered in the 1890s and this is how pressure points were discovered. This was further researched by Dr William Fitzgerald who co-published a book on zone therapy which is considered to be the foundation of modern reflexology, and this was picked up by Dr Riley whose research assistant developed the mapping of the zones on the feet to treat the whole body through the feet.

Clearing Blockages

The entire body is mapped out on the feet and hands through these reflex points and these are connected to the relevant body parts through the meridians, or energy channels. When there is a blockage at these reflexes the relevant body part will be affected.

Blockages can present as energetic blockages, and also physical blockages which are caused by calcium deposits or toxins. Approximately 1% of the body's calcium is found in the blood. This can be deposited at the nerve endings and in particular at the feet due to the gravitational effect on the blood flow. When there is insufficient blood flow, calcium depositing is made worse due to its increased inability to carry the calcium away from the feet against gravity. Furthermore, tension in the body, and pressure from incorrect fitting shoes can also increase the calcium deposits. These deposits present themselves to the reflexologist as grainy 'crystals' under the skin and when these are worked on they break down, sometimes feeling like they actually 'pop'. The lymphatic system is then worked on to carry the blockages out of the body through elimination. For this reason it is important to drink plenty of water for the 24 hours after treatment as it is with all holistic treatments.

Further Effects of Reflexology

Reflexology can bring pain relief as the reflexology massage will help to release endorphins, which are the body's own natural pain relief, in the brain.

The effect of reflexology on the body can be measured by Kirlian photography. This type of photography shows the surrounding energy field or aura. It has been shown that the energy field of the feet is diminished in the related areas where there are imbalances in the body. Further photography has been taken after treatment to show the effect that reflexology has had on the energy field.

The Treatment

Most reflexologists will use a reflexology chair or sun lounger for their client and sit at the foot of the chair. The chair is fully reclined and the feet placed on a pillow so the reflexologist is working on the feet at a comfortable level. If you suffer from a foot condition which is particularly severe, or have an injury to the foot, the reflexologist may work on the hands.

You will not need to undress but will obviously need to remove your shoes and socks. The reflexologist will usually use a light powder such as calendula or a lotion, and will begin and end the session with relaxation techniques. Many will also introduce some oils or moisturiser in the final stage of the massage.

You may feel discomfort when there is a blockage, the level of discomfort will depend on how bad the blockage is. If it is very painful the reflexologist will ask you to breath deeply and reduce their pressure.

CHAPTER 68...Kinesiology

Kinesiology is my favourite therapy, and if I had to give up all of my qualifications and keep only one, this is what I would choose! Kinesiology muscle testing has helped myself and my clients so much over the years and in this sense it has been invaluable. It really takes away the guess-work of anything, even our beliefs and knowledge of nutrition can be replaced with a simple muscle test. I use muscle testing daily, and could not imagine life without this knowledge!

Kinesiology is a holistic therapy that aims to restore balance to the body's energy system and assist the body's own healing process. The techniques tap into the body's energy creating biofeedback responses which reveal the physical, emotional and chemical/nutritional state of the body.

It was discovered by chiropractor Dr George Goodheart in 1964. He used muscle testing to assess his chiropractic work and then began to integrate the philosophy of acupuncture along with nutrition, and the works of Dr Bennett (discoverer of neuro-vascular points) and Dr Chapman (discoverer of neuro-lymphatic points). Kinesiology comes from the Greek word kinesis meaning motion.

It works with the Traditional Chinese Medicine concepts of Yin and Yang, the 5 elements, the meridians and the flow of Chi around the body. The meridians are 14 energy channels which run through the body, each associated with an organ along with Central, Governing, Triple Warmer and Circulation-Sex meridians. These meridians run in the vicinity of nerve pathways and muscles, and when the energy is blocked or restricted in the meridian, the associated muscle will become weak. Therefore, Kinesiology uses a system of muscle tests to ascertain whether there are any issues in the body's health. A basic Indicator Muscle can also be used while focusing on each meridian in turn.

Re-Balancing

If any meridians need balancing, various techniques such as meridian tracing, stimulating neuro-vascular points, acupressure and neuro-lymphatic massage can be performed. The muscles are then retested to see the affects. Further weakness may indicate another underlying issue such as deficiency or toxicity, physical or structural problem or an emotional/mental problem and further muscle testing and assessment will be necessary. These may be remedied by bringing supplements, foods or remedies onto the body to see if this cancels out the weakness, and if it does it would indicate that this particular remedy or supplement is required.

Kinesiology can be practised as a stand-alone therapy or used by health care practitioners or other therapists as a diagnostic tool to find the root of the problem. Sessions are generally carried out with the client fully clothed and either lying on a massage couch or standing up.

Other Benefits

Visiting a kinesiologist can alert simple problems that may otherwise be difficult to diagnose. For example, a therapist I visited discovered that my ileocecal valve (the one-way valve between your small and large intestine) was getting stuck closed. This meant the constipation and swelling I was experiencing after eating was not entirely down to food intolerances as I once thought. She showed me how to manage it with an easy adjustment and this has really helped!

Additionally my mother who had terrible pain for years due to arthritis in her spine, visited a local kinesiologist and osteomyologist, and he discovered she had parasites, prescribed a herbal protocol to her and along with a few alignments to her spine, she has been pain free for years! Kinesiology is an excellent way to uncover the root cause of symptoms and conditions and works perfectly in line with GNM as it is a great way of tapping in to the body to see what it needs at that time!

Testing for the Body's Intolerances and Needs

Using the simple Indicator Muscle test, various substances such as chemicals, supplements and foods can be brought into the body's energy field to see if the energy from that substance will weaken or strengthen the body's energy. Testing supplements in this way can indicate deficiencies, as the muscle will remain strong when holding the supplement closely, and weaken when it is taken away. In this way, a kinesiologist may perform 'allergy tests' on foods and substances.

How to do the Basic Muscle Test:

This is a very simple and handy tool to know for yourself as you can then see for yourself what is good and bad for you. It would not, however replace the benefits of visiting an experienced kinesiologist, as this is just one of the tools that is used!

- Bring an arm of the person to be tested out to the side or front at right angles to the body
- Using 2 fingers, press on the arm, asking them to resist you
- arm stays strong – positive / strong answer
- arm goes weak – negative / weak answer

Before Testing a product / asking a question:

We need to always ask energetic permission to do energy work. You can do this be asking "Do I have permission to muscle test for....."

Then do a 'lie' test to check yes and no answers are correct and to check the amount of pressure to use

> e.g. "my name is *name*", test, "my name is Mickey Mouse", test

If needed, re-balance by tapping in anti-clockwise direction up from heart and around, and try again.

To test a Food / Supplement:

- ask person to be tested to hold a food / product to their chest
- do the muscle test
- tell them to hold it out away from the body
- repeat the muscle test
- bring the product back in to the chest
- test again

STRONG WITH / STRONG WITHOUT – item is neutral, doesn't harm (weaken) but is not necessarily beneficial/therapeutic – if this was a food it is fine to eat, if it was a supplement, there is no point in wasting your money!

STRONG WITH / WEAK WITHOUT – item is therapeutic (better with than without)

WEAK WITH / STRONG WITHOUT – item is not good, will weaken the body, maybe intolerant

To ask a question:

Ask a question that needs a yes/no answer and test the arm straight after asking

> STRONG – yes, WEAK – no

If asking to choose from a list of possibilities, you are looking for the choice that gives a DIFFERENT response to the rest on the list (often all are strong but the chosen one is weak). Then re-test to confirm by asking again in a yes/no format (this time the arm should confirm strong / positive)

e.g.: "Do I have any vitamin deficiencies?" Strong = Yes, Weak = No

> if yes, list A, B, C, D, E, K, testing after saying each vitamin
>
> if D was weak, for example, then ask "So I am deficient in
>
> vitamin D?" Strong = Yes, Weak = No

Assisting Emotional Issues with Muscle Testing

Likewise, we can ask the body questions and receive a yes/no response by the muscle testing. Emotional issues can also be addressed in this way. This works by the body's energy weakening at any stress received by the subconscious mind.

So we can think of an event or trauma, and muscle test to assess whether that particular event or trauma still stresses us. If the response is weak, then we need to do some work!

Ask "Do I need professional help to release emotions relating to this?"

If not, you can learn EFT, use crystals, Reiki, meditation, Back Flower Remedy, or any other modality you have to hand or are able to use. I muscle test to see which would be most effective.

We can also ask if we have a trapped emotion that we can release today, which could be from any event on our lives. To find which emotion, we could use an emotion chart, such as that used by the Emotion Code or you could even make one yourself. Just be creative, but always remember to respect the energies and ask energetic permission so you do not interfere with any universal laws!

CHAPTER 69...Hypnotherapy

Another therapy that I have had great benefit from is hypnotherapy, but I am not qualified in it so I will keep this brief. I have received hypnotherapy both through an 8 week course of treatment, and through a CD course. That is the great thing about hypnotherapy – if you can get hold of a great hypnotherapy healing CD then you can treat yourself, however there is no real substitute for a 1-2-1 session with a therapist.

Hypnotherapy is a bit like guided meditation in that you relax and listen to the guidance, following any instructions given by the hypnotherapist. However it takes you a little deeper into hypnosis in order that the therapist's voice may bypass the conscious mind and access the subconscious mind directly.

Everything we are aware of is going through our conscious mind. It acts like a filter to our subconscious mind, accepting or dismissing information. When the conscious mind is bypassed by creating a distraction or diversion, and the subconscious mind is accessed directly, suggestions and instructions can get deep rooted into our subconscious and become part of our belief system which controls our body and thoughts. Subliminal messaging and imagery can bypass the conscious mind and this is why it is (meant to be) banned from advertising.

Our subconscious mind has a photographic memory so anything it hears or sees stays there. There is further explanation in "Inspiration & Hidden Messages", Chapter 88, as to why I believe it is important that we need to learn of the things we want to dismiss that are all around us like subliminals and symbolism.

But on a more positive note, if a therapist with true intention can access the subconscious, they can correct negative thought patterns, access past events that are causing problems in the present and implant beliefs to do with things like choosing healthy foods or de-programming the addiction to smoking or drugs.

Of course due to the nature of this therapy you need to seek out a therapist you can trust or who comes highly recommended. You don't want to leave your mind in the hands of someone you don't know anything about!!

I have heard stories (and also had experience myself) of remembering something from childhood that the innocent child-like brain has misinterpreted, and this misinterpretation has had a profound effect on the emotions and behaviour. For example, a hypnotherapist friend told me of a client who believed her mother had tried to kill her when she was younger by pushing her out of a car. This memory had caused her to fall out with her mother who was now very ill. During her hypnotherapy session she accessed this memory through her subconscious (remember the subconscious is photographic and will remember exactly as it happened). She saw that the car door had flew open at speed and her mother was holding on to her trying to rescue her and not trying to kill her at all. She made it up with her mother and was able to spend a few months with her before she passed away.

What to Expect

Sessions involve sitting back and relaxing listening to the therapist who will instruct you as you relax. They may also use imagery on a TV. You will be asked to give details of anything you experience usually at the time of being under hypnosis for the therapist to make notes of and help to develop their further sessions with you. Generally the therapist will let you and your subconscious reveal what is holding you back in the first few sessions before assessing the negative thought patterns that require re-learning and correcting. I personally found the hypnotherapy sessions to be life-changing – it was extremely liberating and yet very emotionally challenging at times!

Sessions can cost more than regular holistic therapies and you can expect to pay anything from £50 upwards, although some will offer a discount on a course of 6 or 8 weeks.

CHAPTER 70...Emotional Freedom Technique "EFT Tapping"

Emotional Freedom Technique is a very powerful tool to know. It assumes that every pain, issue and physical condition has an emotional base. Whereas this may be difficult to accept for some people, just think about this.

EFT works with our Meridians, which we have already discussed as being our 'circuitry' through which the energy of life (sometimes called Chi, Prana or Qi) flows. Everything that happens in our lives since we are born determines how we are 'wired', and therefore how we perceive and deal with everything. It is the reason why, when we all found out about the 9/11 Twin Towers disaster, some of us were angry, some were saddened but thankful it didn't happen to them or anyone they knew, some were so traumatised they feared going out and fell into the fear of terrorism. You see, same problem – different reactions which depend on how we are all wired or conditioned.

First Impressions

When I first heard about EFT, and was given some basic knowledge of the technique many years ago, I tried it but it didn't work. I then found a tutorial online a few years later, still it didn't work. I also didn't like the fact that you have to focus on the negative emotions of the situation to be able to release the emotions through the tapping. After all, aren't we told to only focus on positives and never to use negative affirmations? I also steered away from the use of a few gentle NLP techniques included in the more advanced tutorials as I had learned about NLP being used for bad, such as in Common Purpose.

The Original Source

Then, after another few years and while I was studying Kinesiology, I accidentally (or was it?) came across the original founder of EFT, Gary Craig. This was a huge turning point for me. His website takes you through a full course of tutorials and articles free of charge and available to anyone. He has done such amazing work and his seminars are truly inspiring, alleviating all my previous concerns about EFT and explaining why it never worked for me before. Learning from the source gave amazing results for me.

I have completed the Personal Peace Programme and have found freedom from many issues that have previously held me back. I will not share with you the technique in this book, as it is much better and more effective to learn directly from the source! The website to take the tutorials is www.emofree.com – the tapping method is called Gold Standard EFT.

EFT is a great way of downgrading a conflict, and healing emotions that may arise from realising a conflict and dealing with it, but it cannot actually resolve a conflict as this has to be done on the psyche level. Additionally, some long-standing conditions such as those related to heart, kidneys and gall bladder can create serious issues when a conflict is resolved abruptly. So it is best to investigate your condition with GNM in the first instance and consider EFT and other such tools as a supportive therapy if suitable and required.

SECTION VIII.....Physical Exercise & Yoga

CHAPTERS:

CHAPTER 71...Physical Exercise

I must admit I am not a big fan of exercise myself, and I definitely think as with anything, too much can be a bad thing. However it remains an essential part of a healthy lifestyle whether we are 'into' exercising or not! In ancient times, and even more recent history we obtained exercise from hunting, gathering, washing clothes by hand, cooking by hand, gardening to grow our food, walking or cycling for transport, basically doing everything manually. We were so much more active!

So it is particularly important in this convenient modern-day lifestyle to exercise as we do not get the physical activity that our bodies need when we rely so much on electrical appliances, motorised transport and non-physical hobbies and work.

In my very busy lifestyle I personally find it, as many do I am sure, very hard to fit exercise into my routine, and it is especially difficult with the wet and miserable weather we seem to be having so much of most of the year (in my neck of the woods anyway!).

Here are some ideas that may help you to include some activity in your day:

- Do as much housework and cooking by hand without using electrical gadgets, instead use elbow grease!

- Try to reserve a half an hour a day for either going for a walk, practising some Yoga or even a computer game activity such as the Wii Fit.

- Walk as much as possible – if you need to take the car to work or school, park around the corner to give yourself a few minutes walk!

- Use the stairs not the lift

- If you sit at a desk all day, look up some desk stretches and be sure to get up every hour for a walk around the office

- Leave for work or school half an hour early on nice days and stop at a park on the way for a walk

- Have a fun dance night once a week – get those old records out and dance like no-one is watching! This is such fun and a personal favourite of mine!

- Play on the children's garden toys when they are not looking – trampolining, swinging and skipping are great exercise and great fun – and will awaken your inner child!

- Have special time with your partner more often – this will also invoke very positive feelings, self love, increased closeness – and burn some extra calories!

Exercising while Detoxing or Changing your Eating Plan

I would suggest that a gentle exercise is undertaken such as Yoga which will also help with the detox. Do not start any vigorous exercising when beginning a new eating plan as your body will have enough to cope with! Wait at least a week or two to allow your body to adjust. Then build your activity levels up slowly so your body gets used to it.

Walking in nature and doing anything you feel is fun will bring about positive energy and help you in your healing process! Take extra care when getting used to the new eating plan and be kind to yourself!

Above all, exercise must be fun and not a chore – if it is a chore you will not be doing yourself any favours at all! And the good thing is – when you exercise you will actually have more energy, you will raise your metabolism and you will uplift your mood, burn out stress, help your circulation and greatly increase your sense of well-being!

CHAPTER 72...Yoga

My preferred exercise is Yoga – which is not merely an exercise but a complete way of life and belief system. I love it because you can adapt the physical practice to suit anyone's abilities or circumstances, it can be a cardiovascular workout or relaxing and de-stressing gracefulness! You can also take from your practice what you wish, although it is best to practice it in balance – it can be purely meditative and spiritual, or physical and toning. But the thing I love most about Yoga is that it works upon your entire holistic body, on your body, mind and spirit. It helps your mind to connect with your body, helps your balance, corrects your posture and helps you to get to know your body in ways that you never thought possible! It stretches muscles you never knew you had and, despite this, it is possible to attend a 2 hour class and be surprised that it was over so quickly. You feel so energetic and wonderful, feeling like you have really worked out, but didn't even realise how much work you were doing at the time!

Health Benefits

Yoga can benefit the health of the practitioner in many ways. When the muscles are stretched they release toxins and the increased circulation will carry them out of the body. It improves your energy, and promotes a sense of well-being and positive attitude. It stimulates your body, calms and de-stresses the mind, and eases depression. Internal organs are massaged and cleansed during postures and your muscles will gain strength, flexibility and endurance. The far reaching health benefits of Yoga are only just being discovered and more and more people are claiming it as being extremely beneficial to their overall health and well-being.

Classes

Yoga is definitely perfect for those who don't like too much physical exercise, but it can also be adapted for those that do! This is why it is important to find a suitable class. Do not be put off if you go to a class and don't get on with it. There are as many different classes as there are teachers. Some are very spiritual and non-demanding physically, some chant some don't, some are even like drill sergeants!

The class will generally, although not always, be divided into 3 parts. There is the Asana (physical postures), the Pranayama (breathing exercises) and Meditation/Relaxation. Some classes do not cover these 3 but in my opinion they are all as important as each other. Classes can be anything from 45 minutes to 2 hours long – don't let the longer classes put you off as this generally means that the teacher has a very relaxed and thorough approach and often will teach about the other aspects of Yoga too.

For class you should wear loose comfortable clothing that will not restrict your movement, a soft cup bra (unless you are a man!!) and bare feet. You will generally practice on a mat or blanket, and you may need to bring these with you. It is also a good idea to take warm socks and a blanket for meditation, and some water. If you are inflexible you may wish to take a cushion and a belt or non-stretchy scarf to help you in postures, although your teacher may provide these for you. Classes can cost from £5 upwards per class and many teachers offer a discount if you pay for a block of classes in advance.

Yoga at home

Yoga is great for practising at home and I would suggest that 15-30 minutes is practised daily if that is convenient. However I would not suggest you start Yoga practice without first having been shown how to correctly go in and out of postures – this is as important as the postures themselves!

On the following pages I have given an idea of the philosophy of Yoga and the different styles available.

Om

Om is the core of Yoga. Its sound and vibration are believed to be the essence of the universe. Om is a sacred Sanskrit (ancient Indian language) sound that is sometimes chanted to aid meditation at the end of class. Its vibration has a cleansing and relaxing effect on the body, and helps the mind to find space between the thoughts.

CHAPTER 73...Paths & Types of Yoga

Yoga Means Union and has links with the English word 'Yoke'. This can have many meanings and is commonly thought to be the union between body and mind, or body, mind and spirit, however the traditional acceptance is "union between the Jivatman and Paramatman that is between one's individual consciousness and the Universal Consciousness. Therefore Yoga refers to a certain state of consciousness as well as to methods that help one reach that goal or state of union with the divine."

The Paths of Yoga

Traditionally the Yoga student follows one or more of the following paths, also called Margas:

Karma Yoga: the way of right action, serving without the motivation of obtaining the results. Karma Yoga is practised by giving and not expecting to receive. This is believed to cancel out our bad karma that we have from the past and previous lives, and give us good karma so that we may reach our enlightenment more quickly.

Bhakti Yoga: the path of devotion. The Hare Krishna's practice Bhakti Yoga by devoting themselves to Hare Krishna. They are known as devotees. As Yoga is non-denominational, it may be practised by devotion to whichever God is in your belief, or simply to yourself.

Jnana Yoga: the way of knowledge and studying and learning to associate between illusion and reality.

Hatha Yoga: the physical path, using the body through asana and pranayama to control the mind and senses. Many Yoga teachers have devised their own styles of Hatha Yoga some are explained below:

- *Ashtanga (or Power Yoga):* Athletic and fast paced. It uses Ujjayii breath throughout practice.

- *Bikram:* Sometimes called Hot Yoga, athletic, focused yoga practised in a very hot room. Bikram is a rigid sequence of 26 poses. Bikram instructors are often strict like drill sergeants!

- *Iyengar:* Technical yoga focussing on correct alignment and also uses many props. The therapeutic properties of the postures are also emphasized.

- *Sivananda:* This has a rigid class structure of postures, pranayama, meditation and relaxation, with many advanced poses.

- *Viniyoga:* A flowing and therapeutic yoga with repetitive movements flowing in and out of a posture.

Tantric Yoga: the feminine path (but not just for females!), worshipping the goddess energy and seeing the body as the temple of the divine.

Kundalini Yoga: the path of energy, through breathing and movement. Balancing the Chakras is an important practice in Kundalini Yoga and it incorporates pranayama, asana, and chanting.

Raja Yoga: the path of meditation. It is also known as Royal Yoga. Hatha Yoga is a sub-path of Raja Yoga.

Mantra Yoga: the path of chanting and devotional meditation.

CHAPTER 74...*Yoga Philosophy*

The main philosophy of yoga is that the mind, body and spirit are all one and cannot be separated. The following are simple explanations of the different aspects of the Yogic philosophy.

The Law of Karma – Yoga firmly believes in the law of karma – the universal spiritual concept of reaping what you sow. Karma can be passed between reincarnate lives meaning our past lives can affect our present, and our present lives affect our future lives.

The Cause of Suffering: The Kleshas – The Kleshas are ignorance, ego, attachment, repulsion (hatred) and our will to live (fear of death). These are the negative conditioning that affect our mind and perceptions of how we think, act and feel. The kleshas are believed to create our suffering and tie us into the cycle of birth and rebirth. When we conquer the kleshas we can achieve enlightenment.

The Inward Journey Through the Koshas – The koshas can be imagined as layers of an onion, these layers being the planes of consciousness or bodies that make up our complete selves. These are physical body, energy body, mental body, intuitive body and soul. Blockages in the Koshas prevent us from realising our true nature of oneness with the universe. Yoga can release these blockages to bring our awareness deeper into our selves.

Moksha and Maya – Moksha is liberation and freedom, the state of 'non-ego', where duality (me and the universe) vanishes. It is liberation in a complete state of oneness, free from desires, actions and consequences. Maya is consciousness (physical life) and what reinforces our suffering & ego.

Kundalini, Shiva & Shakti – It is believed that Maya is created when the male energy of Shiva moved away from the female energy of Shakti. Shakti is believed to reside in our root chakra at the base of our spine, held down by a spiral of energy, coiled 3 and a half times, called the Kundalini. This is believed to be governed by the individual's Karma and the Kleshas. Shiva (male) is believed to reside in the crown chakra. The aim of Yoga is to release Shakti from the grip of the Kundalini energy by clearing our karma, becoming detached from the kleshas, balancing our chakras and entering a transcendental state. When this happens, the Kundalini energy will rise up the spine, freeing Shakti to meet again with Shiva and banishing Maya.

The 3 Gunas of Nature – In Yogic philosophy, the primal universe is known as Prakriti, and from this are 3 energies or qualities called Gunas which are present in all matter in differing degrees. These (usually present in this order as life unfolds) are Rajas (growth & activity), Sattva (purity & being) and Tamas (death, decay & darkness).

Ultimate Reality – This is the acceptance of our sensory perception as being an illusion and it mustn't be taken for granted that everything is as we see it to be. Everything has an ultimate reality and each person's perception of it is merely their interpretation of the information they are receiving from the universe.

Infinite Cosmic Consciousness - This is the acceptance that there is a oneness, an infinite pure energy, which we are an expression of. We are spiritual beings, connected to an ultimate unified source, having our own human experience through our own unique perception. Put another way, we are merely a small part of the universe as a whole, while still being our own individual self (like a drop in the ocean, although it is said we are also the entire ocean in one drop!). This is why it is considered that we are hurting ourselves when we hurt others. We are all part of the same consciousness, and that consciousness is a part of us. It is why outward experiences and conflict relate to, and can be affected by, our inner state of peace (as above, so below) – as it is the same energy, or at least connected with it. It is why repeated patterns exist in the universe, mathematical phenomenon and sacred geometry throughout nature and existence, from the smallest atom to the largest universal feature, as it is all part of the same code. It is this code that ceases to exist in man-made chemicals, GM foods and other harmful substances that destroy our bodies and the world. They are against the universal code, the natural law or, as some say, the math of God. It is the awareness of the existence of everything, including what is beyond our present realms of perception and awareness. In other words, the impossible may be possible, and just because we can't see/hear it doesn't mean it doesn't or can't exist. We therefore need to open our awareness to acceptance and possibility and not have a narrow, blinkered view that only our conscious can perceive.

Understanding and practising these principles naturally brings us more love, peace and understanding in our world as we become more sensitive to the universe of which we are a part. This in particular helps the individual to live according to the rules and principles of Yama-Niyama, as explained in the 8 Limbs on the following pages.

CHAPTER 75...The 8 Limbs of Yoga

The Eight Limbs are a progressive series of disciplines believed to purify the body and mind, and ultimately lead the yogi to enlightenment. They were compiled by the Sage Patanjali Maharishi in the Yoga Sutras.

These 8 limbs are:

1. **Yamas** – The Yamas are "don'ts" and they are aimed at destroying the lower energies within when practised thoroughly in word, thought and deed.

   - **Ahimsa** – non-violence / compassion

   - **Satyam** - truthfulness / honesty

   - **Brahmacharya** - moderation in all things and control of all senses, including celibacy and faithfulness

   - **Asteya** – non-stealing

   - **Aparigraha** - non-jealousy / non-envy

2. **Niyamas** – The Niyamas are the "do's" and with the Yamas complete the ethical morals. They are:

   - **Saucha** – purity, internal and external cleanliness.

- **Santosha** – contentment
- **Tapas** – sincerity & austerity
- **Swadhyaya** – study, always open to learning
- **Ishwara Pranidhana** – always conscious of the divine nature / universe / God

3. **Asanas** – the physical postures

4. **Pranayama** – regulation or control of the breath and life force, and together with Asanas are known as Hatha Yoga.

5. **Pratyahara** – withdrawal of the senses in order to still the mind.

6. **Dharana** – concentration.

7. **Dhyana** – meditation is that state of pure thought and absorption. There is still duality in Dhyana ('I' and the universe or God).

8. **Samadhi** – the deepest and highest state of consciousness where body and mind are transcended, duality is now oneness or non-duality, and the Yogi is 'at one' with the Self and the universe (or God).

CHAPTER 76...
Pranayama – Yogic Breathing

Pranayama is made of 2 words: Prana is the Sanskrit (ancient Indian) word for 'Life Force', as the Chinese call Chi; Ayama is the Sanskrit word for 'Control'. When we breath it is believed by many that we are not just breathing in oxygen, but also we are bringing the life force into our bodies. This has a profound effect on our bodies, minds and spirits! Yogic breathing practices have been used by many practitioners, doctors and health experts and incorporated into many stress-reducing and self-help programmes. It is better to learn these practices from a Yoga Teacher, however they are detailed here for you to try as they can help to alleviate many common complaints. These practices are very supportive to the healing phase of a disease.

While practising Pranayama:

It is a good idea to imagine the breath as a colour, maybe a bright energetic yellow as it fills your lungs. Then imagine your exhaling air to be a stale colour such as brown, ridding your body of all the 'dirty' impurities and toxins.

Only practice the number of breaths that you are comfortable with even if this is only 2 or 3 breaths to start with.

Please be careful if you:

- have low blood pressure/depression – make sure exhalations are not too long

- have high blood pressure/heart problems – make sure inhalations are not too deep

- are pregnant – take it easy, not too deep with inhalation, not too long on exhalation

- if you feel dizzy or unwell at any time, return to your natural breathing.

Full Yogic Breath or Complete Breath

This can be performed either lying down in Savasana (corpse pose – flat on the back in a star shaped position), sitting in Siddhasana (perfect pose – loosely cross-legged) or standing in Tadasana (mountain pose – standing upright with a straight back). The effect can be enhanced by raising the arms above the head when inhaling, and lowering them when exhaling.

Step 1: Abdominal breathing

First just take a moment to observe your natural breath. Now begin to deepen and lengthen your breath by expanding your stomach completely while inhaling and bringing it into your spine slowly when exhaling. Try to keep the chest still during this practice and only move the stomach. Do 10 breaths and then take a rest.

Step 2: Thoracic (chest) breathing

Start by observing your normal breath again. Now begin to deepen and lengthen your breath by expanding your chest to completely fill your lungs, and when you exhale let your chest relax right down. Try to keep the stomach still and move the chest only for 10 breaths and then take another rest.

Step 3: Full Yogic breathing

This combines the above 2 steps:

First inhale by filling the abdomen and then when it is extended, continue inhaling as you expand the chest. Then as you exhale, empty and relax the chest first and then proceed to relax and breath out from your stomach. This is one round of the full yogic breath. Try to repeat this for 10 complete breaths, but only do what you are comfortable with.

The best way to remember this process is into the tummy, rising up, out from the chest, lowering down.

You may find your breath is uneven and a bit forced and you may even feel yourself yawning! This is normal to begin with. It will soon regulate itself, so do not worry, and never strain or force it.

The full yogic breath forms the basis of Pranayama. But in itself it has huge health benefits. First and foremost it calms the mind, releases tension in all parts of your body, brings much needed oxygen into your body, revitalises your soul, detoxes your lungs, improves circulation and conditions the muscles around your chest and heart.

Rhythmic Breathing

Rhythmic breathing emphasizes the ratio between inhalation, retention, exhalation and relaxation. This ratio is a count of 2 inhalations and exhalations to 1 retention and relaxation as follows:

Inhalation: 1-2-3-4, Retention: 1-2, Exhalation: 1-2-3-4, Relaxation: 1-2

This can be practised as often as you wish, gradually increasing the number of breaths up to a count of about 10 for the inhalations and exhalations, and 5 for the retentions and relaxations.

Rhythmic breathing is excellent when practised along with a flow into and out of postures, or combinations of postures as it allows time in each posture during the relaxation periods. A prime example is the Cat sequence where you are on all fours, using the breath to arch then curve the spine.

The Cleansing Breath

This breath consists of a deep inhale through the nose followed by short sharp exhalations through the mouth.

Stance: Feet hip width apart, knees slightly bent, hands on thighs, lean slightly forward

Practice: Take a deep long breath in. Pucker your lips as if trying to blow up a balloon. Exhale in a short, forceful burst through the mouth, then hold the breath briefly. Repeat the short, forceful exhale again then hold very briefly. Continue with this and each time you exhale, lean forward a little more, bending at the hips. Do this until the lungs are completely empty.

Straighten up to your starting position as you breathe in deeply again through your nose.

Repeat this exercise 3-5 times, but discontinue should you feel giddy.

Effects: cleansing, rids the lungs of impurities and toxins, strengthens and tones the diaphragm, clears the head.

Ujjayii Pranayama (victorious breath)

This practice allows further control of your breath and the flow of Prana into and out of your body.

Stance: Sit in Siddhasana (Perfect pose) – loosely cross legged.

Obtaining the Ujjayii Inhalation:

- Take a deep breath in
- Open the mouth and breathe out making a haaa sound, as if fogging a mirror
- Repeat this twice
- Half way through your third exhalation close your mouth so the breath comes out of your nose. This should create a hmmm noise like a punctured tyre deflating.
- If you cover the ears it should sound like the ocean.

Obtaining the Ujjayii Exhalation:

- Open your mouth to breathe in making a haaa sound
- Exhale normally and repeat this twice
- Half way into the third inhalation, close the mouth making a hmmm sound

Full Breath:

The Ujjayii breath is one full controlled breath in and out with the mouth closed. The methods above are used only to obtain that way of breathing. Practice up to 10 Ujjayii inhalations and exhalations, with long and steady complete breaths, or as many as you are comfortable with.

This breath is good to use throughout your asana (posture) practice to lengthen the effect of the posture and breath. It regulates and controls the breath and is particularly good for flowing (Vinyasa) yoga sequences such as the Sun Salutation. It also allows a better relationship between the breath and the movement and helps to relax the muscles so they can stretch efficiently into each posture.

Nadi Sodhana (or Nadi Suddhi) – Alternate Nostril Breath

As the name suggests this breath consists of breathing alternately through each nostril.

Stance: Sit in Siddhasana. Curl the fingers of the right (or left) hand, leaving your little finger & thumb straight (if it is more comfortable you may use your ring finger and your thumb). Place the thumb of the other hand to the tip of the index finger as you will use this hand to count the rounds you do. To do this, move the thumb to the next section of the finger on each round completed, then begin on the next finger (giving 3 rounds per finger).

The following instructions are assuming you are using your right hand. You may use your left hand if you wish meaning the left/right will be reversed.

Practice:

- Hold the right nostril closed with the thumb
- Breathe in deeply through the open nostril
- Hold both nostrils closed with the thumb and little (or ring) finger for a moment
- Release the thumb and exhale through the right nostril
- Pause for a moment
- Breathe in deeply through the right nostril
- Replace the thumb holding both nostrils closed for a moment
- Release the little finger and exhale fully through the left nostril
- Pause for a moment

This is one complete round. You may now move the thumb of the left hand to the next section of your finger to start a new round. Practice 5 complete rounds, increasing to 10 over time.

Make sure the elbow of the raised arm is held outwards a little so it doesn't restrict your chest. Change your arms if there is tension in the shoulders.

This practice purifies (suddhi) the meridians (nadi), in fact your pingali nadi and ida nadi. It balances the nervous system and is particularly useful when you are uptight and confused. It calms the mind and helps you to settle if practised at bedtime. It has also been known to ease migraine and has a decongestant effect.

Bhramari (Humming or Bee Breath)

As the name suggests, this breath consists of exhaling with a humming sound.

Posture: Any comfortable seated or kneeling posture, you may cover the eyes if you wish. The mouth should be closed, jaw relaxed, teeth apart, tongue softly touching the palate

Practice:

- Inhale fully
- Exhale making a humming sound
- Bring awareness to the vibrations expanding them out of the throat and throughout the head and body
- Practice for 2-5 minutes then rest to enjoy the effects

If you experience any dizziness or tingling return to your normal breathing.

This practice brings constancy to the breath, naturally deepens inhalation and encourages slow, rhythmic breathing. It provides a point of focus and has a soothing effect on the Body, Mind & Spirit.

TIP

For the most benefit when practising any Pranayama exercise, you need to use the complete breath in a slow and controlled manner, unless advised to the contrary.

Try bringing your awareness to how your chest feels after practising Pranayama. Do you feel areas that feel quite cold or cool? These are the parts of your lungs that are not used as often as the rest. The coolness is felt because these areas are used to containing warm, stagnant air. This helps us to realise how much more efficient we may be with increased oxygen intake if we were to breathe more fully!

SECTION IX.....Free your Mind

CHAPTERS:

CHAPTER 77...Stress

Stress is reported to be one of the biggest killers and causes of disease today. There are many stress-busting therapies and practices that are trending recently that claim to reduce, or even banish stress. But before we get carried away, we must understand some points here:

1. From the GNM perspective, stress cannot cause any disease. It can however, greatly hinder and even stop our healing process, and so can cause a 'hanging healing' and chronic conditions.

2. Our bodies actually need stress to a certain extent and many of our inner processes would not function properly without it. Hormones are released when we are stressed which trigger off other processes and reactions in our bodies and these keep us alert and healthy. Organ muscles under no stress will simply die as we all know muscles need to be used to be able to live and be healthy.

3. Focusing on 'killing stress' or 'de-stressing' is actually focussing on stress itself. When we focus on something we actually give it power, as explained in the introduction of Section VII when I talk about positive thinking and the law of attraction. Of course we must address causes in our lives of unnecessary stress such as miserable or unappreciative jobs, relationship worries, etc., but instead of purely focussing on 'de-stressing' at the end of a

busy day, focus on relaxing and appreciating your home. It is a much more positive way of coping with it!

The way I understand it is there are 2 types of stress: necessary & unnecessary. Necessary stress keeps us on our toes, so to speak. It enables the correct and proper functioning of our bodies and exercises our organs, glands and nervous reactors. Unnecessary stress is what we get when there is a deep down unhappiness that has a cause, or when there is a constant or heavy physical stress upon our bodies, often caused by some sort of imbalance.

Fighting Stress

This whole stress propaganda 'fighting stress', is reminiscent of all the 'fights' we are made to have each day – 'fighting against war', 'fighting AIDS', 'fighting cancer', fighting for this and that – this in itself causes us unnecessary emotions purely due to the word 'fight'. When we are in a fight our adrenalin is pumping and our energy is taken from our vital organs and from the inner 'workings' of our bodies to our muscles in what's called a 'fight or flight' reaction. This is extremely detrimental to the healing phase of any biological programme we may be in as it takes us out of the required non-stress state. It is only a thought I've had, but what if talking of and being constantly reminded of all these 'fights' are actually affecting the more sensitive of us by keeping us in this state of 'fight or flight' permanently? I know I have found this with some clients, and this continued stress can cause adrenal fatigue which can weaken the thyroid. If we just change our way of thinking away from the propaganda, into our own natural positive and logical thought patterns, it may just help to reduce the levels of stress we are feeling, without making any other major changes to the way we are thinking or what we are doing at all! So rather than 'fighting cancer' we can 'promote health'; 'fighting for our rights' becomes 'asserting our rights'; 'fighting against war' becomes 'promoting peace'.

Are you REALLY Stressed?

Some may say that today's lifestyles are demanding and stressful, not like they were in the past, and so we are subject to much more stress nowadays. But I disagree. We have busy lifestyles, but in the past people had a different stress – that of survival, and I mean *real* survival not 'surviving in work' or 'surviving the day's obstacles' etc. People had to make everything they needed, hunt for their food – imagine how stressful that could be, not even knowing if you were going to be able to feed your family? What about illnesses that were untreated as there was no convenient access to medical professionals, having to watch people close to you suffer and not knowing what to do. I may sound older than my years when I say this, but we really have it easy nowadays - convenience all the way! Furthermore, it seems propaganda is pushing this fear of stress and TELLING US we are suffering from stress over and over again – and if we are told something enough we will believe it!

When we understand this, if we still feel we are suffering from unnecessary stress then you need to take action. When we look at our lives in balance and with clarity, we can see deep down what the real cause (or causes) of any unnecessary stress is and no amount of de-stressing oils, therapies or meditation will help if the root cause for your stress is not dealt with. We must remove our fears and deal with it! There are the obvious causes such as being unhappy at work or home – these things that I cannot help with, only you can help yourself.

Does the Stress Belong to You?

Many people also take on the unnecessary stress of the worry of the world's problems. I was one of these people, but I overcame this by realising that I needed to focus on protecting my family and bringing about small changes in my own lawful rebellion. I realised that if everyone did this and empowered themselves, it would actually solve

394

many of the world's problems as I explain further in the conclusion.

In addition to all these external stresses and fights, we are also subject to constant stress through propaganda involving moral dilemmas that pressure us to put other issues before ourselves and our families. This is stressful as it is against our human nature and instinct of survival. It's like our compassion is being played off against our instincts. This is seen when we are pressured to vaccinate ourselves and children despite the risks for the sake of 'herd immunity', so those who cannot receive vaccines are protected. We are 'encouraged' to put animal welfare before our own need to eat meat (if we need to do so to be healthy). We are putting environmental issues before our basic needs of warmth and energy (for the sake of climate change propaganda). Even in the December 2019 elections and political debates, certain parties who wanted to remain in the EU were campaigning for people to vote as if they had someone else's circumstances (e.g. 'vote as if your Mum is a refugee')!

I decided to write this book as a way of getting the information and thoughts (and emotions) that were 'stressing me out' to a degree, out of my head and onto paper and into the world. This has also helped me realise that no matter how busy I am, I am not 'stressed' – just sometimes tired as my energy has run out – there is a big difference!!

CHAPTER 78...Finding Balance in Relationships

One of the biggest causes of stress that we may not realise, in my opinion, appears to be relationship stress and this can be simply a misunderstanding of each other. So I have put together a summary of advice that Lloyd and I have found invaluable. Understanding each other helps us to relax and release our unnecessary daily stresses, share our feelings, support each other and find balance and harmony at home.

Defining the feminine and masculine traits

Feminine: The feminine instincts are to nurture their dependants and home, gather (shop) and outwardly talk about their feelings to find peace.

Masculine: The masculine instincts are to provide, protect their loved ones, provide solutions in a logical way to their loved ones when they are not happy, and unlike females, require solitude to solve their problems, or deal with their feelings in their own way.

Problems begin as we do not understand that not only do we speak a different language to each other, but also we have almost opposite needs to each other.

A man needs his solitary place to solve his problems or calm his stress,

John Gray in his book Women are from Venus, Men are from Mars refers to this as being 'in his cave'. Women don't understand this and when their partner is quiet she will think he is a) upset with her, b) has a secret from her or c) doesn't love her enough to share his feelings with her. This is because she thinks he needs to talk about his feelings to release them like she does.

Likewise when a woman is having a little moan to her man to release her feelings, he thinks she is logically complaining to him and that in order for him to make her happy he has to fix her problems for her. But more destructively is that he will feel blamed for not making her happy, due to his instincts that it is his job to do so. This will obviously cause him to become defensive, and when she refuses his solutions to her problems he will also feel rejected and a failure. Little does he realise that his partner just needs to let out her negative feelings – they are not aimed at him, even if it may seem like, it is merely a release. She may make unfair comments or generalisations such as "you are never here for me" but of course she doesn't mean it, she is just releasing her stress.

You could think of it as this: she needs an emotional punch bag in order to release her worries, fears and stress. The best thing a man can do is to be that punch bag, but rather than take what she says literally, dodge the punches! Once his partner feels supported and releases her emotions, he will realise that everything is OK, and was all along – she just needed to release!

Likewise, a woman can offer her partner support by leaving him alone when he is 'in his cave'. She may feel that she wants to find out what is wrong by asking questions, but if a man is left alone, he will emerge more loving and appreciative and be ready with his punch bag suit!

The 'Feminine' side in the 'Masculine' work environment

I instinctively want to nurture my children and make our home loving, welcoming and comfortable. But I am prevented from doing this as I would like as I need to work, which not only uses up my energy, but uses my masculine side and neglects my feminine side. When I arrive home from work I revert to my natural feminine nurturing role and therefore feel I cannot rest until the jobs around the house are done. This is not Lloyd's instinct – his natural male instinct is to find solitude for a little while to release his feelings and stress by creating a distraction like playing with our children or just spending some quiet time on the computer. This resulted in me feeling it was unfair that he could switch off so easily when there were umpteen chores to do – I just couldn't understand how he could play in a messy room that needed a vacuum!

This causes inner stress to women in 2 ways:

1. women cannot rest when they get home as their feminine side wants to then switch to nurturing. Generally their tiredness or lack of energy from burning themselves out working all day prevents them from satisfying their feminine instincts.

2. friction in the relationship caused when a woman doesn't understand how a man can switch off, and likewise a man gets frustrated when he sees his partner unable to switch off despite her stress and tiredness.

It also causes inner stress to men in 2 ways:

1. they are made to feel guilty for not helping more around the house, thereby not able to release their stress in their own way

2. they feel pressured and nagged at by their partner and this turns them away from them, even though they only want to make her happy so they feel they have failed

Also important to note is that abnormal hormone status can cause us to experience the conflicts of the opposite sex. We therefore, in effect, reverse roles later in life. See Chapter 60 on Menopause for more information on this.

The 'Little woman in the House'

Feminism has done a lot for women. Without it we couldn't vote or even begin to be classed as anything but a man's property. However, as with everything, there must be a balance. Along with the increasing rise of feminist approaches, women have been made to almost feel ashamed of being a housewife and full time Mum, feeling like the 'little woman at home chained to the sink'. I was a housewife and full time Mum for the early years of each of my three children. Personally, I felt proud inside that I had chosen this for my children, but admittedly, I almost felt embarrassed to tell people I was a housewife when they asked what I did for a living. Had I realised that it was feminist propaganda and not my instincts that made me feel this way, I would have found much more happiness and peace in being proud of keeping my home warm, comfortable and clean for the family, providing lovely home cooked food and nurturing them when they came home. Women are made to think 'what about me' all the time, but they instinctively and naturally thrive on giving and nurturing, so by being made to think 'what about me' (which is actually a very 'male' way of thinking) it stops them from feeling the ultimate happiness and satisfaction they can feel from allowing themselves to take pride in their feminine instincts. I now only work part time as I have realised how much my own unnecessary stress was based upon my lack of energy and motivation to nurture my family and home, and want to take this opportunity now while I am still needed at home.

I strongly recommend reading the Mars & Venus books by John Gray. I cannot even begin to explain this as well as he does, and I am sure you understand that it is not quite as simple as this! But maybe this small insight will help in some way!

CHAPTER 79...
Common Purpose V Common Sense

Common Purpose is a government charity founded by Julia Middleton that 'trains' people to believe what the government/society wants them to believe, therefore helping them to work towards a 'Common Purpose' ("Working towards a Common Purpose" - that sounds familiar!). There are many other subversive social engineering projects in the UK, some linked to Common Purpose, but all use similar underhand techniques that undermine our common sense and human nature. However, the research I carried out when my children were in school was centred around Common Purpose in particular as this was the most rife at the time.

Common Purpose funded training is used in politics, government, finance, public services such as councils, police, healthcare, etc. and more worryingly it is used upon our children in state schools and other youth groups. It has grown since I originally carried out my research and now is offered worldwide. I really believe this is having a huge impact on the health of our minds.

According to CP Exposed:

> *"Common Purpose (CP) is a Charity, based in Great Britain, which creates 'Future Leaders' of society. CP selects individuals and 'trains' them to learn how society works, who pulls the 'levers*

of power' and how CP 'graduates' can use this knowledge to lead 'Outside Authority'."

And according to Julia Middleton (just for good measure):

""Wherever Common Purpose operates, you will find leaders doing unusual things...to build sufficient trust so that people actually change things."

It is all about 'facilitating change' but the 'change' is always vague and never usually revealed, and often not for the benefit of the people.

CP and our Children

Common Purpose (CP) is testing today's youth, seeing who has the 'potential' to 'fit their way of thinking'. But in reality, the tests that they are performing on our youth contain such tools as neuro-linguistic programming, cognitive behaviour skills and other thought-altering tools to basically see who is the most susceptible. In addition they are setting through an increasingly 'dumbed down' curriculum including extremely disturbing assignments which test the child's compassion and left-brain thinking (that is the logical part of the brain – that does not bow to compassion). I have seen some very disturbing assignments given to my own children and it disturbed me so much that I have removed them from state schooling. More information can be found in Chapter 81 "Education or Indoctrination?".

Brian Gerrish has been working hard to expose Common Purpose for the damage it is doing to our children, and has taken advice from psychologists and other experts regarding the detrimental impact this is having over them. When Brian asked if the techniques used such as NLP were safe for all children, one expert told him it was safe as there was only a 1-2 children in every 1,000 that could potentially be harmed. But wait a moment. If these techniques are used in state schools, upon millions of children, that is 1,000-2,000 per million who will suffer detrimental effects from them!

These tests and selections are carried out mainly through state education and externally funded youth groups and these questionable practices and more which invoke dark emotions in the children, have even been linked to depression, lethargy, lack of motivation, complacency and even the alarmingly increasing rates of youth suicides which are usually found in clusters around the country.

CP and Society

It is not just our children who are under attack here, but our common sense too. It is thanks to Common Purpose 'graduates' that such non-common sense enforcements that have gone way beyond reasoning have been brought in. A prime example is Health & Safety. Yes we need it, and yes most people have the common sense to stick to health and safety procedures naturally, but the legislation has been taken so far that it stops us from thinking for ourselves. Sadly, what has added to this enforcement is the 'no win no fee' mentality of the accident lawyers et al. But is this all part of it – so this overthrow of our common sense approach can be executed? Nothing would surprise me!

To protect yourself from Common Purpose, take care with attending training courses. The type of training courses that commonly involve CP and NLP techniques are Assertiveness and other self-improvement courses, Health & Safety, Customer Services, corporate mindfulness courses and other corporate related courses. I also have a suspicion regarding the courses people are required to attend in order to receive allowances. If you are in work, be wary if these courses are run by outside companies, and also if you are part of a governmental division or large corporation. You can access information on Common Purpose graduates on the website cpexposed.com.

CP in Action

Education and society are fast stripping us all of our logical thinking, common sense and initiative – that is very plain to see. I previously had the misfortune of visiting a hospital with a potential medical emergency. As the Accident & Emergency was always very busy, I thought I would try the new hospital's "Local Emergency Centre". When my name was called, I was told that I had a Medical Emergency so they could not see me. They spoke as if I had been stupid to have even thought they would have seen me as they only dealt with accidents, and the nurse who told me believed it himself, that why on earth would I have gone to an emergency centre with a medical emergency?? But my common sense tells me this: An Accident & Emergency hospital is for Accidents and Emergencies. OK – so surely an Emergency Centre would deal with Emergencies, as if it were to deal with Accidents it would be an Accident Centre?? Now, as I was made to feel stupid (or at least I would have been if I had not been more wise to CP) I may have started to question my own reasoning and common sense. Many times in the past I have felt like my reasoning was questioned and now I know why – it is on purpose! We are required not to think for ourselves as then we would start wanting to ask too many questions on the infringements of our rights, and what's really been going on. An obedient member of society will not question their 'authorities', we will willingly accept unlawful fees and fines, we will believe all we are told by the media, we will accept wars fought for profit and we will accept ridiculous and controlling legislation imposed on us WITHOUT QUESTION!

How many people go through their everyday lives with acceptance and fail to ask any questions at all? I have rediscovered my common sense and logical thinking after years of non-questioning slumber and I will be covering this in the next chapter.

CHAPTER 80...A Guide to
Fallacies & Logical Thinking

What is a Fallacy?

A fallacy is a sort of trick that is commonly used to alter our way of thinking and stop us from thinking logically. Everyday we are surrounded by fallacies, and we even use them on others ourselves sometimes when we are trying to make a point (some more than others). However fallacies can be used to manipulate and control, sell and deceive. There are generally recognised to be 42 logical fallacies, some sources provide more or less as some can be split down to more specific uses and some can be combined as they are similar. If you understand these (or merely even just the concept of them) then you will go a long way to rediscovering your common sense approach and protecting your thoughts and beliefs!

As you read through you will recognise these fallacies and how much they influence us. If anything or anyone uses a fallacy then it may not be speaking the truth, or may have something to hide. The truth does not require fallacies! So any time you hear one of these tactics, start your questioning (even if it appears to be good). Fallacies can be used collectively over time as a "Psy-Op" or Psychological Operation, a technique used by the media to subliminally introduce us to (and 'brainwash' us into) a belief.

404

Sadly, logical thinking is no longer taught in education, but if it was I am sure our world would be a much better place! So I have taught these fallacies to my children to protect them from peer pressure and propaganda. There are many good books, my favourite being "The Fallacy Detective" by Nathaniel Bluedorn and Hans Bluedorn. (Warning: after teaching fallacies to your children, they will catch you out too!!)

Many fallacies can be grouped together in similar types (which I have attempted to do). They were originally introduced to me as the "42 Logical Fallacies" and it has even been suggested that it was the Logical Fallacies that Marvin referred to in the film "Hitch-hiker's Guide to the Galaxy" when he states "42" is the "Answer to the Ultimate Question of Life, The Universe, and Everything"!

FALLACIES THAT ATTACK:

Ad Hominum – An attack made upon a person in order to falsify their belief / statement, etc. Commonly used by politicians. More recently, used by the media by calling free-thinkers "Conspiracy Theorists", a term that has become almost derogatory (see poisoning the well).

> Scientist A: Mobile phones are dangerous!
> Scientist B: That man used to take drugs when he was in university!
> Result: People are discouraged from believing scientist A

Logical reasoning: Just because he has taken drugs in the past doesn't mean his statement is false!

Ad Hominum Tu Quoque (You Too) - An attack made upon a person due to inconsistency.

> Scientist A: Mobile phones are dangerous!
> Scientist B: Last month I saw you buying a mobile phone
> Result: People are discouraged from believing scientist A

Logical reasoning: Just because he has bought a mobile phone doesn't mean his statement is false!

Circumstantial Ad Hominum – This is similar to Ad Hominum but based upon circumstances. For example, someone may say to me "You are bound to say this product is the best because you sell it". Doesn't mean I am wrong – maybe I sell it *because* it is the best!

Guilt by Association – Person A is guilty. Person B works in the same company as A, therefore person B is also guilty.

Personal Attack – Similar to ad Hominum, but with this fallacy, instead of opposing using actual evidence, a personal attack is used.

Poisoning the Well – This is also similar to ad Hominum, however it is usually done in advance. So person A will offer person C a preconception of person B. Now person C will have a preconceived idea of whether he wants to believe person B. The term 'conspiracy' has become derogatory, by its past portrayal in the media in this way, so dismissing non-mainstream news to the non-free-thinker becomes easy, just by calling them "Conspiracy Theories".

IRRELEVANT APPEALS & ASSUMPTIONS:

Appeal to Authority – Someone claims to be expert on a subject so what they say must be right. Commonly used by pharmaceutical companies in their lab testing results, and also the reason people give so much of the power of the health over to their GPs, despite many of them not understanding the basic fundamentals of health which is is nutrition!

Appeal to Belief – Commonly used in religion, "This is what Christians believe, you are a Christian so you must believe it too."

Appeal to Consequences of a Belief – If we don't agree to this, then something bad will happen. Commonly used in many aspects of life, but a great example is the by the TV Licensing enforcements. Many are afraid not to pay their TV Licence (which they do not have to pay) as they believe there is a TV signal detector van (it has been admitted that the **perception** of a detector van is enough to make most people pay). Another similar fallacy is **Appeal to Fear.**

Appeal to Emotion – This is used so much in charity work. Tug on the emotions, we feel bad and think giving money will make us feel better.

Appeal to Flattery – A favourite of salespeople. Flattery makes us feel good, so we are more likely to believe and accept what that person says. "Look at this Porsche, a great-looking guy like you deserves this car"

Appeal to Novelty – Another favourite in sales – be the first to have the new model! An additional very similar one is **Appeal to Technology.**

Appeal to Pity – This was used in a BBC documentary on the 9/11 disaster. A 'conspiracy theorist' had presented an argument that couldn't be answered so they cut to the remembrance plaques and a mother of one of the victims appealing "why can't they let my son rest in peace", then failed to address the argument put forward.

Appeal to Popularity – Very commonly used in advertising and sales "you will have all the girls after you if you wear this after shave!"

Appeal to Ridicule – Used in peer pressure and advertising. "You will be laughed at in those shoes." or "You are weird if you believe that!"

Appeal to Spite – Spite and gossip are substituted for evidence in order to change someone's decision, a bit like the 'Personal Attack' fallacy.

Appeal to Tradition – Something has been done for many years so it is the right thing to do. Many crimes against humanity and children are carried out by religious groups based upon tradition. Also, another example is the annual mass slaughter of pilot whales in Faroe Islands by residents including children, even tourists join in. This was originally for food, but is now only continued in the name of tradition.

Bandwagon – very similar to **Appeal to Common Practice**, and a very common term used is "jumping on the bandwagon". Common Practice and Bandwagon are commonly used in peer pressure and advertising especially directed to children and teens. "Everyone else does it so it must be OK and I'll do it too".

Relativist Fallacy – This is a self-inflicted fallacy when someone rejects a claim because they believe it applies to everyone else but not to them.

ENCOURAGING PRESUMPTION:

Biased Sample (Cherry picking) - Showing evidence which is not a true representative. A prime example of this is Al Gore's 'Hockey Stick Graph' apparently showing the increase in surface temperature of the Earth and encouraging us to believe in global warming. But this was zoomed in to one of many upward 'glitches' in a rhythmic trend which would be clear if he had zoomed out and shown the entire graph.

Begging the Question – This makes a statement then answers a question with an answer that assumes the first statement was true.

> A: There is a God
> B: How do you know?
> A: It says in the Bible
> B: How does that make it true?
> A: Because God wrote it!

Composition – This is also called a whole-to-part fallacy. It judges the whole by the part. A great example is when there is a club or group of people, and one turns out to be a bad apple, the others or the group as a whole should not be judged in the same manner – however it would be good to do some research and be wary I would suggest! A use is in health products such as MMS by Jim Humble. He is subject to massive attacks using all fallacies, but one of them is: Sodium Chlorite is industrial bleach so MMS is industrial bleach as it is made from it.

Confusing cause and effect – This happens when two things occur at a similar time and one is blamed over the other. For example, "chronic illness causes depression" - but how do we know that? Maybe the chronic depression that was undiagnosed caused the chronic illness?

Division – This is also called part-to-whole fallacy and is the opposite of the Composition fallacy. So if you have a team of rugby players and the team is excellent, it doesn't necessarily mean that every player is excellent on his own.
In health, ingredients A, B & C may all be good, but when mixed together they may interact with each other and cause problems!

False Dilemma – This is when 2 possible scenarios, solutions, etc. are presented as being that either one or the other is true. The one is deduced to be false so this means the other must be true. But what if they were both false in the first place?? We should not just assume!

Gambler's fallacy – This is when someone believes that something that is projected in the long term to be a possibility, will happen in the short term as they have been doing it for a while. For example, "If I play the lottery for 20 years the chances are I will win sooner or later – I have been playing for 20 years now so I must be due a win soon!"

Genetic Fallacy – This is when the origins or history of a belief are presented as evidence to alter our reasoning. A great example is when the media actually reports a fact about something, but due to their usual lack of fact in other reports, the fact they have stated is discredited. e.g. "It says in The Sun that homeopathy really works" - "That can't be true if it's in The Sun – you know how they lie about everything!"

Hasty Generalisation – This is when a conclusion is drawn before all the results are collected in, or before there is sufficient time to assess the results fully. Commonly used in pharmaceutical testing.

Ignoring a Common Cause – A & B regularly happen together, (C is ignored or disregarded), therefore A causes B.

Middle Ground – Widely used in politics, and when people judge others, when 2 sides take something to the extreme in opposite beliefs, then a third comes along with a middle ground and states they must be the correct one.

Misleading Vividness – This is when something out of the ordinary happens, and then it is considered that it will be a regular threat or occurrence. An obvious one here is 9/11 and the 'War on Terror'.

Post hoc – This is like the cause and effect, where A occurs before B, and therefore A must cause B. Another very similar is **Questionable Cause**.

Slippery Slope - "This happened, so now this is bound to happen too". Another very commonly used expression. Just because something has happened doesn't necessarily mean that other things will follow.

Spotlight – This states that when something has happened and is placed into the spotlight by the media, then there must be a lot of it happening.

OFFERING DISTRACTION:

Red Herring – A very popular trick in which you are engaged in a debate or argument and the other person introduces a completely unrelated topic and continues the argument on that to steer you away from the original subject (for which he probably doesn't have a good argument for!)

MAKING UNFAIR APPEAR FAIR:

Two Wrongs Make a Right – Another widely used fallacy which really needs no explanation. It is the belief that "he wronged me so I will wrong him back". We believe that we would be justified in taking revenge. No, 2 wrongs do not make a right!!

410

Special Pleading – Very often used in politics, and with the elite – one rule for one, another for everyone else! Also used along with appeal to emotion. This fine is imposed upon person A, but person A has a certain circumstance (is a member of a secret society, or has an unfortunate personal problem) and so is excused from the fine.

Burden of Proof – This is unfairly laying the requirement to prove something through evidence on the uncontentious side (also known as Napoleonic Law). An example is all natural remedies in the EU are banned unless proved safe, which is unfair as there is no record of anyone having died solely from natural remedies. However, pharmaceutical drugs cause hundreds of thousands of deaths per year.

Straw Man - A straw man is a shadow person or associated identity created to impose certain rules or circumstances upon the individual. A prime example: when our birth is registered, a 'corporation' named by our registered name in capital letters is created (our 'straw man'). Law states that a contract can only exist between similar parties, for example a person and another person, a corporation and another corporation, but not between differing parties, such as a corporation and a person. In order to impose contracts upon us (such as fines, legal 'law', debt, etc. which are imposed by corporations) they need us to be a corporation too, hence our straw man 'corporation'. Whenever we sign a 'contract' with a corporation, we are told to enter our full name in CAPITAL LETTERS. By doing so we are assuming the identity of our 'straw man' enabling us to sign equally to the corporation whose contract it is. Veronica Chapman's book "Freedom is more than a 7-letter word" and Youtube cartoon 'Meet your Strawman' explains this further.

We find fallacies everywhere we look, but with a basic understanding of what they are and how they work, we can cut through the propaganda, hype and peer pressure, and rediscover our logical thinking in a positive and protective way – and maybe even win a few arguments!!

CHAPTER 81...
Education or Indoctrination?

It is quite often stated and appealed that we should consider leaving a better world for our children. But what about leaving better children for our world? I don't mean to criticise the children of the world today, of course not! But if they continue to be indoctrinated into society's way of thinking and don't realise they are simply a slave to it, then will anything really change? I am going to reveal some things in this chapter that my family has personal experience with, as sensational as it may seem. But first I will look at what I believe state education to be.

State Education

I really do not think anything in this world comes for free – the NHS is run for pharmaceutical profit, for example. After my research, personal experience and speaking with well-respected researchers such as Brian Gerrish, I firmly believe that education is run by the state for its own ends. It is not the teachers faults, they do what they have been trained to do. Please do not take offence to this if you are a teacher, I think you are wonderful to be able to do such a difficult job. I have worked in a comprehensive school so I know what some teachers have to put up with!

But back to the state's agenda. First they will try to fit every child into a box that they have designed regardless of the fact that every child is beautifully unique and different. Anyone who refuses to fit is either labelled with a condition or 'syndrome', and quite often medicated, or their life is made a misery by being one of the children who just doesn't 'fit in' to the box. Then they 'train' our children to believe in what they want. For example, that they are just a physical body and it is stupid to think otherwise, that history is fact in the way they are taught it, they are taught to obey, that alternative thinking is wrong, to answer questions their way and generally not to truly understand the concept or have their own opinion. They are taught that individualism goes punished (such as not wearing their uniform of conformity). The awareness drives that schools run such as drug awareness, anti-bullying campaigns and the like are simply introducing these things to the children. Brian Gerrish reports of small community schools that never had a bullying problem until the compulsory government anti-bullying campaign was introduced!

CP in Schools

Our children are being stripped of their character and individualism in the state education system. To make matters worse, Brian Gerrish has discovered that Common Purpose has made its way into our schools and this is having a devastating effect on some children. He claims, as confirmed by professionals in the field of psychology, that techniques such as neuro-linguistic programming (NLP) are being used on our children, through teaching methods, usually unbeknown to the teachers, and through assignments. They all contribute to creating instability in our vulnerable young and cause them to doubt their own opinion and beliefs.

The following are some of the assignments that led us to remove our children from state education. They are confirmed to be techniques that could potentially have a devastating effect on the child's mental development and the development of their own values, morals and beliefs with the potential of causing depression, and even suicidal thoughts in a small minority. The assignment wording may not be exact in some cases.

The following was aimed at the first year in 6th form:

- Your baby is in a pram on a train track. There is a train approaching with 20 commuters on it including important society members such as a politician, a policeman and a doctor. Would you a) de-rail the train causing the 20 commuters to die but saving the life of your baby, or b) do nothing causing your baby to die but saving the 20 commuters? Discuss.

We are told by experts that our brain has some parts that do not recognise fact from fiction. In the young adult's vulnerable brain, if this decision was made in the part that cannot separate fact from fiction they may actually subconsciously believe they had caused these people, or their own baby, to die. Imagine the inner turmoil and character destruction this could potentially cause.

- As part of a fairly recent subject called the Welsh (or English) Baccalaureate, which is compulsory in an increasing number of schools and colleges, children are required to debate. However (in our area) the children are required to debate AGAINST their beliefs, rather than for them.

We know that young adults of this age are setting down their morals, values and beliefs. This has been confirmed by experts who have been assisting Brian in his work, and they have also confirmed that this has a huge potential to break the character of the child.

The following was aimed at the middle class of Junior School:

- In the spaces list and draw 5 things you love and 5 things you

> hate – (HATE? Should we be encouraging children of only 8 & 9 years old to think of things they HATE?)

The straw that broke the camel's back, so to speak, was the local primary school discarding all the books in their library (by throwing them into a skip!) and replacing them with "iPads". The library was then furnished like a boudoir complete with red leather sofas and 50inch flat screen TV!

I will not labour the point too much. But hopefully you can get the picture that in my opinion, state education has entered a path I do not wish my children to follow!

University

Children are led to believe once they take their options and enter their GCSE courses in year 10 that it is a foregone conclusion that they are going to attend university, if they say otherwise then they are not the 'norm'. They can be faced with all sorts of obstacles such as difficulty in opening a current account due to lack of credit score, whereas student account are handed out on a plate with cherries on.

The exception is those children who are (what they label as) a below average academic achiever. Then they are encouraged to have a trade (such as car mechanics, which I deem to be a lot more of a useful education!) as they are no use to their 'society' indoctrination. In my opinion, they are fortunate to be immune to their techniques, but sadly this is often presented as a negative rebellion and the child labelled as a trouble maker. I believe this could be because the techniques have upset their minds and made them angry, and as they haven't set their values or morals yet, they do not understand that there are lawful and more constructive ways in which they can rebel. I am not saying this is ALWAYS the case, but I think it could be true in a lot of cases.

I believe there are 2 reasons for university and they are indoctrination and enslavement. Enslavement into the debt system with their student loans. Indoctrination into what society wants them to believe. I could not put it any better than David Icke when he states that the result of a university course is a 'degree', otherwise known as the 'degree of programming' received.

The way I see it is there are 2 types of courses: those which offer further indoctrination into society careers (even the practical engineering courses are mainly based upon old science or furthering the progression of Agendas 21 & 30 in the 'controlled sustainable' field), and those that offer 'interesting but not very useful' courses, a dangling carrot to lead the young adults into debt. I mean the 'fluffy' courses like media studies, humanities, etc.

Fluffy Courses

These have one primary function and that is to get the young adult into as much debt as possible. A debt which they will be burdened with for the majority of their working lives. They will be overqualified for most basic but fairly decent jobs, and many will end up taking more basic, ground level jobs where they are are underpaid and overworked, just so they will remain under the income threshold for paying back their student loan. Or they will become teachers and lecturers in a self-perpetuating cycle.

Society Career Courses

When you think of it, the best paying careers requiring higher education are for society's work, not the work that is really for the rights of the people. For example, teachers are trained to indoctrinate society's beliefs, medical doctors indoctrinated into the conventional, pharmaceutically run way of health management, lawyers indoctrinated into society's man-made legal system, financiers indoctrinated into the corrupt banking and monetary system.

Take doctors for example. They start off as young adults who really want to help people with their health. Then they receive the indoctrination into the pharmaceutical industry, any thoughts of nutrition and natural health are taken from them and they end up as mere salespeople for them. According to Dr Robert Verkerk of the Alliance of Natural Health, the doctor's 7 years of training only contains 1 day of nutrition. Additionally, it is claimed that they are not allowed by law to give any nutritional advice to cancer patients whose treatment would benefit from different diet. Those that have broken through the training while retaining their belief in natural health and nutrition either need to practice privately due to the restrictions imposed by the NHS, or are regularly being summonsed to court over their refusal to comply. A prime example of this is Dr Sarah Myhill from Mid Wales. However, many of the alternative doctors I have come across are not fully immune(!) to the indoctrination, as many are still pro-vaccine because this is so heavily taught in their training.

Alternatives

There are many great alternatives to state schooling. There are private, independent and non-state-funded schools such as the Steiner Waldorf education system which is completely child-centred and focusses on the child's holistic health and happiness. We firmly believe in this system and in our experience it made a huge positive difference. Of course the main sticking point here for many will be the money, but most schools will offer a bursary scheme or scholarships and so it really is worth looking into this. I used positive thinking and affirmations that we will find a way to pay the fees despite starting the application process with no idea how we could afford it! When our daughter attended Steiner School we went without what we didn't need (like Sky TV, holidays and meals out) as we felt it was so important.

Another alternative is home education. I also have experience of this with my son, and have home educated my youngest daughter from age 12-17, after 2 years of Steiner School. It is very rewarding and not as demanding as you may think. As a huge bonus you get to know your children more than you even knew them before and spend such quality time with them! Almost every situation in life and task we do teaches us lessons, we do not have to follow a curriculum or even write down or mark work. As long as the child is learning, then they are being educated, nourished and cherished in a safe and secure environment. I would have loved to have had the courage and confidence to home educate all my children from earlier ages. There are some excellent websites detailing your rights and giving great information and advice on home education such as edyourself.org and educationotherwise.net.

If you cannot find a way out of state education, what we can do is teach our children by explaining our actions and beliefs to them. We can teach them about the logical fallacies using a child-friendly book such as "The Fallacy Detective" and keep reminding them that what they learn in school is only someone's opinion and it doesn't mean it is right!

Whichever path you choose, remember that as parents, WE are the biggest influence on our children and this is how it should always be. Do not leave it in the hands of the state education system. Whether or not they go to school, teaching our children is the greatest gift and legacy we can offer to them, and maybe with this knowledge our children will be the ones who have the confidence and wisdom to really make a positive difference to our future world.

CHAPTER 82...
Mindfulness with Wisdom

Is an ancient and beneficial technique being hijacked?

There is a 'stress-relief' and self improvement method that is so fast-growing in popularity it is almost becoming a buzzword amongst the busy, unfocussed and stressful world of corporate business in the city. It is likewise becoming popular for everyday people who are  simply trying to live simpler and less stressful lives. Mindfulness claims to focus the mind, improve concentration, stop worrying for the future or holding on to the past, slow down the way our lives are going in "fast forward" and in turn provide a much better quality of life for ourselves and those who share our lives. But what exactly is it and where does it come from?

Mindfulness itself is one of the teachings that the Buddha gave around

2,500 years ago. Along with mindfulness he also taught of compassion, wisdom and loving kindness. These are the very essence of Buddhism.

Mindfulness practice involves bringing the mind into the present moment. It teaches how the past has gone and cannot be changed – the future has not even happened yet. This very moment is all that exists in reality, and it is this very moment that we must be mindful of. The saying often springs to mind "when you are cutting carrots, you are cutting carrots" – your mind is not on what is happening later or what happened today but on the carrots and the knife and what you are doing. In this way we are able to train ourselves to stop worrying about future events, and stop letting past issues control us.

'Hidden Dangers' of Mindfulness

Many people have found this practice invaluable in managing their stress levels and have found much improved quality of life from its practice. However, there is another side to mindfulness, as a new strain of mindfulness has recently been seemingly manipulated by the psychiatric research department of Oxford University. This 'new wave' of mindfulness is fast being pushed through corporate channels and it has been discovered on further research by psychologists that it has advanced techniques such as cognitive therapy and neuro-linguistic programming (or NLP) in its practice and training. These techniques are hidden within the practice, the danger being that it is not compatible with everyone's mind. That is besides the human rights issue of having our minds altered without our knowledge. It is even questionable as to whether there is a sinister reason for it being in there.

Another danger of any mindfulness practice is overuse. If there are issues from the past such as suppressed or blocked emotions it is debatable whether practising mindfulness can actually prevent these emotions from surfacing or even further suppress them. It is a firm

420

belief of many that suppressed emotions will manifest into physical or mental conditions if not properly vented to be released.

In the same way over-practising mindfulness can actually prevent us from even considering the future, let alone just worrying about it. If it is not practised wisely then we may become complacent about future issues, and end up being completely impractical when considering our future. If we bring our minds to the present so much that we disregard our future, we may also disregard our dreams and goals. Our inability to organise, plan and keep appointments will not only cause us inner stress but also cause people around us to suffer, and I have seen this.

So how do we practice Mindfulness 'safely'?

If you are considering embarking upon a mindfulness course, I would firstly always seek the origins of the teachings – does it come from Buddha's original teachings or does it come from this questionably dangerous 'new wave' of mindfulness? If you have already been on a mindfulness course from the Oxford lineage, do not fear but please consider the following advice.

The Buddha's teachings are holistic – they involve the whole body: physical, mental emotional and spiritual. They are also holistic in that they cannot be separated. With wisdom, we all know that we cannot cherry pick from a system without destabilising the effects. We must do it as a whole and with balance.

So practising Mindfulness must be done with compassion. We must be compassionate to ourselves – if we have issues that need healing we must help ourselves by seeking that healing. We must be compassionate to others, always being mindful of how our actions are affecting other living beings.

In balance we must also practice with wisdom. We must be wise to

421

know that if we do not have balance, the system will fall down. If we cannot keep to arrangements, we will be causing others to have stress. If we fail to act upon future threats to issues such as human rights, we are setting ourselves and others up for more suffering.

Compassion without wisdom is like being a vegetarian but still buying products that are tested on animals. Or giving to a charity without finding out what that charity actually does, such as Cancer Research that fails to acknowledge the true nature of cancer by embracing Dr Hamer's scientific findings, causing a never-ending search for a 'cure' and funding cruel animal testing in the process. Wisdom without compassion speaks for itself, as we will do what is practical without even considering kindness or anyone's feelings, including our own.

So when mindfulness is combined with compassion and wisdom we get the whole picture and our bodies and minds can begin to benefit. I have personally attended an 8-month mindfulness course at a Buddhist Centre which I have personally found beneficial, but as I am also familiar with compassion and wisdom I have always endeavoured to practice with balance – and with balance comes peace.

A Hidden Agenda?

It is so easy to see how Mindfulness could be such a powerful tool for certain agendas to manipulate and use for their benefit. The techniques such as NLP as mentioned earlier can be misused to control our minds and change our beliefs. What a more effective way of spreading these techniques than by combining them with a beneficial practice that focusses on the current widespread problems of stress and overwork! And encouraging overuse of mindfulness will stop everyone considering or fighting future implications of such threats as the New World Order agenda, or other such violations of our human rights.

By selectively cherry picking the mindfulness whilst disregarding compassion with wisdom, we have a powerful tool that destabilises the mind. In addition, without the teachings of compassion and wisdom, we do not learn to heal our suppressed emotions and we are given the message that the answer to everything is to disregard it by bringing our mind to the present. So if the overuse of mindfulness was taught, we would unknowingly fall into the trap of complacency, thinking of our present moment while our freedoms and rights are being eroded before us. I do believe that many demons can be overcome from within, but we must have balance in also addressing those external forces that are fast trying to trick us into accepting their agenda.

The danger is that the new wave of mindfulness could blacken the name of the ancient teachings and in this way destroy an effective method that can be so valuable in today's hectic lifestyle. We can still find good sources so we may benefit from these effective methods, and must warn those involved of the danger of being hijacked for ulterior purposes so they may protect their lineage and teachings.

The Benefits of True Mindfulness with GNM

Mindfulness practised with wisdom is extremely supportive to the vagatonic state required in the Healing phase. It may also assist in the conflict active phase by offering clarity of mind and thought, potentially allowing you to resolve your conflict more quickly.

Mindfulness has helped me a lot in my journey, and this chapter is in no way intended to turn anyone away from this valuable tool, but we need to learn through an unadulterated source, such as the teachings of Buddhist monks and their students.

SECTION X – Awaken your Spirit

CHAPTERS:

CHAPTER 83...The Ego & Self

I have found much confusion over this subject, with many different phrases and terminology which can leave us even more confused! I will keep this brief and simple, as in my understanding of the concept of ego and self it does not need too much analysis.

Self

The 'Self' is the inner purity that is who we truly are. It is our core, our unconditional and infinite soul, many people believing it is our God within. It is our pure connection to the universe, our universal existence. With the self there is no duality (me and the universe) but there is unity and oneness, that place that is within you as in me, and that part of us we honour when we say 'Namaste'. Despite saying 'within' and 'inner' try not to think of this 3 dimensionally!

Other terms I have come across to describe the Self:

Inner Child, Divine Self, Buddha Nature, Inner Self, Heart Centre, Right Brain, Higher Consciousness, Krishna Consciousness, Inner Christ, Inner Power, Higher Self, Christ Consciousness, Soul, Spirit, God Within

I see these as the same thing, or at the very least all connected to the same thing! The right brain is connected to our 'Self' and is our part of our subconscious mind.

Ego

Unlike the common definition for ego – as in 'big-headed' or egotistical – to me, and in this context, the Ego means the conditioning. Conditioning is what we have learned from our environment and others, a bit like a 'man-made self'. It is not who we really are deep down but the conditioning can lay like layers of an onion smothering our inner self.

Many people see this as a bad thing, and there are many buzz-phrases going around like 'banishing the Ego' but I do not think this is entirely correct. Much of our conditioning is helpful, as we learn not to put our hand in the fire as it is hot, for example. There is good conditioning and bad conditioning – bad conditioning is what we need to try to heal, or at least accept and find a way of making peace with it. Bad conditioning is emotional baggage and unhealthy emotions such as anger, fear, sadness, etc. these emotions that we attach to and find difficult to let go of. The Ego acts like a spoilt but scared child, grasping onto everything, afraid of change and losing its identity (which we very often think is our true selves). What we need to do to heal the Ego is to show it compassion and understanding and find peace with it, while filtering out the conditioning we do not want, or that no longer serves us. To live too much in the ego will prevent us from seeing or being guided by our inner self, and prevent us from being who we truly are. It will make us live in a completely man-made, logical and practical existence, and greatly reduce our compassion and intuition.

Understanding the difference between intellect and wisdom is important. Intellect is very 'ego' – practical, and usually based upon information that we are 'told'. Whereas wisdom is based upon experience, and is truly understood. Put simply, the Ego helps to build our wisdom, as it is like a conditioning that is learned, but deeper than that it is felt from the heart, it enriches and helps our 'self' to mature and develop. It is our healthy conditioning, the healthy side of the ego. So the Self and a healthy Ego in balance is what we need to achieve.

We will never banish the Ego completely as it is the ego that enables us to interact with our world, keeps us grounded in this mortal coil, and as I have explained (or tried to!) it is required for the spiritual development of our soul (or self), but I agree we can have unhealthy attachments that are governed by it. It is my belief that the left brain connects to the Ego or conditioning which is part of our conscious mind.

Other phrases I have come across to describe the ego, or at least an element of it:

intellect, layers of an onion, reptilian mind, will, left brain, 'I', conditioning, conscious mind

When people speak of being too right or left brained and also talk of psychopaths (or the 'reptilian mind' courtesy of Mr Icke!), I understand this very simply as a kind of fuel gauge between compassion (right brain, self) and wisdom (left brain, ego)! In my opinion, a psychopath, sociopath or even a narcissist are operating too far over to the left brain to various degrees. From the GNM perspective, emotional numbness (which could be classed as a psychopathic tendency) is caused by a 'Cerebral Constellation' which is 2 conflicts that are active and which

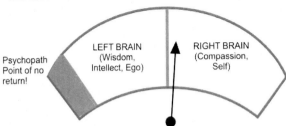

involve both brain hemispheres, one would be a nest worry/argument conflict, and the other would be any other attack conflict. This numbness can be towards a particular person, gender, type of person, race, or humanity itself (which may explain prejudice). This is quite an advanced GNM topic, detailed on www.LearningGNM.com.

CHAPTER 84...*The Aura & Chakras*

Our bodies have their own energy field surrounding us called our Aura. From the base of the spine to the tip of the head there are 7 major energy centres or Chakras. There is a central Nadi (energy channel) that runs down the spine called Shushumna, and 2 more called Pingali and Ida Nadis that cross over at each Chakra (Ida starts at the left nostril and Pingali at the right nostril). The Chakras concentrate and distribute refined life-force energy (Prana or Chi) throughout our physical, emotional and spiritual bodies. The energy at each chakra vibrates at a certain rate, relative to a colour of the rainbow, and affects an area of human life and being. When the Chakras are all balanced and in harmony, we are holistically healthy and full of vitality. The branches of Yoga that mainly work with the Chakras are Kundalini Yoga and Tantra Yoga.

A **Mantra** is a chant - when spoken or sung, the vibrations of that particular sound will resonate at the same frequency as that of the vibration of the relevant Chakra.

A **Yantra** is an image that resonates at the same frequency as that of the vibration of the Chakra.

Using these tools will help to release blockages within the Chakra and help to balance it.

Base Chakra – Muladhara

Colour: RED   **Location:** Base of the Spine
Relates to: Grounding, Survival, Instinct.

Yoga postures: Grounding – Tadasana (mountain), Utkatasana (Chair), Vrksasana (Tree), Virabhadrasana III (Warrior III)

Mantra: LAM   **Yantra:** Golden Square

Crystals: Obsidian, Bloodstone, Black Tourmaline, Smoky Quartz, Red Jasper

Essential Oils: Patchouli, Vetiver, Myrrh, Benzoin

Work on the base chakra if you feel 'spaced out' and ungrounded to reconnect you with the earth and develop and maintain a connection with nature. Also if you have trouble maintaining wealth, relationships, etc., you may need to work on this 'anchor' point.

Sacral Chakra – Svadhishthana or Hara

Colour: ORANGE   **Location:** Just below the navel
Relates to: Sexuality and Creativity.

Yoga Postures: Hip Opening – Virabhadrasana II (Warrior II), Trikonasana (Triangle), Prasarita Padottanasana (Fan), Upavista Konasana (Seated Wide Angle)

Mantra: VAM   **Yantra:** Silver Crescent Moon (opening at the top)

Crystals: Carnelian, Orange Calcite, Topaz, Citrine

Essential Oils: Jasmin, Rose, Sandalwood, Clary Sage, Ylang Ylang, Cardamom, Ginger

Work on the sacral chakra will encourage us to open to, and accept, our sexual selves and our need for pleasure and nurturing. It can also help to unleash blocked creativity.

Solar Plexus Chakra – Manipura

Colour: YELLOW   **Location:** just below the rib-cage
Relates to: Personal power, Individual Will, Divine Will.

Yoga Postures: Twisting & Core Strength – Ardha Chaturanga Dandasana (Plank), Parivrtta Parsvakonasana (Revolved right angle), Parivrtta Janu Sirasana (Revolved head to knee), Virabhadrasana II variation (Crescent)

Mantra: RAM   **Yantra:** Red triangle pointing down

Crystals: Malachite, Jasper, Tiger's Eye, Citrine, Yellow Tourmaline

Essential Oils: Juniper, Vetiver, Geranium

Work on the solar plexus chakra will boost confidence and self-esteem, help de-stress and focus our intentions. It is believed to be where are Ego resides, or at least is governed, and where unnecessary stress accumulates which is why we often get upset stomach or digestive problems when we become stressed.

Heart Chakra – Anahata

Colour: GREEN   **Location:** Centre of the chest, at the heart
Relates to: Unconditional love on all levels, links the lower 3 chakras to the spiritual higher chakras.

Yoga Postures: Back Bending – Biralasana (Cat sequence), Ardha Bhujangasana (Sphinx), Bhujangasana (Cobra), Ustrasana (Camel), Hasangasana (Hare)

Mantra: YAM   **Yantra:** Blue star of David

Crystals: Rose Quartz, Green Quartz, Aventurine, Red Calcite, Peridot, Ruby

Essential Oils: Rose Otto, Rose Absolute, Melissa, Neroli, Ylang Ylang

Work on the heart chakra will encourage the flow of love and compassion in your life, not only for others, but especially for yourself.

Throat Chakra – Vishuddha

Colour: BLUE   **Location:** Throat

Relates to: Expression and communication. Links all other Chakras allowing us to express our creativity, will, intent and the truth in our hearts.

Yoga Postures: Shoulder opening – Ardho Mukha Svanasana (Downward facing Dog), Sirsasana prep (Headstand prep), Chatushpada Pitham (4-legged table), Setu Bandha Sarvangasana (Bridge)

Mantra: VAM   **Yantra:** Egg shape

Crystals: Amethyst, Turquoise, Aquamarine, Blue Topaz, Amber, Blue Tourmaline

Essential Oils: Roman Chamomile, Angelica, Rosewood, Thyme

Work on the throat chakra will improve the flow of communication and support you in reconnecting to your own true voice when using chants or mantras.

Third Eye Chakra – Ajna

Colour: INDIGO   **Location:** in the centre of the brow

Relates to: Wisdom, Intuition and Insight.

Yoga postures: Clearing – Nadi Sodhana Pranayama (no related postures)

Mantra: KE-SHAM (pronounce kuSHAM)   **Yantra:** Violet coloured eye

Crystals: Lapis Lazuli, Sodalite, Purple Fluorite, Diamond, Moldavite

Essential Oils: Helichrysum, Rosemary, Basil, Juniper, Thyme

Work on the third eye chakra will help you reconnect with and trust

431

your inner guidance.

Crown Chakra – Sahasrara

Colour: VIOLET / WHITE   **Location:** Top (crown) of the head
Relates to: Higher Self, Spiritual Centre, connection to Divine/Universe

Yoga Postures: Relaxation – Savasana (Corpse), Siddhasana (Perfect Pose)

Mantra: OM   **Yantra:** Thousand-petalled Lotus

Crystals: Moldavite, Quartz, Selenite, Amethyst

Essential Oils: Lavender, Rosewood, Frankincense, Myrrh, Sandalwood

Work on the crown chakra will help us connect to our spiritual or higher self and help us to reach a state of self enlightenment and bliss.

Shiva (powerful male force) is believed to reside at the crown chakra, with Shakti (powerful female force) at the base of the spine. An energetic coil known as the Kundalini holds Shakti down in human form. The Kundalini is believed to be held down by the effects of Karma and the Kleshas. When a higher state of consciousness is reached during meditation, and the Chakras are all balanced, the Kundalini can be awakened, spiralling up the spine allowing Shakti to meet with Shiva, revealing your true self and enabling you to reach enlightenment, or Samadhi (the aim of Yoga).

Minor Chakras:

In addition to the 7 major Chakras are 3 other Chakras:

Higher Crown Chakra

Colour: WHITE   **Location:** Above the Crown Chakra
Crystals: Petalite, Selenite, Apophyllite

432

Higher Heart Chakra

Colour: PINK   **Location:** Between the Heart and Throat Chakras

Crystals: Dioptase, Kunzite

Earth Chakra

Colour: BLACK/BROWN   **Location:** Between the feet

Crystals: Hematite, Rhodonite, Boji Stone

Major Chakras:

Crown

Third Eye

Throat

Heart

Solar Plexus

Sacral

Root

CHAPTER 85...
Religion, Spirituality & Angels

It is commonly considered that religion and spirituality are the same thing. It is also commonly accepted that science and spirituality are completely different paths. But I disagree on both counts. Religion and spirituality, to me, are completely different and I will explain why in a moment. But likewise, I used to think science and spirituality were entirely different paths. In fact, having such a scientific mind (I began a physics degree once and wanted to be a physics teacher!), I had constant conflicts within myself when I first become interested in spirituality. My first memory of practising any kind of spiritual work was when I acquired a pack of Tarot cards after having my Tarot cards read and being told that I had a future in spiritual work. The reading I received was so accurate – extremely accurate with accounts of past circumstances which the reader could never have known about, and I was blown away as the events began unfolding that were predicted. I tried giving some readings, and I couldn't understand why, but any readings I gave were too accurate to dismiss or ignore. I found myself leaving science behind and following a spiritual path.

Never really 100% comfortable with the Tarot, I quite quickly ditched it for Angel cards. I had never really bothered with Angels as I thought them a bit 'airy-fairy', but I had a dream one night in which two bright beings told me clearly to work with Angels. They gave me their names but they were not very clear – one was 'Serabis Brim' or something, and the other 'Cor----ia'. The next morning I remembered that I had been sent a sample pack of Angel Cards 'The Ascended Masters Oracle' for consideration to add to our shop's range and I felt I had to open them. As I shuffled through the pack, I had to sit down when I noticed 2 cards next to each other – Serapis Bey and Cordelia! From this moment I began working with Angels, receiving Angel Attunements and giving readings and healing. I had left my scientific mind way behind by this time and thought that was a part of me that would never return!

However, it is said we should never say never! As my research deepened, I came to realise the similarities between science and spirituality, especially regarding physics (my main interest), and I explored this further. It was especially pointed out to me through reading some books by H.H. The Dalai Lama, a keen scientist in his younger days. So it seemed I had come around full circle. My scientific mind and spiritual mind met again and I realised that the inner conflict I had been experiencing was arguing about the very same thing!

A teacher at my daughter's old school put this wonderfully:

> *"If 2 people with different beliefs walked in opposite directions around the world they will eventually meet up at the other side"*

When he said this, I realised this is exactly what happened to my scientific mind and spiritual mind. At one point they couldn't be more separate but as my understanding grew, the two views became closer and closer until they finally became one!

Religion

The way I see it, religion is a form of control. I agree there are more open and spiritual religions such as Buddhism. But, to me, this is what religion appears to be – control of beliefs, actions and thoughts. Once these aspects of ourselves become controlled, I believe as many others do that we begin to lose our openness and acceptance of our own individuality, power and spiritual potential. Even in the very open religion of Buddhism, the deeper you follow the more restrictions and rules there are and even though they may be there with good intention and reasons, I believe these things need to be organically felt by us and not imposed.

To demonstrate what I mean, I remember a friend (now a Buddhist Monk!) once asked this question for debate:

> *"If we do something good because we are told to or because it is imposed on us by rules, does that make us a good person?"*

Most religions will teach us to externalise our power, and all will encourage an unhealthy 'clique' or 'part of the group' mentality whereby we have to use certain words, perform certain actions, possess certain items and even wear certain clothes. This prevents us from accepting our own beautiful individuality and uniqueness.

In addition, through my research I have found some extremely disturbing acts performed on the innocent, including babies and children, all dressed up in the name of religion. But dressed up or not, these acts remain violating and unlawful and only those brainwashed into the faith would find them acceptable!

Of course it is the individual's choice whether they choose religion, and I do not think any less of anyone who has chosen this path, as it may be right for them at this moment in time. However, I would suggest that everyone keeps an open and balanced approach to their religion. Recognise that our needs and beliefs may change, and do not adhere to it through any negative emotions. There should be an open and healthy relationship with your chosen religion rather than one of rigidity and fear!

Sometimes in life we need to have faith in something, maybe through a negative experience we seek that external influence, especially when we do not feel strong enough to deal with the problem ourselves. At these times, many people turn to religion to provide that sense of security and belonging. Belonging to a religion provides us with a place to go, people to talk to and relate to, and makes us feel less alone in the universe. However, as lonely and scary as it may first feel, it is important at these times that we look within for our own strength and power and realise that we possess anything we will ever need ourselves. When we realise this we become aware of and open to our spiritual self (see the Deer Story at the end of this section!)

What Spirituality means to me

We have previously looked at how we have a vibration and how this can be affected through vibrations of others such as plants, healers and crystals. If we take this a step further we can see how our whole universe has vibrational energy – colours, symbols, shapes, etc. We are interacting with and exchanging information/vibrations with the universe through our words (as sound has vibration), thoughts (as we realise in quantum physics that our thoughts have energy) and deeds (as what we do affects others and their thoughts and vibrations). We have also looked at this in the Law of Attraction.

We know that vibrations can be different frequencies, so now we can think of the vibrations in the universe on different levels, the highest and purest of which is love – pure unconditional love and heart energy. This is what I am proposing many people believe to be God. We cannot see love but we know it exists. We can feel it – it is real. We also know love (or God) is all around us, both multi-dimensional and omnipresent because more than one person can feel it at the same time. When we raise our vibrations, we are closer to love, and likewise when we have negative thoughts and feelings we are further away. This is why we notice more positive things when we are 'loved up' (like wearing rose-coloured spectacles!), by positive thought or happy emotions creating upward spirals, and when we are down we seem to get stuck in downward spiral as we notice the more negative things. It is almost like we are tuning into that frequency, or radio station and only noticing the things we are tuned in to.

As part of the universe, it is my belief that we actually are the universe and therefore everything we do and think will affect our universe. I think of the universe as an ocean and we are droplets of water in that ocean. We are a part of, or entangled with all the elements of the universe and yet the droplets of water do not cease to exist once they are a part of the ocean, but become part of the bigger picture.

In quantum science and spirituality alike, there is an emptiness, where nothing exists until something interacts with it. It is often philosophised whether a tree still exists in the woods if no-one is there to see it (or interact with it). Bringing back the understanding that vibrations affect each other when they interact, and that we interact with the universe by exchanging our vibrations with it in order for it to exist, in this same way then is it possible that by raising our own vibrations, it will affect the world around us? I believe this is so, and many quantum physicists do too. It will affect the universe not only in our perception of it but in the way its energy (or vibrations) exist for others. This is also how I believe that our own small changes can reflect upon the world and universe, in contrary to what we are conditioned to believe which is that of three-dimensional power in the physical ("one man cannot make a difference alone"). When more than one person raises their vibrations, this collective power is multiplied, and so on.

OK if that hasn't blown up your brain too much (as it has mine in trying

438

to explain it!) we will go a bit further! In addition, patterns are ever existing in the form of cycles, repetitive patterns and circles in time, our lives and our universe. These patterns are usually in fractals, which means every time they repeat they 'scale up' to the next level, such as a larger version of the pattern or a higher vibration of it. They often obey universal codes or laws such as phi, the Golden ratio. Examples of physical fractals can be seen in nature such as in fern leaves, romanesco cauliflower, and even the image of a brain neuron which looks almost identical to how astrophysicists have computer-generated our galactic universe (known as "As Above, So Below"). So by making subtle changes such as a new thought or intention at the beginning of one of these patterns, could we create a change in that fractal, or even begin a new fractal which will in turn scale up each time around? People very often take advantage of cycles and patterns, sometimes instinctively such as starting new diets on a Monday, or resolutions at New Year, etc.

In the book, Choice Point by Harry Massey and David Hamilton, it is suggested by Robert E. Quinn, a professor at the University of Michigan, that by changing the emotion at the start of a vicious cycle we can change it to a virtuous cycle. Likewise, I believe we can apply this to our lives when we find ourselves repeating mistakes in a vicious circle. If we realise what our feelings or intentions were at the start of these repeating patterns, a common theme, we can alter the outcome. Take a person who is always finding themselves with an abusive partner. If this person looks back and realises that in between partners, they were longing for another partner out of fear of loneliness then by altering their intention to something more positive such as attracting a loving life-long partner, they may bring about a different outcome. And as we have learned in the Law of Attraction mentioned in Chapter 63, it is important to focus on what we WANT as opposed to what we DON'T WANT!

Angels

So what's in between the purest vibration of unconditional love (or God) and the frequency that our vibrations are on? I believe that there are other 'interim' vibrations, a bit like a vibrational stairway and I believe that these vibrations are what are commonly called Angels. Angel comes from the Greek word 'Angelos', which also means 'messenger'. As these energies are closer to our vibrational frequency we can access them more easily than attempting to access the purest highest vibration directly. These energies have different vibrations, many resonating at the same vibration as colours and healing frequencies. I also believe that the different aspects of deities could essentially be these same energies (such as the different aspects of Buddha like Green Tara, Chenrezig, Medicine Buddha, etc.). We call these energies whatever fits with our beliefs and whatever feels most comfortable for us. Likewise, we will perceive these energies in whichever way is most agreeable to us and this will also depend on limitations of the individual's mind, beliefs, fears and expectations. They can take the form of mystical beings, symbols, deities, animals, colours, lights or just simply feelings.

These vibrational energies can be invoked to offer healing and guidance in different aspects of our lives. Most commonly worked with are the archangels and our guardian angels, spirit guides, animal guides and other energies who collectively form our 'spiritual support team'.

The 7 archangels most commonly invoked including their associated colour and guidance are:

Archangel Michael – blue – protection and clearing negative energies
Archangel Raphael – green – healing
Archangel Gabriel (pronounced Gabrielle) – white – communication, confidence and purity
Archangel Uriel – golden – interaction with and connection to nature, brings peace and calm to conflicts within

440

These 4 archangels are collectively known as the Archangels of Presence. Then there is:

Archangel Chamuel – pink – unconditional love, relationship harmony
Archangel Jophiel – yellow – illumination and wisdom
Archangel Zadkiel – violet – freedom

Your Guardian Angel

We all have a Guardian Angel, and Spirit Guides to help us through life. Many people have reported feeling a force preventing them from doing something that later would've proven fatal. Some people experience an instinct, or feeling to do something or somehow know they shouldn't do something. There have also been experiences of someone suddenly 'manifesting' into a person's life at a time of crisis, and once that crisis has passed, seemingly vanishing without a trace. We all may have noticed a 'conscience' telling us right from wrong. Could it be that those of us that are more instinctive, or intuitive than others are purely more in touch with our Angel, possibly without even knowing it?

If you wish to meet with your guardian angel, this can be done very easily through meditation. Simply intend and ask that your guardian angel presents themselves to you. Visualise yourself in a sacred place of your choosing in your meditation, protect yourself by surrounding your chosen place with white protective light (and you can also ask Archangel Michael to protect you) and invite your Angel in to meet you. You may also ask questions and request healing from your Angel. Before leaving, make sure to thank your Angel and send them love and gratitude from your heart in an exchange. This helps to give back pure vibrations to the universe.

Asking for Help

You can ask the angels for help any time either directly or through your own Guardian Angel – you just need to ask in your mind or out loud, or simply intend your request to the universe. It is very similar to (in fact I think it is the same as) using the law of attraction. You are simply putting out to the universe what you want with intention and feeling, but it can help to direct your request to someone, or something. Then let it go and let the universe (or Angels) deliver it to you! This last point is very important – let it go out to the universe, do not worry about it or you will hold onto it. In my workshops I often explain this as taking your car to the garage. You must leave it there for the mechanic to fix. If you hold onto the car and drive away in it how can the mechanic fix it for you?

If you want reassurance you can ask for a sign and/or calling cards. Calling cards can be anything you intend such as white feathers, coins, rainbows, certain colours, sounds, etc. You will notice these when it is right for you to do so – although the physical object will always be there! What I mean is, it is not going to manifest itself there specifically for you to see, but circumstances will lead you to become particularly aware of it. Noticing these signs is a great way of reassuring that your request has been accepted and that everything is going to be OK in the end and work out for the best. With faith and belief in this process, it will work – but careful as it can work in ways you didn't realise and it may teach a life's lesson along the way – so you need to be very careful and considerate in what you wish for! Be precise and specific to make sure it is not taken the wrong way.

Finally, if you want to have faith in something, have faith in this statement:

> **Everything will work out well in the end. If it is not well at the moment, it is not yet the end!**

CHAPTER 86...Meditation

It really is difficult to know where to start on such a vast subject, but I am only going to keep it brief and simple, as that is how meditation should be! We can go into it so much that we actually end up 'trying' too hard and the purpose of meditation is not to 'try' but to simply 'be'. There are many different ways for us to meditate and tools that we can use to help, but it all comes down to being able to 'be'.

There is a common misconception about meditation that we need to 'empty our mind' or 'de-clutter our mind'. This is impossible to do as not only are our minds completely active with our busy lives, but if we try to empty our mind we are thinking of trying so our mind will never be empty! This misconception puts us under tremendous pressure and encourages the feeling of failure and hopelessness within us.

Our thoughts are a part of us, they are what makes us and shapes our lives and character. They will always be present in our minds and it would not be right to simply get rid of them. What we should try to do when we practice mindfulness or meditation is to not focus on any particular thought but let them be.

It is like watching a road of traffic, the vehicles being your thoughts and feelings. Normally we would be watching the cars and vehicles and when one catches our eye (or our conscious awareness) we focus on it until it passes and the next one catches our eye. This can cause much confusion and we cannot see clarity or listen to our intuition which lies in the countryside beyond the road. So instead of focussing on the vehicles as they pass, you simply look beyond the line of traffic whizzing back and forth.

If this doesn't work for you, another way to look at it is this. Your thoughts are contained in floating bubbles in your mind. You are seeking to find the space between those bubbles. We have another misconception that our minds are in our brains (see figure 1) - our minds are everything we are and exist throughout our consciousness. When we realise this we can expand the space that was trapped in our previous perception of our minds so the spaces in between become much larger and much easier to find, and so then does our peace and clarity.

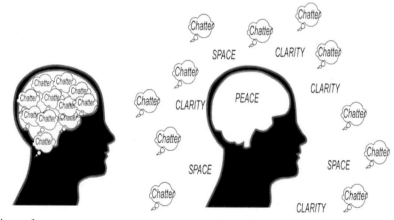

Figure 1

Once you have found the space (or the countryside) simply allow yourself to let go of everything and enjoy this peace.

A lake filled with mud is not clear and you cannot see the way forward.

But if you stop agitating it, the mud will settle to the bottom and the water become clear. Just like the lake, when your mind finds the space in which it can have some peace, it will allow the clutter to settle and we also will be able to think more clearly, rationally and receive valuable guidance from our hearts. Our stress and tension levels will decrease and any blockages begin to release.

Meditation Aids

There are many tools and aids that we can use to help us to find our inner peace and simply be. Some people will use guided meditation CDs and these are particularly good for the novice and also for healing. Some use drumming, dance, singing, chanting, relaxing music, instruments such as Tingsha and singing bowls, all to bring focus, with the addition that the vibrations created by the sound and movement will heal us and help us to focus. Some of these can be extremely soothing and very beneficial.

In the 1970s, a radio engineer called Jose Silva who had devoted his life to researching the mind, developed the Silva Method. His work teaches us to use both hemispheres of the brain, in a balance with the conscious and subconscious, with logical left and the intuitive right. He does this by teaching you how to meditate at the 'Alpha Level', so-called as it is when our mind is vibrating at the alpha frequency. In this state, our both hemispheres are balanced and we have perfect harmony with logic and intuition, and an easy connection with universal consciousness. We can receive guidance and ideas, and learn tools for manifesting our desires and dreams. Jose Silva's work was with his intention "To leave behind a better world for all who follow". More information can be found at Silvanow.com where you will find 5 free introductory lessons.

I have completed both the Silva Method course by Jose's daughter Laura Silva, and the Ultramind ESP course and I find many of the techniques and particularly the 3-2-1 method invaluable. The exercise that programmes this method is called the 'Silva Centering Exercise' and can be found on Youtube. I use the 3-2-1 method daily, and it is also very good for helping me to fall asleep!

Finding Time

Mindfulness is the art of bringing meditation into our everyday lives and is basically being aware of everything that is happening at that particular time. Being focussed on one thing at a time, banishing our ideas of past and future and living in the present moment. You will have read more information on this in Chapter 77, but it is an excellent way to bring meditation into your life. This way we need not set aside any particular time to meditate. However allowing yourself anything from a few moments to a few hours per day will honour your inner self, your mind and allow you to respect yourself in a way that no one else can. I personally wake 30 minutes before I need to and I meditate before I fully wake (first thing before we fully wake, and last thing before we sleep are great times to meditate as we naturally pass through 'Alpha level' at these times!) My favourites are Abraham Hicks meditations, Wayne Dyer's 'I am' meditation, Joe Dispenza and of course the Silva Method!

We have come to a point in life where all our energies are expressed outwards and it is important to take just a little time to honour ourselves, or we might just start calling for attention in ways that are unfavourable such as through symptoms! We can spend so much time healing our bodies, that our poor minds become not only filled with everyday life and worries, but also all the new learning that we are absorbing, so the very least we can do is give our minds a little break and nurturing, whichever way you feel is right for you!

446

CHAPTER 87...
The Dark Side of Alcohol

This chapter is not going to be about what you may think. We all know the damage to the body that alcohol does so I am not going into that here. Instead, this chapter is based upon an even darker side to alcohol which adversely affects our spiritual well-being and vibrations. It was borne from a dream I had, one of those powerful 'realisation' dreams, and this was confirmed the very next day in a completely random conversation Lloyd was having with researcher Ian Crane! As with many seemingly random coincidences in my research and life, I took this as a sign and this lead me to do a little more research. It appears that many people believe what I am going to tell you.

It is probably best to first explain my dream:

There were indigenous people and there was a higher spiritual being (maybe a representative of what many believe to be God). The higher being gave them 2 substances that they could use for recreation and enjoyment – one was a natural herb and the other was alcohol.

The group split by who preferred what substance, and they progressed into the cowboys (preferring alcohol), which I felt represented what is commonly known as civilised society; and the Indians (preferring the herb) representing the indigenous people. Then it fast forward to the

447

present day and we have our society, and the indigenous tribes. I was then presented with rhetorical questions such as:

Who do you think are more spiritual, society or the indigenous?

As being more spiritual = having a higher vibration, therefore does this mean that alcohol lowers the vibrations?

Why do you think it is thought dangerous to read Tarot cards after having alcohol and yet you hear no such warnings for after using natural herbs such as cannabis?

Why do you think it is that people generally feel depressed and sad after or during drinking?

When I woke a lot more questions and realisations entered my thoughts. I began to connect the dots.

This left me with no doubt that alcohol lowers the vibrations and kills our spirituality. In addition, when a person consumes alcohol, his inhibitions and morals are weakened and many turn to negative actions such as physical or verbal violence, crime against others such as stealing, disregard for our own bodies such as eating junk foods, performing daring acts or resorting to indecency and degradation, casual sex, etc. These acts will all further lower our vibrations and add to our negative karma and suffering. And so it becomes a viscous circle as when we feel down we can be led to alcohol again.

How Alcohol Affects Spirituality

When our vibrations are lowered we become spiritually vulnerable. This is common knowledge to anyone who has studied any spiritual subject properly (as opposed to those who have merely 'dabbled'). Combining the lowered vibrations with the lowered inhibitions when consuming alcohol is just like opening the doors to our mind and spirit and giving the bouncer the night off. This is the reason why no good, honest Tarot reader or spiritualist will practice after drinking – in fact many will not consume alcohol full stop.

How this connected with normal alcohol consumption shocked me so much that it has made a lasting impression.

Many believe that there are souls who have not been able to advance spiritually due to their lower vibrational energies, and they are stuck in this realm of existence (like a ghost or spirit). These souls are attracted to our lowered vibrations when we drink, along with other negative energies in our universe. They are attracted as we are on their vibrational level so they become aware of us. This could also be the reason for hallucinations as we are tapping into other realms of existence when our vibrations change. When we are vibrating at a higher frequency, we are not aware of these souls and they are not aware of us as we are on a different frequency to them so we are, in effect, safe – just as I explained in Chapter 63, Vibrational Energy.

When we are at the point where we do not remember what we did the night before, it is believed by many that our body has experienced a 'walk-in' – a kind-of possession by one of these wondering lost souls. Have you ever observed someone who is drinking and found that all-of-a-sudden they have a second wind and start acting out of character? It is a common phrase that is used "He is not himself when he drinks" - could this possession theory be why? And could it be the very reason that pubs and clubs are renowned to be haunted dwellings – lost souls who are still attached to their physical addiction, waiting for the next person to walk-in?

You may remember from Chapter 74, Yoga Philosphy, I mentioned the Gunas of Nature (Sattva, Rajas & Tamas). According to the Spiritual Research Foundation:

"When alcohol is consumed, we are more likely to lose control over our mind and intellect. Negative energies take advantage of this loss of control and infiltrate our consciousness. Even if a single social drink such as beer is consumed, it is enough to reduce the Sattva in the person drinking and increase the subtle Tamas component whereby one becomes more prone to being attacked by negative energies."

In addition, we may be opening ourselves to the influence of negative energies who will pass on their need for alcohol through the drinker due to their need for possession and possible even their love of alcohol when they were in this world.

A Hidden Agenda?

The question is often asked why alcohol is legal and yet so damaging to us in comparison with, say, cannabis – which is claimed no-one has ever died from. If there is an agenda to prevent us from realising our true spiritual selves as researchers such as David Icke suggest, then of course it is understandable that we would be encouraged to enjoy something that is bad for our health and lowers our vibrations, and something that may help our spirituality by heightening our vibrations and also heal us of so many diseases (as is widely claimed) is made illegal. I will leave you with that food for thought and move on!

CHAPTER 88...Inspiration, Intuition & Hidden Messages

What is Inspiration?

We all get thoughts and feelings that lead us or guide us to take action, create or simply just do things. Ideas and 'light bulb' innovations have created the world we live in today. But how come a lot of these innovative ideas have brought us further and further away from our true selves, our instincts, our natural existence and environment and our pure intentions? Have they REALLY done us any good at all?

What I am going to be writing about may sound extreme in some ways, and is probably aimed at the extremely open minded and 'awake' to many controversial truths.

First of all I need to clarify the difference between inspiration and intuition. The way I see it, intuition is felt from within, from feeling, from connection to Source. You feel something is right or wrong, you feel guided to do something, you feel like you need to do something. Inspiration on the other hand is a given thought from something external. It is something that just appears in your thoughts and you don't know how it got there. Sudden inspiration to create, write, do. It's from anything external, such as:

From the Earth's energy: "That beautiful mountain has inspired me to start painting"

From spiritual guides: "I am guided to seek some healing"

From the media: "Reading that book has inspired me to research further into this"

The Darker Side of Inspiration?

In all the conspiracies, crimes against humanity, spiritual attacks, threats to our health, corporate control, brainwashing, elite, secret societies, power struggles, illegal wars, illuminati, and all else that we are subject to, the deeper we delve into these subjects the more we see that it all boils down to good versus evil on a spiritual level. Much of the symbolisms, paedophilia, brainwashing that is happening is linked to satanism. No I am not going to "go all religious" so please read on! If you prefer we can call it dark energies. Dark versus light.

Symbolisms in the media, especially promoted by celebrities by hand gestures, actions, lyrics in pop songs, sounds in music, even the extreme of backwards messaging in some rock (and other) music, were all created with inspiration. People were inspired to write the lyrics which when played backwards gave a dark message. Celebrities were inspired to make certain hand gestures which give powerful negative vibrations. People were inspired to mess with nature and create genetically modified foods and even animals. People were inspired to create ways of poisoning the masses, disconnecting us from our spirituality and stopping us from developing (to quote Rudolf Steiner):

> *"foolish inclinations connected with spiritual life, 'foolish' here, of course, in the eyes of materialists."*

Of course I am talking vaccines, fluoride, aspartame, etc.

452

Inspiration is a given thought – but who or what gives it to us? It is my opinion that inspiration can come from a dark place as well as a light place.

Subliminals

On a spiritual level, the dark place can be very subtle, so subtle only those that know what to look for can see the signs. It can be very cunning, so cunning that the subtle signs, messages and symbolisms are not recognised by the conscious mind but are absorbed subliminally into the subconscious mind, which can interpret symbols, sounds and words that are written in any direction or at any speed due to its photographic memory, unlike our conscious mind. This is extremely dangerous as our conscious mind is a sort-of filter for our subconscious mind, and if we are conscious of the information we can decide how our brain should process it. For example, factual and fictional information is stored in different parts of our brain. When we receive information into our conscious mind, our brain can decide which category it fits into before it is passed to our sub-conscious mind, or if it needs to be discarded. Without this decision our brain may decide something fictional is fact or vice versa and trigger our emotions accordingly. This can be so detrimental to our state of mind especially when it is regarding dark information.

The Importance of Symbols

It is worth understanding the importance and effects of symbols and images. Symbols hold vibrations. This is why they are so widely used in religion, belief systems and secret societies. Visualising symbols (such as Yantras) and images (such as that of the Medicine Buddha) can help us to heal, spiritually protect us, and cleanse our Chakras. These symbols, images and Yantras have high vibrations so they affect our vibrations favourably. So it is obvious then that symbols and images with low vibrations like those used in the occult and satanism, and masonic symbols will affect our vibrations unfavourably.

Protecting Ourselves

Images, symbols, suggestions and messages that enter the sub-conscious mind directly are processed and de-cyphered raw by the brain. When we recognise them as something we do not want to take notice of, we can store the memory of them in the relevant part of our brain that stores what we want to dismiss. So I therefore believe that we can protect ourselves by being aware of what to look for. If our conscious mind recognises what is happening, it does not absorb into our subconscious with a detrimental effect.

An example of this is looking through a magazine which has some hidden satanic symbols in the photos. If we can recognise these with our conscious mind (which of course does not want to have anything to do with these dark energies) we can send the signal to dismiss the symbol, so it is stored in our brain's 'recycle bin'!

I am no psychologist but I have studied some psychology on the conscious and subconscious mind in my Yoga diploma, studied a distance learning psychology diploma as a part of home-schooling my daughter, and have also gathered some knowledge from professionals as to how our brain can process information, so this is my interpretation and how I have pieced it all together!

When I first started learning of the various Satanic, Masonic and other dark symbolism in our media and all around us I thought "but if we are noticing it surely we are giving it energy and maybe I don't want to give this dark stuff my energy". But as I have continued with my research I have realised that learning about these things really is the only way (as far as I understand) to protect ourselves from their messages to us.

454

If you intend to research into this controversial subject, a great place to start is 'the Vigilant Citizen' (www.vigilantcitizen.com). It is actually quite a fascinating subject, especially once you begin to recognise the plentiful symbolism all around us that we never even noticed before! But you do need to take care as you can get drawn into it. I would consider it good practice to protect yourself before researching such as surrounding yourself in spiritual protection such as white light, and holding the intention that you are learning the symbolisms for the greater good. When Lloyd and I did a small amount of research into backwards messaging in certain popular rock songs, one Satanic phrase in particular got caught up in our heads for a while afterwards, a bit like one of those annoying songs – but the danger with this is it becomes a powerful chant when repeated many times in your mind. Is that why certain songs are so 'catchy'?

Speaking of which, I was also wondering recently why so many songs have tunes with the singer just chanting Na Na Na. I felt uncomfortable with singing along to these songs, so I did a little research and discovered Na is Sanskrit for death! When used in chanting it is generally said alongside Mah which is rebirth, as in Shiva's chant "Om Namah Shivaya". I still sing along to songs I like, but sing La La instead so I am not chanting "death" and lowering my vibrations!

A more subtle protective approach may be to visualise your mind as having a 'firewall' and intend this firewall to filter out any symbols, hand gestures, subliminal messages, lighting and effects, strange or inaudible lyrics, and other things that may be giving you unhealthy messages. Then, if you feel curious, or notice something recurring quite a lot, you may wish to do some research to see if it has any unfavourable significance. If your suspicions are correct then you have an efficiently working firewall! I believe this method simply is a tool for tapping into your intuitive consciousness as deep down we really know what is good and bad for us! I have found this method very helpful.

CHAPTER 89...An Inspirational Story

I'd like to share this story with you. I first heard this story during a Yoga class and it has made a lasting impression on me, helping me through some of life's hurdles. The story is about a deer who lives in the forest.

One day it catches a beautiful scent on the wind. It becomes obsessed with this scent, mesmerised and enchanted by this captivating aroma. The deer starts to become restless for it feels it cannot go on unless it finds where this perfume is coming from.

It starts chasing after it, searching and searching. No matter where it goes, or how hard it looks, it can never seem to get any closer to the intoxicating scent.

At the end of each day it collapses with exhaustion, until the morning when it awakens and catches the scent once more, beginning its frantic search again.

It eventually becomes crazy, getting more and more frustrated, feeling more and more depressed with each disappointing, unsuccessful day.

It appears that the more it searches for the scent, the more distant it becomes, and the deer begins to lose hope. It begins to become less aware of the beauty around it, and starts to feel quite sad and yet even more determined that it must know where this perfume is coming from.

The deer's focus is so much upon the scent and the determination to find its source, that its life simply passes it by without it realising.

As time goes by it becomes increasingly weary, and even though its search continues with increasing determination of mind, its body becomes weaker and weaker. And yet still it struggles to continue its relentless search for the scent that it has become so obsessed with.

Then, one day, the deer collapses with exhaustion – feeling incomplete and unfulfilled as it never finds the source of this perfume, the scent it has been so desperately searching for its whole life through.

What the deer didn't realise is the very perfume that had driven it crazy, and sent it chasing all over the forest, was actually the musk that it produced from its own body.

The Moral of the story

We are all very much like the deer, ever searching, never seeming to get closer to what we consider is true happiness. We may think sometimes that we are close, we may even think we've found it for a moment, but it doesn't last. There is a feeling inside us that there is more to life, and if we keep changing and searching we will find what it is we so desperately need. We look further and further, widening our search, which in fact takes us further and further from where it actually is.

If we stop and look inside ourselves, actually believe in who we are, respect the person that is 'us', we will realise that what we are looking for has been here all the time. We are everything we ever wanted to be, everything we could possibly want and need can be found if you look in the right place. We can feel empty, worthless and disappointed by looking in the wrong direction, and finding nothing.

As hard as it is to believe, this is the Greatest Truth you will ever hear.

SECTION XI – IN CONCLUSION

CHAPTERS:

CHAPTER 90...Connecting the Dots

I want to stress that the focus of physical health and nutrition in the majority of the book is not intended to place the emphasis of importance on the physical body. On the contrary, when you read through this book, you will realise that everything ultimately comes down to a balance between our physical, mental & spiritual bodies.

However we must realise that in the same way that holistic remedies are beneficial to us holistically – on all levels, in the same way the things that are bad for us that we learned of in Section IV are holistically detrimental to us – on all levels. A prime example is that Fluoride calcifies our pineal gland at our Third Eye Chakra. How can we spiritually progress when we are being holistically attacked? So it is of paramount importance that we protect ourselves from these attacks. Furthermore, you may feel that knowing about these negative things may be lowering your vibrations and causing physical stress as you may experience negative emotions by learning of them. But this is only temporary. Understand that wisdom holds very high vibrations and we cannot be wise to something that we do not know about!

In addition, if our bodies are not in a state of well-being, our vibrations will be lowered thus preventing our spiritual progression. So as you can see this book so far has been intended to form a basis for any further spiritual, **emotional** and mental healing and practice that you follow on your spiritual path.

As you are aware by now, it is important to have a balance of compassion and wisdom. To have wisdom we need to know exactly what is going on so we can use this knowledge as wisdom to protect ourselves from the potential threats and wrong-doings, and to make a difference, no matter how small, to providing our children and grandchildren with a better future. This is an invaluable inheritance to them, more so than material items! If we do not understand what is going on behind our backs, how can we know what is potentially in store and how can we set about preparing solutions so that it does not affect us and our loved ones too much, or even stop it from happening in the first place?

Therefore, I do not apologise for the content of this book not being all love and light and positive! Many would say that I am giving power to the negative subjects by writing and talking about them, and if the love brigade want to bury their heads in the sand, then that's their choice. I agree that we shouldn't give the power of our thoughts and emotions (where our *real* power lies) to these things. However, holding this knowledge as positive wisdom and showing compassion to ourselves and families by seeking positive solutions is a far cry from being all doom and gloom and just complaining endlessly about these subjects without taking any action. Again we must find balance! In other words, we need to embrace things, including ourselves, in its entirety, warts and all. We need to accept the dark as without it there wouldn't be light, the evil as without it there wouldn't be good. After all, we live in a dualistic word.

It would be no good to have all the knowledge that I have attempted to portray in this book without realising that the supplies of these products and information were under threat. What is the point of knowing you need 50,000iu of vitamin D3 if it is illegal to sell or obtain that potency?

So we must be aware of the impending threats, spread the word, and do what we can to ensure that ours and our families needs are met, and maybe even leaving a better, freer future for our grandchildren! Whether this is stocking up, writing to MPs and MEPs, joining with others in your area to raise awareness and organise lawful rebellion or non-compliance.

The latter is my personal belief to be the best way to tackle this. For a few years, Lloyd and I have been running an 'Awakening' group in South Wales for like-minded people to meet up and share information and solutions (contact me or my shop if you want more information!). It has been said that a revolution takes only 10% of the population to wake up to what's *really* occurring and stand up for their common law rights (which by the way are completely different and mostly contradictory to the 'legal' system imposed by the state – which is a corporation, but that is another story!). While we are on the subject, if you want more information on the state, common law rights and the corrupt legalese system, grab yourself a great book by Veronica Chapman called "Freedom is more than a 7-letter word".

So, getting back on track...we must now look at the impending threats to our Health Freedom. We must get to know what is happening behind our backs in order that we can protect ourselves and take the correct action when needed.

CHAPTER 91...The Threats to our Health Freedom

On the following pages, I have written a summary, in simple English, of the threats to our health freedoms at the time of writing. Some of these have already come into play and some are waiting in the wings to be enforced. This information has been checked by Scott Tips of the National Health Federation as being a good explanation of what is actually occurring – please be aware that there is much fear-mongering and misinformation on the internet regarding this!

Even though the UK has now voted to leave the EU which should now be happening imminently (I hope!), the EU Directives remain in force until they are replaced by UK law. What we need to do is petition the government to ensure the new UK laws will not be as restrictive, or biased towards corporate interests. Read on for more information!

EU Supplements Directive

This EU Directive came into force in January 2010 in a bid to control what is regarded as 'safe upper limits' of potencies (or strengths) of supplements that are available to us. The levels that have been proposed are extremely low and are of no benefit to our health. This Directive has failed to have an impact as yet and this is due to the failure to agree on on 'daily reference values' on a global level, which are used to calculate the 'daily recommended allowance' for supplements. Of course until this latter figure is set, they would be folly to set levels for upper safety limits, as there is potential that it could work out that the upper safety limit is actually lower than that of the RDA – which would make everyone realise that the levels are not based on true science, but biased studies and 'bargaining' discussions.

EU Directive for Traditional Herbal Medicinal Products

This EU Directive came into force on 1st May 2011. There is much confusion and ambiguity regarding the effects of this directive as nothing as yet appears to have changed (well not as much as it was once thought). But many therapists, practitioners, re-sellers and personal users of natural herbal products are now worried about the future availability of these products.

Many products such as some homeopathic remedies, herbal supplements such as Slippery Elm, have slowly become more and more

463

difficult to source, some have even disappeared from sale. This is because re-sellers and importers need to register the product in order to keep selling it. This requires similar extensive testing that is required of pharmaceutical drugs making this prohibitively expensive for most independent manufacturers and distributors to keep their products available.

However, at the moment, many products continue to be OK to be sold as long as there are no medical or health claims made – which is fine for those of us who know about them, but not so good for people who need to educate themselves and make informed choices on how they manage their health.

It is still unclear how much impact this will have in its entirety, as it is a very slow process, and I believe this is purposeful so we do not notice. My suggestion is to stock up on your essential supplements and herbs, or even better look into growing and making your own. I believe self-sufficiency is the answer here if that is possible. I understand that future implications of further legislation may try to take our right to grow our own away (as is happening in some parts of the US & Canada) – but if millions of us are doing it, surely it would be impossible to police?

EU Nutrition & Health Claims Directive

This EU Directive was agreed in 2006 but came into full force on the 1st June 2012, when companies had to remove all their 'pharmaceutically unapproved' health claims and bring their information in line with the new legislation. The Directive states that any health information given on a product or in the process of the selling or promoting of a product, must only be those statements on the EU's approved list. Of the 2037 health claims submitted, only 241 have been approved to date. It is complete control over what we are allowed to say about a product. At present it is just the likely candidates with very soft wording that are allowed, for example, "iron contributes to normal function of red blood cells". Many of the more unusual products have not even been submitted, and in true EU law style (i.e. guilty until proven innocent), the claims have to be removed until they are approved. Furthermore, to submit a claim for approval the EU requires expensive and extensive scientific and technical support for the claim which most independent health shops and natural health suppliers are unable to afford to supply.

Codex Alimentarius

The driving force behind these Directives is a global entity entitled the Codex Alimentarius Commission. The UK have a delegate seat at the Codex Commission, but as yet the UK are not compliant with the guidelines Codex sets. The term actually means Food Code and the commission was set up in the early 60s in an attempt to control anything that enters our mouths, or the mouths of animals that we use for food. The commission consists of an unelected representative (or bureaucrat) from each country and various other delegates from other corporations and organisations, many of which have Pharmaceutical, Agribusiness, Biochemical and Biotechnical interests.

The National Health Federation won a delegate position at the Codex Commission at the turn of the millennium as an unbiased health freedom and consumer education organisation. To this day they remain the ONLY unbiased organisation that is concerned with our health freedom who is present at the commission and can actually speak out for us.

The Commission is run by the World Health Organisation, The Food and Agricultural Organisation and more recently the World Trade Organisation. To begin with the commission just set up a load of guidelines, but since the WTO became involved many non-compliant countries are having to deal with heavy penalisation which will

465

eventually force them to become compliant with their guidelines.

As of 2013, the EU was not 'Codex compliant' but the WTO were fining them 150 million Euros per year for not importing genetically modified meat from Canada, with the figure set to rise every year so they will soon be forced to comply. The aim is to get all countries to eventually comply. There was a date set for April 2012, but it appears that they are way behind schedule – thanks to the non-compliance of many and to the NHF for putting forward good arguments encouraging other countries to disagree with the propositions, and forcing the decisions to be carried forward to the following year's meeting. This may only be pushing the goal posts forward, but it is giving us more time to spread awareness and possibly create a revolution to overthrow this corporate control in all areas of our lives.

ACTION PLAN

Until we voted to leave the EU, there was not much that could be done. However, now we have the chance to make our voices heard, to ensure that the UK laws that will eventually replace the EU Directives will not be as restrictive! We can contact our MPs, councillors, etc. to show our discontent and concern at the current system, and to make them aware of Codex and that it is not in our best interests to become Codex compliant. Tell them about its biased stance and that we, as citizens, do not want to bow to these guidelines, put in place to protect corporate interests. It is worth signing as many petitions as possible (but bear in mind many have been set up by controlled opposition to act as comfort blankets). We almost have a blank canvas now we are set to leave the EU so we really have a small window here where we can make a difference.

Distraction

Many therapists, re-sellers and users of natural products have been far too busy campaigning to get the EU directives overthrown, but now we need to change our tactic and tell our MPs what we want instead. We can also support the NHF in their work with Codex, so if we ever do become compliant by stealth, it may not be as bad as it could have been.

Writing to your MP about Codex

If you inform any MP about Codex they will generally come back with a reply such as "it's nothing to worry about as it is just a set of optional guidelines" - actually this is just what both my MP and MEP said! But this is what they are told, and they are not told the underhand way in which we are being forced into this. But by contacting these people who are meant to work for us, at least we are telling them we are not happy. And the more people who contact them, the more they will understand what a big issue it actually is.

Implications

Although the immediate EU-lead threat is now imminently over, the natural health industry may eventually be driven underground if our UK laws remain as restrictive as the EU Directives, or we are forced into Codex compliance. This would potentially open the market up to more cowboys, snake oil salespeople and con artists than there are now in natural health (although it could be argued that the most dangerous are those in pharmaceuticals!) But if we can channel our energies in following the only path that can actually work – the only path that can attack the belly of the beast – maybe there is hope after all.

Attacking the Belly of the Beast

You may not actually realise this, but as consumers we have so much power – we GIVE these corporations their power! The way I see it is:

"Every £ we spend is a vote for that product, that manufacturer and that store from which we purchased it"

We can CHOOSE to NOT VOTE for these corporations who control us! If you don't want to give a corporation power, then do not give them your vote! Simple! Here are some ideas:

- grow our own food (and even medicinal herbs), or at least source your products locally from reputable independent companies such as health shops, markets, grocers or farms (see the tip below)

- take control of our own health whenever possible

- vote for the type of company that YOU want – check out their ethics, their stand on issues such as animal testing, fairly traded products, etc.

- know your basic human and common law rights and let them work for you

Every time we visit a shop we are voting for that shop. Stop voting for the things you don't want and start concentrating on what you do want.

Shopping Tip

Instead of using a supermarket, why not try an organic farm delivery service such as Abel and Cole or Riverford, see if there is a local farm shop or visit farmer's markets? I find both Abel and Cole and Riverford both excellent for service, and value for money.

When you first look at these they may obviously appear more expensive than basic non-organic supermarket foods. But as I mentioned in the Veggie Debate chapter, not only do you actually find you need less food, but also this is how I believe the cost of food SHOULD BE.

Animals should be treated well and fed naturally with no routine pharmaceutical drugs; vegetables and fruit should be grown naturally without routine use of harsh chemical pesticides and herbicides. When you think of it, the organic prices are more in line with inflation when you compare them to the price of similar foods before all this corporate interference and mass production in the food chain. The producers would need to be making a sacrifice of some sort to offer the cheaper prices found, such as mass production which lowers the quality of the food, less welfare for animals or other inferior practices. If you wish to use a supermarket, I have found Waitrose to be the most ethical, and as previously stated, are the ONLY supermarket to uphold their ban of GM foods in their products or in the feed of the animals used for their meat or dairy! Recently, Aldi have announced they are banning GMOs from their own brand products, and moving more towards organic in their EU stores – let's ask them to do it here by supporting (buying) their organic range!

Take Back YOUR Power!

We all must realise how much power we all have to choose a better future. If we do not give these people our money – we will eventually be able to watch them crash and burn! So protect your health with high quality supplements, avoiding all that can compromise your resistance, reduce your unnecessary stress, happiness is a fantastic cure! We don't have to be what they dictate we should be!

We can overthrow these corporations by taking back the power they have taken from us. Empower yourself and protect yourself and your family. Also share this information with others and maybe they will too! The more people that are talking about these issues the better.

CHAPTER 92...*Conclusion*

I really hope that some, if not all the information in this book will help you on your journey to well-being and empowerment. I am very happy to advise you in any way I can if you need help or guidance, or if there is anything in this book that you do not understand.

There is much I could have explained more clearly and convincingly by going into greater detail, and in contrast some subjects that I have gone into much depth over. I must say that this is certainly not that I give more importance to those subjects I have written more fully on, it is simply those lengthier topics are more in my areas of thorough research and/or expertise. The chapters and topics that are mentioned more briefly I feel are extremely important to be aware of, and I believe being unaware of these issues could potentially have an effect on our overall holistic health. An example of this is chemtrails or geo-engineering. I personally feel that this may be one of the most important subjects of all. I could easily write a book solely on this subject yet I have only really mentioned it briefly. The reason I feel this topic is of such importance is this. We can (at present) choose how to keep ourselves healthy. If our food is highly processed and contains harmful chemicals we can choose to eat organic or grow our own, if we do not like allopathic medicine we can maintain our own health, if we feel our TV is brain-washing we can switch it off, if our water is fluoridated we can choose to distil or filter our water, etc. – but we cannot choose the air we breathe and neither

470

can we grow organic foods if toxic aluminium, barium and strontium is rained down onto the earth. There is much research into many other reasons for chemtrails, but I will not go into that here – please research this further for yourself if you wish!

Speaking of which, I have written some guidance that may help you if you wish to research any subject further in the reference section along with many excellent sources of information and references in addition to those mentioned throughout the book. I would highly recommend that you carry out your own research reading both sides of the story and come to your own conclusions. It is very empowering to do this and it will give you a much deeper understanding of the issues. I also appreciate that you may at first be resistant to some of this information, or it may conjure up some unpleasant feelings. As I previously mentioned, this is natural. Just think how angry and hurt you felt when you were first told by a friend that there was no Father Christmas! First denial, then suspicion, then realisation – and then the hurt experienced when you realised your parents had lied to you all these years!

You may think you have no time for all this especially if you care for others. I am a mother and grandmother, I have a mail order company, Yoga class, I have studied many diplomas, researched into truth issues, natural health products and health issues avidly and home educated my son and daughter. You can do it no matter how busy you are. Two of the biggest time-savers I have experienced are getting rid of T.V. (I just use it to watch DVDs in my own time, and not when programmes dictate it to me!) and reducing the use of my smart-phone. I am on Facebook but I allocate time to it now instead of being a slave to emails and notifications on my phone – and the bonus is that getting rid of the T.V. and only minimally using my phone also saves money, and I have less 'programming' and radiation! It's win win for me and a loser for them! Time is an illusion and always 'not having the time' is therefore also an illusion (and an excuse!). I schedule these things into my day and stick to it! I plan meals, shopping, etc. If you fail to plan you really do plan to fail! Just think – if you fall ill who will be able to do your job of mother, wife, father, keeping your home together, etc. as well as you can? You owe it to everyone in your life as well as yourself to be well and happy!

All you need to do is recognise that you and your body has needs, and deserves your compassion and wisdom. We very often give compassion and loving kindness to all living, sentient beings, while failing to have the wisdom that we ourselves are living, sentient beings too!

I am very grateful for feedback, success stories, or hearing if something didn't work for you. This will help me to further develop and improve my information in the future.

Oh and one more thing – If you think you are too small and insignificant to make a difference, try sleeping with a mosquito!

References
& Further Research

Some Advice for Further Research and Explanations of my Referencing

Some of the articles included in this book were written over the last few years when it didn't even occur to me that they may one day be included in a book! Therefore I unfortunately did not reference much of my research. Besides, it would have been a mammoth task to reference everything as a lot of information was obtained through talks and personal discussions with the people I have mentioned in this section. I have attempted to substantiate facts and figures quoted, however rather than labouring over proving the accuracy of every piece of information (which is only correct to the best of my knowledge at time of writing), I highly recommend that you carry out your own research and accept what feels right for you. Anyone in the field of spreading awareness of non-mainstream information will agree that this is very important.

I do not think I have found a single person I agree 100% with, and I am sure there are some chapters of this book, or opinions I have presented, that may not sit right with you. That is perfectly acceptable and natural as everyone is different and I do not believe that anyone, including myself, is going to be 100% correct on everything as there is always still so very much to learn and discover and it all boils down to individual perception. We have our areas of expertise and can offer explanations in our own ways of understanding which may help others understand the topic, but in many areas there is no right or wrong (unless absolutely proven by unbiased scientific studies or trends of course).

There are some excellent websites and books that I have read and studied over the years, many lectures and talks, and personal discussions with the people mentioned. It is mainly from these sources including my diploma studies that I gather the information to write this book. I have endeavoured to give as factual an account as possible without bias – as my firm beliefs are only based upon the facts, otherwise they are merely my humble opinion (but I would like to think of this as an educated and informed opinion nonetheless!).

If my writing has whetted your appetite for more and you wish to extend your research, these websites, books and people are those I have found most trustworthy, independent and unbiased. So, based upon my own conclusions from research, recommendations and personal feelings upon meeting the people involved, I have no hesitation in recommending the resources in this section for you to obtain further information.

It is important to obtain your information from unbiased sources, and you can be assured that most, if not all, mainstream, government and 'official' sources have vested interests, such as pharmaceutical funding or sponsorship. So I read what they say, but I always try to establish if their research could be biased before deciding whether to accept what they are saying!

I must finish by giving a warning about Wikipedia as many think it provides us with unbiased information as it can be contributed to and edited by anyone. Well that is just the point – you will have much information on there that is not well-researched, but also I have been told of many controversial facts that mysteriously vanish, including entire pages. I will look at Wikipedia subjectively as I do with all sources, but always with a critical and logical mind with the awareness that what I am reading may not necessarily be so. Something else to be aware of is that a source may appear very open and controversial in its view but can still be controlled, so that much important information is held back or biased.

BOOKS:

The Metabolic Typing Diet by William Wolcott and Trish Fahey

Health & Nutrition Secrets that can Change Your Life by Russell L Blaylock

Living Dharma by Ven. Lama Yeshe Losal Rinpoche

Secrets of Planet Earth by Tony Neate

The Universe in a Single Atom by H.H. The Dalai Lama

Transdermal Magnesium Therapy by Dr. Mark Sircus

Autobiography of a Yogi, Paramhansa Yogananda

Chakra Yoga, Alan Finger

Puzzling People by Thomas Sheridan

Remember Who You Are and Where You Come From, David Icke

Physics, the Human Adventure: From Copernicus to Einstein and Beyond by Gerald James Holton, Stephen George Brush

The Reflexology Bible by Louise Keet

A Synoptic Key of the Materia Medica by C.M.Boger

What's Really in Your Basket by Bill Statham

The Truth Agenda by Andy Thomas

Codex Alimentarius Global Food Imperialism by Scott C Tips

Freedom is More Than a 7-Letter Word by Veronica of the Chapman family

How To Cure Breast Cancer Naturally by Dr Veronique Desaulniers

Breast Care Manual by Brian H Butler

References & Further Research

A Course in Miracles by Dr. Helen Schucman

WEBSITES:

EFT Founder (Gary Craig) tutorials, www.emofree.com

Natural Health Research Documents, www.greenmedinfo.com

German New Medicine resources, www.LearningGNMcom, www.drrykegeerdhamer.com

Common Purpose Exposed, www.cpexposed.com

Dr Mercola, www.mercola.com

David Icke, www.davidicke.co.uk

Jim Humble & MMS, jimhumble.is, mmsnews.is, genesis2church.is

Richard D Hall, researcher, www.richplanet.net

Andrew Johnson, www.checktheevidence.com

Neil Sanders Mind Control, www.neilsandersmindcontrol.com

UK Column newspaper, www.ukcolumn.org

West Midlands Against Fluoridation, www.wmaf.org

Alliance for Natural Health, www.anhcampaign.org

Dr L Wilson, www.drlwilson.com

Mike Adams (The Health Ranger), www.naturalnews.com

What Doctors Don't Tell You, www.wddty.com

www.chemtrailsprojectuk.com

www.uk-skywatch.co.uk

Betty Martini, Mission Possible World Health International,

http://www.mpwhi.com/main.htm (Dr. Betty Martini paid me a personal compliment through Scott Tips for my article "The Innocent Poisoning of our Children" when it appeared in the Health Freedom News magazine!)

Dr Mark Sircus, www.drsircus.com

Clifford Carnicom, www.carnicominstitute.org

South Wales Awakening, www.southwalesawakening.org

PUBLICATIONS:

What Doctors Don't Tell You

Nexus Magazine

Health Freedom News

PROGRAMMES:

The following used to be aired on Sky Channel 200 or 192. They will now only be found on Youtube and internet TV.

Rich Planet, now on richplanet.net

Conscious Television Network

On the Edge with Alex G (R.I.P. Alex)

On the Edge/One Step Beyond with Theo Chalmers

DVDs/YOU TUBE VIDEOS/DOCUMENTARIES:

Spirit Science

We Become Silent, Kevin P. Miller

What in the World are They Spraying? And Why in the World are They

Spraying?

Meet your Strawman

The True History of Marijuana

The Truth about Cancer (Series)

Vaxxed

Vaccines Revealed (Series)

Betrayed (Series – Autoimmune disease)

Anything by Truthseeker444

PEOPLE:

Ian R Crane, geo-political analyst

Brian Gerrish, UK Column

Richard D Hall, researcher & TV host

Scott Tips, National Health Federation

Andrew Johnson, researcher & lecturer

Stephen Lovering, Reiki Master/Teacher

Ven. Geshe Damcho Yonten, Spiritual Director of Lam Rim Buddhist Centre in Wales.

Dr. Akong Tulku Rinpoche, Kagyu Samye Ling monastery, Scotland

Lama Yeshe Losal Rinpoche, Kagyu Samye Ling monastery, Scotland

Specific Data Sources

Further to the websites that I receive a lot of my information from, I have included some links, direct or otherwise, to some of the facts I have stated in this book. **These website are not necessarily recommended in their entirety for further research**, as many I have simply visited to substantiate some facts and figures. In addition to these links I have also stated where I have found the data mentioned in the body of the article where this was deemed appropriate.

Section I – Nourish your Body

www.Cacaoweb.org
www.gojijuices.net
www.chlorellafactor.net
www.goforlife.eu
www.boxingscene.com
www.hadousa.com
www.vegetariansociety.org
Http://www.soilassociation.org/frequentlyaskedquestions/
yourquestion/articleid/2404/is-organic-vegetarian-cheese-non-gm
http://www.dailymail.co.uk/health/article-147606/How-cleanse-air-breathe.html#ixzz2MkedVB7R

Section II – Nutrition & Supplementation

www.hippocratesinst.org
www.VitaminDCouncil.org
www.europa.eu
www.livestrong.com
www.drsircus.com

Section III – Detoxification

www.himalayaninstitute.org
www.healthandyoga.com
www.yoga-age.com

Trading Standards

www.wolfcreekranch1.tripod.com

www.magnesiumoil.org.uk

http://aussiezeolite.com.au/yahoo_site_admin/assets/docs/
Zeolite_Study_Powder_v_Liquid.23212827.pdf

www.aboutclay.com

Patent of Synthesis of molecular sieve catalysts

EP 1301274 A2, Hyperphysics, Dept. of Physics & Astronomy, Georgia State University.

Section IV – Avoiding Toxins in Everyday Life

http://aspartame.mercola.com/

http://www.wnho.net/fda_92_symptoms_on_aspartame.htm

Www.fda.gov

http://seedsofdeception.com/genetic-roulette/65-health-risks/

http://www.bbc.co.uk/news/uk-england-hampshire-19197261

http://www.southamptonhealth.nhs.uk/aboutus/publichealth/
improvement/water-fluoridation/

http://www.naturalnews.com/Report_HPV_Vaccine_2.html

www.mercurypoisoned.com

www.organic-farming.europa.eu/

www.cdc.gov

www.organicconsumers.org

Section V – Natural Remedies

www.howstuffworks.com

http://www.rdmag.com/news/2012/07/ions-not-particles-make-silver-toxic-bacteria

www.silversafety.org

www.customprobiotics.com

www.saltworks.us

Section VI – Common Chronic Diseases

www.cancerresearchuk.org

Cancer: The Hidden truth & Suppressed Cures,
http://www.youtube.com/watch?v=Fo7uqQTFAs0

www.cancertutor.com

www.thetruthaboutcancer.org

www.arthritis.org

Jane Thurnell-Read, www.lifeworkpotential.com

Section VII – Holistic Therapies

Www.kinesiology.co.uk
www.nicola-schramm.co.uk

Section VIII – Physical Exercise & Yoga

British School of Yoga diploma course
www.yoga-age.com

Section IX – Free your Mind

http://www.nizkor.org/features/fallacies/

Section X – Awaken your Spirit

www.vigilentcitizen.com
http://www.spiritualresearchfoundation.org/articles/id/spiritual-research/spiritual-science/effect-of-alcohol

Alphabetical Index

Danielle's Websites & Contact

Danielle's Blog website: www.DanielleBryant.co.uk
(with a section detailing updates to this book)

Danielle's Therapy website: www.HolisticDani.co.uk

Shop Holistic website: www.ShopHolistic.com

Shop Holistic phone: (029) 2085 2222

Danielle is available for public talks, book signing, workshops, therapies and advice. She can be contacted through Impetus Books, or by direct email through her website. When you make contact, please state that you are a reader of her book!

Lloyd at Impetus Books

Email: info@impetusbooks.co.uk

Phone: (029) 21 660 901

Website: www.impetusbooks.co.uk

Also Available

Meditations for Yoga CD

Guided meditation CD written and recorded by Danielle M. Bryant, containing 6 guided meditations inspired by Yoga and Mindfulness. Great for beginners to meditation, Yoga students and teachers to use in class!

Available on Amazon, at Shop Holistic and on Danielle's websites.

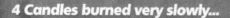

4 Candles burned very slowly...

The First candle said "I am Peace. No-one is interested in me any more" and it went out.

The Second candle said "I am Love. Everyone forgets how very important I am " and it went out.

The Third candle said "I am Freedom. While people sleep, I am being taken away, and no-one seems to care" and then it went out too.

A little girl came along and started to cry when she saw 3 of the candles had gone out.

The Fourth candle said "Do not cry, for I am Hope, and while I still burn the other 3 can always be re-lit."

Never let your flame of hope go out, no matter how bad things may seem.